Special Forces Hero

To Lene, my stroke of good fortune

Special Forces Hero

Anders Lassen VC MC**

Thomas Harder

Translated from Danish by Tam McTurk

Pen & Sword
MILITARY

First published in Great Britain in 2021 by
Pen & Sword Military
An imprint of
Pen & Sword Books Ltd
Yorkshire – Philadelphia

Copyright © Thomas Harder 2021

ISBN 978 1 52678 751 4

The right of Thomas Harder to be identified as Author of this work has been asserted by him in accordance with the Copyright, Designs and Patents Act 1988.

A CIP catalogue record for this book is available from the British Library.

All rights reserved. No part of this book may be reproduced or transmitted in any form or by any means, electronic or mechanical including photocopying, recording or by any information storage and retrieval system, without permission from the Publisher in writing.

Typeset by Mac Style

Printed and bound in the UK by TJ Books, Padstow, Cornwall.

Pen & Sword Books Limited incorporates the imprints of Atlas, Archaeology, Aviation, Discovery, Family History, Fiction, History, Maritime, Military, Military Classics, Politics, Select, Transport, True Crime, Air World, Frontline Publishing, Leo Cooper, Remember When, Seaforth Publishing, The Praetorian Press, Wharncliffe Local History, Wharncliffe Transport, Wharncliffe True Crime and White Owl.

For a complete list of Pen & Sword titles please contact

PEN & SWORD BOOKS LIMITED
47 Church Street, Barnsley, South Yorkshire, S70 2AS, England
E-mail: enquiries@pen-and-sword.co.uk
Website: www.pen-and-sword.co.uk

Or

PEN AND SWORD BOOKS
1950 Lawrence Rd, Havertown, PA 19083, USA
E-mail: Uspen-and-sword@casematepublishers.com
Website: www.penandswordbooks.com

Contents

Preface		viii
Foreword		x
Introduction – 9 April 1940		xii
Chapter 1	Childhood and Family	1
Chapter 2	M/S *Fionia*, January–May 1939	7
Chapter 3	Bækkeskov, May–June 1939	11
Chapter 4	The Art of Guerrilla Warfare 1 – MI(R)	13
Chapter 5	M/T *Eleonora Mærsk*, 1939–40	15
Chapter 6	The Art of Guerrilla Warfare 2 – The Snowballers, November 1939–March 1940	20
Chapter 7	'Good luck – aim between the eyes' – February–March 1940	22
Chapter 8	M/T *Eleonora Mærsk*, 1 January–9 April 1940	23
Chapter 9	M/T *Eleonora Mærsk*, 9 April 1940–October 1940	25
Chapter 10	The Art of Guerrilla Warfare 3 – Independent Companies and Operation Knife	31
Chapter 11	M/T *Eleonora Mærsk* in British Service, 4 May 1940–October 1940	35
Chapter 12	The Art of Guerrilla Warfare 4 – Commandos	39
Chapter 13	M/T *British Consul*, October–December 1940	43
Chapter 14	Britain, December 1940–January 1941	46
Chapter 15	The Art of Guerrilla Warfare 5 – SOE – "Set Europe Ablaze"	51

Chapter 16	In the SOE	53
Chapter 17	The Art of Guerrilla Warfare 6 – The SOE Schools	55
Chapter 18	'Good with an out-and-out independent nature'	57
Chapter 19	The Art of Guerrilla Warfare 7 – Commandos	61
Chapter 20	Special Training School 21, Arisaig House	67
Chapter 21	Gumley Hall	72
Chapter 22	The Art of Guerrilla Warfare 8 – *Maid Honor*	75
Chapter 23	Operation Postmaster	85
Chapter 24	Small Scale Raiding Force	108
Chapter 25	SAS/SBS – Jellicoe	140
Chapter 26	The SSRF – The End	143
Chapter 27	Special Boat Squadron	147
Chapter 28	Operation Albumen, Crete, 23 June–11 July	154
Chapter 29	The Battle for the Aegean Sea – 1	175
Chapter 30	The Battle for the Aegean Sea – 2	186
Chapter 31	Raiders in the Aegean, 1944	216
Chapter 32	Fatigue and Addiction	250
Chapter 33	The Adriatic, July–August 1944	255
Chapter 34	Back to Greece, September–October 1944	261
Chapter 35	Thessaloniki, October–November 1944	275
Chapter 36	Senforce, Crete, December 1944–February 1945	287
Chapter 37	Italy	303
Chapter 38	Legacy	331

Anders Lassen's Service in the British Army — 337
Acknowledgments — 338
Glossary — 342
Notes — 345
Bibliography and Sources — 371
Index — 382

A moonless night. Eighteen British soldiers and two Italian fishermen are crossing a huge lake. The soldiers row their storm boats as silently as possible. Their Italian helpers punt their long, flat-bottomed boat through the shallow, cloudy water.

The soldiers have spent most of the day lying in muddy holes on a small, low-lying mosquito-infested island. Anybody who stands up will be visible from the observation post in the church tower on the opposite side of the lake and draw fire from the German 88 mm guns.

Most of the men are veterans of numerous landing operations, but they have never before seen a battlefield quite like this.

Commanding the patrol is a 24-year-old Dane. In a few hours, it will be exactly five years since the Germans occupied his homeland. He has been at war ever since.

Preface

Anders Lassen was very young when his war began in 1940. He was still young when he died in action five years later. He became an adult during that time, and the war allowed him to express himself. Fervently patriotic, Lassen fought for his country – but he also had a strong desire to prove his worth. War presented challenges that he could face on his own and with honour. Although not greatly enamoured by life at sea, he loved 'the feeling of sole responsibility – when you zigzag in a convoy – and feel the ship obey you and you get to steer her as hard as you want … and the Skipper and Mate … don't bother you at all but let you get on with your job.'

Anders Lassen did not want to be a soldier, but became one because he felt it was the right thing to do. He was highly decorated, receiving the Military Cross three times for gallantry in action. He was also awarded a posthumous Victoria Cross, Britain's highest award for military valour. His courage, spirit of self-sacrifice, strength and military skills were legendary. In death, he has become an almost mythical figure. But he was also a human being, a man of flesh and blood. Like everyone else, he was the product of his family, his childhood and the people he encountered during his formative years. Although in many respects he thrived in wartime, it also wore him down. He was a historic figure and his movements, actions and life can, to a certain extent, be reconstructed from various sources. This book attempts to do just that. It also seeks to put his life and military career into a wider historical context.

I have endeavoured to get under the skin of the man, as far as the sources permit, but still have much to learn about him and his war. I have not sought to fill these gaps with fictitious accounts, and where I do resort to speculation, assumptions or hypotheses, I make this clear.

Whenever I quote from sources in English, I retain the spelling and standards of the original. Every effort has also been made to preserve Lassen's somewhat idiosyncratic style and spelling, including in quotes from his letters and journals, so these may differ somewhat from contemporary norms and expectations. Translations of sources in other languages conform to modern English standards and conventions.

Preface ix

There are two types of notes in this book. Source notes are references few will be interested in looking up as they read the book. Text notes are references that provide further detail about circumstances or relationships, tell a spin-off story or explain what subsequently happened to a minor character. Source notes have numbers; text notes have numbers and an asterisk.

Copenhagen, 22 January 2021
Thomas Harder

Anders Lassen in Else and Vagn Hoffmann's garden in Helwan. The photo and Lassen's signature are from the Hoffmann family's guestbook and are dated 29 August 1943.

Foreword

It is a great privilege to be invited to contribute a foreword to this fascinating and meticulously researched account of the life of one of the SAS's great wartime heroes. Anders Lassen indisputably merits such distinction; in a few short years his single-minded pursuit of being wherever the action was hottest brought him a trio of Military Crosses, one of only twenty-four officers to be awarded the MC three times during the Second World War. His final act of sacrificial gallantry within days of the end of the war elevated him into the pantheon of wartime legends, earning him posthumously what to this day remains the SAS's only Victoria Cross, a record unmatched in the three-quarters of a century since his death beside Lake Commachio in Italy in April 1945.

Although Anders Lassen might not be a household name today, in Denmark and in the close-knit community of British Special Forces he remains a heroic figure, cast in bronze outside the headquarters of the SAS at their base in Herefordshire. I count myself fortunate to have known some of his contemporaries with whom he fought including some under whose command he served: George Jellicoe, David Sutherland and Fitzroy Maclean. It was Bill Stirling, brother of the regiment's eponymous founder David Stirling, whose eye Lassen first caught on his estate at Keir and who sent him on his way to join Jellicoe's marauders under the shade of the Crusader castle at Atlit in April 1943. These were not easy men to impress but much later in life they all still recalled in primary colours Lassen's natural charisma, restless energy, infectious charm and ruthless ferocity in action.

He was a natural soldier seemingly indifferent to hardship, fear, fatigue and danger, the normal yardsticks by which such men are measured; his nature perfectly tuned to the demands of unconventional warfare, intrepid, adventurous, and resourceful. In a regiment notable for its legion of buccaneers, for whom audacity and risk-taking was a way of life, Lassen stood out and his men learned to love him for it.

He died tragically young, not yet 25, and what follows is a magisterial account of a young heroic Dane at war. His story deserves to be illuminated for another generation, not least because in bringing Anders Lassen back to life Thomas Harder paints a vivid and compelling picture of an extraordinary tribe of irregular citizen-soldiers whose spirit, panache and élan still lives on amongst those to whom that wartime generation passed the baton.
Who dares wins.

                General Sir Mark Carleton-Smith KCB CBE ADC Gen

Introduction – 9 April 1940

Anders Lassen's war began on the morning of 9 April 1940, when news that the Germans had occupied Denmark reached the tanker *Eleonora Mærsk* in the Persian Gulf. At the time, he had been at sea in wartime conditions for seven months, but the war declared by Britain and France on Germany on 3 September 1939 had not been *his* war.

He thought about volunteering to fight for the Finns in the Winter War with the Soviet Union in November 1939, but that probably had more to do with frustration and boredom with life on board the tanker, and a lack of interest in a career as a ship's officer, rather than ideology or a lust for war and the military life. He was tempted to prospect for gold in Brazil, and emigrating to the United States also crossed his mind. Both options required seed capital, and Lassen welcomed the war supplement – 250% of the standard rate – that allowed him to save up and enjoy life at sea and in port. He was annoyed when *Eleonora Mærsk* was sent to waters not classified as war zones and he had to smoke a pipe or roll-ups instead of cigars, and drink beer instead of brandy.

Then Germany occupied his homeland – and for Anders Lassen, the world war suddenly became a personal matter.

Chapter One

Childhood and Family[1]

The squirrel said: 'I've been lying along a branch, shaking with fear, while a tall boy fired pointy sticks up at me – I've no idea how he spotted me, as I didnot stir at all.' Bente was displeased – no doubt the tall boy was one of her brothers.

(Suzanne Lassen: *Bente og Skovens Dyr*, 1936)[*]

Høvdingsgaard and Bækkeskov

Anders Frederik Emil Victor Schau Lassen was born 22 September 1920 at Høvdingsgaard manor in South Zealand. His younger brother, Frants, was born in 1922. Their father, Emil Victor Schau Lassen, had inherited the estate from his father in 1917 – two years before he married their mother, the author and illustrator Suzanne Marie Raben-Levetzau. In 1929, financial difficulties forced Emil Lassen to sell Høvdingsgaard. He instead bought the nearby estate Bækkeskov, but it proved just as difficult to run a profitable agricultural enterprise there. The boys' younger sister, Bente, was born in 1931.

Anders and Frants on a fishing expedition.

---

[*] The Danish book has never been published in English. The title translates as 'Bente and the Animals of the Forest'.

Anders and Frants were keen hunters. At an early age they developed a formidable ability to move quickly and quietly in the wild. They honed their marksmanship and archery skills on chickens, pigeons, sparrows, rats, leaping roe deer, wild birds in flight and even a fully-grown tomcat.

The boys often camped in the woods with their friends and the family's large dog. They sailed the local lakes and caught brown trout by tickling them or shooting them with a bow and arrow. They experimented with jumping out of a bathroom window on the second floor, using a garden umbrella as a parachute. One of their favourite playgrounds was the roof of the main building – but only when their mother was not home. Once when Anders and Frants saw a wall of death at a market they dragged a moped up onto the roof and drove it around the gutters.[2] Sometimes the boys would practise shooting indoors – which, like Anders' knife-throwing, inflicted much damage on the fixtures and fittings.

Emil Lassen apparently had no qualms about his sons' free and occasionally wild lifestyle. Perhaps he was too busy trying to put the estate onto a stable financial footing to pay much attention to what his offspring were up to when they were out of sight. Although burdened by the family's financial difficulties, Emil was an energetic and outgoing personality with a pronounced sense of humour. He came from a family with strong military traditions. His great-grandfather, Emil Victor Schau, was one of the famous seven Schau brothers, all of whom were killed or died of typhus in the Schleswig Wars of 1848–9 and 1864 – and he himself was a second lieutenant in the Royal Life Guards Reserve. Part of his election platform as a Conservative candidate for parliament was to strengthen the armed forces. The electorate were less keen and he was defeated in the general elections of 1932, 1935, 1939 and 1943.

Emil Lassen instilled a strong sense of patriotism in his children, teaching them that they had a duty to their country – a duty that might well mean putting their own lives at risk.

Anders' mother, Suzanne, was born in 1888, the daughter of Count Frederik Raben-Levetzau – one of the biggest landowners in the country, with estates on

Suzanne and Emil Lassen with Rufus.

The main building of Bækkeskov was erected 1796–98 when the estate was owned by the Englishman Charles August Selbys. (Illustration by Suzanne Lassen in *Bentes Fuglebog*, 1932)

Lolland and in South Zealand, and who served as Minister of Foreign Affairs 1905–8 – and his American wife, Suzanne (better known as Nina) Moulton.

Suzanne was artistically gifted and made her debut as a writer and illustrator in 1915 with *En Billedbog* (A Picture Book). In 1929 she published the verse novel *Den uartige Caroline* (Naughty Caroline), one of the most popular Danish children's books of the day. This and subsequent publications made a significant contribution to the family finances. Suzanne illustrated her own books with black-and-white drawings and elegant watercolours. Both the text and images reflected her fresh and humorous approach to life.

Before the outbreak of the First World War, Emil Lassen's two sisters, Jenny and Estrid, had married German landowners, from whom they later separated. When Jenny's two young sons, Axel and Cuno von dem Bussche-Streithorst, visited Bækkeskov, Anders took charge of their war games and decreed that the Danes had to win every battle – a somewhat tiresome ritual for the guests.[3]

Among the many visitors to Bækkeskov was Karen Blixen's brother, Thomas Dinesen, who had fought in the Great War as a private in the Canadian army. He was awarded the Victoria Cross during the offensive at Amiens in 1918,

> for most conspicuous and continuous bravery displayed during ten hours of hand-to-hand fighting, which resulted in the capture of over a mile of strongly garrisoned and stubbornly defended enemy trenches. Five times in succession he rushed forward alone, and single-handed put hostile machine guns out of action, accounting for twelve of the enemy with bomb and bayonet. His sustained valour and resourcefulness inspired his comrades at a very critical stage of the action, and were an example to all.[4]*

Other guests included the well-known hunter and explorer Count Gregers Ahlefeldt-Laurvig-Bille. He taught the 13/14-year-old Anders and his younger brother to make bows and impressed upon them that a proper hunter carefully records his every kill. Anders was fascinated by the history and traditions of archery and decorated the title page of his 1934 hunting journal with a drawing of an ancient Assyrian relief depicting a lion struck by four arrows, below which was a detailed drawing of another arrow. On the name label on the cover he drew his own personal emblem – a silhouette of an animal skull, vertically pierced by an arrow. From then on, Anders recorded all of his kills and how he had despatched them.

School

Anders and Frants spent their first year of education at the local school in Mern, near Høvdingsgaard. When the family moved to Bækkeskov, the boys were home-schooled until Anders turned 11. He then attended the exclusive Herlufsholm boarding school for four years, which gained him admission to the upper-secondary school. Herlufsholm was a popular choice for sons of the landowning class and Emil Lassen had also been a pupil there.

As Herlufsholm was about 12½ miles from Bækkeskov, Anders often returned home at weekends, which must have been bright spots in an otherwise difficult period for him. Anders' grades from October 1932 to the summer of 1935, and not least his teachers' comments, show a boy who despite making an effort – which according to his teachers he did in some subjects – found it hard to live up to the school's academic demands. It did not help that he contracted a kidney disease that, according to his mother, set him back half a year, and would plague him for the rest of his life.[5]

Anders' teachers wrote about him: 'nice but slow, ... surprisingly ignorant, ... immature compared to his class ... has great difficulty being attentive in class ... has difficulty getting used to regular, thorough work ... it seems as if his bodily growth stands in the way of his mental development.' A Science teacher was pleased that Anders 'at least shows an interest in Zoology', and an English teacher was glad

Anders Lassen at Herlufsholm.

that 'he has pulled himself somewhat together, and some small progress may be traced.' A history teacher found that Anders 'is interested and keeps up quite well', a Geography teacher noted that 'his inability to absorb the subject matter is coupled with quite a reasonable judgment', and a Woodshop teacher remarked that he 'is interested mostly in the fabrication of weapons! It is hard to get him to do any other kind of work with care.'[6]

When Frants joined him at Herlufsholm in 1933, the brothers found themselves in the same class because Anders' poor grades meant he had to repeat a year. They remained at the school until summer 1935, when Emil Lassen informed the headmaster that he was aware that Anders' grades were too poor for him to continue. He and Suzanne had therefore decided to withdraw both of their sons, 'because as far as possible we want them to stay together, and we hope to have them placed at Haslev High School after the summer holidays'.[7]

It was not to be. In autumn 1935 the boys started at Lundby Lower Secondary, studying for a Standard Preparatory Exam (leaving certificate) with three languages. The certificate would not only qualify them for upper-secondary school, but also for a position in the Civil Service, and was a prerequisite for access to both the Royal Agricultural College and the Polytechnic. Lundby was within cycling distance (10 miles) of Bækkeskov, so Anders and Frants could again live at home. The brothers rode to and from school on a tandem, Anders at the back acting as tail gunner and taking pot shots with his gun at the many targets that popped up along the way.

Anders was one of the oldest in his class – two years older than the youngest – and one of the biggest and strongest. At Herlufsholm he had acquired a reputation as an aggressive and vicious tearaway. While he was involved in many fights at Lundby, he also had a reputation of never kicking or using dirty tricks, and always backing off once his opponent was down.[8]

Academically, Anders was a poor student, but he was well liked, enterprising and a natural leader, who impressed his peers with his archery and the other skills he had acquired in the forests around Bækkeskov.[9]

Always ready to defy authority, his rebellion often took the form of innocent – albeit not necessarily harmless – schoolboy pranks. For example, during a bike ride around Funen in the summer of 1937, Anders led all of the

Anders Lassen, 18 years old.

boys in the class on an illicit night-time swim in a pond behind the barn in which they were supposed to be sleeping.[10] On another occasion, he used a teacher's brief absence from the classroom to trace a mirror reflection of the word 'pussy' in the chalk dust on her seat. The prank had the desired result, the word was clearly legible when she stood up again and turned around. The class fell about laughing. Somebody told on him though, and Suzanne Lassen was summonsed to a meeting with the headmaster. When she arrived at the school, Anders hid – and while she was talking to the headmaster, he stole her car and drove home to Bækkeskov.[11]

Anders' three years at Lundby ended in May–June 1938, when he was awarded a leaving certificate with the lowest possible pass grades.[12]

What next?

Frants did well at Lundby and had no difficulty obtaining a position in the East Asiatic Company – the biggest and most respected enterprise in the country at the time, with a portfolio that included a worldwide shipping operation. His appointment to the highly selective EAC may have been helped by the family's close friendship with Prince Axel, cousin to King Christian X, a member of the board since 1927, managing director since 1934 and made chair of EAC in 1938.

Anders went down a different path. On 3 November 1938 he started at the Ollerup Academy of Physical Education, an institution favoured by the parents of the more unruly element of upper-class youth at the time. It is not known whether Anders made a conscious choice to become a PE teacher or whether it was an attempt to knock some discipline into him. He excelled at the physical aspects but was frustrated by the sedentary academic side, which must have felt like being back at Herlufsholm and Lundby. He dropped out, leaving Ollerup on 22 December to spend Christmas at home with his family, and never returning to complete the course.

Emil and Suzanne had sold Bækkeskov to Suzanne's oldest brother, Siegfried Raben-Levetzau, who let them have a house, *Skygholt*, in the grounds. Anders was still able to roam his forest paradise, but the family's reduced circumstances were all too clear.

In 1938, Emil Lassen was appointed to the International Non-Intervention Commission's corps of observers, which was under the command of the Danish colonel C.D.O. Lunn. The corps guarded the border between France and Spain in the Pyrenees during the Spanish Civil War, and secured Emil paid employment well into 1939. During his absence, Anders went to sea.

Chapter Two

M/S *Fionia*, January–May 1939

Since storms are less frequent at sea than some landsmen suppose, the life of a sailor is principally made up of the daily performance of certain tasks, in certain manners and at certain times.
(Nordhoff & Hall: *Mutiny on the Bounty*)

Despite his family background, and his seemingly natural inclination towards the life of a soldier, Anders showed no interest in a military career. If he had turned up at the draft board in 1938 (the year he turned 18) and – kidney condition notwithstanding – completed his national service, it might have opened the door to a career as an officer. But Anders chose to postpone his appearance in front of the board. Instead, perhaps again with Prince Axel's intervention, he signed up as a cabin boy on one of EAC's ships, *Fionia*, which set sail from Copenhagen on 19 January 1939 on a four-month round-trip to Bangkok via Antwerp, Portsmouth, Dunkirk, Gibraltar, Port Said, Port Sudan, Aden, the Red Sea and Colombo.

The East Asiatic Company's ship M/S *Fionia* was built by the Burmeister & Wain shipyard in Copenhagen in 1914.

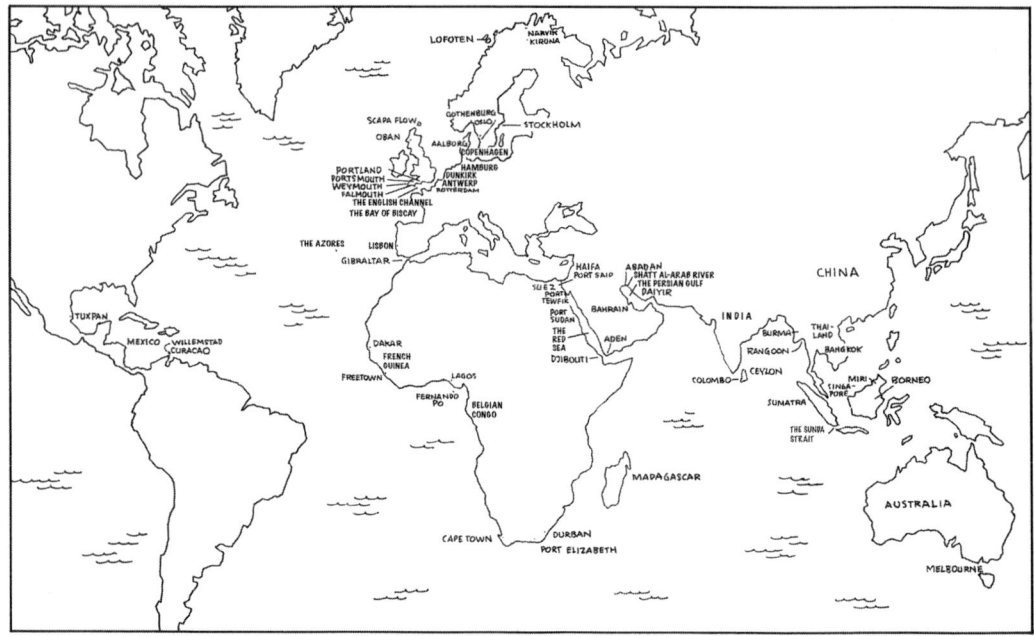

Anders Lassen's travels before joining the SBS.

In each of the sixteen weeks of the voyage, Anders wrote at least one letter to his mother. These letters express his pleasure at seeing the big, wide world, but also quite a severe degree of homesickness and a distaste for the 'indescribably boring' and menial work, which offered no prospect of advancement. If Anders were to make a career for himself at sea, it would not be by working his way up through the ranks, but by sailing with the training ship *Danmark*.[13]

Prince Axel's son, Prince Georg, in whose home Anders had sometimes been a guest before joining *Fionia*, reported that Anders rarely drank. Or, more accurately, he was rarely drunk – but when he was, he always wanted to fight. Not that he needed alcohol to be belligerent. The prince described him as an aggressive loner who 'frightened people'.[14]

Anders' letters to Suzanne, which were otherwise so open and plain speaking, contained little mention of drinking and fighting. When the ship was in port, the crew would get drunk, 'because spirits costs next to nothing', but Anders reported that he did 'not like being drunk, and only liked to drink when it is done with style, as you know'. While tempers sometimes boiled over – such as during a pub quarrel with some Norwegians about the right to Greenland – Anders, unlike most of his crewmates, was rarely embroiled in actual violence. He suspected that this was because of his size and his 'Ollerup muscles that suggest I've been a boxer or wrestler'.

Anders was from a different social class than his crewmates and spoke a different language. Towards the end of the voyage he wrote to his father: 'I will soon have had enough of mixing with the riff-raff.' The 'riff-raff' were the rank-and-file crew, whereas the officers, while they too would get drunk, were people with style and a sense of decorum.[15]

Bit by bit, Anders began to abandon his plans for a future in the merchant navy. 'Sailing is shit,' he wrote time and again.

He had a clear vision of the sort of life he wanted:

> Hope some day ... to earn enough to buy a nice old place. Go hunting with bow and arrow ... and in the evening smoke cigars – drink slowly and stylishly, enjoying a vintage brandy – talk about the day's hunt and play cards.[16]

Agriculture may have seemed an obvious route back to the lost paradise of his youth, but it held no particular allure for Anders. Running his own farm or company, rather than being an employee, would require funds – of which he had none. He asked his mother to use her connections, hoping that Prince Axel would find him an office job, as he had done for Frants.

Time and again, Anders wrote about Prince Axel and getting a job in 'Land EAC', but with less optimism as time wore on. Perhaps Prince Axel shared his son's view of Anders as an aggressive, scary loner. Or maybe he just considered Anders' exam results too poor for EAC.

By March 1939, Anders could see the end of the voyage approaching and he received cheerful news from home – not about potential careers, but about the dinner the family was planning to celebrate his return.[17] On 1 April 1939 he wrote to Frants and their mutual friend Frede. Next to his signature he drew his emblem – the animal skull with the arrow:

Anders Lassen aboard M/S *Fionia*, Copenhagen 11 May 1939.

> ...a glorious May evening with blackbirds whistling and doves cooing to go out with big bows, a quiver with half a dozen heavy broadheads, good food, find a good camp in the Deer Park. Lay down around campfire, light pipes, talk about things about foreign countries, about knocking

off, about foreign folk, about hunting while the shiny long narrow knives … flash in the glow of the crackling and flaming fire. Up and out early next morning, shoot the biggest and strongest deer in the park before the first rays of sun light up the tips of the trees. Gentlemen and archers, you should get arrows, even though it is a bit difficult you can be sure it is only a fraction of the difficulties I face. … in the 'Old Park', Uncle Siegfred has given me hunting rights there. So no excuses for laziness like it's 'not on', 'too dangerous', or the likes. Remember what it means to spend about half a year without touching a bow or seeing a piece of game, let alone shooting one … It will delight me greatly and be a great homecoming gift if the kit is ready. I'll bring <u>the knife</u> and whatever else I can.[18]

Chapter Three

Bækkeskov, May–June 1939[19]

The beaters drove the hens out, and when almost the whole of the brood had passed by, a dishevelled specimen appeared, I pulled back the string, let go and killed it instantly.

(Anders Lassen, *Hunting Journal*, 29 January 1935)

When *Fionia* docked in Copenhagen on 11 May 1939, Anders' family met him on the quayside. He withdrew his holiday pay (DKK 6.63) and spent the next month at Skygholt in the company of family and friends, including his German cousins Axel and Cuno von dem Bussche Streithorst, and the 17-year-old landowner's daughter Varinka Wichfeld, who had been the model for Suzanne's 'Naughty Caroline'. She would later describe Anders, who demonstrated his marksmanship by using old gramophone records as clay pigeons, as 'striking-looking, totally blond with big lavender-blue eyes', but also pretty wild, restless, disquietingly boastful and aggressive.[20]

It is not difficult to imagine this as an idyllic summer, during which elegant young people enjoyed their beautiful surroundings and each other's company. However, reality soon intruded. Prince Axel had not found Anders a desk job in EAC. And Anders had abandoned the idea of a career as an army officer – possibly because he did not want to return to education or perhaps he could not wait for the autumn draft board. Whatever the reason, his only option for quickly earning some money and perhaps carving out a career in the long term was the merchant navy. On 1 June

Anders, Bente, and Frants Lassen.

he signed a contract to train as a ship's mate with the shipping company A.P. Møller, which obliged him to serve on the company's vessels for four years. According to the contract, the four years would include time spent at a navigation school, and a minimum of one year of service after Anders had passed the navigation exam.[21] He would then be a qualified ship's mate.

Other – and bigger – shadows loomed over south Zealand that summer. Europe was gripped by fear of war. Anders' cousin Axel von dem Bussche Streithorst noted gloomily: 'This is the last time we will gather as a family. Next year we will be at war.' Cuno – who, like Axel, was an officer in the German army – replied: 'Yes, and I will be in command of a mass grave.'[22]*

Chapter Four

The Art of Guerrilla Warfare 1 – MI(R)

Your creed must be 'Shoot, burn and destroy'.
(Gubbins, *The Partisan Leader's Handbook*)

In autumn 1938 the British War Office set up a working party to study recent guerrilla warfare in China and the Spanish Civil War. The idea was to learn how to deal with uprisings or war anywhere in the Empire. At least that was the official brief. The real purpose was to devise ways of supporting resistance movements in any country the Germans might occupy. As the Nazi threat grew, so too did the small working party, eventually becoming part of the Directorate of Military Intelligence, where it was dubbed Military Intelligence (Research) (MI(R)).

The head of MI(R) was Lieutenant Colonel J.F.C. Holland, a First World War pilot who had provided air support for T.E. ('Lawrence of Arabia') Lawrence's guerrilla war against the Turks in the Middle East. Later he served in Ireland, where the Irish Republican Army (IRA) used bombs, assassinations, ambushes and raids to great effect against the forces of the Crown from 1919 to 1921. Seriously wounded in an IRA attack, Holland saw and felt at close quarters just how serious a threat a small band of irregulars with popular local support was to an occupying power.

One of Holland's closest colleagues was Lieutenant Colonel Colin McVean Gubbins MC. A Scot from a long line of officers, Gubbins had been wounded and awarded the Military Cross during the First World War. He had served in the British forces that came to the aid of the White Army during the Russian Civil War of 1919–20, and, like Holland, he had served in Ireland 1920–22. At the time of the German invasion of Poland in 1939, Gubbins was head of the British military mission in Warsaw. When Poland

Brigadier Colin McVean Gubbins.

surrendered, he escaped to Bucharest, taking with him important information about Polish intelligence's efforts to break the German Enigma code.

What Gubbins saw and learned in Russia and Ireland had aroused his interest in irregular warfare. At Holland's behest he wrote a series of textbooks on the subject, along with explosives expert M.R. Jeffries: *The Art of Guerrilla Warfare* (on guerrilla warfare in a whole country or region); *The Partisan Leader's Handbook* (on tactics and training for individual guerrilla groups); and *How to Use High Explosives* (a practical handbook by Jeffries).

In *The Art of Guerrilla Warfare*, Gubbins formulated 'The Guerrilla's Creed':

(a) Surprise first and foremost, by finding out the enemy's plans and concealing your own intentions and movements.
(b) Never undertake an operation unless certain of success owing to careful planning and good information. Break off the action when it becomes too risky to continue.
(c) Ensure that a secure line of retreat is always available.
(d) Choose areas and localities for action where your mobility will be superior to that of the enemy, owing to better knowledge of the country, lighter equipment, etc.
(e) Confine all movements as much as possible to the hours of darkness.
(f) Never engage in a pitched battle unless in overwhelming strength and thus sure of success.
(g) Avoid being pinned down in a battle by the enemy's superior forces or armament; break off the action before such a situation can develop.
(h) Retain the initiative at all costs by redoubling activities when the enemy commences counter-measures.
(i) When the time for action comes, act with the greatest boldness and audacity. The partisan's motto is 'Valiant yet vigilant'.[23]

In early summer 1939, while Gubbins and Jeffries were working on these pamphlets, their colleagues in MI(R) started recruiting future agents and guerrilla leaders, as well as people to train them. The recruitment process consisted of contacting personal acquaintances and making confidential enquiries to military units and the admission committees of various universities. Approximately 1,000 prospects were selected for their proficiency in languages, knowledge of relevant countries, or other special talents and skills. Polar explorers and mountaineers were in particularly high demand. Civilian candidates were sent on a short training course and then assigned the rank of officer in the regular army.

Chapter Five

M/T *Eleonora Mærsk*, 1939–40

June–September 1939

'Dash it all, old man!' exclaimed Vernon, when his chum had confided his plans; 'it ought to work. If it doesn't, nothing else will. I'm on it happen what may!'

(Percy Westerman, *The Submarine Hunters: A Story of Naval Patrol Work in the Great War*)

At midnight on 20 June 1939, Anders Lassen boarded a train at Næstved Station, near his home at Bækkeskov, and headed for Hamburg to join the new crew of the A.P. Møller tanker *Eleonora Mærsk*.

The vessel was built in 1936, making her 22 years younger than *Fionia*. At 16,500 dwt, she was the company's biggest vessel and the second-largest single-screw ship in the world.

Lassen still thought that 'sailing is shit', but he preferred *Eleonora Mærsk* and A.P. Møller to *Fionia* and EAC. Conditions on board were better and the work less arduous. What he liked most though was his shipmates, especially the bosun:

> … the type you only meet at sea, and even then not very often – made for a Viking film – strong, fair and handsome with good manners but hard and brutal over the smallest thing, and a sense of humour. Suits my and your idea of a modern gentleman a 1,000 times more than Siegfried [Raben-Levetzau] Snob.[24]

It is striking how this description of the bosun as Viking-like, handsome and strong, quick-tempered and brutal, yet humorous, fair and gentlemanly corresponds almost word-for-word to many of the descriptions of the soldier Lassen would become. Undoubtedly it meant a great deal to him to see some of his own traits and characteristics – some of which had often landed him in trouble – reflected in an adult male who exuded authority and commanded the respect of those around him.

On *Fionia*, Lassen had harboured reservations about his shipmates' drinking. Now he accepted it as part of life at sea – and was even proud of being better at it than some of his new friends: 'Was ashore yesterday. Everybody legless except me. Incredible how little some can take. Falmouth boring by the way.'[25]

From Falmouth, *Eleanora Mærsk* sailed to the Mexican oil port of Tuxpan, where she moored offshore and was hooked up to an oil pipeline. A lack of shore leave did not prevent Lassen from describing Mexico, in a letter home, as a country where the girls were pretty, cars dotted with bullet holes, and people sauntered about with big guns stuck down their belts.[26]

Adopting the patois of his shipmates bit by bit, Lassen started to mix his Danish with more and more English words and expletives. 'Foggen' (Danified pronunciation of fuckin'), and 'black bastards', for example, tripped off his pen – in letters home, in the diary that he started to keep in his hunting journal – and, presumably, off his tongue as well.

From Mexico they sailed back to Hamburg. On 5 August, Anders sent a telegraph: 'Expect to see family Hamburg 8th.'[27] Suzanne Lassen took him up on it and they spent four 'happy days' together, despite the uneasy atmosphere caused by the threat of impending war. Anders bought presents for the family, but also for himself and for the ship's cook, who liked to hunt, a couple of big, powerful catapults that they would use to shoot seabirds. In Hamburg, Anders targeted passers-by from his hotel room window.

On 11 August, Anders accompanied his mother to her train. They agreed to meet again when *Eleonora Mærsk* next docked in a European port within reasonable travelling distance.[28]

After Hamburg, *Eleonora Mærsk* headed for the oil port of Willemstad on Curaçao in the Dutch West Indies.[29]

In a letter to his family, Anders mentioned that he had seen six British destroyers in the English Channel, but the visible signs of war that loomed over Europe otherwise went unmentioned. He was more preoccupied with the silver lining: 'As far as I can make out, if it comes to it, people only sail for very high wages during war – not bad.'[30]

Incidentally, Willemstad was 'quite good fun – except that we were all so terribly drunk.'[31]

September 1939–January 1940

Eleonora Mærsk set sail from Willemstad on 1 September 1939. The following morning, at 04:40, fifty-seven Wehrmacht divisions totalling 1.5 million men attacked the Polish army, the Luftwaffe struck Polish airfields, and the

German training ship *Schleswig-Holstein* shelled a Polish base in Danzig. On 3 September, Britain and France declared war on Germany.

When *Eleonora Mærsk*'s radio operator, Arne Bennike, heard the news, the captain, P. Juel Pedersen, set the crew to work painting big Danish flags on the deck and sides of the vessel to show that the *Eleonora Mærsk* was neutral. He also gave orders to fly the flag at all times of the day and night and to make sure that it was brightly illuminated in hours of darkness – and with good reason. Immediately after the outbreak of war, the Allies had begun a blockade of Germany and started seizing merchant ships. On the first night of the war, a German submarine sank the British passenger steamer *Athenia*, which was en route from Liverpool to Canada, killing more than 100 passengers.

The oil from Curaçao was intended for Hamburg, but when *Eleonora Mærsk* entered the English Channel she was spotted by a British convoy of 10–15 ships, accompanied by two destroyers and a reconnaissance aircraft. The plane flew low over the ship, which was stopped and searched by the two destroyers, and ordered to dock in Weymouth on the south coast of England. She remained there for a week, along with several other vessels detained in the port.[32]

Lassen watched torpedo exercises off the naval base on the artificial island of Portland, and the constant flow of aircraft and supply ships to France, where the British Expeditionary Force was being deployed. It was all very exciting, and the money was excellent. As he put it, 'I now earn a princely wage three times as much as otherwise without doing the least bit more. It is extremely appealing.' For the first time in his life, Lassen forgot his own birthday. He turned 19 on 22 September.[33]

From Weymouth, *Eleonora Mærsk* crossed the Channel, docking in Antwerp on 28 September and remaining there for six days. In Antwerp, Lassen read in a Danish newspaper that a German submarine had sunk the Danish coal steamer SS *Vendia* in the North Sea. Eleven people lost their lives and six survivors were rescued by another Danish vessel.

Lassen wrote that he had seen another ship 'be done for in much the same way'. Not that he was profoundly affected by it, as in the next sentence he reported that he had bought a meerschaum pipe that was 'fine as hell'.[34]

He also wrote about a 'really sweet – in fact exceedingly sweet girl' he had 'had' … for the six days in Antwerp, who was also 'fine as hell'.[35] Together they saw a 'brilliant … hunting film from Poland'. Her thoughts on the film went unrecorded, but he noted that 'the river outside the city is full of ducks, cormorants, snipe and everything'.[36]

In Antwerp, Lassen briefly stepped out of his able seaman persona in favour of the lifestyle to which he had formerly been accustomed, and spent time 'eating an exquisite dinner at the finest hotel in Antwerp'. He was amused by the thought of 'what the Maid or Driver would think if they saw me cleaning tanks, hosing down decks or the like'.[37]

While in Antwerp, the crew went on strike, resulting in an almost-total breakdown of on-board discipline. After three-quarters of the crew signed off voluntarily or were put ashore, Captain Juel Pedersen – with great difficulty – assembled a new crew, most of whom had previously sailed under other flags, many on American ships.[38]

> …nobody wants to sail tankers – so they're a hardy bunch, rough bastards. Maybe there'll be extra cash for cleaning tanks [and (?)] because of the mines – suits me – as soon as the men in the shipping offices hear it's a tanker, they say stop.[39]

Lassen did not say 'stop', nor did he join the strike. He considered signing up on a British ship ('Fortune to be earned – no work – become a real sailor'), but stayed on *Eleonora Mærsk* where he made careful note of the particularly responsible and difficult tasks, some of which triggered a bonus, that were entrusted to him: 'Wax man most of Sunday, extra DKK 15, not to mention war and tanker supplements – spent time with the binoculars looking at pretty girl in yellow and red shoes on a Belgian boat on the port side.'[40] He also enjoyed, from time to time, being 'invited to drinks with the steward and mate, great honour'.[41]

From Antwerp, *Eleonora Mærsk* again sailed through the minefields in the English Channel, through the Bay of Biscay and the Strait of Gibraltar, 'with a moderate gale and heavy seas from astern'.[42] After an uneventful voyage through the Mediterranean, the tanker docked in Port Said.

> The other day in Port Said I was on guard on the gangway (an honour Skipper chose me). Skipper's orders nobody to board – merchants, maybe about 60 of them, swarmed like flies cursing pushing threatening making signs across their bellies and screamed like crazy when I slapped one and the clumsy clot fell into the water – Reaction didn't take long – tall black bastard pulled a marlin spike up from the bottom of his boat and aimed it at my bonce but I preferred to duck. Still got it.[43] … then I rigged up the deck hose and held it between all four limbs as the rabble approached.[44]

Enjoying a good brawl and making a fine job of an 'honourable' task were recurring themes in Lassen's diary entries and letters. His condescending (to put it mildly) term for the Arab merchants was in a similar vein to other prejudiced and racist descriptions that flowed from his pen and mouth: Frenchmen were comically servile, Mexicans were lazy, Africans were smelly 'niggers' and so on.

The voyage through the Suez Canal had been 'very exciting',[45] but slow, because the tanker had to moor several times to let oncoming vessels pass. Like Port Said, most of the ports at which *Eleonora Mærsk* called – Port Tewfiq, Aden, where they took bunker oil on board, and Bahrain in the Persian Gulf – were British territories. Oil was loaded in Bahrain, after which the ship sailed south towards Melbourne, Australia. 'No war supplement the next 3 weeks – Hell.'[46]

Christmas 1939 was celebrated at sea with typically Danish rice pudding, roast pork and a makeshift Christmas tree with presents in the officers' mess. Lassen sent a radio letter home: 'Warmest Christmas greetings. My thoughts are with you at home.'[47] Via the shipping company, his family sent Lassen a package including Charles Nordhoff's and J.N. Hall's *Mutiny on the Bounty* trilogy.[48]

Eleonora Mærsk saw in the New Year at sea, shortly before docking in Melbourne, where the oil was unloaded.

Chapter Six

The Art of Guerrilla Warfare 2 – The Snowballers, November 1939–March 1940[49]

'It sounds a preposterous outfit,' Alan said when Burge had gone.
'Perhaps,' Amos said, *'but doesn't it sound fun!'*
(John Verney: Going to the Wars)

On 30 November 1939, while *Eleonora Mærsk* was somewhere between Bahrain and Melbourne, the Soviet Union attacked Finland, following the rejection of its demands for changes to the border on the Karelian Isthmus and a base on the Finnish coast. The conflict dragged on for a surprisingly long time. The small but highly mobile Finnish forces caused the Russians unexpected difficulties and inflicted heavy losses.

In December 1939, British and French political and military leaders started planning to send an expeditionary force to Finland. Apart from coming to the aid of the hard-pressed Finns, it was to have the equally important mission of putting a stop to Swedish exports of iron ore to Germany via the port of Narvik in the north of Norway.

The French had a corps of *chasseurs alpins* (light mountain infantry), known as 'the Blue Devils', but the British would have to train and equip from scratch a force capable of operating in the Finnish winter. Instead of deploying an existing mobilised unit, they decided to set up a new one, the 5th (Supplementary Reserve) Battalion Scots Guards (5th Scots Guards), made up of volunteers from all parts of the army, as well as civilians with experience of skiing, dogsledding and mountaineering. The highly traditional Scots Guards may not have been the most obvious setting for this new type of unit, but on the other hand, like the other Guards regiments, the Scots Guards had a high concentration of wealthy officers, so it is safe to assume they had a correspondingly high proportion of people used to winter sports.

The 5th Scots Guards were placed under the command of winter sports star Lieutenant Colonel James S. Coats of the Coldstream Guards, while two polar explorers, mountaineers and writers – Martin Lindsay and Freddy Spencer Chapman – were put in charge of equipment. The flood of volunteers was overwhelming, including so many officers and NCOs that many enlisted as privates rather than miss out on this snowy adventure. The keen amateurs were propped up by NCOs from other Guards regiments and enlisted men from the Scots Guards, who may never have skied before but were reliable soldiers.

The volunteer 'Snowballers' included David Stirling (24), a son of Scottish landed gentry, and George Jellicoe (22) who would go on to play a key role in Lassen's military career.

Stirling had served as an officer in the Scots Guards. He had also studied at Cambridge, unsuccessfully trained as an artist in Paris and architect in England, and spent time as a cowboy in Canada and the United States. He was a frequent visitor to the racetrack at Newmarket and White's Club in London (the members of which also included the writer Evelyn Waugh, film star David Niven and Winston Churchill's son, Randolph). When war broke out in September 1939, Stirling was in the Rocky Mountains, training to climb the as-yet-unconquered Mount Everest.

George Jellicoe was the only son of Admiral Sir John Jellicoe, who commanded the British fleet at the Battle of Jutland in 1916 and was made an earl for his exploits. On his death in 1935, the title passed to George, aged 17. Jellicoe had been called up on 27 October 1939, but contracted pneumonia after only a few months at Sandhurst. He was an excellent skier and, like James S. Coats, was one of the British stars of the extremely fashionable tobogganing event at the Cresta Run in St. Moritz. He heard about the new ski battalion while he was convalescing and volunteered right away.

January was spent kitting out the battalion, working on their fitness, and weapons training. Once these basic skills had been mastered, the 5th Scots Guards boarded a train to Southampton and sailed to France, where the regiment was to train in winter warfare at Chamonix with the *chasseurs alpins*. Spirits were high and the Snowballers left a trail of empty champagne bottles in their wake along the railway track.

All did not go to plan in Chamonix though. It proved unexpectedly difficult to transform civilian sportsmen into soldiers – a task not made any easier by the avalanche warnings that kept the *chasseurs alpins* down in the valley, so the British were unable to benefit from their teaching. After an enjoyable but ultimately pointless week in the Alps, the Snowballers returned to Britain. They had spent a single night on board the passenger ship that was supposed to take them to Finland when the Finns capitulated on 12 March 1940 and the expedition was called off. It was probably just as well for the enthusiastic but ill-prepared volunteers. Strong forces in the War Office had always been opposed to the idea of a skiing battalion in the British army, and it was not long before the 5th Scots Guards was disbanded.

Chapter Seven

'Good luck – aim between the eyes' – February–March 1940

'My husband isn't home,' explained the wild duck, 'he's out flying with friends.'
(Suzanne Lassen: *Bentes Veninde*, 1932)*

Lassen knew that both his father and his brother Frants would be attracted by the Finnish cause, but he showed no interest at first. He wrote to Suzanne:

> I hope Frants ... hasn't gone up to shoot Bolsheviks in Finland. You won't get fat from that and it leads nowhere. Better prospecting for gold.[50]

Frants was too young to serve in the Finnish Army, but Emil Lassen was one of approximately 1,260 Danes who volunteered. Suzanne wrote to Anders:

> I understand him doing it ... I wouldn't dream of trying to stop him. Although I am really unhappy about it and worry about him all of the time.[51]

Emil set off on Friday, 9 February 1940, and was appointed second-in-command of 1st Company, the Danish Battalion. In March he was transferred to the 2nd Company under the command of a fellow officer from the Life Guards, Captain C.F. von Schalburg, a Nazi who was to fall on the Eastern Front in June 1942 while commanding the Danish Waffen-SS Legion *Frikorps Danmark*.

When Anders received the news that his father was on the way to Finland, he sent him a telegram: 'Good luck – aim between the eyes.'[52] Emil never did get the chance to 'shoot Bolsheviks'. Like the vast majority of the Danish volunteers, he was still training for winter warfare when the Finns surrendered.

---

* The Danish book has never been published in English. The title translates as 'Bente's Friend'.

Chapter Eight

M/T *Eleonora Mærsk*, 1 January–9 April 1940

Remember also that it is at sun-up and sun-down that you cast the longest shadow.

('Yank' Levy: *Guerilla Warfare*)

From Melbourne, *Eleonora Mærsk* sailed west from Australia and through the Sunda Strait to Miri on Borneo, where she anchored in the roadstead for a few days.

Once loaded, she sailed through the Strait of Singapore to Aden and Djibouti on the Horn of Africa, where the oil was unloaded. The next port of call was the major Iranian oil centre of Abadan on the island of the same name in the Arvand River, at the northern end of the Persian Gulf. The voyage continued with a new load, south of India and up to Rangoon, where Lassen and his companions went on a drink-fuelled shore leave marred by a violent incident.

> It's now a long time since you've heard from me – which is why you are now – firstly the high wages allow for cigars and cognac every day. … Been made (honourable) 'mine shooter' if we get rifles on board by Skipper himself much to chagrin of Cook. On land the other day with Sparky and Chippy in place called Rangoon in India somewhere – nearly ripped to pieces for throwing some black bastards out of the joint we wanted to be in. Whole street in uproar, and had to beat up several to get out – the bitches on our side screaming like crazy – Chippy good with fists Sparky too despite being totally sloshed.[53]

The next port of call was Cape Town in South Africa, where Lassen found time for an affair with a local woman. As luck would have it, her husband turned out not only to be the customs officer but was on his way down the gangway from *Eleonora Mærsk* just as Lassen was saying goodbye to his new friend down on the quay. To escape the wrath of the customs officer, Lassen boarded the ship by clambering up one of the hawsers and hiding while the couple discussed the matter.[54]

> Anders made his way ashore along one of the hawsers mooring the ship to the dock. One slip would have meant certain death at the bottom of

the dry dock. Cook wandered out onto the deck, saw Lassen dangling out there, turned a ghastly pale shade and had to sit down. Lassen made it back on board laughing and said he just wanted to see if he could do it.[55]

From Cape Town, *Eleonora Mærsk* sailed to Durban, where the ship entered the dry dock.

* * *

Although he thought that shooting Bolsheviks in Finland was unlikely to make you fat, Lassen did consider signing off early to join the Danish volunteers. However, before he could put his plan into action, the Winter War came to an end. His letters from early 1940 indicate that this sudden desire to go to war was motivated by aversion to life at sea rather than any sudden enthusiasm for the Finnish cause. In them, he muses on how much longer he had to serve at sea before he could sign off, and requests that money be deposited in his company account so that he could pay for any breach of contract and have something to live off. He was tempted to go to Brazil with the ship's carpenter to prospect for gold, but also considered going to the US where he expected to be able to rely on Suzanne's family and friends – at least whenever he was not thinking about all the money he could make as a whaler.[56]

By 20 March, Lassen had once again resigned himself to life on board *Eleonora Mærsk* – so much so that he wrote:

> Boarded 20 June. Now 20 March so been here 9 months under Seamen's Act 9 more left. Time will tell if I last that long.
>
> Thanks for sending money right away not needed this time but still in company account it feels much freer knowing some kind of chance of escape when it suits (feeling better about it all actually) but <u>think</u> I'll see out the 9 months at the moment but who knows?[57]

Chapter Nine

M/T *Eleonora Mærsk*, 9 April 1940–October 1940[58]

As in all guerilla projects, it is essential that every allowance be made by the guerrilla leader for the original plan miscarrying. Steps will always be taken in advance to overcome difficulties if and when they arise, and the leader will always be prepared for the worst.

(*SOE Syllabus*)

Occupation and mutiny – 9 April to 4 May 1940

On the afternoon of 9 April 1940, while *Eleonora Mærsk* was sailing north through the Persian Gulf, the radio operator, Arne Bennike (aka 'Sparky' with the good fists), received news via Boston Radio that the Germans had occupied Denmark. The crew listened to him with disbelief. Only when told personally by Bennike, or when they heard it on the radio with their own ears, did they begin to accept the fact that their country really had been occupied.

Bennike was unable to get through to Denmark, but received a telegram from a head of department in A.P. Moller, who had left Denmark early on the morning of 9 April before the Germans closed the borders, and was now in Helsingborg, Sweden. He instructed the captain to contact the company's representative in New York – Ismolco, a joint venture company owned by Arnold Peter Møller, the founder of the shipping company, and his cousin Hans Isbrandtsen – and await orders from there. However, when Bennike was unable to make contact with New York, Captain Juel Pedersen opted to continue towards Abadan.

On 10 April, the crew of the *Eleonora Mærsk* received a message from the Ministry of Trade in Denmark instructing Danish vessels to proceed to neutral ports. The very next day, on a BBC transmission from Bahrain, they heard the Danish Consul Knudsen in Colombo encourage them to proceed to British ports. The British authorities and the International Transport Workers' Federation called – in both English and Danish – on officers and crews on the 244 Danish ships that were outside Danish waters to make for British or French ports. They were promised all necessary protection and assistance, plus payment for their services, if they chose to sail under Allied flags.

On 12 April, Captain Juel Pedersen received an order from Ismolco in New York to sail to a neutral port. He tried to comply with the order by continuing to the ship's original destination, Abadan in neutral Iran. However, at the mouth of the Shatt al-Arab river, which connects the Gulf to Abadan, *Eleonora Mærsk* was stopped by a British patrol boat, at which point the captain dropped anchor in neutral waters. A day later, the British gave the captain permission to continue to Abadan, on the condition that he promised to then proceed to Melbourne as planned. Shortly afterwards, however, *Eleonora Mærsk* was again stopped and this time ordered to dock in Bahrain.

On 14 April, Ismolco ordered Captain Juel Pedersen to await new orders in neutral waters. Two days of uncertainty and unease followed, with heated discussions between the crew and officers, and the men downed tools temporarily. A ship's council was held, and all but Captain Juel Pedersen and the chief engineer, C. Mærsk-Møller (a cousin of the owner of the shipping company), declared that they wanted to sail for a British port. Despite this, the council decided to leave the captain in charge until such time as the company issued new orders. The next day, Juel Pedersen sent a note to the commanding naval officer in the Iranian port city of Daiyir, and moved his vessel closer to the shore. In the days that followed, he made preparations to sail even closer to the Iranian coast.

M/T *Eleonora Mærsk* at anchor in the Persian Gulf.

Two days later, Lassen and the cabin boy, S.N. Christiansen, were asked to row the captain and the third officer to Daiyir, where the two officers were to hold talks with local military and customs authorities. When they reached the shore, Lassen saw camels on the beach. Using gestures and drawings in the sand, he persuaded one of the herders to lend him one, and then proceeded to gallop up and down the beach. Eventually the captain called him to order so that the party could make their way to the commandant's residence. Here, Lassen and his companion enjoyed refreshments in the cool shade of some trees while their superiors met with the Iranians.

The ship remained where it was for a few days and the crew spent their time fishing and performing routine duties. As a safety precaution, the captain had the ship's name painted over. This required dangling off the outside of the ship while large sharks circled in the water below, but Lassen saw it as another special assignment and a great honour.

The crew became increasingly frustrated with both this enforced passivity and being kept in the dark about their fate, especially as British radio continued to broadcast more and more news about the German subjugation of their homeland. On 21 April, the BBC reported that the Danish ship *Jessie Mærsk* had, at the request of the crew, docked in an English port, where both the authorities and the unions had welcomed the Danes. This caused a stir among *Eleonora Mærsk*'s seamen and stokers. The officers tried to calm the crew down while still waiting for orders from Ismolco. On 22 April, the captain, at the crew's request, asked the company how long they would be anchored outside Daiyir and whether their wages were guaranteed.

The answer came on 23 April. Isbrandtsen ordered the captain to wait until the situation was clarified, and guaranteed all wages as long as the vessel remained in neutral waters. However, that same afternoon, the BBC broadcast a message from the Danish captain, H.C. Røder, who had docked his ship *Tasmania* in a British port. Røder strongly urged all Danish ships to proceed to British ports, seek protection and help the Allies liberate Denmark. When the message was broadcast again at 21:30, the whole crew gathered round the radio. Røder's words were the spark that ignited the simmering tensions on board. At 22:00, the ordinary crewmembers confronted first mate R. Skov and second mate C.A. Lang in the latter's cabin and declared that they would take over the ship unless it sailed to Bahrain the next morning. The first mate delivered the ultimatum to the captain, who then called the whole crew to a meeting in his cabin. With the exception of chief engineer C. Mærsk-Møller, all of the officers agreed to the men's demands. Pedersen promised to inform Ismolco and sail to Bahrain the next morning if answers were not forthcoming during the night. The response from Ismolco came in at 03:40

the following morning: 'Remain neutral territory until otherwise instructed – Hans Isbrandtsen.'

At 04:00, Juel Pedersen called in his two officers and conferred with them for an hour. They strongly advised him to make for Bahrain, stressing the risk of mutiny should he refuse. All of the advice from their trade unions and from the British authorities meant the crew were in no mood to be persuaded to stay put and await orders – which they suspected might be treasonous or dictated by the Germans anyway. The captain said he did not think the crew would use force – although he had asked the chief steward to lock away all the knives just in case. He had also agreed with the military in Daiyir that they would send help if a particular signal was heard from the ship's whistle. The officers advised him not to call for help, as that would only inflame the situation.

A watchman placed on the bridge by the crew eavesdropped on all of this. He roused the others, told them what he had heard and somebody disconnected the air supply to the whistle.

After meeting with his first and second mate, Juel Pedersen summoned all of the officers and two representatives of the ordinary seamen to a ship's council in the saloon. The entire crew soon turned up, and the meeting lasted for six hours. The captain recommended that they keep waiting, but an overwhelming majority were disinclined to heed his counsel. Eventually the captain asked all present two questions, the answers to which would be recorded in the logbook: What did they think about the demand to sail to Bahrain? And, if necessary, would they use force to oppose the captain's orders if he did not comply with this demand? All present stated that they wanted to sail to Bahrain – some for their safety, others (the officers) to avoid violence, and most in order to serve the Allies. Of the seven officers, only the second mate, Lang, was unequivocally prepared to use force if the captain insisted on remaining in neutral waters. The third engineer, Birch, wrote that he would use force if a flag other than the Danish, British or French were hoisted on board, or if the ship undertook actions that were contrary to British or Danish interests.

The three boys aged under 18, to their great regret, were not asked their opinion. The 23 ordinary seamen in the crew, except the chief steward, who said he would not use force as long as the ship did not sail for German interests ('but only to help England and Denmark'), all declared themselves unreservedly willing to use force if the captain refused to sail to Bahrain. Lassen wrote:

> Trainee ship's mate and ordinary seaman A.F.E.V.S. Lassen demands immediate departure for Bahrain, as he sees that as the only immediate option he has to serve his country. If the Captain opposes this, I am ready, if necessary, to impose this by force.

At 16:00, *Eleonora Mærsk* weighed anchor and set sail for Bahrain, where she cast anchor again at 08:15. A few hours later, a military patrol boarded the ship, and Captain Juel Pedersen and engineer Mærsk-Møller were taken ashore with the logbook. Many of the crew thought that the captain planned to accuse them of mutiny but the pair returned at 15:00 and the captain issued orders to leave port at 15:45.

Eleonora Mærsk now had a British prize crew on board made up of two lieutenants, an NCO, a telegraph operator and four soldiers. The soldiers were posted around the ship with loaded rifles. However, the mood on board was distinctly pro-British, so they relaxed and spent their time on target practice, shooting at anything they could find to throw into the water. The crew were allowed to join in, no doubt to the great delight of Lassen.

On 26 April, the British ordered *Eleonora Mærsk* to set sail for Colombo in Ceylon. On the same day, second mate Lang, the officer who had the best relationship with the crew and the British officers, was handed a list of those who wanted to volunteer for active military service. Six able and ordinary seamen expressed a preference for serving at sea, three on land. Lassen was one of the three, but it would be almost a whole year before his wish became a reality.

Hunting journal, diary, novel…

Many Danish sailors started keeping diaries on 9 April 1940 or in the days following the occupation of their homeland. Lassen was not one of them, but he did jot down scattered notes in the hunting journal that he had received as a confirmation present from Kristine Carlsen, known as 'Dida', who had been nanny to both Anders and his father. He also used it to store photographs, telegrams, newspaper clippings, etc, sent from home. Some of his entries were short and sometimes obviously written in haste or without concentrating. Others were long and detailed, and perhaps served as a substitute for the more reflective letters he could no longer send home. He wrote mostly in Danish, but sometimes in English. Many of his entries were written in a mixture of the two, which probably reflected the way that he and his Danish colleagues on board spoke. Later he also used the hunting journal as a scrapbook in which he saved newspaper clippings related to his own service career, as well as postcards, photographs and other souvenirs.

On the first page of the journal, Lassen reiterated:

> Mutinied in Persian Gulf. Wrote – the undersigned 'declares that if the captain opposes this, I am ready, if necessary, to impose this by force.'

* * *

On board M/T *Eleonora Mærsk* in the summer of 1940. The picture on the right shows Anders Lassen.

The hunting journal possibly also served as a repository of ideas for a project that he had embarked on at some point in the spring of 1940. In a telegram to his parents on 1 March 1940 he said, 'ALLRIGHT NOW ORDINARY SEAMAN WRITING NOVEL ANY NEWS'. The novel was never mentioned again in the few letters and telegrams he sent before links with home were severed on 9 April. Nor do letters from his family shed any light on this novel that he had started. Maybe it was based on him. Maybe he wrote to while away the hours of boredom or to reflect on himself and his life. Or perhaps he hoped that a novel would generate so much income that he would be able to escape the clutches of the merchant navy. In December 1941, Suzanne Lassen wrote to him: 'Did you really rip up the novel you had written? Really sorry about that. Would have liked to read it.'[59]

Chapter Ten

The Art of Guerrilla Warfare 3 – Independent Companies and Operation Knife

<u>Safety-razor blade, or blades, in cap peak.</u>
May be shown, in order that students may know what to expect, but the use of this device is not to be encouraged.

(SOE Syllabus)

Norway, April–June 1940

Shortly after the expedition to Finland had been cancelled and the Snowballers returned to their original units or civilian jobs, the rest of the British-French-Polish expeditionary force originally earmarked for deployment in Finland was instead sent to Norway to help halt the German invasion which had begun on 9 April 1940. A total of 10,000 Allied troops fought alongside the Norwegian army, but they could not prevent the Germans from occupying the whole of the country.

Under the command of Colin Gubbins, MI(R) set up ten 'independent companies' that would operate as lightly armed guerrillas, able to fight under their own steam for up to a month. Each company consisted of 20 officers and 270 privates and NCOs, all of them from the Territorial Army. The volunteers were supposed to have some experience of skiing and mountaineering, but there was no time for special training. Only five of Gubbins's independent companies made it to Norway, where they were almost immediately caught up in the Allied retreat and ended up functioning as regular infantry.

On 8 June the last British troops were evacuated from northern Norway. King Haakon and the government left with them to form a government in exile in London. The following day, the Norwegians commenced negotiations for their capitulation.

As well as the independent guerrilla companies, MI(R) also set up a dedicated sabotage unit that was to be put ashore from a submarine in the Sognefjord to blow up the road and rail bridges that linked Oslo with the north of the country.

Operation Knife, as it was dubbed, comprised six men under the command of Lieutenant Colonel Bryan Mayfield of the Scots Guards. Mayfield had been Jimmy Coats' second-in-command in the 5th Scots Guards. The other members of the team were Captain Peter Kemp, who had fought on the nationalist side in the Spanish Civil War; David Stirling's older brother William 'Bill' Stirling, who had been one of the 1,000 names in the MI(R) files, a fellow officer with Mayfield in the Scots Guards and his hunting buddy; James 'Jim' Gavin, a sapper and explosives expert who had attempted to climb Mount Everest in 1936; Ralph Farrant, who was an officer in a regiment of the line; and David Stacey, who was a stockbroker in civilian life. Apart from Kemp and Stirling, they had all been Snowballers.

The team left the naval base at Rosyth on the Firth of Forth on board the submarine HMS *Truant* on 23 April 1940. However, they were not at sea for long before *Truant* was attacked by a U-boat and hit by two torpedoes. *Truant* made it back to Rosyth, but Operation Knife was postponed. After some delay, which the group spent on impromptu guerrilla and sabotage training in the grounds of the Stirling family estate in Keir, nineteen miles from Rosyth, word came that Operation Knife was to be abandoned altogether. Stirling and Mayfield, who feared that the team would be split up and sent to conventional regiments, made an alternative proposal to their superiors in MI(R): set up a school to teach irregular warfare so that future operations would be better prepared. Holland and Gubbins, who were now back in MI(R), were thinking along the same lines – and in fact, had already secured funding for such a school.

STC Lochailort[60]

Stirling and Mayfield put themselves and their comrades from Operation Knife forward as instructors at MI(R)'s new school, and suggested that it be located in Scotland – specifically, in the Northwest Highlands, with which Bill Stirling was intimately familiar from countless hunting trips. Sparsely populated and noted for its harsh terrain and inhospitable climate, the region offered all sorts of invaluable challenges, as well as large numbers of remote buildings for billeting and training. Another advantage was that the Northwest Highlands had been one big security zone, encompassing a third of Scotland, since 1939. The zone was set up to protect the huge naval base at Scapa Flow and to facilitate surveillance of the long and sparsely populated coastline. Even locals needed special permission to be there. Holland and Gubbins approved the proposal, and Stirling and Mayfield were given free rein to commandeer properties. They were aided by Lord Lovat (Simon 'Shimi'

Fraser), who was not only Bill Stirling's cousin and a fellow student of Peter Kemp, but owned substantial portions of the Northwest Highlands. During the Boer War, his father had set up a rifle regiment of volunteers known as the Lovat Scouts, consisting of marksmen and *ghillies*, mainly drawn from his own estates. The Scouts' emphasis on mobility, marksmanship and the ability to merge into the landscape made them in many respects a precursor to the ideas MI(R) would develop more systematically and on a larger scale.

With the help of Lord Lovat, Stirling and Mayfield discovered Inverailort House, south of the village of the same name. It was located on the old 'Road to the Isles', between Fort William and Mallaig, on the mainland coast facing the Isle of Skye. The surrounding countryside provided abundant opportunities for hard marches, climbing, survival training, sailing with landing craft and small boats in rocky waters, and landing on difficult coasts, as well as training in close combat, shooting with live ammunition and sabotage under realistic conditions. Lochailort was also conveniently close to a railway line that could transport trainees and supplies to and from the school, and also be used in sabotage training.[61]

The new school, which opened in May 1940, was named Special Training Centre Lochailort (STC Lochailort). Administratively, it was a confusing collaboration between the War Office's Directorate for Military Training, which was in charge of admin and management, and MI(R), which was responsible for the training. Trainees were not told who was behind the school.

Within a few months, STC Lochailort had swallowed up many large and small buildings within an approximately thirty mile radius of Inverailort House. By late June, the school had eighty-two instructors – most from the Army, some from the Navy, and a number of civilians, including six local *ghillies* – as well as a few hundred other employees. The local Home Guard often played the role of the 'enemy' and guarded sabotage targets or chased trainees around the area. The school could train 150 officers and 2,500 NCOs and squaddies at a time.

The original six members of the Knife force taught at STC Lochailort. However, in June, Peter Kemp was transferred to other special duties and replaced by Bill Stirling's younger brother David (the mountaineer), who had grown bored of life in the Scots Guards. After completing the school's training, David Stirling became a fully-fledged instructor.

The instructors at STC Lochailort included all sorts of people whose talents, skills and ideas were often far removed from what was normally considered good form in the British army of the day. The most famous were two former police officers, William Fairbairn and Eric A. Sykes. They had returned to Britain after many years of service in Shanghai, where they had become experts in various forms of lethal close combat and developed an 'instinctive' shooting technique they considered faster and more accurate than the traditional 'aim and shoot' method.

One of Fairbairn and Syke's students was I.C.D. Smith, who later served in the Commandos, the SOE and the SBS, achieved the rank of major, and was twice awarded the Military Cross. He described the two Shanghai policemen as 'tough as old boots, but quite charming'.

> Maybe the most unusual aspect of their teaching which ran contrary to all orthodox instructions was in their method of aiming a revolver or pistol. When firing from the hip they were adamant that the average pistol firer was bound to be inaccurate because the effort of pulling the trigger, which in the case of a revolver was considerable, dragged the weapon off target. But on the other hand if you point your finger at any object and then check the line of sight you will find that inevitably your finger is spot on target. Therefore if you align your finger along the barrel and pull the trigger with the second finger at least the weapon will be correctly aligned. They maintained that this was just as accurate as the two handed method ... They also taught that a quick response was vital and firing from the hip was a lot quicker than the two handed pose. Personally I found that their theory gave much improved results not only with a revolver but also with a submachine gun, about the only weapon with which I was reasonably competent.[62]

Working with Wilkinson Sword, Fairbairn and Sykes also developed the legendary dagger known as the *F-S Fighting Knife*. It had an almost 7.5-inch long blade and a fluted brass handle with a crossbar. The long, thin double-edged blade, which opponents could not grab hold of, made the F-S dagger suitable for knife fights – and in particular the 'silent kills' that were one of Fairbairn and Sykes's specialities. The F-S was put into mass production in early 1941 and became standard issue for British special forces. Very few were ever used in combat, but it became an important symbol of the aggressive spirit and uncompromising willingness to kill without hesitation that were so fundamental to the ethos of the special forces.

Chapter Eleven

M/T *Eleonora Mærsk* in British Service, 4 May 1940–October 1940

Colombo is one of the most beautiful cities I've been to, and the climate down there is unusually lovely.

(Arne Bennike: *Gnisten paa Eventyr*)*

Eleonora *Mærsk* arrived in Colombo at 08:00 on 4 May. In the early afternoon, the British naval flag, the White Ensign, was hoisted on the fore-top, a sign that the Danish vessel was now a British prize.

The crew of *Eleonora Mærsk* passed the time swimming in the harbour – until they realised that sharks liked to do the same – and visiting other Danish and Norwegian ships. The Norwegians liked to tease the Danes with stories about their exploits against the Germans. 'It was not nice hearing that the Danes had offered no effective resistance,'[63] wrote cabin boy N.S Christiansen. Lassen would undoubtedly have concurred.[64]*

* * *

On 10 May, news reached them over the radio that the Germans had attacked the Netherlands, Belgium and Luxembourg, and that Winston Churchill had replaced Neville Chamberlain as British prime minister. On 15 May, news arrived of the Dutch capitulation.

Two days later, Captain Juel Pedersen, the Danish consul, Knudsen and a British officer assembled the whole crew and asked each one in turn whether he would serve under the British flag. All answered yes, albeit some of them adding the caveat that they would resign if the opportunity of active military service arose.[65]

* * *

---

* The Danish book has never been published in English. The title translates as 'Sparky's Adventures'.

After some time in port, the crew were granted shore leave. Anders went ashore with able seaman Hummer and a bunch of other crewmates. 'After getting half-pissed', the group, dressed in dirty khaki shorts and not wearing ties, descended on a posh hotel where 'despite furious bellboys and gesticulating managers', they forced their way in, sat at the best table and ordered beer. The other guests looked at them 'with disgust'. An anxious-looking manager asked the noisy sailors to leave, but to no avail. When a 'haughty manager' announced that they would not be served, a drunken Lassen beat him up. A couple of guests tried to intervene and Lassen's companions joined in the fray until 'everybody backed off and we retired in good order' to the sound of 'the posh bitches' cries'. The next item on the evening's programme was a visit to a brothel:

> Hummer and I drove up country in a taxi to find some good stuff not that we did I was half-cut and Hummer well gone but at the sight of the girls we both woke up and he jumped out and was nearest, so grabbed the youngest and prettiest one and left me with a horrible old witch – we crashed into the place and as always no matter how drunk I am I remembered to stash Grandpa's cigarette case and money away.
>
> Next morning Hummer found they had robbed him of 50 rupees – paid some layabout to show us where they lived – found them and threatened to smash the place up, call the police, etc. Eventually they paid up – but the bitch's husband was so mad that he stabbed the layabout in the shoulder Hummer kicked the bastard in the face we drove off and dropped the guy in the middle of the street in the next village Quite amusing, what with Hummer's zeal for the lass – that he ended up riddled with the clap.

It may have been this scrap that cost Lassen his front teeth. Not that he wrote about it in his letters or hunting journal, but sometime between parting with Suzanne in Hamburg in August 1939 and the spring of 1941, he did lose his front teeth. A friend wrote:

> I … assumed that he had parted company with them during his Merchant service days. Andy was a bright lad and his usual method of enforcing his (strong) will upon others was to enforce said thought with physical persuasion and I wouldn't be surprised if the Tale of The Two Teeth is embroiled in some such enforcement.[66]

* * *

After about three weeks in Colombo, *Eleonora Mærsk* was fitted with a crow's nest, a big gun platform on the poop deck at the stern, and a bridge from the new platform to the deckhouse. Lassen had to move out of his cabin, which was turned into an ammunition depot. On 2 June the gun was mounted. Over the next few days, ammunition and other supplies were loaded on board.

* * *

At noon on 11 June, *Eleonora Mærsk* finally set sail for Singapore. The ship was now registered in Colombo and those members of the original crew who had decided not to remain on land or sign up on one of EAC's bulk carriers had now signed on under British rules, with British wages and war supplements. Lassen's monthly wage was now £5 16s 3d, a bit less than his previous Danish income.

He was now not only an ordinary seaman and trainee ship's mate, but one of the seven men selected to operate the new anti-submarine gun:

> We docked in Colombo and got the loveliest gun 4.7 Inch. Guncrew was chosen by Second Mate [Lang] who the Admiralty and us thought was the only real man among the officers and an instructor said do such and such. After that we sailed off – shoot, he said. Alright. I was the one who drew and aimed the height and very apprehensively pulled – a helluva bang – I don't think there are very many who have fired a big heavy 4.7 incher requiring a seven-man crew knowing so little about it as I did that day.

Only four test shots were fired off Colombo, but Lassen and his mates in the gun crew practised several times en route for Singapore. He was, if he said so himself, a 'fine gunner'.

The gun crew of M/T *Eleonora Mærsk*. Anders is mostly hidden by the gun, but can be glimpsed under the cross, behind the man in white.

After a few days in Singapore, the ship continued to Sumatra, where it picked up a new cargo before returning to Singapore.

Eleonora Mærsk left Singapore again on the morning of 26 June. The same day, news came that France had capitulated and that the evacuation of British and other Allied forces to England had been completed.

From Singapore, the ship sailed to Cape Town and Port Elizabeth in South Africa, where its cargo was unloaded in late July. Along the way, the gunners trained twice a day and the whole crew performed repeated lifeboat drills – because even in the South Pacific and Indian oceans, German warships were a real threat.

Once *Eleonora Mærsk* had discharged her load in Durban, the ship docked to prepare for British military service. The A.P. Møller funnel marking was removed, the vessel was painted grey all over, concrete was cast around the bridge, enclosing the wheelhouse, radio rooms, etc, and live cables were wrapped around the whole ship to protect it from magnetic mines.

On 5 August, *Eleonora Mærsk,* now prepared for the hardships of war at sea, left for Abadan and a new cargo of oil. The tanker berthed in the Iranian oil port on 27 August. It was 40° in the shade and crew were not allowed on deck without headgear. Two days later, the ship set off back to South Africa.

* * *

Lassen had previously viewed the war with a certain degree of detachment, but the German occupation of Denmark had made it a deeply personal matter. He wanted to fight for his country's freedom and honour, and he was in no doubt that the best way to do this was under the British flag. He was proud of being a 'fine gunner' and an accomplished sailor, but he would have preferred to fight on land.

On the other hand, he was not sure that the war would have the outcome he wanted. At the back of his hunting journal, he wrote a rough draft of a letter to his Aunt Lila and her husband, the American diplomat Lithgow Osborne, who lived in the United States. In the letter he asked his aunt and uncle about the possibility of obtaining US citizenship 'if England has to sue for peace or God forbid, suffers the same fate as France'.

Chapter Twelve

The Art of Guerrilla Warfare 4 – Commandos

When the exotic name 'Commando' was at length made free to the press it rapidly extended its meaning to include curates on motor bicycles. In 1940 a Commando was a military unit, about the size of a battalion, composed of volunteers for special service. They kept the badges of their regiments; no flashes or green berets then, nothing to display in inns. They were a secret force whose only privilege was to find their own billets and victuals. Each unit took its character from its commander.

(Evelyn Waugh, *Officers and Gentlemen*, 1955)

'Butcher and bolt'

In the weeks immediately after Churchill took over as PM on 10 May 1940, the situation deteriorated in Norway, and France collapsed, culminating in the evacuation of 338,000 Allied troops from Dunkirk between 27 May and 4 June. The Germans were now poised on the other side of the English Channel, and every effort had to be made to defend the British Isles. At this moment, with Britain alone and with its back to the wall, it was important for Churchill to show the world and the British people that the armed forces still had the will and the ability to strike back.

MI(R) carried out a sabotage operation on the French coast on the night of 2/3 June. Three officers sailing on a trawler made available by the Royal Navy were put ashore between Boulogne and Étaples. They set fire to 200,000 tons of fuel and returned safely on 10 June, rowing twelve miles with a German prisoner of war. The mission was a success, but Churchill demanded more and bigger operations.[67] On 5 June, he instructed the Chiefs of Staff Committee to see to it that Britain had the capacity to launch regular guerrilla attacks on the French coast as soon as possible: 'Enterprises must be prepared with specially trained troops of the hunter class, who can develop a reign of terror first of all on the "butcher and bolt" policy. I look to the Chiefs of Staff to propose me measures for a vigorous enterprising and ceaseless offensive against the whole German occupied coastline.'[68]

Churchill's orders triggered an immediate response from the Imperial General Staff. That same day, Lieutenant Colonel Dudley Clarke submitted a memorandum calling for the establishment of a force of 5,000 men, divided into ten independent units known as Commandos, which would carry out small frequent raids along German-occupied coasts. This would tie up German resources along the entire periphery of the occupied territories and hinder their efforts to build up an invasion force to attack Britain. Another important aim was to promote the aggressive spirit that Churchill saw as essential to prevent further disasters.

The 41-year-old Clarke was an unconventional officer with a great flair for stage setting and disguises. He had served in the British Mandate for Palestine, where he learned first-hand how difficult it was for the regular British forces to defeat Arab guerrillas. However, his main source of inspiration was the Boers' small, mobile 'commando' units, which had caused the British no end of trouble during the war of 1899–1902. Churchill had originally suggested the name Leopards, but having served as a cavalry officer in the Boer War (and been made a PoW), he liked Clarke's suggestion of 'Commandos'.

The name aside, it was not so much the Boers who inspired Churchill but the German 'Stormtroopers' deployed during the First World War. These were specially trained, heavily armed infantrymen whose shock attacks broke through enemy lines and penetrated deep into the rear, spreading fear and confusion. It then fell to slower conventional units to overrun positions that could not be taken right away. The Italians had succeeded with a similar tactic in their trench warfare against the Austrians when the elite corps *Arditi* ('the Daring Ones') made frequent lightning attacks on the enemy before withdrawing again. In the campaigns against Poland in 1939 and France, the Netherlands and Belgium in 1940, the Germans' victorious *Blitzkrieg* strategy was based on the same principles as the Stormtrooper operations in the First World War.

Churchill enthusiastically embraced this tactic of shock, surprise and terror, which he alliteratively dubbed *butcher and bolt*. 'Butcher' was not a word that the British army liked, and many officers were far from enamoured by the pirate-like image of the Commandos, which quickly took hold of the imaginations of both the armed forces and the general public. Many also doubted the wisdom of devoting resources to special forces, who required special training and (on Churchill's express orders) the best equipment, and might drain regular units of their best fighters.

Although not everybody was equally enthusiastic about Churchill and Clarke's idea, it was swiftly put into practice. On 14 June, Lieutenant General Alan Bourne of the Royal Marines was appointed 'Commander of Raiding Operations on coasts in enemy occupation, and Adviser to the Chiefs of Staff on Combined Operations'.

The first unit, 3 Commando, was established on 5 July 1940 and headquartered in Plymouth. It was under the command of the newly promoted Lieutenant Colonel John Durnford-Slater, a former captain at a training unit. In the following weeks, 4, 5, 6, 7, 8, 9 and 11 Commando followed.

To make sure there was no weakening of defences against invasion, existing units were not converted into commandos. Instead, a new volunteer force was set up, with the promise of special service of an unspecified, dangerous nature.

Not all commanding officers were willing to release trained manpower to the commando units. Others, however, saw it as an opportunity to rid themselves of more troublesome elements. According to Durnford-Slater: 'We never enlisted anybody who looked like the tough guy criminal type as I considered that this sort of man would be a coward in battle.'[69] On the other hand, he had no qualms about accepting people who had committed minor offences, because the threat of sending them back to their units was usually enough to deter them from causing trouble. *Return to Unit* (RTU) became a familiar notion in the special forces, and an important means of maintaining discipline among people who, in many cases, had volunteered in order to escape the stricter discipline of their regular units.

The first raid

The first commando raid took place even before the units had been set up. On the night of 23 June 1940, 120 men of 11 Commando/Independent Company, under the command of Major Ronnie Tod, landed on the coast of France, south of Boulogne-sur-Mer and Le Touquet.[70*] The official purpose of the hastily cobbled together Operation Collar was 'offensive reconnaissance'. Tod's men did in fact engage the enemy. Two Germans were killed, and Dudley Clarke, who was there as an observer, lost most of one ear to a bullet. The operation provided the newspapers with a positive story at a time when good news was at a premium.

A week after Operation Collar, the Germans occupied the Channel Islands – 15 miles from Normandy and 139 from England, which had been English since 1066 and William the Conqueror. On 2 July, Churchill demanded a raid on the islands, preferably by the commandos, as a matter of urgency. The War Office started planning right away. The plan was to go ashore on Guernsey – at 30 square miles, the second biggest of the islands (Jersey is 36 square miles) – and attack the airfield. The mission was codenamed Operation Ambassador.

It was to be carried out by a force of 140 men, composed of troops from the as yet untrained 3 Commando and 11 Commando/Independent Company (100 men). Unlike the Normandy mission, the Guernsey landing was meticulously planned. Three officers with local knowledge were set ashore from submarines to reconnoitre and act as guides for the commando units to follow. The landing was originally scheduled for the night of 12/13 July, but postponed for two days because of the weather. Shortly before the troops boarded the two destroyers that would take them to Guernsey, word came that the Germans had reinforced several of the planned landing sites. The plans had to be changed at the last minute. At 17:45 on 14 July the force departed on board the two destroyers, accompanied by six fast RAF rescue launches which were to transport them from the warships to the shore.

Despite all of the preparations, the operation was an ignominious failure, partly because the planners had failed to take into account that the two-day delay meant that tidal conditions had changed. Technical problems put a couple of the RAF boats out of commission, while others had problems with their compasses – possibly because the metal in the soldiers' weapons affected the magnetic needles. The 40 men from 3 Commando, who were to create a diversion while 11 Commando/Independent Company attacked the airfield, made it ashore more or less according to plan, albeit soaking wet. However, half of the main force landed on the neighbouring island of Sark, while the rest ran aground on rocks off Guernsey or encountered problems with their RAF launches.

The forty commandos who made it ashore searched in vain for Germans to fight, but soon ascertained that their training, equipment and knowledge of local conditions were not up to the job. The only damage they managed to inflict was to sever a couple of telegraph wires and erect a roadblock made of boulders. Leaving Guernsey did not go to plan either. The high tide meant they had to swim about 100 yards out to the boats. Although it was an explicit requirement that commandos could swim, three non-swimmers had to be left behind on the beach. One man disappeared, presumably drowned, while ferrying weapons to the boats.

Churchill reacted to the debacle by replacing Bourne with Admiral of the Fleet Sir Roger Keyes, who was given the title of Director of Combined Operations. The 68-year-old Keyes moved into the office of the chief of the Directorate of Combined Operations on 17 July 1940.

Commando operations more or less ceased for the next eight months, while the units trained intensively and the Directorate of Combined Operations refined their techniques and methods. MI(R)'s independent companies were disbanded, and the men were assigned to the new commando units. As Combined Operations became more established, the commandos opened their own schools in the Northwest Highlands – including at the newly commandeered STC Lochailort.

Chapter Thirteen

M/T *British Consul*, October–December 1940

Anders Lassen visited the other day. He looked splendid, healthy, cheerful and engaging. We had a long talk and I thought very highly of him.
(Eduard Reventlow)

Eleonora Mærsk docked in Cape Town on 26 September. The ship was unloaded and remained in port for most of October while mechanical problems were dealt with and various other work was carried out. Lassen spent every day ashore.

South Africa, October
Painted outside with old Jørgen and we were talking about how much better and stronger sailors was when he was young than they were now – I has been pretty drunk the night before and was still a good deal i suppose, therefore i told him i couldn't agree with and than I was readdy to Bet a Pund than i was able to climb up on one the wire Stage which goes up to the Raa in the Mast.
 We betted and i started and half up i felt i couldn't do it
 But the Thought of the £ lead me go on and when only one yard from the end i couldn't keep the grib more and felt like a Stone on the iron Deck. They all laughed, I lost my £ and couldn't move for 2 Days so it seems like old Jørgen was right.

Although Lassen was still getting on very well with his crewmates, he had had his fill of *Eleonora Mærsk* and resolved to sign off.

Second mate Lang lamented his decision, which he did not understand. As he said, 'Anders was not the type who told others what he intended to do.'[71]

Captain Juel Pedersen did more than just deplore the ordinary seaman's decision. He refused point blank to sign him off. Although Lassen could be unruly, he was an accomplished sailor and the head of the gun crew. He would be difficult to replace.

Lassen was not to be moved. He did systematically shoddy work, feigned illness and was insubordinate. When threatened with three weeks in prison, he immediately accepted the 'offer', at which point the captain finally gave in and signed him off. He was paid his last seaman's wage, minus a penalty for being 'absent from work', on 25 October. He wrote in his diary: 'The first man for a very long time to have been payd of in prober manner in Cap-town in regular manner.'

His description of the signing off is followed by some partly illegible and even less coherent notes. Only certain words are decipherable:

> Ran away … train … police … sentenced to hard labour … pardoned … signed on Greeks outsailed really drunk … robbed of sub … signed on MT 'British Consul'.

On 24 October, Anders signed on with the tanker SS *British Consul*, under Captain J.D. 'Dusty' Miller. Built in 1924, the 6,900-ton *British Consul* was twelve years older than *Eleonora Mærsk* and less than half her size. Conditions on board were also far more basic than both *Eleonora Mærsk* and *Fionia*.[72] Lassen, unaware that there were two Norwegians in the crew, and in no doubt as to his own maritime prowess, wrote in his hunting journal: 'Was only Scandinavian, so best sailor on board.'

On 26 October, *British Consul* left Cape Town for Scotland. Her route would take her through areas where German submarines lay in wait, or where she risked being seized by the Vichy French navy operating out of ports in the French colonies in West Africa or attacked by German aircraft from bases in France.

* * *

Two days after *British Consul* set sail from Cape Town, Italian and Albanian forces crossed the border between Albania and Greece, and the Italian air force began bombing targets in Greece.

During the Italian-Turkish War of 1912, Italy had seized the Dodecanese Islands from the Ottoman Empire. In 1925 the people of the islands were made Italian citizens and Italian was introduced as the official language. Mussolini now wanted to extend Italy's dominion in the eastern Mediterranean to the whole of Greece. The Greek forces only had obsolete equipment, but provided unexpectedly stiff resistance. On 2 November, the Italian invasion stalled. The next day, British military personnel arrived on the mainland to establish bases from which the RAF would be able to support the Greek army.

* * *

The convoy voyage from South Africa to Scotland, and *British Consul*'s subsequent service as a supply ship for British navy vessels in the waters around Scotland, was full of dangers to the ship and her crew, and full of new challenges for Lassen. As an experienced able seaman and trainee ship's mate, Lassen was allowed to take the helm. He was proud of the trust that Captain Miller and his mate showed him, and he enjoyed

> [...] the feeling of sole responsibility – when you zigzag in a convoy – and feel the ship obey you and get to steer her as hard as you want so the ship aft can't keep up and the Skipper and Mate don't bother you at all but let you get on with your job.

At some point on the journey, Lassen wrote that, for the first time 'things were really happening'. Hitherto, only the escort ships had been attacked, but *British Consul* had now been attacked twice, and had fired eight shots that were 'very close' to hitting their targets. The ship also fired four more shots at – and luckily missed – a plane that turned out to be 'friendly'. Lassen was annoyed not to have been in the gun crew during the shooting, as he was on lookout duty in the crow's nest.

Towards the end of the voyage, he wrote:

> damned hard month at sea in bad weather – water everywhere always and air attacks every other day. Started with 38 shells and only two left when we arrived. ... Now I know a lot about artillery. Expert in 3 types and a really fine Gunner.

Arriving in Scotland did not mean the danger of air raids had passed. While *British Consul* lay anchored between a Norwegian and a Dutch ship, its two neighbours were attacked by a pair of long-range German bombers, 'and a gang of Norwegians went to hell'. Lassen noted that the two ships had not been properly blacked out, and thought it would never have happened on a ship commanded by British officers.

He admired British officers in general, and *British Consul*'s Captain Miller in particular. Lassen enjoyed Miller's robust sense of humour – like when he gave the order to shoot at a British plane that flew over his ship in a no-fly zone – and his firm leadership. Miller's hard-hitting style commanded respect, but he also knew how to reward good work. 'Great honour,' noted Lassen in his diary, when the skipper had drunk a glass of rum with him in recognition of his proficiency as a helmsman.

Chapter Fourteen

Britain, December 1940–January 1941

The success of the organization is going to depend on the quality and work of the individual members, therefore it is impossible to over-estimate the importance of picking the right people.

(SOE Syllabus)

'What the hell else is there to do?' – Newcastle, December 1940–January 1941

Anders Lassen signed off from the *British Consul* in Oban on 23 December 1940. Captain Miller offered to take him on as a regular able seaman (as opposed to a wartime seaman), but did not stand in Lassen's way when he said no.

From Oban, Lassen made his way south to Newcastle, which had been designated as the home port for exiled Danish seamen. It was here that the union leader Børge Møller, who had fled to Britain in May 1940, had been running the Danish branch of the British National Union of Seamen. Lassen joined the NUS on Monday, 30 December. He wrote about the early days in Newcastle in his hunting journal:

> had a great time, hung about in 'Princes' full of Scandinavians especially Norwegian Teddy Bears legless every night for 14 days. It's no good, but what the hell else is there to do?
>
> One evening I was about to go home with some girls and wanted to buy a half bottle of whisky before I left when I realise that I don't have any more change so I get out my money belt to pay the lovely Stella behind the bar. When Stella sees it she says: Ay you silly fool now you are showing your Monney here and about 10 Men are looking at you in this Moment better give me the Mony and come and get them the Morrow when you are sober. Drunk as I was, for the first time in my life I gave a girl money without getting something back right away and of course anyone would think you would never see it again but lo and behold the next day I walk in and Stella gives me back my money every

Great Britain.

cent or penny. Stella is now bank, really like Stella, as it were the first bit of stuff … I've met who hasn't tried to rob me.

* * *

It may come as a bit of a surprise that a brave, dynamic and patriotic young man, who had proven his willingness, in both word and deed, to fight for his country – and had even indicated that he wanted to do so in the army – did not just march straight from the train station to the nearest recruiting office. Instead he spent two weeks 'hanging around' in the pub. Maybe he was worn out after two months on convoy duty, or unsettled by the anti-climax of life on land, which was relatively safe and where there was nothing in particular to do. Maybe he thought about signing on at sea again. Maybe he was unsure what use he would be, or maybe he was having more fundamental, existential doubts about what to do with himself now that he was no longer surrounded by shipmates united in their desire to fight the Germans. Lassen spent two to three weeks in wet, blacked-out, wintry Newcastle. It was the first, indeed only, time that his life was that unstructured – no family, friends, school, ship's crew or military unit. It is by no means clear what path Anders would have chosen had he not met another Dane, a 29-year-old second engineer, in the pub one evening.

About six feet tall and nearly as wide, champion swimmer Kjeld Mogens Aage Hammer was an engineer in the merchant navy. Following the German occupation of Denmark, he signed off in Newcastle, where he too was eager to join the war effort. Like Lassen, Hammer was brave, bordering on the reckless, never afraid of a challenge and a fervent patriot.[73]

Mogens Hammer.

* * *

The other day in Prinses I met a young 2 Master Hammer and we got talking politics and found out he had very fine news. Hammer and I talked about all sorts among other things about the great significance it would have for Denmark's future after the war if it could be ascertained that free Danes had been ready and willing to do their bit for the British cause and as a start we decided to try the Royal Air Force the next day. The reception was extremely friendly and welcoming. The following, however, got in the way of these plans.

A few days later I was standing chatting with Stella over the bar in Princes at about 8 in the evening when Hammer comes in and asks if I fancy going to London that night to join the army. I said right away to hell with the damn army I'm going to be an airman. But I agreed to go with him and talk to the man in charge.

It was a Cap'n Iversen – who turned out to have completely the same idea of the tremendous significance it would have politically later on if Denmark could say that so and so many put their lives on the line side by side with Englishmen and the men of other nations who fought to win back their countries' freedom – and – my hope is later perhaps to set up a Danish regiment here in England … Cap'n Iversen asked what I thought about this and that and after learning what he wanted to do and seeing that it was much like what I thought and believed – I told him that I would be ready to leave in half an hour – that same evening we went to London.

Cap'n Iversen[74]

Since April 1940 the 57-year-old Werner Michael Iversen had devoted his time to encouraging Danes around the British Empire to support the war effort. Regardless of the outcome of the war, Iversen believed that supporting Britain would give Denmark the 'moral right' that it was otherwise in danger of losing by not resisting the German occupation, and not even protesting vigorously enough about it. Since early October 1940 he had been head of a recruitment office for the British run by the newly established Danish Council in London.

Captain Werner Michael Iversen (right) with another Dane, Pilot Officer A.G. Frandsen, RAF.

In 1919, Iversen had travelled to Malaya to work on a plantation, and went on to manage several others in the country. In 1939, following the expiration of a contract and the outbreak of war, he moved to England with his British-born wife, Muriel Lilian Robinson. Shortly before his meeting with Lassen, Iversen, a lieutenant in the Danish Army Reserve, was finally – after several unsuccessful attempts – accepted as a captain in the British army. He threw himself into the recruitment drive right away.

Iversen was a pedant, a stickler for the rules and highly reluctant to delegate responsibility and authority. He was also extremely secretive, but enjoyed using what he knew, or his hunches, to cut an interesting figure in Danish circles in London. He was not easy to work with, but he was highly energetic and spared no effort in his recruitment drive.

During this phase of the war, while the Battle of the Atlantic raged and threatened to cut off the convoys that were the nation's lifeblood, the British were just as interested in volunteers for the merchant navy as for the armed forces.[75] The real reason Iversen was allowed to travel to Newcastle in January 1941 in search of volunteers was that he was working for the British Lieutenant Commander Hollingworth, who had just been put in charge of a newly created organization that needed Danish volunteers. The working relationship between the two men was somewhat awkward. Hollingworth could neither tell Iversen what kind of work the volunteers would be asked to do, nor tell him what organization he represented.[76]

Commander Ralph C. Hollingworth, RNVR, head of SOE's Danish Section, 1940–45.

Chapter Fifteen

The Art of Guerrilla Warfare 5 – SOE – "Set Europe Ablaze"

Early in October I received a letter from a room number in the War Office, which began, as far as I remember:

'Your name has been given to us by Mr. Dodds-Parker as having qualifications which may be of interest to this Department.'

(Peter Kemp: *Without Colours or Crest*)

Around the same time as the Combined Operations Directorate, another new organization was set up at Churchill's behest. In the PM's words, the purpose of the Special Operations Executive was to 'set Europe ablaze' using sabotage, guerrilla warfare and propaganda. It was the result of a merger of MI(R), the secret service SIS/MI6's Section D, and

SOE Headquarters in Baker Street, London.

the Foreign Office department Electra House. Like MI(R), Section D had been set up in 1938, and with more or less the same purpose, but its focus was on sabotage, intelligence work, and the promotion of anti-Nazi activity in Germany and the occupied countries. Electra House was a propaganda unit.

While the War Office and Foreign Office squabbled over ownership of the new organization, the Labour politician and Minister of Economic Warfare Hugh Dalton made the post of political head of the SOE his own. Throughout the war, MI6 considered the SOE little more than a bunch of amateurs who put the intelligence service's own agents at risk. The War Office and the military also looked askance at the SOE, if not with outright antipathy.

The SOE was a secret organization and preferred to operate under the pseudonym Inter-Services Research Bureau (ISRB). Its staff and first agents were recruited from the War Office, Foreign Office and the Ministry of Economic Warfare, as well as via MI(R)'s index of potential agents and via private contacts. The SOE needed all sorts of people with all sorts of talents, and recruited 'everything from pimps to princesses'.[77]

In November 1940, Dalton brought Colin Gubbins to the SOE. Gubbins had been training civilian 'stay behind groups' to wage guerrilla warfare against the Germans in the event of an invasion of the British Isles. He was promoted to brigadier and put in charge of training and operations.

The SOE had a special section for each of the European countries in which it operated – sometimes more than one (there were six French sections, all working with different Resistance groups). The Danish section was set up in October 1940.

Gubbins recruited a handful of diplomats, naval officers and other British citizens who had been living in Denmark when the Germans occupied the country on 9 April 1940, but had been allowed to leave in a sealed train. One of them was Ralph C. Hollingworth, who had lived in Denmark for years and worked in the bicycle industry. In his spare time, he sang in the Anglican church choir, but also worked for the intelligence services. He had been keeping an eye on German minesweepers in Danish waters since March 1940.[78]

Chapter Sixteen

In the SOE

I still recall from the early days the two empty trays with outgoing and incoming correspondence and a certain sense of loneliness.
(Hollingworth)

Recruitment drive in Newcastle

One of Hollingworth's first jobs as head of the Danish section – which at this time consisted of just himself and a staff of two – was to travel to Newcastle to seek out SOE recruits among the Danish seamen. The head of the Danish branch of the National Union of Seamen, Børge Møller, was very helpful, despite the fact that Hollingworth could not tell him the name of the organization he represented, nor the nature of the work for which potential volunteers would be signing up. Secrecy was and remained a major problem. To get the ball rolling, Hollingworth defied the rules and confided in the local chief of police in Newcastle. The chief kept files on the exiled seamen, all of whom had to sign in regularly at the police station. He also had personal opinions on many of them. He chose 60–70 men and had them brought in so Hollingworth could talk to them individually and assess their suitability. This was how Mogens Hammer was recruited – and through him, Anders Lassen.[79]

London

The following morning, Iversen, Hammer and Lassen arrived in London and went to the Royal Hotel on Russell Square, which became their base in London.

Iversen told Lassen and Hammer of his plans and ambitions – and also of his frustration that so many of the leading members of the Danish Council in Britain were reluctant to openly disassociate themselves from the government's policy of cooperation with the Germans and join the British war effort.

While the British had more sympathy for the 'progressives' (as they called Iversen's activists), that did not mean they were prepared to give them *carte blanche* to implement their ideas. For example, the Admiralty rejected a proposal to man a British destroyer, or perhaps just a corvette, with a purely Danish crew, preferring that the Danes continued to serve in the merchant navy.[80]

In his hunting journal, Lassen vents about the Danes' incessant parleying and discussions and the fact that they were merely 'looking out for their own interests'.

> … all this about being open about what we want here in Britain will come when the time is right but many big names with something to lose are still opposed.
>
> The unfortunate thing is that as long as we aren't officially recognised the hundreds of Danes around the world will hold back from joining.
>
> Yet when the Day comes it will mean a lot that there is a core that can be built around.

No. 1 Special School, Brockhall

In addition to Lassen, Iversen and Hammer, the original core group of Danish volunteers consisted of twelve others, who began two weeks of basic training at No. 1 Special School on Saturday, 11 January 1941. Some had been recruited in Newcastle, others via British consulates around the world, or through the Royal Victoria Patriotic School in Wandsworth, where refugees were interrogated and screened.[81]

No. 1 Special School in Brockhall near Flore, a village near Northampton about sixty miles north-west of London, was under the command of Major T.G. Lindsay, who was on secondment from the Irish Guards.

* * *

Lassen and his comrades spent the Sunday settling in at Brockhall before training started the next morning. The working day was 08:45 to 19:30. Apart from square-bashing, the programme included lectures on guerrilla warfare, map-reading, explosives in theory and practice, hand-to-hand combat, shooting with pistols, rifles and automatic weapons, and the use of gas masks.[82]

The trainees may have wondered why they were required to spend so much time on disciplines like guerrilla warfare and explosives. What the Danes were not told was that No. 1 Special School was no ordinary British army training camp, but elementary training for agents of the Special Operations Executive. Captain Iversen may have dreamed of a Danish unit in the British army under the Danish flag and with 'DANMARK' emblazoned on their shoulders, but the main priority for the British was to recruit Danes to the SOE. Although he was kept in the dark for security reasons, Iversen was able to put two and two together as time wore on.

Chapter Seventeen

The Art of Guerrilla Warfare 6 – The SOE Schools[83]

Personally, I have to admit that I'm absolutely terrified every time I have to jump. I know it doesn't show, but inside – my God how I am shaking!
(Mogens Hammer)

The SOE training programme was on four levels. Level one was spent at *Preliminary Schools*, housed in six manor houses dotted about the countryside in the south of England. Trainees spent three to four weeks there, learning the rudiments of guerrilla warfare and sabotage, while the schools decided whether they were suitable candidates. Those found fit then moved on to one of the five *Paramilitary Schools* or *Group A Schools* (STS 21-STS 25) in Invernessshire in the north-west Highlands, where they spent five weeks getting fit and learning how to survive in the field – and how to kill. The paramilitary training included a stint at the Royal Air Force's No. 1 Parachute Training School at the Ringway air base near Manchester.

Level three consisted of a number of *Finishing Schools* or *Group B Schools*, just outside the village of Beaulieu in Hampshire. The use of so many country mansions and other large and often quite sumptuous stately homes for training purposes gave rise to the jocular interpretation among those in the know that 'SOE' really stood for 'Stately 'omes of England'.

Unlike the *preliminary* and *paramilitary schools*, which focused on sabotage and military and paramilitary skills, the Beaulieu schools taught the trainees how to cope with life as a secret agent. Subjects included life underground, personal safety, secret organizational work, secret communications, the recruitment and use of agents, the organization of enemy forces, propaganda and the use of codes, invisible ink, etc. It was only at the *Group A* schools that the volunteers were told what it was they were being trained to do, and that the SOE even existed.

Level four consisted of an in-depth briefing just before agents were sent into the field. This took place in a flat in London, and was given either to individuals or to small teams that would be deployed together.

At the very end of the training there were a number of *Specialist Schools* focusing on particular types of sabotage, making explosive devices, the use of carrier pigeons, street fighting, advanced radio communications, microphotography, gauging public opinion in enemy and occupied territories, etc. Last but not least, there were a number of *Country Section Schools* and seven *Holding Schools*.

The SOE also set up what were known as ISRB workshops (as mentioned previously, Inter Services Research Branch was one of the SOE's aliases). The workshops, in Inverlair in Invernessshire, were known within the SOE as 'the Cooler'. Trainees found unfit for service in the SOE were interned there until what they had learned no longer posed any danger to SOE agents or their operations, or might otherwise hinder the war effort.

Chapter Eighteen

'Good with an out-and-out independent nature'

There are plenty of genuine patriots willing to take risks for anyone working against the enemy. The danger here is that in order to persuade such a person to do the service for you it may be necessary to disclose information about your organization and activities.

(*SOE Syllabus*)

STS 1

No. 1 Special School, Brockhall, one of the SOE's 'stately 'omes' was known internally as 'Special Training School 1'. For practical and security reasons, each school only took in one nationality at a time. In the second half of January 1941, the Danes were the only trainees at Brockhall.

At this stage, the recruits had no idea what they were being trained for or that the SOE even existed. This made it rather difficult to make the training relevant, and the national sections often tried to rush their people through the basic courses.[84] The first Danish team left Brockhall on 27 January, after just two weeks of basic training.

Iversen followed this first team closely, and described Lassen as 'Good with an out-and-out independent nature. Good in theory and practice and suitable for special service.'[85]

The head of the school, Major Lindsay, wrote about him:

> Speaks English (fluently), German (well), Norwegian & Swedish (fair). Description: Height 6', weight 11st. 7. Eyes blue, hair fair. Commandant's remarks: Determined and keen. Comes of very good Danish family. Well educated. Failed an exam when studying forestry and, I think, ran away to sea. Considerable experience of hunting and shooting. Should do well as an individual or as a leader of a patrol. Might develop into a good officer later. Has missed much of the training due to a poisoned foot.

No other sources specify the nature of the 'poisoned foot' that prevented Lassen from taking part in the training. Nor do we know the source of the information that Lassen had run away from home after failing a forestry exam. Perhaps it was based on a misunderstanding – perhaps his English was not as fluent as Lindsay thought – or perhaps Lassen had reinvented his own past.

After the course, the participants swore a triple oath of allegiance to Christian X and 'any authority that works against the enemy which has occupied my country … so help me GOD.'

Lassen wrote later in his hunting journal (with characteristic inaccuracy for numbers and dates):

> On 2/1 1941, 17 men who had decided to do everything in their power to fight for Denmark's Freedom swore an oath to Captain Iversen who we for the most part can thank for it all getting as far as this ~~without him and 2nd Commander Hallingwood? and Dr. Leutnant Bruhn~~. And everyone's hope is now that this will be the beginning of a coming together of all free Danes and a revolt in Denmark itself later on.

Carl Johan Bruhn

Carl Johan Bruhn, or 'Dr. Leutnant Bruhn', as Lassen called him in his diary, was born in 1904 to a well-off business family in Frederiksberg. After training as a forester, in 1929, like Iversen, he travelled to Malaya, where he managed a rubber plantation. In 1932 he married the Scottish-born doctor Anne Connan. The couple returned to Denmark the same year and Bruhn took over the running of a sawmill. The business failed and in 1934 the couple moved to London where Bruhn started studying medicine. A religious man, he wanted to return to Malaya as a medical missionary, but changed his mind following the outbreak of war and the occupation of Denmark. Shortly after 9 April 1940, at a meeting of the Danish Club in London, Bruhn met the newly appointed head of

Carl Johan Bruhn.

the SOE's small Danish department, Lieutenant Commander Hollingworth, who was on the lookout for a reliable man. The two became close friends, and Bruhn went on to be a key figure in the SOE's Danish activities.

In January 1941, Hollingworth selected Bruhn for the first Danish team to undergo SOE's training. Hollingworth later described Bruhn as:

> the best man we ever had in the SOE, full of energy, with a talent for organization, winning the respect and devotion of all his comrades and exercising great influence upon all who worked with him. His determination may be judged from the fact that he passed his final medical examinations when already training for parachute jumping at Ringway.[86]

'Cannot stand being kept in', January–March 1941

In Iversen's absence, it was Bruhn who addressed the passing out ceremony on the morning of Monday, 27 January, after the Danish contingent's final drill and parade. Bruhn thanked the staff of the school on behalf of his comrades. He said that while the course had appeared daunting in scale, thanks to the instructors' 'interest, enthusiasm and patience', he now felt well equipped for further training. Bruhn said that the Danes were proud of the opportunity to serve as British soldiers, and that they would not only fight for Denmark's freedom but also help Great Britain in its 'heroic struggle for the freedom of nations and of individuals'. He rounded off his short address by promising Major Lindsay that he would be proud of the trainees' future achievements.

At 13:00 the Danes left Brockhall, arriving at the Royal Hotel in London three hours later. Here they changed into civilian clothes and were sent on leave. Their orders were to meet at the hotel, in uniform and ready to travel, at 00:00 on Wednesday, 29 January. Later that morning they set off for the next camp, where they were to be billeted temporarily before heading to the SOE's Paramilitary School at Arisaig House (STS 21) in north-west Scotland.[87]

* * *

After the passing out parade on 27 January, Lassen was briefly separated from his companions because he was sent to hospital to have his inflamed foot treated. He was admitted to Leavesden Hospital, in the village of Abbots Langley, Hertfordshire, approximately ten miles north-west of London. This was actually a mental hospital, but parts of it were now being used to treat the wounded from the fighting in France and victims of air raids. In his hunting journal, Lassen wrote of his admiration for the resilience and humour of the British.

However, despite the good company, he quickly tired of lying about in a hospital. In mid-February, he was discharged when his restless behaviour became too disruptive.

This meant that he had some spare time before he could proceed to Arisaig House – but being idle was not in his nature. He missed the activity, independence and recognition of his prowess from the time spent on *British Consul*. In his hunting journal he wrote, 'if it turns out that I can't do anything real in the Army there is still a chance [as a sailor].'

In his frustration, Lassen asked Børge Møller, head of the Danish section of the National Union of Seamen in Newcastle, to help him get out of the SOE so he could go to sea again – but without success.

In early March 1941, Lassen was reunited with the rest of the Danish contingent. Once more under the watchful eyes of his superiors, his suitability as a secret agent was evaluated regularly.

On March 11, '1340' (perhaps Iversen, perhaps Bruhn or Captain Carl Johan Starup, who served as Iversen's assistant and instructor for the Danish team), wrote:

> 2379 [Anders Lassen] is the weakest character of the party, he is the black sheep of a good family who has run away from home and become a sailor. He is keen enough on the job, but cannot stand being kept in, he would definitely not be reliable enough for special duties; he might not keep sober when on leave and give away secrets.

Despite the reservations in these assessments, Lassen was allowed to continue training along with his fellow Danes at Arisaig House (STS 21).

Chapter Nineteen

The Art of Guerrilla Warfare 7 – Commandos

It's the grandest job in the Army that one could possibly get, and it is a job that if properly carried out can be of enormous value. Just think of operating under direct orders from the C. in C.! No red tabs, no paper work, none of all the things that are so cramping and infuriating and disheartening in the Army. Just pure operations, the success of which depends principally on oneself and the men one has oneself picked to do the job with you. It's terrific! It's revolutionary.

(Geoffrey Appleyard, letter to parents)

Raids

The commando forces were set up to carry out *raids*, i.e. attacks that always ended in withdrawal no matter their scale or the nature of the target. Four main types of *raids* were envisaged: 1) hit-and-run attacks designed to alarm the enemy and make them expend resources by putting large areas on high alert; 2) reconnaissance missions aimed at gathering intelligence through observation, photography and taking prisoners, preferably as part of the preparations for a landing or major attack; 3) sabotage raids against factories, military installations and energy infrastructure, which could not be attacked from the air; 4) attacks in support of a larger operation, either as a diversion or to subdue isolated targets and pave the way for the main attack.[88]

In the spring of 1941, the commando forces were finally ready to go into action. On 3 March 1941, 3 and 4 Commando landed on the Lofoten Islands, where they destroyed fuel depots and fish-oil plants. When they left they took with them 216 German prisoners of war and 315 Norwegians who wanted to fight for the British, as well as German code books and encryption equipment.

Layforce – From Scotland to Syria

A few days before the attack on the Lofoten Islands, a mixed force of men from 3, 4, 7, 8 and 11 Commando set sail from Scotland, heading to Egypt via South Africa and the Suez Canal. Originally known as Z Force, the group was later renamed Layforce (after its commanding officer, Colonel Robert Laycock).

The ranks of 8 Commando were bolstered by a small force of skilled kayakers, who were to reconnoitre enemy shores before the commandos landed to commit minor acts of sabotage. 'Folboat Section' – named after a type of collapsible two-person kayak or *folboat*[89]– was founded by Captain Roger Courtney, who had previously spent time kayaking on the Nile, among other exotic locations, and as a big game hunter in East Africa. Courtney had enormous energy, indomitable willpower and a formidable gift of the gab, all of which helped him to convince the higher echelons of the military establishment of the military value of kayaks.

He was also well known for his ability to drink anyone under the table, which was a useful skill in 8 Commando.[90] The officers included George Jellicoe, Winston Churchill's son Randolph, the author Evelyn Waugh, and David Stirling, who spent so much time in his bunk that he earned the nickname 'the Giant Sloth'. Stirling spent most of his waking hours playing poker, roulette and baccarat with the other young socialites. Randolph Churchill lost £850 in two evenings, while Jellicoe lost almost three years' wages, only to win it all back on a single lucky card.[91]

Folboat.

Layforce was to join up with General O'Connor's XIII Corps and build on his successes in North Africa. When the Italians invaded Egypt in September 1940, O'Connor inflicted heavy losses on them and drove them back. He now appeared to be in a position to conquer the whole of North Africa. Layforce was to attack Italian-occupied Rhodes as part of a larger plan designed to ensure the Allies had control of the Aegean and the eastern Mediterranean, which would pave the way for attacks via the Balkans.

However, before the plan could be put into action, the military situation changed dramatically. Rommel's *Afrika Korps* counterattacked in Libya and reached the Libyan-Egyptian border on 12 April. Six days earlier, German forces had attacked Yugoslavia and Greece. The Greek army, reinforced by British troops sent to the country in early March, was unable to withstand the onslaught, and the troopships that were supposed to carry Layforce were instead used to evacuate 45,000 British and Australian-New Zealand (ANZAC) troops from Greece. On 27 April, King George II and his government left for Alexandria before proceeding to London. On 30 April the Germans occupied the last part of the Greek mainland, effectively dominating the whole of the Balkans. On Crete, 42,000 Greek, British and ANZAC troops held out.

Layforce was now part of the general reserve that was to defend Egypt if Rommel continued his advance. However, Laycock allowed his old friends in 8 Commando to operate as special forces closer to the front. A series of small attacks were planned on the enemy's long and vulnerable coastal supply lines, but they were all cancelled – except for one rather unsuccessful attack on Bardia.

When German airborne forces invaded Crete on 20 May 1941, 800 men from Layforce were transferred to the island. Layforce only fought in the final battles on the island, during the chaotic and humiliating evacuation of the vanquished Commonwealth forces. Some of the Layforce men left on one of the last ships to depart from the port of Sfakia on the evening of 31 May, but about 600 were killed or captured.

British and ANZAC losses amounted to 15,000 dead, wounded and captured. The Germans lost 6,000 men – more than in the whole of the rest of the Balkans campaign. Around 17,000 Commonwealth troops were evacuated from Crete, while others hid in the mountains, intending to escape from the island later.

* * *

Greece was divided into Italian, German and Bulgarian zones of occupation. The Italian zone encompassed most of mainland Greece, the Peloponnese, the easternmost part of Crete, Corfu, Cephalonia and Zante, and most of the Aegean islands. As mentioned previously, the Dodecanese islands, including Rhodes, had been Italian since 1912. The Germans and Bulgarians divided the north and north-east mainland between them. The Germans also occupied Athens and the port of Piraeus, as well as a handful of strategically important islands in the Aegean and the western three-quarters of Crete.

* * *

After Crete, Layforce was disbanded and the men were invited to serve in the newly created Middle East Commando. Those who did not accept the offer, and who did not join one of the myriad special units and 'private armies' that began to emerge in North Africa and the Middle East, were assigned to various infantry regiments.[92] Jellicoe was transferred to his old regiment, the Coldstream Guards. Roger Courtney's Folboat Section was transferred to the supply ship HMS *Medway*. Renamed the *Special Boat Section,* and with a force of about eight officers and thirty other ranks, it was to work with No. 1 Submarine Flotilla on reconnaissance, sabotage and landing missions.[93]

SAS[94]

David Stirling remained in Alexandria, where he spent several weeks dividing his time between a playboy lifestyle and military training. In June he was accepted into a newly created group, inspired by the German success in Crete, that was to learn to parachute. Hospitalised after a training accident, Stirling wrote a memo on desert warfare and the potential role that special forces could play in the offensive planned for the end of the year by the British commander in North Africa, the Stirling family's old friend General Claude Auchinleck.

Stirling thought that Rommel's supply lines and airfields, which lay a short distance from the 600-mile Libyan coast, were ripe for attack. He argued that the reason for their relative lack of success so far was that the commando units were too cumbersome to achieve the element of surprise so crucial to guerrilla warfare. This could be remedied by deploying small groups of no more than five carefully selected and trained men, who could be parachuted behind enemy lines and attack thirty different targets in a single night. Stirling suggested setting up an independent unit to train these small groups and plan their operations. He stressed that these new units were not tactical, but a strategic resource whose commander (Stirling) would report directly to the Commander-in-Chief North Africa (Auchinleck).

Stirling knew full well that the staff officers in the Middle East Command were unlikely to welcome his plan – but Auchinleck, on the other hand, was a man who appreciated unconventional initiatives and grand gestures. In true guerrilla style, Stirling sneaked through the fence surrounding the Middle East Command's HQ in Alexandria. He managed to reach Auchinleck's deputy chief of staff, the Scottish Major General Neil Ritchie,

David Stirling. The cap badge is the winged dagger of the SAS with the motto 'Who Dares Wins'.

who skimmed the memo and promised to pass it to his superior. Three days later, Stirling was summoned to meet Auchinleck, who gave him permission to recruit and train sixty-five men from the remnants of Layforce, as well as the use of five Bombay bombers to drop them behind enemy lines two days before the start of the autumn offensive. As head of this new force, Stirling was to report directly to Auchinleck. It was given the name 'L Detachment, Special Air Service Brigade'.

'A' Force

At the time, there was no 'Special Air Service Brigade' and no 'detachments' A–K. The designations were invented by Lieutenant Colonel Dudley Clarke. The previous year, he had devised the basis for the commando forces, but had since found his true vocation as head of 'A' Force. This was a highly secretive unit, based in Cairo, which devised and coordinated a variety of fantastic deceptive manoeuvres to fool the Germans and Italians into making wrong moves based on misconceptions of Allied strength and intentions. Among Clarke's most important weapons were military units that only existed on paper or in rumours, spread by false radio traffic or by small but highly visible groups of men whose uniforms and activities gave the false impression that they were part of something big and dangerous.

'Special Air Service Brigade' was originally fictitious – a force that was supposed to be in Jordan, where it could quickly be transferred to North Africa and dropped behind German lines. The full name of Clarke's own

Lieutenant Colonel Dudley Wrangel Clarke photographed by the Spanish police in October 1941 when he was arrested in Madrid wearing women's clothes.

unit, 'Advanced HQ A-Force', was meant to give the impression that it was an advance party for the airborne brigade. Stirling's new force gave Clarke a welcome opportunity to add a little more substance to his hoax by disguising it as part of 'SAS Brigade'.[95]

Chapter Twenty

Special Training School 21, Arisaig House

… the attack must aim at surprise, speed, ingenuity, and forcefulness.
(*SOE Syllabus*)

The School

Arisaig House was one of the properties near the coast at Cuillin Sound in Invernessshire that the SOE had appropriated and disguised as 'ordinary' commando schools. When Lassen and his comrades started their paramilitary training there in the middle of March 1941, they thought that they were going to join the commandos or perhaps be assigned to garrison duty in the Faroe Islands.[96]

The school curriculum was based on that of STC Lochailort, but adapted to suit the needs of the SOE. The recruits learned fieldcraft, armed and unarmed combat, navigation, sailing with small boats, and tactics. They also underwent strength and endurance training (in particular long marches across the rugged landscape) and preliminary parachute training.

Arisaig House.

Much of the timetable was taken up with the use of radio transmitters and Morse code, along with tactics and the art of drawing up plans, orders and reports clearly and concisely. This was all new for most of the recruits from civilian life – but most of the military men were just as unfamiliar with planning an operation from scratch.

The teaching of tactics covered small groups' attacks on secure targets that were to be blown up or set on fire. They learned about timing, communications, explosives, weapons and other types of equipment, advancing on the target, the final reconnaissance before the attack, and how to allocate tasks and position members of the force once they reached the actual target:

> In a case where the sentry or sentries are killed by fire, the sound of that shot is the signal for the assault to go in. Whether the shot was fired by the sentry party or the sentry will not matter, for if it was fired by the latter, the covering party … will kill him immediately.[97]

And the withdrawal:

> The leader will have ordered a time limit for arrival at [the] rendezvous after which any member of the party not present will be considered a casualty.[98]

Real houses or special training facilities were used when teaching street fighting and how to attack buildings. When storming a building, the first thing to consider was access: Should you go in through the front or back door, or perhaps through the roof? Or blast your way in? The approach depended on conditions, but the rear entrance was usually best. Generally speaking, the attacking force should always consist of a commander, a bomber, two entry men and a landing man.

> The two entry men take up position on either side of the door while the leader and the landing man either cover the door from the front (if there is adequate cover) or from the side. The bomber is with the leader.
>
> The door is then forced (either kicked or blown open with a small charge over the lock). The entry man then throws in a grenade and waiting til it explodes they dash into the house.
>
> When the entry men have crossed the threshold, they must not pause in the door way but should slip right and left and make their way across the hall to the staircase clearing any opposition as they go. Grenades may effectively be thrown through appropriate windows

In long corridors, rooms were to be systematically cleaned one at a time to avoid the risk of suddenly finding the enemy behind you.

If the man who opens the door finds no opposition the leader enters and makes a thorough search. Cupboards and locked doors can be dealt with by firing the tommy through the wood. It is also a good idea to fire down through the floor. This will bring down large lumps of plaster on the heads of anyone in the room below. …

When entering a room occupied by an unsuspecting enemy, either fling open the door and rush in or throw in a grenade.

For buildings with more than one floor, it was important to make your way upstairs right away and attack while moving downward. This gave the attack more speed and energy, made it easier to attack the enemy with hand grenades and other missiles, and made it more difficult for them to return fire. An attack from above also afforded defenders the opportunity to flee through the building's normal exits, so they would usually put up less resistance. Once they had left the building, the covering force waiting outside could 'take care of them'.[99]

William Fairbairn and Eric A. Sykes, who had incorporated the Chinese underworld's fighting techniques, the F-S knife and 'instinctive shooting' into the curriculum at Lochailort, also taught at Arisaig in the first few weeks of the school, as the SOE did not yet have enough of its own people to cover all of the topics. The short standard speech with which the school's close-combat teachers introduced the course in 'silent killing' was straight from Fairbairn and Sykes:

At some time or other, most of you, probably, have been taught at least the rudiments of boxing, under the Queensbury rules. That training was useful because it taught you to think and move quickly and how to hit hard. The Queensbury rules enumerate under the heading of 'fouls', some good targets which the boxer is not trained to defend.

This, however, is WAR, not sport. Your aim is to kill your opponent as quickly as possible. A prisoner is generally a handicap and a source of danger, particularly if you are without weapons. So forget the Queensbury rules; forget the term 'foul methods'. That may sound cruel but it is still more cruel to take longer than necessary to kill your opponent. 'Foul methods' so-called, help you kill quickly. Attack your opponent's weakest points, therefore. He will attack yours if he gets the chance.[100]

The instructors recommended that each man practise the blows, kicks, grips and parries that suited them personally. It was better to master just one of the many methods of killing demonstrated on the course.[101] It made for faster decision-making in real-life situations: the fewer the options, the faster and more decisively they would react. It was also an economical way of learning.

Frisking of prisoners was preferably to be done as follows:

> Kill him first. If that is inconvenient, make him lie face to the ground, hands out in front of him. Knock him out, with rifle butt, side or butt of the pistol or with your boot. Then search him.[102]

If you had to take a prisoner with you, somebody – possibly the prisoner himself – should cut his belt or braces. He should then be led away with one hand on his head and the other holding his trousers up. If the prisoner was to be detained for some time, his hands should be tied behind his back and he should be gagged by stuffing something – e.g. a lump of peat, a handkerchief or his cap – into his mouth and then tying a piece of cloth over his mouth and chin and behind his neck, and another under the chin and over his crown.[103]

The trainees at Arisaig House learned to use the British army's standard firearms – from the Webley revolver to the Lee Enfield rifle, Bren gun and heavier weapons – and as many as possible of the foreign weapons that they might chance upon behind enemy lines. The emphasis was on pistols and revolvers, and on sub-machine guns like the US Thompson ('Tommy gun') and the British Sten.

They trained by day and night on ranges and in open countryside, in special houses or on streets where moving targets suddenly popped up and had to be neutralised. They often shot at silhouettes of human figures with targets on their bellies.

> To kill a man it is not necessary to put a shot through his heart. The vulnerable part of a man's body is from the crotch up to the top of his head. Two fast shots anywhere into that area are going to dispose of him permanently.
>
> The object of Pistol Training is to obtain maximum speed in attack with sufficient accuracy to hit the vulnerable areas.[104]

The firearms instructors at Arisaig House did not teach the trainees to point along the barrel with the index finger and pull the trigger with the middle finger, the way Fairbairn and Sykes did at STC Lochailort, but they did teach the Shanghai policemen's instinctive aiming method. The idea was to make the burst of fire as much of a rapid reflex as possible. The ability to react at lightning speed to any threat was an obvious advantage, but 'instinctive' shooting also helped solve what was increasingly recognised as a problem – that a surprisingly large number of soldiers who had received standard training in the conventional armed forces had never fired a weapon in anger.

Normally the chances of actually shooting at the enemy increase the larger the troop concentration and the more closely they work together. However, these future SOE agents were being trained to operate alone, without the social influence of comrades. Like the practical training in killing with their bare hands, a knife, or other available tools, the firearms training, with its emphasis on instinct, was not just about *how* to kill, but about breaking down the instinctive reluctance most people have to kill fellow human beings, even those who present a danger to their own lives.[105]

'I want that one!'

Lassen was in his element for the three weeks at Arisaig House. Here his talents came into their own – all of the things that he was good at and liked to do were appreciated. The paramilitary school was distinguished by a sense of purpose, of doing something meaningful, and of preparing for battle (even if the recruits did not quite know under what circumstances).

Anders Lassen had an extraordinary ability to move silently – as if he 'moved without touching the ground'. In the dark, he could sneak all the way up to a man without being noticed. He was not just silent, but also lightning-fast, decisive and adept with a knife:

> Once we were out on an all-day exercise to learn how to make use of the compass, sun, map reading, and so on. We were working in small groups and on the way back we joined up and went home together. Suddenly we saw two stags at a distance of about 50 yards. The ground was covered by small patches of bushes. Before any of us had seen them, there was one who reacted, and that was Anders:
>
> 'I want that one!' he shouted.
>
> We knew that Anders was a hunter and seeing that one stag was moving off, we stayed clear and left him to it. He ran round the bushes, got close up to it and stabbed it with his knife. It was a fine, big animal, and the next few days we had lovely roast.[106]

Chapter Twenty-One

Gumley Hall

Andy hated bullshit, was foulmouthed, did not suffer fools gladly and I realised that we had this in common. Perhaps that is why we did not get along.
(Dick Holmes MM, SBS)

Rebellion

After graduating from STS 21, Lassen and his group transferred to Gumley Hall in Leicestershire. This elegant residence was the location of Special Training School 44, one of SOE's 'Holding Schools', under the command of a Major Grayson.[107] Another 20 Danes joined the Arisaig team there, bolstering the ranks to 32 men.

Conditions in the manor house in the English Midlands were far more comfortable than at Arisaig House, but Lassen found his time there disappointing, and it brought out the rebel in him.

SOE's *Holding Schools* were more *holding* than *schools* – almost a kind of storage unit for agents while they waited to go into action. Almost no teaching was done at them. Instead, highly motivated young people, whose eagerness to make a difference was at its height, were left bored and frustrated.[108]

Their time was spent on square-bashing and other activities that Lassen found pointless. The recruits were never informed of the purpose of their stay, nor how long it would last. They were not told that they were once again being evaluated by the British – primarily by Major Grayson – to determine who should remain in the SOE and who should be booted out.

In April 1941, Captain Iversen and the Danish Council finally succeeded in reaching an agreement with the British military authorities that the Danish volunteers, as far as possible, would be included in the Royal East Kent Regiment ('The Buffs'), which had a traditional connection with the Danish royal family.[109] This gave Iversen and the SOE a story to tell Danes when they tried to enlist them, and a place to dispose of volunteers who could not or would not continue in the SOE. Iversen also felt that this brought him a step closer to his dream of establishing a purely Danish unit.

Iversen's idea of a Danish unit within the regiment never came to fruition, partly because too few Danes joined the Buffs. Many of the 731 Danish volunteers who signed up for British service during the war[110] applied for other parts of the Army, the RAF or the Royal Navy, and many of the seamen stayed with the merchant navy. The Danes who did join the Buffs were incorporated into regular battalions. Nevertheless, the British authorities still regarded them mainly as potential SOE recruits, so most of them were never sent to the front – much to the frustration of Iversen and many of the volunteers.

* * *

The apparently aimless waiting gave rise to considerable discontent among the Danes at Gumley Hall. Lassen was one of the most vocal.

> Anders called us together to ask us whether we had noticed what was wrong … and said that we had to submit a collective complaint. He could get all het up, in an amusing manner, but keep smiling when we lined up on parade, he could laugh at one of the adjutants who had a nasal voice so he had to turn his back because he was laughing too. Anders had a complete lack of respect for his superiors. If he thought something was wrong, he said so. … Then came the day we called dark Monday, when Lassen stood up and gave Iversen what for because he had promised all sorts that had come to nothing. Lassen acted as if he had been giving orders all his life. I have never heard anyone speak so well. He was very handsome, a tall, beautiful figure. He had something about him everybody liked and he talked in a slow and careful manner. Yes, he was one of the most handsome and best guys ever to wear the Danish flag on his shoulder. … One day he said to us: 'Don't you see that we are just square-bashing sheep … we don't want to be square-bashers, we want action.'[111]

Lassen eventually escaped life as a 'square-bashing sheep' when Captain Iversen responded to Brigadier Gubbins's request for men for a special assignment at sea. On 15 April, Captain Starup noted in Lassen's papers:

> The Brigadier needed a man for Patrol-boat work. I recommended 2379 [Lassen] who is quite clever and well mannered and speaks English fairly well. He would fit into a job like that better than a regiment as his nature does not like drill and military discipline.[112]

Gubbins accepted the offer, as did Lassen. He left Gumley Hall while Iversen and the head of the school pondered who would serve in the SOE, who would be transferred to the Buffs or to other services, and who would return to civilian life.[113]

"Perfectly all right", April–May 1941

Suzanne and Emil Lassen had heard nothing from their son since 9 April 1940. In her letters to Anders, Suzanne told him all the news, big and small, about the family and their friends – about Emil's return from Finland, where he had been promoted to captain, about her books, about weddings, dinner parties and social calls, the family's move to an apartment in Nyhavn in Copenhagen, and so on. She had nowhere to send the letters, but hoped to show them to Anders one day. From time to time, she sent short (maximum 25-word) messages via the Red Cross, which may or may not have reached her son. She also sent a few telegrams and a single letter via acquaintances in Sweden, including Christian X's sister Princess Ingeborg, who was married to the Swedish Prince Carl.

Anders did not write home, as the occupation had interrupted the normal postal service between the UK and Denmark. A smuggled letter from a British address intercepted by the German authorities would have put his family in danger.

On 22 April 1941, the silence was suddenly broken. Suzanne and Emil Lassen attended a dinner party with an acquaintance who had just arrived from Sweden bearing a telegram from Anders. The content was related by mouth because German checks at Elsinore made it too dangerous to bring the actual telegram. It read 'Perfectly all right, Anders'.[114]

* * *

On 13 May 1941 the SOE sent a routine inquiry about Lassen to the security service MI5 with a view to him 'serving as a crew member under the ISRB'. On 22 May, MI5 responded that they had no black marks against his name. Lassen was sent to Poole in Dorset to train at another SOE Special Training School – a completely different type from the ones he was used to.

En route from Gumley Hall, he spent a few days in London, where he visited the Danish ambassador, Count Eduard Reventlow, who knew his parents. They spoke, among other things, about conditions for Danish seafarers in the UK. Lassen thought the conditions were abysmal and asked the ambassador to do something about it. It would be another six months before Reventlow broke with the Danish government's policy of cooperation, but he sympathised with the volunteers – especially Lassen.[115] The two kept in touch, and when Lassen later found himself in London he visited Reventlow and stayed with the family several times. He would later boast that he had slept with two of their three maids.[116]

Chapter Twenty-Two

The Art of Guerrilla Warfare 8 – *Maid Honor*

Colvin was startled. 'What in hell kind of a ship is that?' he asked. 'A fishing-boat?'

(Nevil Shute: *Most Secret*)

Spirit of adventure

One of the most serious difficulties with which the new SOE had to contend was its lack of a transport wing. It was completely dependent on help from the Royal Navy and RAF, who were not always fully on board. As a consequence, the SOE quickly started building up its own fleet of fishing vessels and other vessels for clandestine operations, primarily to and from the Norwegian fjords and the cliffs off Brittany.[117]

In March 1941, the 35-ton, 70-foot ketch *Maid Honor* joined the SOE fleet. It was built as a trawler in 1925 or 1926 in the fishing port of Brixham in Devon, but in 1936 it had been sold to a yachtsman, who converted it and installed a four-cylinder auxiliary engine.[118] *Maid Honor*'s incorporation into the SOE fleet was the result of a bold move by one of its most daring and enterprising officers, Captain Gustavus March-Phillipps.

Gustavus Henry March-Phillipps.

* * *

The tall, dark, athletic Gustavus Henry March-Phillipps was born in 1908. He had served in the British Indian army but left the military in 1931 to become a professional hunter and racing driver. He was also a keen yachtsman. March-Phillipps, who had a rather heavy stammer when he became excited, was of a romantic, literary disposition and a deeply pious Catholic. At the outbreak of the war he volunteered for the army and later distinguished himself as a staff officer during the fighting in France. Following Dunkirk, he applied to join the commandos, where he was placed in charge of 7 Commando B Troop (a force of about fifty men, approximately a platoon). As was standard practice in the early days of the commandos, March-Phillipps had great freedom to choose his own people and organize their training. Among the first recruits was Lieutenant Geoffrey Appleyard, whom he knew from Dunkirk.[119]

John Geoffrey Appleyard.

John Geoffrey Appleyard was born in Bramley, near Leeds, on 20 December 1916. He was the eldest son of J. Ernest Appleyard, one of the pioneers of the British automotive industry and a Morris, Jaguar and Daimler dealer. The family went skiing in Switzerland every year, and both Geoffrey and his brother Ian (who became Britain's leading rally driver of the immediate post-war era) were Olympic-standard skiers. Geoffrey, like his brother, was a passionate nature-lover and ornithologist, and was personally acquainted with every single dipper in Upper Wharfedale. He graduated in engineering from Cambridge, and were it not for the war he would doubtless have taken over the family business. The Appleyards were Quakers, but their pacifist principles did not stop Geoffrey joining the army three days before the declaration of war, nor did they prevent Ian from enlisting in the Royal Electrical and Mechanical Engineers and becoming a teacher in tank technology at the Military College of Science and a major at the age of 23. Nor did they prevent their sister, Joyce, from signing up for the voluntary women's organization First Aid Nursing Yeomanry (FANY), which among other things provided secretaries for a range of types of intelligence work. Geoffrey's technical aptitude led him to the Royal Army Service Corps, where he became a second lieutenant and head of a workshop group responsible for maintaining 160 vehicles. 'Apple', as his friends called him, thrived in this work, but fared less well with the army's rigidity, regulations and bureaucracy. So when his friend March-Phillipps offered him a place as a squad leader in 7 Commando B Troop, he signed up right away.[120]

Appleyard, who was just as enthusiastic and as much of a romantic as his friend and superior, wrote about March-Phillipps:

M-P is a great worshipper and disciple of the Knights of Old, believes that the spirit of Drake and Raleigh, of Robert the Bruce and of Oliver Cromwell is the spirit that will save England to-day and give her a name that the world will once again look up to. And I'm sure he's right. It isn't a spirit of Safety First, but it's a spirit of adventure, of giving instead of getting, of clean living and physical fitness, of comradeship and unity, and, above all, it's God's spirit. Of that I'm sure. Don't you see what this show can mean?[121]

Despite his zeal, Appleyard was generally very quiet, and one of the few people untroubled by March-Phillipps's often highly-strung behaviour or intimidated by his sharp tongue – which, combined with his stammer and a disfigured upper lip (he had once been bitten by a horse), was used as an effective weapon against any subordinate who did not immediately follow orders or live up to expectations. The stable Appleyard was a necessary counterpoint to the flighty and intense March-Phillipps.[122]

March-Phillipps's focus was on preparing B Troop for amphibious operations. Around Christmas of 1940, the whole platoon chipped in £35 to buy the yawl-rigged 32-foot, 5½-ton sailboat *I'm Alone*, whose owner, a local fisherman, had been called up by the Royal Navy. The boat was in need of some repair, and so served as both a communal leisure project and an important bonding and training tool. March-Phillipps and Appleyard planned to buy the crew's shares after the war and use *I'm Alone* as their private yacht. 'We are already planning our voyages,' Appleyard wrote to his parents.[123]

'So much to see and do here'

In February 1941, 7 Commando was incorporated into Layforce and sent to North Africa. However, a month earlier, both March-Phillipps and Appleyard had been transferred to the SOE to train a small, select group in amphibious operations. They suggested that a Brixham trawler be acquired for this purpose – a robust, relatively fast two-masted wooden sailing vessel, traditionally built in Brixham (Devon) and used by local fishermen. They sailed silently at night, and the wooden hull would not trigger magnetic mines. The proposal was approved in principle in March 1941.[124] March-Phillipps, without waiting for the money to buy a ship or any kind of permission, set off for Brixham right away, commandeered *Maid Honor*[125] and tasked the captain, Blake Glanville, with sailing it and training the crew.

March-Phillipps sailed *Maid Honor* to Poole, where his new force was billeted in two houseboats. His HQ was in a 400-year old coaching inn, the

Antelope Hotel – the proprietor of which, Arthur 'Pop' Baker, had taken March-Phillipps and his men under his wing. Once *Maid Honor* was moored, March-Phillipps told his superiors about the purchase. The news caused some consternation, but Brigadier Gubbins chose to endorse his actions.

Maid Honor, which was moored at the remote Russel Quay on the north side of the wooded Arne peninsula,[126] had bunks for a crew of five to eight men. They were quickly filled with March-Phillipps and Appleyard's old friends and comrades, as well as men from the SOE system – like Lassen. The first recruit was Appleyard's childhood friend the cabinet maker Graham Hayes, who was now a captain in the British army's first (and at that time, only) parachute battalion.

Maid Honor photographed from the bowsprit by Graham Hayes. Appleyard is shown in bathing trunks and next to him the Yugoslav 'Marco', a great ladies' man. In the background are March-Phillipps, bent forward, Buzz Perkins with hands on hips, and the group's navigation instructor Blake Glanville wearing a hat.

Before the war, Hayes had sailed on the Finnish four-master *Pommern*, carrying grain from Australia, and he brought valuable knowledge and skills to the table.[127] Next came the SOE man Sergeant Leslie Prout, followed by the Frenchman André Desgrange, who was extremely popular among his peers, despite the fact he did not speak a word of English and was apparently unable to learn it. Desgrange, a huge, strong man with dark, curly hair and a big, ever-present smile, was a former diver in the French Navy and had a particular aptitude for engines. He had been with Appleyard on the submarine HMS *Tigris* (*N63*), on the night of 4/5 April 1941, when they picked up two agents on the Normandy coast – an operation that led to Appleyard's first Military Cross. Appleyard described Desgrange as 'the most un-French Frenchman one can imagine', always calm, composed, impossible to rile, and also always willing to do the hardest and dirtiest work.[128]

* * *

Anders Lassen arrived at Poole in late May 1941. After his very first chat with Lassen, March-Phillipps noted to Prout: 'Unless I am very much mistaken, that youngster will go a long way.'[129] Appleyard later described Lassen as 'a crack shot with any kind of weapon, and a splendid seaman.'[130]

* * *

The next to arrive was 23-year-old Denis Tottenham, 6 feet 3 inches tall and of Anglo-Irish landed stock. He was in the Royal Navy Volunteer Reserve (RNVR) and, like several of his ancestors, had attended Harrow. Tottenham and Lassen were soon joined by the 22-year-old Sergeant Jan Nasmyth, who had read PPE at Oxford before the war, and the cook, Ernest Evison, whose cuisine helped generate camaraderie in the small team. The youngest member of the group was Frank 'Buzz' Colbourn Perkins. He was only 17, but strong, tough and technically gifted. Perkins' admission to the team was due to his cousin, Captain Harold. B. Perkins, who himself had run away to sea at 16 but was now one of Colin Gubbins's closest associates. Captain Perkins had recommended Buzz for the *Maid Honor* Force, and Buzz had lied about his age to get in. While it is unclear whether March-Phillipps believed the lie or not, he accepted the eager young recruit nevertheless.[131]

In August 1941, the final member of the crew arrived when March-Phillipps finally succeeded in persuading the head of the parachute battalion to let go of Company Sergeant Major Tom Winter, whom Hayes considered an indispensable part of the *Maid Honor* Force. Winter had taken part in all sorts of difficult operations all over the world and was a great mechanic. When Winter joined, he and Hayes forged a solid partnership.[132] Appleyard asked the experienced Winter to keep a close eye on the unruly Lassen and, '[b]e as strict as you can with him, but don't go too far because he's good-hearted and good at everything – even if he does dislike discipline.'[133]

This motley crew did not look like a military unit. The soldiers and naval officers wore their old uniforms, and those who came directly from civilian life or from the SOE schools wore battledress without insignia. They mixed and matched bits of uniform with civilian mufti acquired on shopping trips to London.

* * *

During the summer, two of Lassen's comrades from the SOE school at Gumley Hall – sales rep Alfred Jørgensen (an accomplished ham radio enthusiast) and architect Børge Franck – joined *Maid Honor* Force. Franck had arrived in England via Greenland, where he had been part of an expedition in autumn 1940 organized by the Danish Nazi Curt Carlis Hansen to provide the Germans with meteorological intelligence. The expedition masqueraded as a hunting trip, and Franck was probably unaware of its true purpose when he agreed to go. On 7 Sept 1940, the four members of the expedition were arrested by the Norwegian coastguard ship *Fridtjof Nansen*, which was working for the British. They were brought to England, where Franck and his colleagues – professional polar hunter and businessman Jørgen Tvermose and radio operator Carl J. Starup – ended up serving in the SOE.[134*]

Lassen's two countrymen were clearly just as unaccustomed to military discipline as he was. The three stood out right from the start due to their aversion to authority, manifested in a sarcastic, slightly aggressive attitude.[135*]

* * *

During a visit to Bournemouth, Lassen was embroiled in a pub brawl that required police intervention. He and the other two Danes were also arrested on at least two other occasions, not – or at least, not primarily – because they caused trouble, but because their unconventional uniforms, language and lack of normal military ID aroused suspicion that they were enemy spies. During a rowing trip up the Frome, they were apprehended by a Home Guard patrol under the command of 67-year-old Captain Percy Westerman, whose boys' books about adventures at war and on the seven seas were well known in Denmark. Once the misunderstanding was cleared up, Westerman invited Lassen and his comrades to his houseboat and gave them a few signed Danish editions of his books.[136]

* * *

Maid Honor Force's training consisted of lectures on seamanship and basic navigation at the customs office in Poole, as well as practical sailing exercises in all weathers in Poole Harbour and along the south coast, led by Blake Glanville. The team also spent time rowing along rivers and hiking in the nearby moorland. The extensive rush beds in the area were rich in bird life and provided plenty of opportunities for hunting. Glanville turned out to be a tireless trainer, and his reassuring calmness and inexhaustible store of maritime yarns made him something of a father figure to March-Phillipps's young crew.

While Lassen was not unconditionally keen on all of his companions, and although his health was again causing him problems, he enjoyed the relative freedom of serving in the *Maid Honor* Force, and welcomed the chance to try new things and improve his skills as a sailor.

> Am now sailing again, even though it's in a different way from before – you can't just do what you want – cos am still the feckin boy – but can do almost what I want and if I was to go back to the land it would be hard to find a job for me; I'm probably staying by the way. Had a row the other day with the skipper (Cap'n in the Army) but like him. And so much to see and do here, things so interesting people in Denmark can only dream of. And if I don't cause trouble and get sent back ashore there's a chance to learn navigation sooner or later. The navigation officers are fine chaps. Unfortunately I can't say the same of the crew but I could be wrong. Time will tell. At the moment in hospital by the way a horrible place.

As the weeks went by, and they all worked and learned together, Lassen lowered his guard and became more attached to his comrades. His liking for the charismatic March-Phillipps evolved into a warm friendship, borne by deep admiration for the older man's courage, dynamism and patriotism. Among the rank and file, he became particularly good friends with Alfred Jørgensen and Denis Tottenham – so much so that when Tottenham married Winifred Susanne Tate on 7 July 1941, Lassen was his best man.[137]

Lassen and Tottenham had long and passionate discussions about the advantages and disadvantages of the merchant navy and the Royal Navy, and not least about the war:

> Andy was fanatical in his positive hate and abject loathing [of the Germans] – his one wish was to kill, kill those Huns. I think it was this hate that made him such a perfect fighter, utterly fearless and quite unselfish. For myself, I was … a peace loving man. I hated killing, the futile waste & destruction and loss that war in any form entailed. I fought because I had to – not because I wanted to. Andy the reverse.[138]

Most Secret

March-Phillipps set his sights higher than just transporting agents. He was preparing his men to carry out amphibious assaults on German positions along the coasts and sabotage enemy shipping. During the summer he started to equip *Maid Honor* for guerrilla warfare. Major C.V. Clarke from the SOE Technical Research and Development Station, along with a representative of the Royal Navy Department of Miscellaneous Weapons Development

(DMWD), visited *Maid Honor* to oversee the installation of four rocket launchers (spigot mortars or Blacker bombards) that would be used to engage targets at sea, as well as steel plates on the deck to minimise the risk of fire. The idea was that *Maid Honor* would lay off a hostile port and wait for a German warship to investigate, at which point the concealed weapons would open fire on the enemy vessel and its inquisitive crew.[139]

The officer from the DMWD was First Lieutenant Nevil Shute Norway, a novelist with a dozen books to his name. His novel *Most Secret*, written in 1942 but not published until 1945 due to wartime censorship, is about a French fishing boat (with two Danes in the crew) that the British equip with a hidden flamethrower so that it can sneak up on German vessels off the French coast and set them alight. Unlike the good ship *Geneviève* in Nevil Shute's novel, *Maid Honor* never lured German naval ships to their doom, because March-Phillipps's imaginative plan was rejected when he submitted it to the Admiralty in June 1941.[140]

This setback came at a time when the SOE was in desperate need of success. The organization had been around for about a year but with little to show for it – and it had plenty of enemies in the corridors of power.

To prove the SOE's worth, Gubbins proposed that March-Phillipps and his ship and crew be transferred to the SOE department in West Africa, which operated from Lagos and Freetown in the British colonies of Nigeria and Sierra Leone. Here, it was hoped, *Maid Honor* would earn SOE the victories it needed without any conflicts of interest with the Royal Navy.

On 16 July, the SOE office accepted the idea, and on 30 July the Admiralty agreed. Five days later, Lassen and the rest of the crew were officially transferred to the SOE's W Section (West Africa).

Exactly what *Maid Honor* would do in Sierra Leone was by no means clear. Possible operations included hunting down a secret German radio transmitter thought to be operating in the south of neutral Liberia, locating German submarine bases on the Portuguese (and therefore neutral) Cape Verde Islands, or attacking ships in the port of Dakar in the Vichy French colony of Senegal.[141]

March-Phillipps was undeterred by this apparent lack of clarity and started to kit out *Maid Honor* for its new role. The rocket launchers were removed, lookout posts were added to the masts and served as machine-gun posts, part of the deck was lowered so that the crew had a line of fire through the scuppers, and a two-pound Vickers Mark VIII gun was concealed under a bogus deckhouse of plywood that could be lowered at the pull of a handle. In the stern, a pile of fishing nets hid a supply of depth charges. From a distance, and even during a cursory close-up inspection, *Maid Honor* appeared to be a peaceful leisure craft or fishing boat – only now it had teeth. Not very big teeth admittedly, but if the opponent was not too big or well-armed, and on the surface or just underneath, *Maid Honor*, the rebuilt Brixham trawler, might stand a chance. The Vickers Mark VIII was an anti-aircraft gun, but the masts and rigging made it difficult to engage targets in the air. This made the only defences against air attacks the machine guns in the masts and, perhaps more importantly, the camouflage, including the Swedish flag under which the ship would sail.[142]

Bow and Arrow

Anders Lassen had been relatively good at English at school. He spoke the language often on *Fionia* and *Eleonora Mærsk*, and since October 1940 he had lived in completely or predominantly English-speaking environments. His English was now fluent but still heavily accented, with a consistently monotone intonation that the British considered very Germanic. While this underlined how different he was, it also had the positive effect of, at least partially, setting him apart from the British class system that exerted such a huge influence on relationships between the officers and the other ranks in the British Army – and between the officers themselves. His character and manners were the product of a Danish upper-class background, but the way he spoke English made it difficult to pigeonhole him automatically. This enabled him to mix with other classes more readily than a British serviceman.

While *Maid Honor* was being fitted out and the crew trained, Lassen wrote a letter to the British War Office on an issue close to his heart: the use of the bow and arrow in modern warfare. He argued his case systematically, clearly informed by what he had learned at Arisaig House – and with idiosyncratic spelling that gives a vivid impression of how his English may have sounded at the time:

> BOW AND ARROW USED IN MODERN WARFARE
> The idea must seam ridicolous and even stupid for an ordinary man vhich dont know vhar a vonderful veapon it really is.
> Alone than we should in 1941 take up again the same sort of veapon vhich vhich England won the hundred-year war vith must seam a bit cracy vhen you compare a bow with a maschingun and a tommygun.
> However, after now having been at these different schools and after what I now know about gurilla-warfare skhouting-patrols fighting-patrols and that sort of thing I amin now doubt than a bow and arrow inmany cases could be of great value. I have a great deal experience in

hunting vith bow and arrow and have schot all from spur to stags and though I never has tryed a man it is my absolut opinion than the effecht vill be just as good as vith the stags.

Advantages
1. It is nearly noiseless
2. It kills vithout schok or paine, so than it is not likely, than say a man vould schream or do any of that sort of thing.
3. A veltrained man can schoot uo to 15 schot in a minnut.
4. It is as deadly as an ordinary riffelbullet.
5. You actually dontaim, vhat is a great advanteg at night time (more like the way a man through a stone).

Disadvantages
1. Itis extremely difficult and require a good deal training and at the same time absolut interest and going up in the job.
2. A good for that purpose bow would to day cost in London from 2 to 6 £, training arrow about 4 schilling each and they may be used 100 of times. Hunting arrows vill be about tvice as expensive.[143]

Appleyard too was interested in the idea of using bows and arrows and suggested to the War Office that it equip landing forces with steel bows to silently do away with enemy lookouts.[144] However, the War Office ruled the bow and arrow inhumane and unfit for combat. There is nothing to suggest that Lassen ever violated this ban.

Chapter Twenty-Three

Operation Postmaster[145]

She was proud and haughty and handsome
(As Italian Duchesses go)
And when I looked over her transom
I whispered softly and low
'T'amo molto bene ma duchessa
Come with me where the sea winds blow',
And she softly answered 'oh yessir!
Anywhere, to leave Fernando Po.'
(*Addio a Fernando,* by Neucols' 'Tame Poet',
Attachment No. 18 to Report by Head
of the West Africa Section)[146]

The voyage[147]

On Sunday, 10 August 1941,[148] the crew of the *Maid Honor* gathered for a slap-up farewell lunch at *The Antelope*. The host, Arthur 'Pop' Baker, served champagne, and none other than Colin Gubbins travelled from London to be the guest of honour. The mood was somewhat mixed. While March-Phillipps looked forward to finally seeing action, Appleyard was frustrated that he would not be going. Nasmyth noted that 'everybody was obviously maintaining a stiff upper lip in the usual British way and wishing to see the last of them as quickly as possible'. Lassen, however, was 'quite eloquent':

> He said 'We're doomed. I'll never see you again, our commander is mad.' Which of course, other people thought about Gus too. And I said, 'Well, it's not as bad as that, Andy, there's a chance.'

But Lassen was not convinced. 'He looked very, very miserable.'[149]

In the late afternoon, the crew – March-Phillipps, Hayes, Tottenham, the young Buzz Perkins, Lassen, the radio operator Alf Jørgensen and Børge Franck – boarded *Maid Honor* with their guests. The engine was started and Hayes (with some difficulty, perhaps due to nervousness or the effects of

From Bækkeskov to Fernando Po by way of Poole.

"P. & O. R.M.S. STRATHMORE, 23,500 Tons. Carrying First-class and Tourist-class Passengers. India and Australia Mail Service." Souvenir postcard belonging to Ernest Evinson.

the lavish lunch) set sail. The pilot then navigated *Maid Honor* out to the limestone rocks known as Old Harry, off Handfast Point. Here, the crew drank a champagne toast, after which the pilot and guests disembarked and *Maid Honor* headed south-west.

A Brixham trawler's usual crew consisted of six men – with seven on board, space was at a premium. The rest of the force – Appleyard, Leslie Prout, Tom Winter, Desgrange and the cook Ernest Evison, were to sail in civilian clothes to Freetown with the passenger ships *Strathmore* and *Stuyvesant*, which now served as troop ships.[150]

Maid Honor was not long at sea before it became clear that Jørgensen suffered chronic seasickness – and that Franck's seamanship did not live up to expectations. The two Danes were set ashore in Dartmouth, about 70 nautical miles (80 miles) further west along the coast. A month later, they sailed from Newcastle to Freetown on the Holland America Line's SS *Delftdijk*. *Maid Honor* stayed in Dartmouth for two days, partly for repairs to its gun. On Tuesday, 12 August, at 18:00, the voyage resumed with a crew of only five. It meant more work for the remaining men, but also reduced the risk of exhausting the supply of fresh water.[151]

The next day, proceeding westward through the English Channel, *Maid Honor* proved less seaworthy and watertight than expected, perhaps because the gear in the mast and the weapons on board had shifted its centre of gravity. The cabins, the wheelhouse and the storeroom all took on water. On 15 August, *Maid Honor* sailed into the Atlantic, where fierce winds made for a highly unpleasant voyage. On 21 August, March-Phillipps, who was getting to grips with the art of navigation using a sextant, determined *Maid Honor*'s position to be about halfway between the Azores and Cape St. Vincent. By Monday, 25 August, Madeira was in sight. *Maid Honor* cast anchor in Funchal and took on fresh water and supplies. The Portuguese authorities showed no particular interest in the vessel, which was fortunate. *Maid Honor*'s cover story – that it was a Swedish yacht and the owner did not want the crew to go ashore because he was impatient to set off again – would hardly have convinced any reasonably alert harbour master.

After two days in Madeira, March-Phillipps headed west around the Portuguese Cape Verde Islands, keeping a safe distance from the Vichy French naval base in Dakar. Short bursts of favourable trade winds and good speed (albeit in unpleasant, choppy conditions) alternated with long windless periods. A threatening leak was, with some difficulty, localised to a valve in the storeroom and repaired. The engine then seized up due to a rusty piston, but the young Perkins, assisted by Hayes, managed to repair the damage and get the vessel going again. However, the engine was never completely stable and *Maid Honor* lay still for several days at a time. This increased the risk of running out of fresh water, but freed up time to scrape barnacles and other marine life off the ship's side. This was an uncomfortable job, as it meant sitting in a boatswain's chair hoisted over the railing – but it also gave Lassen a chance to demonstrate a trick he had learned on board the tanker. He put some water in an empty tin can, added a lump of carbide from one of the ship's lamps, replaced the lid and stuck a lit match through a hole in the side of the can. He then threw it into the water, where it attracted a number of fish before exploding and adding a few welcome additions to the by now somewhat monotonous diet.

On the morning of 19 September, *Maid Honor* spotted an Allied convoy and was flagged down by one of the escorting destroyers, which confirmed that Freetown was barely two days away. That same afternoon, the crew spotted more ships and one of the RAF's big Sunderland seaplanes, which had flown out from Freetown to have a look at the vessel. At 11:00 on Sunday 21 September 1941, the day before Lassen's 21st birthday, the pilot from Freetown came on board. Since leaving Poole 41 days earlier, March-Phillipps and his crew had covered 3,185 nautical miles.

Suitable employment?

Geoffrey Appleyard and his men had been in Freetown since late August. Freetown was, in Appleyard's words, 'very one-eyed, ramshackle, and quite

'Hard job', Anders Lassen wrote on the back of a photograph of 'The Old HMS "MH"', which was beached for some much-needed maintenance.

an outpost of the Empire'. It rained almost incessantly, and in the rare dry periods, thick clouds of steam rose from the ground, roofs and roads. Appleyard nevertheless managed to set up a comfortable camp for the crew and their fellow newcomers on the beautiful Lumley Beach, about ten miles from Freetown. It had palm, banana and coconut trees, and the crew spent three or four hours a day swimming, diving and harpoon fishing. Meals were taken in the local officers' mess, where the hosts were 'a most awfully nice and hospitable crowd' from the Royal Artillery.[152]

For a while, the only thing to disturb this idyll – and add some variety to everyday life – was the work needed to make *Maid Honor* seaworthy again after the long journey. Perkins was despatched to the local navy store to obtain supplies of gun oil, tar, putty, cotton waste, sandpaper, polish, etc. The ship was then hauled up onto the beach, and Lassen, Tottenham and Perkins, helped by some locals, set about scraping the sides and bottom, repairing woodworm damage and painting the hull.

Maid Honor and its crew were now under the command of the SOE office in Sierra Leone, where an agent codenamed W5 was responsible for the small force. While Anders and his companions enjoyed beach life, W5's superiors in Lagos discussed with HQ in London what to do with the new arrivals.

* * *

The SOE mission in West Africa was set up in November 1940 under the cover name *Political and Economic Research Organization* (PERO). By summer 1941 it had been divided into two sections: *Frawest* (French West Africa), under Lieutenant Colonel R.S.L. Wingate, and *Neucols* (Neutral Colonies) under the Belgian banker Louis Franck. *Frawest* was tasked with spreading propaganda in the Vichy French colonies, establishing contact with pro-Allied factions, and sabotage. *Neucols* did much the same in the Spanish and Portuguese colonies.

Franck may have held a British passport, but any resemblance to a typical British banker or civil servant ended there. He would saunter around Lagos dressed in silk shirts with puffed sleeves and a blue body belt, which only partially concealed a Malayan *krish*. He was an imaginative agent, but some found his ruthless mindset hard to take, for example when he suggested contaminating the drinking water on enemy ships with typhoid bacteria. The colourful and energetic Franck enjoyed a good working relationship with the Governor of Nigeria, Sir Bernard Bourdillon. Despite an understaffed administration, Bourdillon permitted several of his officials to attend classes at the SOE school at the Olokemeji forestry research station, about 75 miles north-east of Lagos.[153]

* * *

On 25 September 1941, when Gubbins and his people received the good news that *Maid Honor* had arrived safely, they sent a telegram to *Neucols* in Lagos:

> 'News of safe arrival M A I D H O N O R causes us to occupy our minds with problem her suitable employment.'

Various suggestions followed, including searching for U-boat bases in the Cape Verde Islands or German radio transmitters in Liberia, and attacking ships in the Vichy French port of Dakar. Four days later, Franck's people received the discouraging response that the existence of these German facilities was in doubt, that the SOE management had banned 'bangs' on neutral ships, and that the other proposals for the use of *Maid Honor* sounded unfeasible. The Lagos office did not feel that the ship would be suitable for intelligence work – on the contrary, it risked giving itself away – and there were strong doubts that it was suited to operations in the Tropics at all.

Having torpedoed Gubbins's plans to use *Maid Honor* in the twin battles with the Germans and with the SOE's enemies in London, *Neucols* then identified where March-Phillipps and his people might be able to do some good without the ship. In August 1941, Franck had suggested to the London office hijacking the German tug *Likomba* and sabotaging the Italian freight and passenger ship *Duchessa d'Aosta*.[154] When their countries went to war, the vessels had sought refuge in the port of Santa Isabel on the Spanish – and therefore neutral – island of Fernando Po (now Bioko in Equatorial Guinea,

Duchessa d'Aosta at anchor in Fernando Po.

460 miles south-east of Lagos). *Duchessa d'Aosta* did not in itself constitute a danger to the Allies. However, according to British agents on Fernando Po, the ship's radio station was still in working order and could be used to send intelligence to German or Italian operatives.[155] The 70-ton *Likomba*, which belonged to a German plantation company in Cameroon, was ideally suited for operations along the West African coast.

If this plan were not approved, and the ban on 'bangs' against Vichy ships not lifted, *Maid Honor* and its crew would lack purpose, and might instead be put to work preparing border defences in Sierra Leone or Nigeria.[156]

Coastal sailing

While life on Lumley Beach was pleasant, it was also something of an anti-climax after the intensive training in England and the long and perilous voyage. When faced with disappointment, Lassen's impatience caused him to react violently and aggressively. When Perkins told him that the dog Loopy, which lived in the camp, had killed *Maid Honor*'s mascot, the monkey Chico, Lassen went in search of it with a large knife in one hand, a Colt .45 in the other and a wild look in his eye. While the dog's fate remains unknown, Appleyard wrote in a letter to his parents that 'the future did not appear so good for Loopy'.[157]

Similarly frustrated by the lack of activity, March-Phillipps also turned out to have a very short fuse. Among the friendly, hospitable artillery folk whose mess his crew frequented was a Lieutenant Ian Warren, who was bored in Sierra Leone and kept pestering March-Phillipps for a place on *Maid Honor*. Warren also annoyed March-Phillipps with his love of Hoagy Carmichael's *Stardust*, which he incessantly whistled or played on the mess gramophone. March-Phillipps was so sick of *Stardust* that he broke the record over Warren's head. When Warren persisted in whistling the tune, proper fisticuffs ensued – which March-Phillipps lost. However, the fight cleared the air, and March-Phillipps promised to take Warren on as part of the crew. Although it was not possible right away, Warren joined March-Phillipps and his team when they returned to the English Channel in summer 1942.[158]

The enervating monotony was finally broken on the afternoon of Friday 10 October, when *Maid Honor* left Lumley Beach to embark on the first of several week-long trips north to Portuguese and French Guinea, south through independent and neutral Liberia, and on to the Vichy French colony Ivory Coast. One such trip involved March-Phillipps and Appleyard sailing up the Pongo River in French Guinea in a two-man folboat to look for a rumoured German submarine base. The trip lasted two days. The two men rowed at night and hid in the swamps during the day. Mosquitoes were a constant nuisance, but the expedition also encountered larger predators. One night, when the boat was proving hard to paddle, it turned out that a big crocodile was lying across the bow. Appleyard hit it hard with the oar, after which it disappeared into the water without capsizing the light and fragile boat.

Maid Honor mostly sought to avoid contact with the local population – especially the Portuguese and French authorities. However, it was put into service as a mail boat, taking shipments from Bathurst in Gambia to Liberia or South Africa, and sometimes the crew had to answer questions. On one occasion, *Maid Honor* sent a dinghy into port in Liberia, allegedly to buy fruit for a sick crewman. The real purpose was to find out what was going on in

Detail of the *Duchessa d'Aosta*'s trellis mast and deck machinery. Pen and ink and watercolour by the artist Peter Anson who sailed from Venice to Vancouver on the *Duchessa d'Aosta* in 1926.

The bridge of the *Duchessa d'Aosta*. Watercolour by Peter Anson.

the harbour. When Appleyard and Hayes went ashore, they were questioned by the local authorities, who insisted on boarding *Maid Honor* to see the sick sailor. Appleyard deliberately bungled the boarding, giving Hayes time to jump on board *Maid Honor* before the colonel who was head of the port authority. He quickly told his comrades that the skipper was called Johnson, and that the rest of the crew were called Green, Brown and Jones, and that Green was ill. One of the crew was sent to bed and told to powder his cheeks with flour to imitate a sickly pallor. When the colonel finally made it on board, he conceded that Green did indeed look ill and probably needed fresh fruit, but also asked to inspect the hold. As mentioned previously, the deckhouse was a plywood mock-up concealing *Maid Honor*'s gun. Captain 'Johnson' deflected attention by explaining that the hold was sealed because it contained mail heading to South Africa. The colonel was content with the explanation, luckily for him – his gullibility probably saved his life, or at least stopped him being kidnapped and taken to Lumley Beach.[159]

While Lassen and his comrades kept themselves busy, the telegram traffic between Lagos and London was intense. On 12 November, *Neucols* was finally given the go-ahead for the hijacking mission. London was very clear that the main target was *Likomba*, and that *Neucols* must not be distracted by the more ambitious mission of hijacking the much larger (7,872 GRT) *Duchessa d'Aosta*. Everything possible was to be done to conceal the fact that this pirate raid on vessels in a neutral port was carried out by British forces. The heads of the British Army and Navy in West Africa initially objected to the plan, but ultimately allowed themselves to be persuaded. The Governor of Nigeria, Sir Bernard Bourdillon, was in favour from the outset.[160]

Spies on Fernando Po

The British had an effective network of spies on Fernando Po. The most active was Vice Consul Charles W. Michie, who had been sent by Governor Bourdillon to ensure that the 18,000 Nigerian workers on the island's coffee

British intelligence photo of the port of Santa Isabel. The aerial photo shows *Duchessa d'Aosta* (left) and *Likomba* (right) moored side by side.

and cocoa plantations were treated properly. Richard Lippett (SOE agent W25) was an engineer who represented the trading house John Holt & Co. Lieutenant C.A.L. Guise (W10) travelled as a royal courier between the English, French and Spanish colonies in West Africa, and used his frequent visits to Fernando Po to obtain detailed information about local conditions.[161]

Thanks to these and other agents, the British knew that *Duchessa d'Aosta* (which, despite admonitions from London, quickly became *Neucols*' main focus) was carrying wool, fur, asbestos and copper worth a total of £220,000 – not to mention the ship's potential value to the British war effort. They also knew that the crew of *Duchessa d'Aosta* were pretty demoralised by the many months of inactivity, that the two ships were not moored along the quay but out in the harbour basin, and that all lights in Santa Isabel were turned off at midnight. Aerial photographs from British reconnaissance aircraft supplemented the agents' reports.

British intelligence photo of the port of Santa Isabel. The photo appears to have been made from some high point ashore. *Duchessa d'Aosta* is marked 'D.A.'

Once the go-ahead was given, preparations began for what was dubbed Operation Postmaster. However, Franck was not convinced that his own people or the *Maid Honor* crew – while he considered them 'admirable in their own way' – were capable of planning and carrying out such a complex operation. He also thought March-Phillipps lacked common sense. Eventually, Franck and his colleagues agreed that March-Phillipps probably could do the job if he received the necessary assistance from Appleyard. One factor in his decision was the *Maid Honor* crew's unwavering faith in their skipper.[162]

The operation was to take place immediately after midnight on the night of Thursday, 15 January 1942. The timing was critical – not only was it a moonless night, but Lippett had arranged a dinner for eight Italian officers from the *Duchessa d'Aosta*, two German officers from *Likomba* and fourteen local Spaniards, Italians and Germans in the casino in Santa Isabel.[163] The casino restaurant had a view out over the harbour basin, but the table plan had the Germans and Italians sitting with their backs to the windows. Lippett had also ordered such generous food and drink that by midnight the diners would be rendered more or less insensible. To divert attention from himself, Lippett had a Spanish agent, Agustin Zorilla, make the practical arrangements. Zorilla did the job so well that a Herr Luhr, whom the British suspected of being a German spy, had the honour of hosting the event.[164]

Christmas 1941 – Olokemeji

In early December, *Maid Honor* departed Lumley Beach for the last time, bound for Lagos.[165]* Lassen was not on board. Due to a lack of room on the *Maid Honor*, he and other members of the group waited in Freetown to board the M/V *Mary Kingsley*, which sailed for Lagos on 12 December. Lassen's application for an exit visa listed his employer as the Royal Navy and his position as 'Civilian Research Staff (Navy)'. On the back of the visa, he noted that he brought three pairs of shorts, three white shirts, three pairs of khaki shorts and a pair of socks.

* * *

While Lassen and his companions waited in Freetown, the announcement came that on 7 December Japanese aircraft had attacked the American naval base at Pearl Harbor and the British fortress of Singapore, and that Japanese troops had landed in Malaya. On 10 December, Japanese aircraft sank the British battleships *Prince of Wales* and *Repulse*. On 11 December, Germany declared war on the USA.

* * *

Alfred Jørgensen and Børge Franck probably remained in Freetown. Of the participants in Operation Postmaster, the *Maid Honor*'s crew were listed as March-Phillipps, Appleyard, Hayes, Prout, Winter, Desgrange, Tottenham, Lassen, Perkins and Evison and a Taylor (who had not been mentioned previously).

As part of the preparations, Lassen and his comrades spent Christmas Day in the SOE training camp in Olokemeji, hiking in the mountains, hunting, fishing with dynamite, and enjoying fresh fruit and:

> There were nine of us up there for Christmas […] We had a very jolly Christmas Day [and a] grand Christmas dinner at night with turkey and etceteras, plum-pudding (on fire!), mince pies, etc. and all the additions of crackers, a Christmas tree (with presents!), chokolates, nuts, etc. Great fun, and all very unexpected.[166]

The *Maid Honor* team celebrated New Year in Lagos, and Lassen took the opportunity to visit Danish ships in the harbour. He had a lively time with his countrymen.[167]

The coup

In Lagos, the Nigerian colonial administration made two fully manned tugs available, *Vulcan* and *Nuneaton*. The local SOE team and *Maid Honor*'s eleven men were also supplemented with civil servants from the volunteer Lagos Defence Force or Nigerian Local Defence Volunteers. These men had politely but emphatically been asked to sign up for an unspecified, secret and potentially highly dangerous operation. (When the civilian 'volunteers' turned up, they were told roughly what the mission was about, and were then given twenty-four hours to opt out. Nobody did.) The total force numbered thirty-eight men – or, as agent W10 (Guise) would later call them in his report, 'The Forty Thieves' and 'our black brothers in the engine room'.

The two tugs left Lagos at 05:00 on Sunday, 11 January 1942. *Vulcan*, with Lassen on board, had the smaller *Nuneaton* in tow. *Nuneaton* danced 'along behind like a naughty puppy on the end of a lead,' wrote Guise. On Monday, *Nuneaton* became quite unruly. It lurched so far to starboard that the engine room was partially flooded and the skipper stood in water up to his neck in the wheelhouse. All of the crew members who were able to do so made a 'by no means panicky, but somewhat disorderly evacuation onto the port side of the hull … where the bilge keel was plainly visible'. *Vulcan* was pulling the smaller tug down, and:

until Lassen on *Vulcan* cast her off, it was 100 to 1 that *Nuneaton* was finished.

Vulcan's tow watch was ready but Lassen was the only professional and took immediate action without which there is little question that the strain of the high speed tow on the flooded ship would have pulled her over.[168]

The two tugs sailed on under their own power. On Tuesday, 13 January, both crews began preparations for the coup. The kayaks that the *Nuneaton* team would use to board *Likomba* were painted grey. *Vulcan*'s bridge was kitted out with planks to put a boarding party onto the deck of *Duchessa d'Aosta*. The teams practised shooting with Tommy guns and were given clear instructions on what to do when they boarded the two vessels – the engine rooms were to be occupied, the *Duchessa d'Aosta*'s radio was to be put out of commission, etc. That same night, *Nuneaton* lowered its folboats into the water and the crews sailed right up to *Vulcan* undetected.

Vulcan and *Nuneaton* reached the approach to Santa Isabel on Wednesday, 14 January, just before midnight Lagos time, only to find out that the city and port remained brightly illuminated. Nobody had told March-Phillipps that the Spanish possession Fernando Po, despite being in the same time zone as Lagos, followed Madrid time and was an hour behind the clocks on board *Vulcan* and *Nuneaton*. The two tugs waited at a safe distance from the island. The waiting was almost too much for March-Phillipps. As per the plan, *Nuneaton* started to creep towards the harbour entrance, ready to make its move once the lights were turned off in Santa Isabel. Just then, a familiar voice roared through the darkness: 'Will you get a b-b-b-bloody move on or or g-g-g-get out. I'm coming in.' The *Nuneaton* skipper feared that the whole operation would be scuppered if *Vulcan* sailed into the brightly lit harbour, so he placed his ship across *Vulcan*'s bow and blocked its way. After a heated exchange of views, common sense prevailed. *Vulcan* turned back and waited in the dark.[169] Midnight finally arrived and darkness descended on Santa Isabel. *Vulcan* and *Nuneaton* prepared to sneak into the harbour. *Nuneaton* lay just inside the harbour mouth and lowered its two folboats into the water. *Vulcan* continued into the basin and elegantly glided up to the 164-yard *Duchessa d'Aosta*.

The crew of *Nuneaton*'s first folboat boarded *Likomba* without difficulty. A local watchman briefly challenged them but was fobbed off when a voice from the boat, speaking in pidgin, explained they had a letter for his boss. The stranger climbed aboard while the other kayak crews used bombs to destroy *Likomba*'s anchor chains. The watchman and his colleague swiftly leapt

Among the participants in Operation Postmaster were a group of civil servants from the volunteer Lagos Defence Force or Nigerian Local Defence Volunteers. One of them was the acting principal of King's College, Lagos, H.H. Jeffers. Jeffers had studied at Cambridge where he had rowed as 'stroke' for Selwyn College when Selwyn won against Christ College in 1926.

overboard, leaving the now-abandoned ship to its uninvited guests.

Boarding *Duchessa d'Aosta* was almost as easy. The biggest problem was that the teams who were to occupy the radio room and the officers' mess were delayed by the unexpectedly large number of prisoners they took on their way. Demolition teams placed specially designed explosive charges on the ship's anchor chains. Others searched the cabins and engine rooms to ensure nobody on board would mount any resistance.

H.H. Jeffers (2nd from left, front row) with a group of unidentified colleagues some of whom may also have been among the "Forty Thieves", presumably in Lagos.

Lassen led a group of eleven men tasked with fixing *Vulcan*'s tow rope to the bow of *Duchessa d'Aosta*. It was difficult, but Lassen managed it quickly, efficiently, and with great authority.

Six Italians did not understand an order to lie down and were knocked out with foot-long iron bolts wrapped in rubber – the boarding party's main weapon. But throughout the operation, not a single shot was fired on either ship.

The British spies on Fernando Po had predicted that the attackers would face no resistance, and the whole plan was based on this assumption. It turned out to be true, but it could easily have been so different:

> Though Bren guns were ready on both 'Vulcan' and 'Nuneaton''s decks, any quite mild form of resistance might have caused disaster. The manoeuvering of 'Vulcan' alongside the 'Duchess' was good; but a couple of machine guns aboard the latter would have seen off the entire boarding party. Similarly in 'Likomba' they could thank another man that no German remained aboard as the design of the ship makes it almost certain that great losses would have been suffered by an attack against force. It is in fact not easy to imagine what would have happened, but few came away from the party with any idea that they could have done anything at all if the enemy had been prepared or shown fight.[170]

By 00:30 both tugs had left the harbour with their prizes in tow. *Nuneaton* even had a bonus, in the form of the small German vessel *Bibundi*, which was towed by *Likomba*. No one in Santa Isabel had any idea what was going on until it was all over. After the first explosion, a bugler had sounded the alarm. But when several other alarms followed in quick succession, people in the city assumed an air raid was imminent and took cover indoors. As planned, the two ships' officers were intoxicated, and did not return to the harbour until their ships had long since disappeared into the darkness.

Lassen remained on board *Duchessa d'Aosta*, where he took a shift on the bridge. He was also responsible for guarding the deck and setting up light machine guns to keep potential pursuers at bay. For the rest of the voyage back to Lagos, Lassen led a team of Italian sailors tasked with cleaning *Duchessa d'Aosta* and, as far as possible, repairing the damage that the ship had suffered over the previous eighteen months of increasingly perfunctory maintenance. The twenty-nine prisoners were cooperative and even seemed happy to finally leave Fernando Po.

The trip back to Lagos was beset with problems. *Nuneaton*'s engines malfunctioned, and the British corvette *Violet*, which had been sent to 'find' *Duchessa d'Aosta* and *Likomba* drifting in international waters, ran aground and then had trouble locating the two ships. When it finally succeeded, the head of the party sent on board *Duchessa d'Aosta* was convinced that he was actually seizing an enemy ship, and reported back that the Italian ship's captain (March-Phillipps) spoke exceptionally good English.

After multiple difficulties with *Violet* and the tugboats, the convoy finally arrived at Lagos on the afternoon of Wednesday, 21 January. Guise (W10) described the scene in his official report:

> By midnight all was over and the crews of both ships except for the members of M.H. who stayed aboard on duty, were ashore. They left the scene in a pleasantly happy state of mind, but comment was free about the navy, and laughter was freer when they learnt that 'Violet' had been aground near Forcados during the rendezvous time.
>
> So, rather drably, with naval officers guarding their every move ended a pleasant adventure from [for] the volunteers, and a good aperitif for the professionals. The word loot is unworthy, but souvenirs were not uncommon, and the fact that H.E. [Governor Bourdillon] was alleged to have been standing at the end of his landing stage with a whisky and soda in his hand, cheering loudly as the 'Duchess' came in, gave a good finishing touch.[171]

* * *

The 'accidental' encounter with *Violet* was one of several decoy strategies employed to mask the fact that Postmaster was a British operation. Before *Vulcan* and *Nuneaton* left Santa Isabel, the crew threw Free French caps into the harbour basin so that General de Gaulle's supporters would be blamed. This account of a Free French operation off the coast of Fernando Po took hold long enough for the German news agency to announce that De Gaulle's men had sent a destroyer into the port of Santa Isabel, where it had blown up the German and Italian ships' anchor chains and then boarded them, shooting Italian and German seamen.

However, the Spanish newspaper *Arriba* accused Britain of being behind the incursion into Spanish territory, and declared: 'Spain will not tolerate such a situation.' In Madrid, a demonstration was held in front of the British embassy and ambassador's residence, and the Spanish government lodged an official complaint about the violation of neutrality, demanding compensation.[172] The British denied any link with the coup, insisting that *Violet* had found *Duchessa d'Aosta* and *Likomba* drifting in international waters and had taken them as legitimate prizes. When the German news agency accused the British of being behind the operation, the Royal Navy sent warships to the area to look for a mysterious ship that was rumoured to have been seen in the waters around Fernando Po when *Duchessa d'Aosta* and *Likomba* disappeared. As late as October 1943, the Spanish ambassador in London again complained to the Foreign Office about the incident. The allegations were again flatly denied by the Foreign Secretary, Anthony Eden.

Likomba's captain, Specht, had no doubt about who was behind the kidnapping of his ship. Half an hour after the coup, he turned up – still 'very drunk' after the dinner party at the casino and 'very quarrelsome' – at the British Consulate in Fernando Po, where he attacked the assisting Vice Consul, Peter Ivan Lake (W 53) and the acting Vice Consul, B. Godden (W 51). This gave the two agents a welcome pretext to 'knock the stuffing out' of Specht. He was then removed by the Spanish authorities, who after a formal complaint by Lake to the Spanish Governor General apologised for the incident, stationed a guard in front of the consulate and provided various other British citizens (some of whom were SOE agents or spies) with police protection.[173*]

* * *

'Caesar', the head of the SOE's W Mission, which was responsible for all of the organization's activities in Africa, expressed in his report on Operation Postmaster the hope

> that S.O.E. will be permitted to demonstrate that what was possible in Fernando Po is possible elsewhere.

He concluded, on a slightly sour note, that

> perhaps on the next occasion, it will not be found necessary to preface twenty-five minutes compact and decisive action by over four months of prolonged and desultory negotiations.[174*]

The SOE leadership in London noted with satisfaction that the success of Operation Postmaster had earned the organization considerable recognition – from Churchill at the top, down through the government apparatus, and among the military and civilian authorities, where it had previously been regarded with scepticism. The fact that the Spaniards had figured out who was behind the operation was not considered disastrous either. It would serve as a useful warning to other neutral countries that the British were prepared to take action against anybody who worked too closely with the Axis powers.[175]

* * *

For Lassen, Operation Postmaster was yet another honourable task – his most difficult, most independent and most exciting to date – and he had acquitted himself well. His efforts were duly rewarded when, during the voyage back to Lagos, March-Phillipps promoted him to second lieutenant. Unfortunately March-Phillipps did not have the authority to promote his subordinates, but Lassen was no less proud of his new rank. He glued his souvenirs from the mission into his hunting journal – a postcard of *Duchessa d'Aosta* and a playing card with the ship on the back, along with two newspaper clippings with the headlines 'Navy goes to Fernando Po' and 'Mystery "theft" of three Axis ships'. Alongside these trophies, he wrote:

> Have been in many funny Stunts. The last one of the best, run right into a forreign Harbour punched a big ship and disapeered with it Jerrys and Italians kiched up a hell of a Row. Was promoted to Officer on the bridge of the kaptured ship by Kapt. Marsch Phillips.

Aftermath in Nigeria

As soon as they arrived in Lagos, the 29 prisoners from *Duchessa d'Aosta* (27 Italian men, one Italian woman and a Spanish man) were examined by a consultant at the European Hospital, who confirmed that they were all well and unharmed. On Friday 23 January at 21:15, the 27 Italian men left Lagos by train. At 08:30 on the following Monday, they arrived at an internment camp in Umuahia in south-east Nigeria. The travel order for the prisoners, as well as the 24 British officers, soldiers, police officers and orderlies who accompanied them to Umuahia, emphasised:

> THE NECESSITY FOR ABSOLUTE SECRECY with regard to this operation should be repeatedly impressed on everyone concerned (including personal servants). The composition of the Party, the origin, strength and disposal of the Internees should be kept as secret as possible, both during and after the operation.[176]

On 15 September 1943, following the Italian capitulation, the British War Office decided that the 27 internees, many of whom had succumbed to illness, could be transferred to South Africa where conditions were better. On 16 October 1943, the Colonial Office decreed that the last member of the crew still interned, the Spanish cook José Segura, could be released, albeit in Nigeria. Work was to be found for him there, and he would not be allowed to return to Fernando Po.[177]

* * *

Operation Postmaster   105

In addition to prize money all those who had taken part in the operation received a Defence Medal and a silver ashtray, presented without formal ceremony. H.H. Jeffers' daughter, Mrs Philippa Field, has bequeathed her father's Postmaster ashtray to the present day SBS. A guest room at the SBS in Poole is named after Operation Postmaster.

Most of *Maid Honor*'s crew spent a few more weeks in Africa. They probably did another – unfortunately unrecorded – job in the Belgian Congo and were then granted leave in Cape Town. It was thought that they would remain in South Africa and train for more operations similar to Postmaster – indeed, the SOE had plans to repeat the success in another African port – but it was not to be. March-Phillipps and Appleyard arrived back in Britain on 11 February 1942.[178]

Lassen stayed in Nigeria somewhat longer, where he was attached to the SOE school in Olokemeji. He helped Major Leonard H. Dismore – who had taken part in the hijacking of *Duchessa d'Aosta* (and, in the dark and confusion, had told a pig

Playing card taken as a souvenir by Anders Lassen and kept in his Hunting Journal.

to put its hands up!) – train members of the Yoruba tribe in sabotage and guerrilla warfare. Dismore dressed his troops in a uniform consisting of khaki shorts and shirts with blue epaulettes, blue sashes around the waist and a blue fez. He had a local silversmith produce a unit badge consisting of the dragon from the badge of his old regiment (The Buffs), above which was a crown, reflecting the rank on Dismore's shoulder. The dragon proved a useful ally when Dismore ran into problems with a local witch doctor, who was driven off with stink bombs and 'Powder, itching, MK II' from the SOE's comprehensive catalogue of special materials: '"*Dragon he be strong ju-ju too much*" – and our witch doctor was last seen going for the bush at a rate of knots.'[179]

In his hunting journal, Lassen wrote:

> Had a temporary Job in Africa which consisted of training Niggers in different ways to wage wars.
>
> It lasted a couple of months and was very interesting and very responsible and very independent. Had more than a hundred black bastards under me without a single NCO so it was pretty heavy going.

But Olokemeji also offered relaxation, in the form of hunting. Lassen spent time both sitting idly on the porch, shooting Dismore's poultry with his Colt .45, and out in the wild, stalking deer, monkeys, crocodiles and hundreds of birds.

While he enjoyed the freedom, responsibility and sense of accomplishing something on his own, Lassen missed what, for him, the war was primarily about:

> Refused a while back an offer of a really interesting job – but it didn't involve slaughtering any of the swines, so I turned it down.

Shortly after making this decision, he was called back to England, where March-Phillipps was reassembling the *Maid Honor* crew.

> Unfortunately I left Africa just as my negotiations to buy an unusually beautiful wife were about to fall in place. The Father originally wanted the abominable price of £15, and I would only give £10. He had agreed that I could [get] her on trial and if she was good I was to give him £10 and 2 bottles of trade gin, if not the deal would be off with the exception of the gin. A great shame for that and other reasons that I was called back. First time since the ships that I really had something to do and say something to organize, arrange care of and give advice, go out and fight put dozens of men to work and the likes –

On 31 March 1942, Lassen flew from Lagos to Freetown in a Pan Am Clipper seaplane, and then continued by ship to Liverpool, arriving on 19 April 1942.

Operation Postmaster 107

Anders Lassen in Olokemeji.

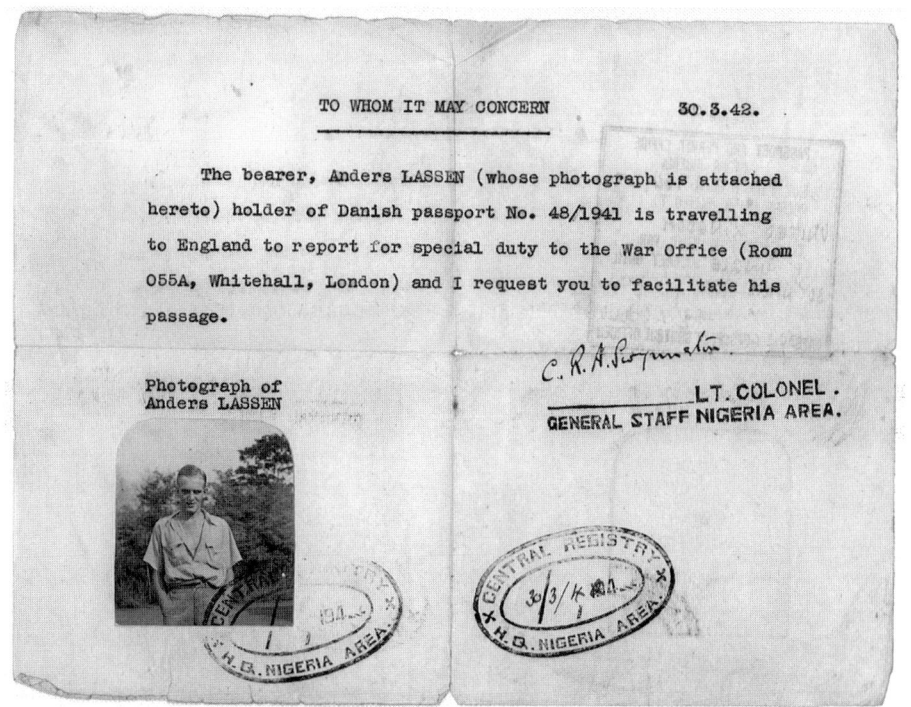

Chapter Twenty-Four

Small Scale Raiding Force

The British Commando raids at different points along this enormous coast, although so far only the forerunner of what is to come, inspire the author of so many crimes and miseries with a lively anxiety. His soldiers dwell among populations who would kill them with their hands if they got the chance, and will kill them one at a time when they do get the chance.
(Winston Churchill, speaking in Edinburgh, 12 October 1942)

Back to the roots

On 27 October 1941, Churchill replaced the 69-year-old Admiral Roger Keyes as Chief of Combined Operations with Lord Louis Mountbatten, 28 years his junior and commander of the aircraft carrier HMS *Illustrious*. Mountbatten was one of the prime minister's special protégés, and under his leadership Combined Operations grew markedly in both scope and ambition.[180]

On the night of 27/28 February 1942, under Mountbatten's overall command, around 120 men from the newly created Parachute Regiment launched a successful attack (Operation Biting) on a German radar installation near the village of Saint-Jouin-Bruneval in Normandy, fourteen miles north of Le Havre. The attackers landed by parachute and were evacuated by the Royal Navy. They took with them important components from the German Freya-Würzburg radar system, which the British only knew about from spies, interrogations of prisoners of war, aerial photographs and equipment found on downed German bombers. The British losses amounted to two dead, six wounded and six taken prisoner.

Lord Louis Mountbatten.

A month later, Combined Operations struck again, this time on a much larger scale. On the night of 27/28 March 1942, commando and naval forces attacked the French Atlantic port of St. Nazaire (Operation Chariot). They damaged the German U-boat base and destroyed the big dry dock, the only one along the Atlantic coast that had the capacity to receive ships as large as the German battleship *Tirpitz*. However, of the 611 men who took part in the operation, only about 200 made it to the harbour – and of those, only 27 were not killed or captured.[181] Mountbatten's success was expensive, but it greatly weakened the Germans in their battle for Atlantic supremacy. The attack was also part of a strategy to draw German forces away from the Eastern Front by making them think that the Allies were preparing an invasion in the Calais area. In December 1941, Hitler started talking about a line of fortifications along the Atlantic coast. On 23 March 1942 he issued Führer Directive no. 40, ordering the fortification of the Atlantic, North Sea and Channel Islands coasts. In the aftermath of St. Nazaire, he also ordered that all ports and naval bases be more heavily defended.

Shortly after the attack on St. Nazaire, Combined Operations started planning an even bigger raid – Operation Rutter, an attack on German fortifications, radar installations and port facilities in and around the northern French town of Dieppe. The operation was to serve several purposes. It would fuel Hitler's fears of a landing in northern France, and (again) draw German resources away from the Eastern Front. It would also show the Russians and the Americans – who, unlike the British, were very keen to open a 'second front' in Western Europe in 1942 – that it was not a lack of fighting spirit and determination that was holding the British back. Finally, it would provide valuable experience of large-scale amphibious operations. Rutter was scheduled for 4 July 1942.[182]

Since their inception in summer 1940, the commandos had far outgrown their original purpose. They were no longer small, highly flexible forces capable of carrying out pinprick attacks anywhere along the German-occupied coasts of Europe. Colin Gubbins was, therefore, highly receptive to the proposal drawn up by Geoffrey Appleyard and March-Phillipps and presented to him by the latter less than a week after his return from Africa. The idea was to set up and train a small amphibious force capable of carrying out numerous small-scale attacks in rapid succession in order to force the enemy to spread their forces thinly – in line with Gubbins's recommendation in the *Partisan Leader's Handbook* and the strategy of ensuring that Hitler focused his attention on Calais. The success of Operation Postmaster meant that March-Phillipps and Appleyard's new project enjoyed Lord Mountbatten's support. On 21 March, the Chiefs of Staff Committee also approved it.[183]

March-Phillipps was promoted to major and given extensive freedom to assemble, train and lead his unit, which was named *Small Scale Raiding Force*. The SSRF, which received its official 'charter' from Mountbatten on 27 March 1942, would not only carry out attacks on targets in northern France, but also train officers and NCOs to train other raiders. Over time, the members of the original SSRF would form the core of a chain of similar units operating from bases all along the English coast.[184]

The SOE's Department M, under Gubbins, was responsible for administration, supplies and training, while Mountbatten's Combined Operations had operational control. However, it was agreed that Combined Operations would not launch raids without the consent of the SOE. In the SOE system, the force was called Special Training School 62 or Station 62, while Combined Operations called it 62 Commando. The members wore the commandos' green beret.[185]

As a home for the new unit, March-Phillipps and Appleyard chose the beautiful Anderson Manor, near Blandford Forum, 9½ miles inland but handy for the ports of Portsmouth, Poole and Portland.[186]

In the weeks and months that followed, SSRF's ranks swelled to approximately fifty-five members. From *Maid Honor* – in addition to

Anderson Manor, home of the SSRF.

March-Phillipps and Appleyard – came Graham Hayes, Tom Winter, André Desgrange and Denis Tottenham, as well as 'that Bloody Man' Ian Warren, with whom March-Phillipps had ended up fighting in Freetown and who was summoned to Anderson Manor while on leave in England. Other members included Peter Kemp, who had been a member of the Knife force; Captain Lord Francis Howard, who felt that there was too little to do in the SOE's Belgium Department; Lieutenant Tony Hall, who had been a sergeant in the London Irish Rifles before leaving to write for *Punch* and several popular radio programmes but volunteered again when war broke out; the Polish-Jewish refugee Abraham Opoczynski (codenamed Adam Orr); the Dutchman Hellings; the Sudeten-German Czech Richard Lehniger (Leonard); and the Czech-Jewish Ján Ludvik Hoch, codenamed Ian Robert Maxwell, who would go on to build one of the world's largest media empires.

Lassen joined this motley but fine crew on 5 June 1942.

'Am now an officer in the English Army'

Shortly after his return to England, Lassen submitted an application for an 'Emergency Commission'. March-Phillipps, now a newly appointed major, was of high enough rank to grant the request and say that he found Lassen fit to serve as an officer in the British Army. Lassen named R.C. Hollingworth and another officer as guarantors of his moral and professional conduct. He became a second lieutenant on 20 May 1942. On the same day, he was transferred to 'special service' in the Inter Services Research Bureau (SOE's alias). Two weeks later, he officially joined STS62/62 Commando.

> Have now by own abilities and definitively without protection since no one here knows anything about me other than that I am Andy who was A.B. Seaman before he joined the Army obtained the King's Commission and am now an officer in the English Army. I doubt there are many sailors serving as officers in the English Army.

* * *

In practice, Lassen's paramilitary SOE training and his experience in West Africa put him on a par with most new second lieutenants, although he lacked their systematic, albeit relatively superficial, training in military organization, leadership and tactics.

His class and family background may not have set him apart greatly from the majority of his new colleagues, but his lack of an upper-secondary education, his two years in the merchant navy and, not least, his experience from the SOE schools and West Africa nevertheless made him something of a misfit in the British officer corps. Unlike his British colleagues, he had not acquired the shared values, style and language that permeated the British Army, despite the cultural breadth of the different regiments and corps. And then, of course, there was his accent – on the one hand, as mentioned previously, it put him outside the rigid class system; on the other, it underlined his status as an outsider. Lassen may have become an officer, but he was no *gentleman* in the traditional sense. For a whole variety of reasons, the same could also be said of quite a few of the other members of March-Phillipps' small force.

* * *

While Lassen waited for the bureaucrats to do their job so that he could transfer to Anderson Manor, he spent his time in London, partly on visits to friends of the Raben-Lewetzau family, Lord and Lady Hambleden. The Hambledens, who owned the WH Smith bookshops, lived at Greenlands in Henley-on-Thames. Here, Lassen was briefly able to resume the kind of activities he enjoyed during his year at Bækkeskov, such as horse riding, fishing and shooting pheasants and squirrels – the latter causing Lord Hambleden's mother a certain degree of unease.[187]

Other regular fixtures in Lassen's life during this period included the Danish ambassador Count Reventlow and his family (and maids), as well as Emil Lassen's sister Estrid. Like her sister Jenny, Estrid had married and divorced a German landowner. She had since married the German engineer Peter Reichenheim. The couple had settled in London where Estrid ran a physiotherapy clinic for children in one of the poorest parts of the East End. To protect themselves from the anti-Semitism that was also widespread in the UK, Estrid and her husband went by the surname Dane, rather than the Jewish Reichenheim. In 1942, Lassen spent some of his leave between SSRF raids as a guest of the couple. He would sometimes turn up unannounced in the middle of the night, restless and quivering with tension, clearly affected by what he had been through and what lay ahead. Although a good night's sleep and a generous helping of Estrid Dane's spaghetti calmed him down, the stress symptoms returned as the time to leave again approached.

'It is strange to receive letters from Denmark…'

In December 1941, the Lassen family's good friend Fritz Emmerich Hoegh-Guldberg was appointed Secretary of Legation in Lisbon. Shortly afterwards, Suzanne Lassen started to write letters to her 'Dearly beloved Fritz'. On receiving these letters, Hoegh-Guldberg forwarded them to the Danish Embassy in London, where Anders picked them up. From December 1941 to August 1942 he received at least eight letters from his mother. He was afraid of exposing his family to the risk of reprisals by writing letters that might fall into German hands (later volunteers from occupied countries were forbidden to send letters home), so he wrote only a few telegrams and a single letter, in May 1942: 'I assure you there is no reason at all for you to worry…'[188]

* * *

In autumn 1941, Suzanne informed Anders that his German cousin Cuno von dem Bussche Streithorst had fallen on the Eastern Front, and that his brother, Axel, had been severely wounded by a bullet to one of his lungs. Otherwise, she mainly talked about the mundane, everyday details of the lives of their family and their circle:

> Axel Thott studied forestry this winter at Petersgaard … Varinka is so sweet – pretty to look at and bright. … Uncle Siegfried wintered in an atelier here in Nyhavn – He enjoyed it – it was a terrible mess… You know I write to you about all this insignificant stuff to give you an impression of what our lives are like – But I can't, of course, write about what is really on our minds.[189]

However, in the spring of 1942 she hinted that Anders' brother Frants planned to follow in his footsteps: 'He told me to say hello to you and tell you he does not think it will be long before he sees you again.'[190]

In his hunting journal, Anders was somewhat indignant about the stories of Siegfried's studio, Axel's studies and other matters:

> It is strange to get letters from Denmark and hear about the way people live exactly like four years ago, untouched apparently, and getting on with all sorts of trivial things like learning farming, keeping chickens, having terribly messy lofts in Copenhagen.
>
> All the while we or at least I weekly risk my life and concentrate all my ability energy on fighting and dying for Denmark all quite unnoticed and quite indifferently as far as [those] filthy pigs and pricks are concerned.

Anderson Manor and London, May–August 1942[191]

The atmosphere in Anderson Manor was both relaxed and intense. Little distinction was made between officers and men. Everybody was on first-name terms, and they wore civilian clothes when they visited the local village hall, the *World's End* pub in Bere Regis or *The Antelope* in Poole, or went to Bournemouth. Although traditional military discipline appeared to be lacking, the actual training was tough and focused. The programme followed the pattern established at the commando schools in Scotland. It included shooting with pistols and automatic weapons, knife-fighting, the use of hand grenades and explosives, fieldcraft, cutting through barbed wire, kayaking in Poole Harbour, navigation with and without maps and compasses, and parachute training at the air base at Ringway. The men also went on long marches, locally and as far north as Cumberland. This improved their endurance and fieldcraft, and taught them to improvise and live off the land. For example, they would drink ditch water disinfected with chlorine tablets, or eat clams and sea snails scraped from the rocks when they finally reached the sea after a 60-mile march from an unknown starting point, over Exmoor to Lynmouth in north Devon. The instructors advised the future raiders to blacken their faces on night raids, but March-Phillipps refused: 'If I am to die on one of these parties I'll die looking like an Englishman and not like a damned nigger.'[192]

The countryside around Anderson Manor offered excellent opportunities for hunting, and Lassen liked to roam the land with the two bows that the War Office had sent him in response to his memorandum on archery as a weapon of war. In shooting competitions with his comrades, Lassen proved time and again that in the hands of a skilled archer, a bow was every bit the equal of conventional small arms.

Life at Anderson Manor suited Lassen well. He impressed his peers with his strength, endurance and ability to move quickly and quietly. He was an excellent marksman, and in knife fights he was decisive and lightning-fast. The one thing he did not like was the parachute training.

Like Peter Kemp, he often pointed out that he was really keen to see combat, but Lassen seemed more intense – one of the wildest in a group not short of wildness.[193]

Lassen and March-Phillipps were close friends, and Lassen also got on well with the other members of the force, especially Hall, Kemp and Appleyard, although he was reluctant to discuss himself and his background. Appleyard in particular liked going to Poole and Bournemouth with him in search of girls. However, his comrades had to come to terms with the fact that Lassen's impressive physique, mischievous nature and strange accent, combined with the big gap where his front teeth used to be, made him the ladies' favourite. He had quite a long relationship with a twice-widowed woman in Bournemouth, whom he called his 'widow with a bar' (a bar on a medal ribbon showed that a decoration had been awarded twice).

Occasionally Lassen found the time to take a trip to London, where he would visit not only Estrid and Peter Dane, the Hambledens and the Reventlows, but also Henning and Elli Karsten, both of whom were very active on the Danish Council. On Sunday 31 May, their 17-year-old daughter Ellen wrote in her diary:

> Have now met Anders Lassen – the famous. He is very handsome, blond and tanned. … Anders asked if I would like to go out and eat lunch with him … I think he will forget to call – it might be quite cosy.

The lunch did not happen because Ellen was not feeling well, but Lassen was by no means short of diversions. He was a member of the *Rye and Dry Club* in Bury Street in St. James, *Le Bar Alexis* and *The Swizzle Stick* in Mayfair and the *Wellington Club*, a favourite watering hole of Danish and Norwegian volunteers in the British armed forces. He also frequented the fashionable artists' pub *The Fitzroy Tavern*.

* * *

Ellen wrote about Lassen several times in her diary and in letters to her brother Henrik, who was an officer of the 3rd King's Own Hussars in North Africa and later in Italy. She noted that Anders 'was almost unable to write' and called him a strange, stupid boy, but found him sweet and admired his attitude to the war. She noted that the English girls all had a crush on him and wanted to know about his background, and it amused her that despite coming from such a distinguished family, he introduced himself as a simple sailor. At that point, the snobbish girls lost interest in him and he would laugh at them behind their backs.[194]

MTB344

During the summer of 1942, the SSRF became a fully amphibious force when the Royal Navy put the motor torpedo boat *MTB344* permanently at the disposal of March-Phillipps's unit. *MTB344* was a 60-footer with two Thornycroft petrol engines totalling 1,200 hp, giving it a top speed of 40 knots, and an auxiliary engine with its exhaust fitted below the waterline to make it almost noiseless when sailing close to enemy shores. Removing all of the armaments except two 0.303 machine guns behind the bridge freed up space for an 18-foot Goatley boat (a wide, low-sided and collapsible 12-man boat made of canvas stretched over a wooden frame) which could be launched from a ramp on the aft deck. *MTB344* was nicknamed *Little Pisser* because of the jet of cooling water that spurted from a tube at the rear. The crew consisted of the captain, Lieutenant Frederick 'Freddie' William Parnall Bourne (RNVR), a mate and seven sailors. Working on the bridge or in the engine room offered some form of protection from the elements, but there was virtually no shelter for anybody else on board.

Operation Barricade, Cap Barfleur, 14–15 August 1942

As soon as *MTB344* was adapted for use by the SSRF, the men started training to sail it and use dinghies and inflatables for landings. March-Phillipps had hoped to launch his first operations in mid-June, but was thwarted by technical problems with the boat, by bad weather, and by his own inability to draw up plans that convinced the head of Royal Navy Portsmouth Command, who was in charge of the maritime part of thre SSRF's activities, to give the go-ahead for the operation. It further complicated matters that operations could proceed only on moonless nights, and that for two weeks every month *MTB344* was not allowed to sail in the Channel, to avoid collisions with convoys.[195]

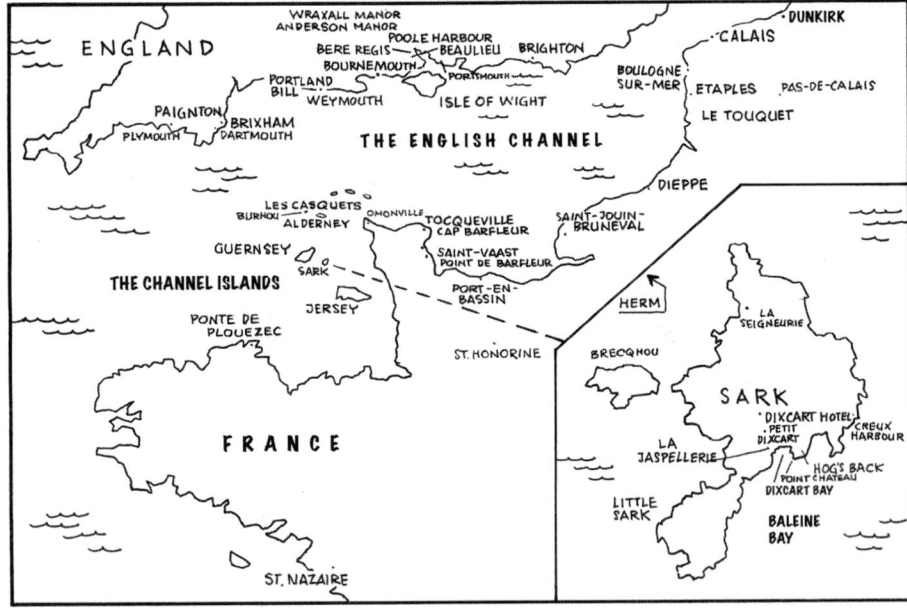

On the night of 14/15 August 1942, the SSRF finally made its first raid on the French coast (Operation Barricade).

The target was a German radar station at Cap Barfleur. *MTB344* – with March-Phillipps and his eleven raiders, including Lassen, on board – set sail from the naval base HMS Hornet in Portsmouth at 20:45. It was a calm but cloudy night. After an hour, *MTB344* reached the Nab Tower lighthouse which marks the entrance to the deep shipping channel between the Isle of Wight and the English coast. From there, Bourne set a course for Pointe de Barfleur on the east side of the Cherbourg Peninsula. Unfortunately, the port engine failed, and he had to make do with just the starboard engine as the crew worked to fix the problem. A radio signal from the naval base at Portsmouth announced that *MTB344* was a good bit further east than Bourne and his team had calculated, so they changed course. By 23:00, the crew could finally make out the lighthouse at Cap Barfleur, fifteen miles away. Sailing at an average speed of 18 knots, the boat arrived at a point three nautical miles due east of Barfleur. Bourne switched the starboard engine off and continued with the quieter auxiliary engine at a speed of 7 knots against a tide of 2½ knots. The landing was scheduled for midnight but they were running late because of the engine problems, because the low featureless coastline made it difficult to determine their position, and because *MTB344*'s only compass was fixed, which meant that the boat had to lie still with its bow pointed towards Barfleur lighthouse every time the navigator took a bearing.

MTB344.

At 01:30, *MTB344* finally dropped anchor, and the eleven raiders boarded the Goatley boat. Four men rowed on each side, one manned the rudder at the stern, and one kept a lookout at the bow. Around 100 yards from the beach or the surf, a kedge anchor was cast, which meant that the boat could be brought to an immediate halt by tugging on the anchor rope and a motor winch could be used later on to haul the boat off the beach again. On this last stretch in, the lookout wielded a boat hook, ready to push off from any rocks that appeared in front of the bow.[196]

It was a very dark night with a visibility of max. 30 feet and a light westerly wind. It took March-Phillipps's force 20 minutes to row the last nautical mile between their torpedo boat and the shore. When they finally made it, they were not on their planned landing spot on Pointe de Fouli beach but three-quarters of a mile further north, because they had failed to take account of the strong northward current along the coast. March-Phillipps decided to forge ahead anyway. He left a man armed with a Thompson sub-machine gun to guard the boat and led the rest of them off the beach. Moving in single file, they crossed the fields behind the beach and made their way inland to look for their target – a small building surrounded by four 55-foot-high masts. Before long, they encountered a barbed wire entanglement, which they cut through with little difficulty, making sure to leave a path for a rapid retreat. They then reached an approximately 200-foot-wide field where some cows were grazing. When the attackers entered their space, the animals started to stir and make a noise, which dulled the sound of the raiders' movements. More barbed wire awaited them on the other side of the field. Behind it, they could make out something that looked like a house, but might have been a vehicle or a technical installation, covered with camouflage netting and emitting a faint bluish light. They could also see some sort of guard hut and a sentry's head. This time the barbed wire was thicker and stronger. The raiders found it difficult to cut with their small, portable tools. March-Phillipps divided his men into two groups and ordered one to keep cutting – about quarter of an hour later they were only halfway through. The other group, meanwhile, was to bypass the obstruction and attack a building off to the right. The second group returned soon after, reporting that the building was the size of a hangar, and that the camp also included other smaller wooden buildings, aerials and possibly more fortifications. The German camp seemed to be significantly larger than first assumed. March-Phillipps thought it would still be possible to attack at least a part of it, and gave the order to continue clipping the barbed wire.

Whatever the buildings and structures were that the raiders thought they had identified in the dark, they were certainly not about to attack the radar station they were supposed to destroy. In fact they had chanced upon a small German fortification, 'Post 4', manned by two officers and fourteen men, five of whom were on a routine patrol heading towards the next German position. As well as rifles and handguns, the German defenders had a light machine gun and a heavy one. The attempts to cut the wire eventually made so much noise that the Germans sent two men to find out what was going on. They could see nothing suspicious, but shouted 'Password' anyway and cocked their guns. The raiders responded with seventeen machine-gun bursts and three charges of plastic explosives, totalling 5 lbs.[197]* The raiders thought they had killed at least three Germans – perhaps six – and wounded three or four. In fact, a single German suffered a flesh wound.[198]

The rest of the Germans in Post 4 then charged out, firing white star shells. The raiders were now clearly visible, but managed to retreat into the surrounding darkness before the four Germans sent after them came within shooting range.

The commotion alerted other nearby sentry posts. Post 4 sounded the alarm to 9th Company, 587th Infantry Regiment, which was guarding this stretch of coastline. Eighteen minutes after the clash by the barbed wire, a reserve unit in Tocqueville was ordered to advance towards Post 4 immediately. Over the next half hour, other German units in the vicinity were alerted, as was a nearby coastal battery. For the next hour, shots were fired at random from German positions and by patrols in the area.

In the meantime, March-Phillipps and his men had hurried back to the beach. Fifty minutes after going ashore, they were back on board the Goatley boat. Due to the strong current, it took half an hour to row out to *MTB344*. They reached it at 03:45. Ten nautical miles from the French coast, an unidentified twin-engine aircraft flew very low over *MTB344*, but did not attack. Sometime later, once the boat had reached the middle of the English Channel, the aircraft flew along the port side. The long, thin silhouette indicated a German Dornier Do 17. The crew and raiders opened fire with everything they had and the plane disappeared into the darkness again. At 07:00, *MTB344* could see the lighthouse at St. Catherine's Point, the southernmost point on the Isle of Wight. An hour later, the force landed in Portsmouth. The whole operation had lasted about twelve hours.

* * *

Operation Barricade was a failure. The in-depth planning, which included careful studies of aerial photographs of the target area and the preparation of detailed descriptions of potential routes from the landing site to the target, was all to no avail because the raiders had failed to take into account the strong current that forced them to land in completely unknown territory. The raiders were fortunate that the Germans in Post 4 took so long to realise that the attackers came from the sea. In June, two members of the German civil and military engineering group Organisation Todt, who were on their way home from a pub late at night, had their throats cut by persons unknown – probably the French Resistance. At first, the Germans thought that this too had been a raid. The German military authorities later determined that the response by the head of Post 4 and his men was largely correct, but that if they had been more dynamic and battle-hardened, and adopted a more offensive approach, they could probably have wiped out the landing party.[199]

Although Operation Barricade failed to achieve its targets, Combined Operations HQ remained optimistic:

> The effects of such raids, though small in itself, can be cumulative if they are continuous. If carried out frequently and over a wide area they would have a most demoralizing effect on the enemy and corresponding heartening effect on our own troops. They present the best form of training both for commandos and home forces.[200]

'Killed two with deliberate and calculated fire.'

After Operation Barricade, Lassen wrote in his hunting journal: 'Killed two with deliberate and calculated fire. Weapon Tommy gun.' However, in the darkness and confusion, this deliberation and calculation amounted to firing in the general direction of shouting voices, fleeting shadows and the sound of men and weapons. He was not to know that, at best, he may or may not have inflicted a flesh wound on a single German. Nevertheless, as far as Lassen – and possibly his comrades – were concerned, he had for the first time taken another person's life.

* * *

Most people find it hard to take the life of a fellow human being. But with the proper training – such as Lassen and his companions received at the SOE schools – anybody can learn to kill in situations where it is not only appropriate to do so but seems morally justified and is done in the name of a system that both requires and rewards it.

A small group, estimated at about two per cent of the male population, find it easy to kill in battle. Some members of this group, but by no means all, even derive pleasure from it. Most of these 'natural killers' are neither psychopaths nor people who would be particularly dangerous outside a combat situation. Rather, they are individuals who, under extreme stress, keep a cool head and act as the situation requires.[201] Men who volunteered for operations such as those planned by March-Phillipps were unlikely to have harboured great concerns about killing, although they may not necessarily have liked doing it. Some, like Lassen, expressed eagerness to fight and 'slaughter bastards'. Some of them actually believed their own bravado, and continued to believe it after they had killed for the first time. One of Lassen's comrades later said of him: 'He liked to fuck and he liked to kill.'[202]

* * *

On the same day that Lassen returned from the raid on the French coast, he wrote a letter to Lady Hambleden. After first apologising for the length of time since his last letter or visit, he told her that he had received

> some very interesting news since last we met. [His brother] Frants has succeeded in escaping to Sweden, and if all goes well he will soon be in this country. How he has done it I do not know, but that doesn't matter anyhow as long as he gets here.

Operation Jubilee, Dieppe, 19 August 1942

In the early hours of 19 August 1942, some 6,000 troops (approximately 5,000 of them Canadians) landed on the beaches around Dieppe to attack German forts, radar stations and port facilities. The German defences turned out to be far stronger and better prepared than expected. About 4,300 of the attackers were killed or captured. The survivors withdrew, largely without achieving any of their objectives. Operation Jubilee was an abject failure, but it provided important lessons that were used in the planning of later Allied landing operations. It also strengthened Hitler's resolve to fortify the whole Atlantic coast.

As mentioned, a previous attack on Dieppe, Operation Rutter, was supposed to have been carried out on 4 July 1942. It had been cancelled due to a sudden storm in the English Channel and disturbing intelligence from France that the German 10th Panzer Division had been moved to the area around Dieppe, suggesting that the Germans had wind of the impending attack. After German planes attacked some of the ships that were part of the Rutter armada, it became obvious that they had been observing the convoys assembling in the Channel ports. The planners recommended aborting the operation – but it was not abandoned entirely.

Churchill considered a major amphibious operation during the summer of 1942 to be a necessary precursor to the landing in 1943 for which the Americans were still pushing. Since it was impossible to cobble together a brand-new operation at such short notice, he demanded that Rutter be dusted off. Churchill has subsequently been accused of forcing through the attack on Dieppe, knowing that it would fail, to show the Americans that the invasion they craved would be a disaster for the Allies. There are good reasons to believe this claim. For one thing, the British rumour campaigns and other forms of misdirection that had been going on for months to fool the Germans into thinking that there would be an attack in northern France during 1942 had not been suspended, nor were they adjusted to make the Germans concentrate on parts of the coast far from Dieppe. Similarly, nothing was done to mislead the Germans as to the purpose of the vessels assembling in the Channel ports.[203]

Regardless of Churchill's ulterior motives regarding Operation Jubilee (as the new version of the Dieppe raid was dubbed), the need to emphasise the dangers of an invasion disappeared when the British, at a meeting in London on 24 July 1942, managed to persuade the Americans to shelve plans for the north of France in favour of a landing in French North Africa not later than 10 October.

The mission in North Africa, codenamed Operation Torch, did not make Jubilee superfluous. It still fulfilled the strategic objective of drawing German air power away from the Eastern Front, and enabled the Allies to study how their land, sea and air forces worked together in practice. There was also the brand-new purpose of concealing Torch by deceiving the Germans into thinking that the Allies were planning attacks on the north of Norway and the north of France, as well as operations in the Middle East.

Since the spring, a whispering campaign had been fostering the impression that the Allies were preparing an attack across the Channel in 1942. This continued at full blast, as did the radio broadcasts warning the people of northern France that their region could be transformed into a battlefield at any moment. As was the case with Operation Rutter, nothing was done to conceal the preparations for Jubilee. The fact that Operation Barricade was allowed to go ahead only four days before the attack on Dieppe meant the Germans were on high alert.

Perhaps there really was an ulterior strategic motive for letting Barricade go ahead so soon before Jubilee. Perhaps it was just a side effect of military secrecy, which meant that one hand did not know what the other was doing.

Or perhaps it was erroneously believed that the Germans would *not* expect a raid to be followed so soon by a big attack. In any event, both Barricade and the other SSRF raids in the weeks and months that followed effectively formed part of a major campaign of diversions that paved the way for the landings in North Africa by getting the Germans to concentrate on the Channel coast.[204]

Operation Dryad, Les Casquets, 2 September 1942

At 21:00 on 2 September 1942, *MTB344* sailed from Portland Bill, heading for the small handful of rocks known as Les Casquets, eight nautical miles west of Alderney. March-Phillipps commanded the force, which comprised Lassen and another ten men, including officers Geoffrey Appleyard, Graham Hayes, Peter Kemp and Francis Howard, CSM Tom Winter and the German-speaking Private Adam Orr, who was responsible for looking after the prisoners they intended to take.

The raiders had studied a detailed model of Les Casquets and the buildings they were to storm. However, only Lieutenant Bourne, March-Phillipps and, presumably, his confidant Appleyard knew the name of their target and its exact location.[205]

Since 1724 the lighthouse on the largest of Les Casquets had warned seafarers of danger. The crew of the lighthouse and its radio station were the target of the raid on this otherwise uninhabited rocky outcrop.

The attack had been postponed numerous times due to bad weather. On 2 September, the conditions were less treacherous, with a wind speed of between 3 and 5 on the Beaufort scale (or 'Dryad weather', as the raiders called it). Bourne and March-Phillipps decided to go ahead. Despite difficulties with the port engine, *MTB344* had Les Casquets in sight at about 22:45. The two main engines were then turned off and the silenced engine used instead. At 00:05 the Goatley boat was launched. The engine problems had delayed arrival at Les Casquets significantly, and the north-easterly tide was stronger than expected. It took the eight rowers a whole 20 minutes to cover the 875 yards. To avoid guards and minefields, the raiding party went ashore at the foot of a cliff and climbed 25 yards up to the lighthouse. Hayes, who had navigated the boat through the violent and unpredictable whirlpools between the rocks, stayed with the boat, while the rest of the force stormed the buildings. The German crew consisted of seven men: two were on duty at the generator, three were asleep, and the two radio operators were heading to bed. They were equipped with old Steyr rifles, but also had an Oerlikon 20 mm cannon and crates of grenades. March-Phillipps noted in his report that had a proper watch been kept, or if the raiders had moved less silently, the seven Germans could have made their rocky outcrop virtually impregnable. Instead, they were caught in their pyjamas – one of the sleeping men was wearing a hairnet, and March-Phillipps thought at first that he had captured a woman – and herded down to the boat. At first, a small group of raiders stayed behind to disable the radio equipment and look for papers and other booty. To save time, March-Phillipps and Hayes decided not to wait for *MTB344*'s lifeboat, which was to have been used to transport the prisoners from the coast. Instead the twelve raiders and their seven prisoners crammed into the Goatley boat – which, although it had been built to carry 12 people, turned out to be capable of carrying 19, albeit sitting worryingly low in the water. At 01:35 the boat reached *MTB344*, which then docked in Portland at 04:00. The prisoners were sent for interrogation and the booty (coding and signal books, lighthouse and radio logs, personal letters, photographs and service records, ration books, etc) was handed over to military intelligence.

Despite engine problems and difficult weather and seas, Dryad was a success, with no losses and plenty of results. The only injuries sustained were by Peter Kemp, who hurt his leg, and Geoffrey Appleyard, who fractured his tibia when sliding down a cliff to jump into the boat – the last of the raiders to do so.

Operation Branford, Burhou, 7–8 September 1942

Three days after Operation Dryad, a new team of lighthouse keepers was in place on Les Casquets, but it was some time before the broken radio was replaced. Out again on the night of 7/8 September, Lassen saw the new crew of this exposed and tedious outpost exchanging Morse signals with their counterparts on the larger neighbouring island of Alderney.

Second Lieutenant Anders Lassen was second-in-command of a force of eight men under Captain Colin Ogden-Smith that landed near the southern tip of Burhou, an outcrop roughly midway between Alderney and Les Casquets, at 00:28. The purpose of the expedition (known as Operation Branford) was to examine whether Burhou was inhabited, and whether it would be possible to place artillery there.

It took Ogden-Smith an hour to ascertain that the site was suitable for mortars and artillery positions. After accomplishing their mission, the landing force left Burhou at 01:38 and rowed in the Goatley boat, with Lassen as helmsman, out to *MTB344*, which docked in Portland at 04:30.[206]

While Operation Branford involved no engagement with the enemy or particularly severe weather, it was always risky and difficult to navigate the

Goatley boat into unknown rocky coasts in the dark, in waters with strong and somewhat unpredictable currents. In his report, Ogden-Smith notes: '2/Lt Lassen, as cox of the landing craft, displayed excellent judgment and seamanship throughout the operation.'[207] In his hunting journal, Lassen wrote: 'Did another one. As 2nd in command. Very honourable mention in report.'

After Operation Branford, Lassen took weekend leave in Bournemouth, where he went into town or visited his 'widow with a bar'.[208]

Operation Aquatint, St. Honorine, 12–13 September 1942 – 'Biggest sorrow I have felt in this war'[209]

While Lassen tried to relax, the SSRF embarked on another expedition – this time to Normandy, close to the village of Sainte-Honorine-des-Pertes, near Port-en-Bessin, north of Bayeux. The purpose was to reconnoitre the terrain and German defences, and take prisoners. The force, under the command of Major March-Phillipps with Appleyard as second-in-command, included the captains Graham Hayes, John Burton and Francis Howard, the lieutenants Tony Hall and André Desgrange, the sergeants Tom Winter and Alan Williams, and three privates: the Dutchman Hellings, the Pole Adam Orr and the Sudenten German Leonard. Appleyard, who was still unfit for action, was to remain on board *MTB344* along with Lieutenant Bourne and his crew while the rest of the raiders went ashore.

To avoid the German minefields, *MTB344* first sailed from the Isle of Wight to Barfleur, east of the Cotentin Peninsula. They reached this point in dense fog at 22:00, and then continued in a south-easterly direction across the Seine Bay, bypassing the minefields. As midnight approached, the boat was close to the coast, where Bourne had to sail very slowly to avoid the risk of running aground. The fog lifted slightly, but it was still pitch dark and difficult to identify the fissure in the steep slope where they were to land. At 00:05, Appleyard discovered an opening in the cliff that he thought must be the planned landing point. March-Phillipps decided to go ashore. In reality, what they had found was not the Sainte-Honorine gap but the St. Laurent gap at Les Moulins, half a mile along the beach – and in the middle of the area that two years later would become known as the D3 section of Omaha Beach.

At 00:20, the Goatley boat was launched. *MTB344* also had a lifeboat (a 'Dorey') that could have accompanied the Goatley boat and served as a reserve boat for the subsequent evacuation. However, given that the Goatley boat had carried nineteen people during Operation Dryad, March-Phillipps decided to leave the Dorey behind. At approx. 00:25, the Goatley boat reached the beach, but March-Phillipps gave the order to sail a few hundred yards further east before landing, to put some distance between them and some buildings. March-Phillipps and nine men went ashore and spent about fifty minutes exploring the beach and the foot of the cliff. In the dark they could see no more than five steps ahead, and had no idea that they had landed between two German positions, very near the one that was closest to the beach and right next to a path that the Germans used on their nightly patrols.

While on the beach, the raiders heard a patrol approaching and took cover in a small hollow in a thicket at the foot of the cliff. The patrol consisted of a corporal armed with a machine gun and four soldiers, three of whom were armed with rifles, while the fourth was carrying a light machine gun and had a dog on a lead. Each of the soldiers also had four hand grenades. The dog barked once it got wind of the raiders and a chaotic firefight ensued. In the confusion, Howard and Hall almost managed to drag a German down to the Goatley boat, but he freed himself by throwing a grenade that exploded, wounding Howard in the leg, and used another one to knock out Hall (the German stick grenades, which had a wooden handle with a heavy head filled with explosives, made effective bludgeons).

The alarm was raised, and the British patrol came under fire not only from the German position right next to their landing spot, but also from neighbouring positions on both sides, 500–600 feet away. The Germans peppered the beach with machine-gun fire, sent up star shells and summoned reinforcements from other positions nearby. The firefight lasted for almost half an hour until March-Phillipps and Hayes got the whole force back on board the Goatley boat – except for Hall, whom they thought was dead. When the boat was about 300 feet from the beach, it was fired upon from the German positions. The raiders were exhausted, many of them wounded, and they were incapable of rowing out to *MTB344*. Instead they sailed in an arc along the coast in a westerly direction. They came under renewed fire, not just from machine guns, but from a 75 mm anti-tank gun in one of the fortifications. The first shot capsized the Goatley, and then the artillery turned on *MTB344*. The torpedo boat was close to the shore and the German gunners were unable to aim low enough to hit it. Although the shells flew over the boat without doing any harm, Bourne and Appleyard still chose to act as if they were withdrawing. A machine-gun bullet had taken out the starboard engine, but the port engine started and *MTB344* sailed two nautical miles straight out from the beach. At first they sailed at full speed, but gradually slowed down so the enemy would think that the boat was out of earshot – in reality it was heading back towards the beach to rescue the survivors. They did not manage it. March-Phillipps, Williams and Lehniger, all three of whom were wounded, drowned while trying to swim out to the boat. At 02:25, *MTB344* was fired on by a German patrol boat, and ten minutes later Appleyard gave the order to sail one nautical mile east and then make straight for the Nab Tower off the Isle of Wight. Due to its damaged engine, *MTB344* had a maximum speed of twelve knots. Appleyard and Bourne thought it would be too dangerous to sail the long way around the minefields via Barfleur. They chose instead to sail directly through the minefield. It was a risky decision, but luck was with them and *MTB344* reached Portsmouth at 10:35 without further incident.

Back at the beach, Howard, Desgrange and Winter had made it ashore and were taken prisoner by the Germans, along with the badly injured Hall. Burton, Orr, Hellings and Hayes had also made it ashore. The first three were captured on 17 September. Hayes, who was a very strong swimmer, tried in vain to save March-Phillipps, and then swam for some considerable distance along the shoreline until he found a spot where he could sneak into the country. He was helped by French civilians and resistance fighters who kept him hidden and gave him false papers. In November 1942 he made it across the border into neutral Spain. However, shortly after crossing the Spanish border he was arrested and handed over to the Germans.[210*]

* * *

The SSRF had never before experienced such losses. Almost a third of the raiders were gone – including its charismatic founder and inspiration. Combined Operations immediately promoted the 25-year-old Geoffrey Appleyard to major and appointed him interim head of the SSRF, to which a group of experienced people from 12 Commando were transferred. To boost morale in the SSRF and help integrate the new recruits, Combined Operations recommended an operation on Sark (the fourth largest of the Channel Islands, located between Jersey and Guernsey) as soon as possible – around 20 September. Combined Operations' evaluation of Operation Aquatint states, 'The fact must be faced that we are certain to have some mishaps.'[211]

* * *

For Lassen, Aquatint was a personal disaster: 'The biggest sorrow I have felt in this war. My best friend is killed and many other good friends dead or missing.' In one fell swoop he lost eleven comrades, several of whom he had known since his *Maid Honor* days. They had shared training, adventures, fun, danger and (or so they believed) kills. They had become as close as only soldiers at war can be. This sense of comradeship was important for everybody in the force, but undoubtedly meant something special to Lassen, who, except for his parents' friends and family in London, was cut off from any contact with home and his old circles.

The loss of March-Phillipps in particular shook him deeply. As well as his companion and friend, March-Phillipps had been his mentor and role model. Lassen had admired and learned from this man twelve years his senior, just as he had looked up to and respected the boatswain on *Eleonora Mærsk* and Captain 'Dusty' Miller on the *British Consul*. But March-Phillipps had meant more to him than any of the others. March-Phillipps had given Lassen's life direction by letting him see action at a time when he felt trapped in the endless limbo of training and waiting. March-Phillipps's ardent and eloquent idealism, his initiative and death-defying dynamism, and his leadership style, characterised by informality and concern for his men and, of course, his desire to lead from the front, made a huge impression on the 20-year-old Lassen.

> Major March-Phillipps is dead now. The only man I really liked and respected. He died fighting at the head of his men a dignified death for him I sometimes wish that I had been with him when things went wrong, all the other times we fought together just not the last time.

Operation Basalt, Sark, 3–4 October 1942

An initial attempt to raid Sark, on the night of 19/20 September, had to be abandoned due to an unfortunate combination of wind and currents. Appleyard and his men tried again on the night of 3/4 October. The mission was preceded by the usual study of aerial photographs, guidebooks and multiple other sources, including the Appleyard family's own cine films from a holiday on the island.

MTB344 sailed from Portland Bill at 19:03. The wind was light and variable but mainly south-easterly, and the sea was calm with a light swell. Visibility was four nautical miles, but, due to mist, only one along the coast. The force under the command of Appleyard consisted of seven men from the SSRF, including Anders Lassen and his companion Denis Tottenham from *Maid Honor*, Captain Colin Ogden-Smith, Captain Patrick Laurence Dudgeon, who had also been involved in Operation Dryad, Ogden-Smith's brother Bruce (a sergeant) and Captain Philip Pinckney from 12 Commando, along with four of his men, Lance Sergeant (a corporal acting in the rank of

Sark seen from the south with Dixcart Bay and Derrible Bay in the foreground.

sergeant) Joseph Henry 'Tim' Robinson, lance corporals Jimmy Flint and Horace Stokes and gunner Eric Forster, making a total of twelve raiders. Captain Warre from 'M.E. raiding group' went along as an observer. The purpose of the expedition was to take prisoners and gather intelligence about German defences.

Pinckney was a talented and brave officer. He was also an avid ornithologist, botanist and hunter, passionately preoccupied with finding new ways for soldiers to 'live off the land'. He had taught at the commando schools in Scotland, where his penchant for grasses, beetles, raw snails and other unorthodox foodstuffs had made the otherwise very well-liked officer widely feared.

MTB344 dropped anchor near Point Château, where the steep Hog's Back promontory juts out into Baleine Bay. Moments before this, a German observation post on the southern peninsula, Little Sark, had asked *MTB344* to identify itself using a Morse lamp. Appleyard had replied that they were Germans seeking shelter for the night in the bay. The Germans took no further action.

The raiders rowed ashore, and Lassen, acting as lookout on the bow, guided the boat right up onto the beach. For once his comrades landed with dry feet. Less fortunately, they had landed in the wrong place – not on Sark, but on a small rocky island off the tip of Hog's Back. A second, successful attempt was made, and by 23:30 everybody was on dry land and in the right place. Second Lieutenant Young and Tottenham were to guard the boat, which lay in deep water, a safe distance from the rocks, secured by a kedge anchor and a rope fastened to the shore.

Lassen was sent to scout ahead, climbing the steep 160-foot crag to the top of Hog's Back to look for a rumoured machine-gun position. The rest of the men followed slowly in his wake. The darkness and loose rocks hindered this dangerous progress, but by midnight the whole force had reassembled at the top. Lassen told them that he had found no German positions anywhere on Hog's Back. The raiders now moved north, along the top of the promontory, until they saw something that reminded them of British army prefabricated Nissen huts and an aerial mast. They immediately stormed the site, but the antenna turned out to be just a flagpole and the Nissen hut was part of a shooting range. The advance continued through dense thickets of bracken and gorse. The raiders proceeded in single file with Appleyard taking point, Lassen in the middle of the column, along with Corporal Flint and another raider, and with Captain Pinckney at the rear. After some time, they heard a German patrol approaching. They scurried off the path and hid in the bushes until the Germans passed by and disappeared into the darkness. No more patrols were encountered, but there were several false alarms whenever one of the men stepped on a dry twig or something moved in a thicket.

At 01:15 they reached the group of small buildings known as Petit Dixcart, the main target of the raid. Two men were sent in to reconnoitre. All of the buildings turned out to be empty and abandoned. Appleyard led the men through the dark towards the secondary target, La Jaspellerie – a larger, detached building atop a small hill, approx. one mile inland, on the other side of a small gorge. The main force remained hidden while three men searched the outhouses and the exterior of the main building. They found a French door to the south-east. The raiders stormed it at 01:50. The ground floor was empty, but Appleyard and Corporal Flint found the owner on the first floor. Forty-one-year-old Frances Pittard seemed unperturbed by being awoken by two armed men with blackened faces – she was the widow of an army doctor and the daughter of a naval officer who lived in England – as did her daughter. She may have had family connections to military intelligence, and it is possible that Appleyard knew her from his holiday on the island. At any rate, he and another member of the force spent about an hour talking to her while the rest of the men secured the building. Mrs Pittard brought out a map and told them in detail about the German fortifications and minefields, the number of soldiers, where they were billeted, their morale, etc. She gave Appleyard the latest edition of the local newspaper, *Guernsey Evening Star*, which reported that the Germans intended to deport 2,000 able-bodied men from the islands, as well as other pamphlets and interesting papers.

There were around twenty German soldiers on Sark, divided into a heavy machine-gun group, a light mortar group and three anti-tank guns, all belonging to 6th Company, Regiment 538 of the 319th Infantry Division. They also had three anti-tank guns in fixed positions, three flamethrowers and a light machine gun, as well as 939 S-mines (anti-personnel landmines that, when triggered, launched into the air and exploded at waist height in a hail of steel fragments), spread over 22 different minefields. Mrs Pittard said that the German soldiers were billeted at the nearby Dixcart Hotel, while five sappers who worked at the port in Creux lived in the hotel annexe.

The raiders set off again, heading towards the hotel. They had already been on the island for an hour longer than planned, so a corporal was sent back to the Goatley boat to signal to Bourne on *MTB344* that everything was in order and that he should keep waiting on them.

What then happened on the way to the hotel is unclear. One of the raiders later gave an account of the events. He and Lassen were sent ahead to reconnoitre the hotel's surroundings. They spotted a German guard and reported back to Appleyard, who sent them back to take care of him. Lassen remarked jokingly that it would have been helpful to have a bow and arrow with him.

In Arisaig, Anders had learned that, ideally, two men were required to kill a sentry – one to hold him while the other stuck a knife into his kidneys (or stomach if his equipment got in the way). The helper could also seize the victim's rifle to stop it making a noise as it hit the ground. It was also easier for two people to hide a corpse. Lassen, however, insisted on dealing with the German on his own. He and his comrade hid for a while, watching the sentry and working out how long he took to go back and forth along his route. They could hear his footsteps, but otherwise nothing but deathly silence. The other raiders arrived just in time to catch a glimpse of the German before Lassen crept up on him. There was a stifled scream, and then Lassen returned.

Appleyard sent his men towards the annexe. They advanced in formation, but there were no more Germans to be seen. Breaking the door down made a noise, but not enough to alert the occupants. They forced their way into a room with a door at the far end. Lassen opened it. It led into a corridor with half a dozen doors along the two sides. Appleyard ordered his men to take one each and enter at his signal. The five Germans in the building were sleeping in separate rooms and the raiders overpowered them with little difficulty. The prisoners were brought into the hall. A raider kept them covered while their hands were tied behind their backs with rope, and their uniforms and rooms were searched. They were then led outside.

However, in violation of SOE procedures, the prisoners had not been gagged. Once they emerged into the moonlight and saw how few attackers there were, they began to shout. Appleyard yelled, 'Get the prisoners to shut up!' In the ensuing mêlée, a prisoner managed to break loose. His guard felled him with a rugby tackle, but the much larger German broke free again. The raider grabbed him, and as they rolled around in a cabbage patch one of the officers said: 'If they try to escape, shoot them!' Captain Pinckney's prisoner also wriggled free and ran shouting towards the hotel. Pinckney pursued him and shot him. The raider in the cabbage patch and another raider could no longer cope with their prisoners, and so shot them. At one point Lassen was holding two Germans – one of whom was so unruly that another raider beat him with a gun, which went off and hit the prisoner in the head. Four Germans had been shot in a matter of minutes. The fifth, petrified, fell silent and offered no resistance.

Shouts were heard in the dark, and more Germans poured out of the main hotel building. Appleyard gave the order for immediate withdrawal. Lassen wanted to throw grenades through the hotel windows, but Appleyard told him to save them for later.

The fighting outside the hotel annexe lasted from 02:30 until 02:50. The raiders made it back to the beach after a frantic dash over difficult terrain. The exhausted, pyjama-clad German had to be dragged along for the final stretch. At the boat they met the corporal who had been sent to report the delay. The terrain's dense vegetation had delayed him too. Had Lieutenant Bourne not decided to wait beyond the scheduled time – he opted for 03:50 but not a minute longer – *MTB344* would have been on her way back to England.

The raiders left Sark with their German prisoner at 03:35, and were back on board *MTB344* at 03:45. Bourne set sail for England immediately, and they docked in Portland at 06:33.[212]

Operation Basalt – Loose ends

The story of Lassen killing the German sentry is based on his own very brief note in his hunting journal and on a later eyewitness account by a 'Gunner Redborn', who is quoted by Winston Ramsey in *The War in the Channel Islands Then and Now*; by Mike Langley in *Anders Lassen, VC, MC of the SAS*; and by Sir Peter de la Billière in *Supreme Courage*. Redborn was first quoted by Suzanne Lassen, who described him as a modest little man with a large black moustache, a ladies' milliner in civilian life. His account forms the basis for many of the details in the description of the capture of the five Germans and the shooting of four of them. For example, it was Redborn who said that the prisoners' hands were tied behind their backs. Appleyard did not mention it in his report. On a number of points, Redborn's account is more expansive than those of the other witnesses, but in no way contradicts them.

The problem is that it has not been possible to confirm that a soldier called Redborn took part in the raid – or that he ever existed. In fact it is probable that Suzanne Lassen invented Redborn, and his account was then repeated by Langley, Ramsey, et al. She may have wanted to combine information from several sources in a single narrator's voice, or perhaps for reasons of discretion or confidentiality she felt compelled to conceal the identity of her source. Whatever the truth about his identity, Redborn's account – like all the others about the raid – leaves important questions unanswered.

Like Operation Barricade, the raiders overestimated enemy losses. Two of the four Germans who were shot in the yard in front of Dixcart Hotel survived (corporals Just and Klotz). The German losses amounted to two prisoners who were shot while trying to flee (28-year-old Sergeant August Bleyer and 30-year-old Corporal Heinrich Esslinger), as well as the man Lassen killed with his knife. His victim was probably the 35-year-old Senior Corporal Peter Oswald, whose gravestone is in the cemetery in Creux on Guernsey, alongside those of Bleyer and Esslinger, and is also dated 4 October 1942. The fifth prisoner, who was taken to England, was Senior Corporal Weinreich.

The German reports only mention Bleyer and Esslinger. The death of the sentry is mentioned neither in the German material nor in Appleyard's report, in which it would otherwise have been natural to mention the number of enemy dead.

The official SOE historian M.R.D. Foot theorised that a German prisoner was stabbed to death while resisting being dragged off to the boat. Peter Kemp tells the same story in his own war memoirs.[213] If this is the case, the story of Lassen killing the sentry may have been invented to cover up the execution of an unarmed prisoner. This might explain why Appleyard did not mention the killing in his report, but not why the Germans failed to mention it. The German report stated that the two prisoners were killed with 'bullets and bayonets'. They may have mistaken knife wounds for the work of bayonets, but that still does not explain why they only mention two dead men rather than three.

No matter why the Germans kept silent about the third casualty, this alternative version of the story presumes that the raiders took not one but two prisoners from Dixcart Hotel, only one of whom made it to the boat alive, while the other was stabbed to death when he refused to obey.

It is fairly certain that the official reports (at least those that are preserved and accessible) do not contain the whole truth. It is likely that the surviving participants' later accounts are flawed and uncertain. Nor is it inconceivable that the raiders agreed a cover story to mask less than commendable actions.

It is possible that they were ordered to concoct such a story, because apart from the fact that they neglected to gag their prisoners, the raiders probably did not think that they had done anything wrong. Even if they actually had stabbed an obstreperous prisoner to death, it would have been entirely consistent with the teaching at the SOE schools and the recommendations in Brigadier Gubbins's partisan handbooks.[214*]

* * *

Regardless of why Lassen killed Peter Oswald, there was a world of difference between this and the two killings he thought he had perpetrated during Operation Barricade. During the fighting in front of Post 4, Lassen fired his machine gun into the darkness in the direction of voices or shadows. But on Sark he crept right up on his prey. Here too the killing took place in the dark. If Lassen stabbed the sentry or prisoner from behind, he avoided looking him in the face, but he cannot have failed to notice Oswald squirm, twitch and tremble, or avoid being smeared in his warm blood.

Lassen's last note in his hunting journal reads: 'Was on again the other day trickiest and hardest work I've ever done used my knife for the first time.'

Operation Basalt – Aftermath

The confusion about what actually happened on Sark on 4 October 1942 stems in part from the propaganda war waged in the weeks that followed Operation Basalt.

Hitler was already furious about secret instructions the Germans had found on Canadian troops involved in the attack on Dieppe on 19 August 1942 that any prisoners were to have their hands bound so that they could not destroy secret papers. This was interpreted as a violation of the Geneva Convention on the protection of prisoners of war (which the Wehrmacht itself had violated on countless occasions). Nor did it help that it turned out that some German prisoners actually did have their hands tied behind their backs – and some were even shot by British or Canadian troops who had taken more prisoners than they could cope with.[215] There were also rumours that the commandos who took part in the raid on the Lofoten Islands on 3 March 1941 had been encouraged to shoot German soldiers before they could surrender. (The British took 216 prisoners at Lofoten, many of whom had their hands tied.) In addition, much of the rhetoric that surrounded the commandos contributed to the impression that they were criminals – an image Hitler probably believed in, and which his propaganda machine certainly found easy to exploit. Now there was the treatment of the prisoners on Sark.

On 7 October the Führer's HQ proclaimed that all the British soldiers the Germans had captured at Dieppe would be 'shackled' or 'bound' ('*Fesselung*') until the British confirmed that they would comply with the ban on tying up prisoners of war.[216]

The British government threatened to retaliate. On 9 October, the Germans announced that 1,376 British soldiers had been shackled. The next day, the British shackled a similar number of German PoWs in Canadian camps. The Swiss government offered to mediate and suggested that both parties remove the shackles at the same time. The British did so on 12 October, and the Germans followed suit once they had received an assurance that the British would ban the practice completely.

'The shackling crisis' was over, but Hitler was not finished with the commandos. On 18 October 1942 he issued the 'Commando Order', which instructed the Wehrmacht to kill every last man involved in 'so-called commando operations', whether they wore uniforms and were armed or not, whether they were engaged in combat or on the run, and even if they 'appeared to make moves to surrender, in principle no mercy is to be shown to any of them'.[217]*

* * *

The German military authorities carried out an in-depth investigation of the events on Sark of 3–4 October 1942. They believed that the islanders had helped the raiders. When they interrogated Frances Pittard, she confessed that she had given them detailed information on the garrison and defence installations.[218]

Mrs Pittard, Miss Duckett and Miss Page (who owned the Dixcart Hotel) and other specially selected Sark residents were deported to France. To prevent further attacks, the Germans sent reinforcements to Sark and extended the minefields, further restricting the residents' already limited freedom of movement. As elsewhere in occupied Europe, there was widespread reluctance among civilians to help saboteurs, partisans or, in this case, raiders whose actions triggered reprisals and counter-measures.[219]

The SSRF expands – Fahrenheit and Batman (October–November 1942)

Despite the fuss about the treatment of prisoners, Mountbatten was so pleased with the SSRF that in mid-October he agreed with the SOE to increase the

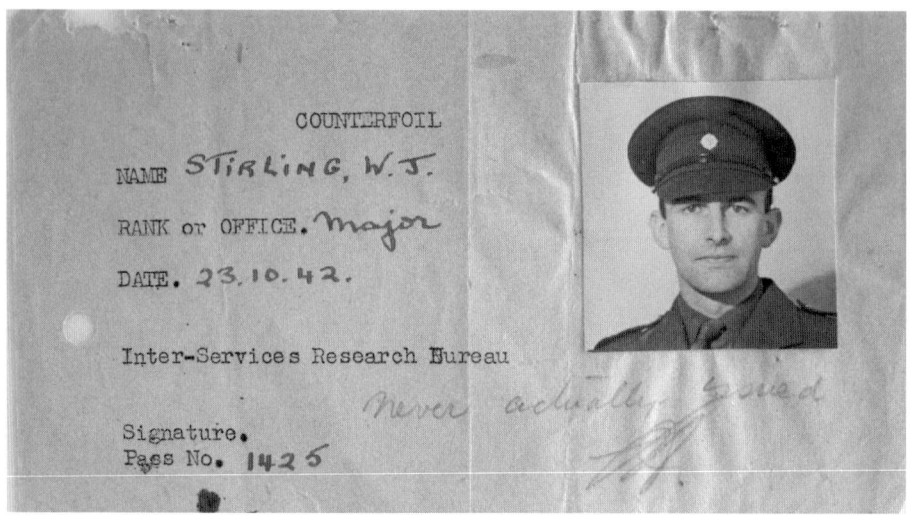

William 'Bill' Stirling.

force to four troops, headquartered at Anderson Manor and with four camps scattered across the south of England.[220*] The enlarged force would consist of a cadre of 'original' SSRF men, complemented from raid to raid by personnel from the commandos or the regular army. The SSRF's maritime capabilities were also expanded, with *MTB344* backed up by six patrol boats from Royal Navy Coastal Command.

The new, bigger force required a commander of higher rank and with greater experience than Major Appleyard. Bill Stirling, at that point an acting major in the Scots Guards, was brought back to the SOE, promoted to lieutenant colonel and placed in command of the new SSRF as of 17 October 1942.[221*] Appleyard was the operational commander.

While the SSRF was being reinforced, the new Force J was also set up. This included all of the ships and smaller vessels that had participated in Operation Jubilee, which were now part of the new 102 Royal Marines Brigade.

Stirling was given command of all raids, but the head of Force J had 'operational command' over them. Stirling had to seek approval from Mountbatten for all proposed raids. However, the proposals also had to be sent to the head of Force J, who would seek approval from the head of the naval command in whose area the operation was to take place.

In the midst of these complicated changes, Combined Operations HQ and the SSRF were planning a new operation (Fahrenheit) for the night of 11/12 November 1942 – a more classic SSRF operation. A force under the command of Peter Kemp of the SSRF and Captain 'Mickey' Rooney from 12 Commando landed at Pointe de Plouezec on the north coast of Brittany to reconnoitre the German defences, attack a signal station, and take prisoners.

The raiders chanced upon two German sentries. Captain Rooney threw a hand grenade, injuring the two soldiers – one a young man. As they lay on the ground, one was silent and hid his face in his hands while the other shouted 'Nicht shoot, nicht shoot. Kamerad!' – but they were killed by a burst from a Tommy gun. The explosion and the shots alerted the other Germans at the signal station. In the ensuing firefight, two Germans were wounded and probably killed. The raiders withdrew without losses before the Germans had time to cut off their retreat to the beach. The signal station remained unscathed, but the raiders cut its telephone lines in several places.[222] Sabotaging the telephone lines forced the Germans to use the radio, which the British were, for the most part, able to intercept and decipher.[223]

> [Peter Kemp] was feeling the reaction from the excitement of the last few hours; although relieved that I had brought our party back intact I could feel no elation at our small success: instead, I could not rid my ears of the terrible screams that had come from the mangled, wounded sentries, or my mind of the grim memory of our return through the minefield and the wait in the dory under the blazing Very lights. At the same time I could not shake off a nagging, persistent worry that perhaps I had not acted with sufficient resolution; that if I had pressed home my attack instead of giving the order to withdraw we might have made prisoners of the entire garrison.[224]

On 12 November, Mountbatten wrote to Churchill: 'I gave orders that no prisoners' hands were to be tied. None were taken.'[225] Two weeks later, Combined Operations HQ sent a memorandum to 62 Commando reiterating the value of prisoners and the importance of the element of surprise and caution:

> If initial surprise is lost it will usually be wrong to proceed with the landing. ...
> Shoulder straps, buttons, tunics, documents, equipment etc. removed from the dead Germans should be brought back whenever possible. One prisoner is worth about ten dead Germans. ... Until orders to the contrary are received, prisoners will, on no account, be bound.[226]

The SSRF planned another raid for 1942, Operation Batman, scheduled for the night of 16/17 November. The plan was to reconnoitre German coastal defences in the north-east corner of the Cherbourg peninsula, but fog and strong winds scuppered the operation. Bad weather prevented any further raids for the rest of the year.

October–November 1942

In the autumn of 1942, Lassen was sent to Scotland to decide if sixteen Danish volunteers undergoing training at the commando school in Achnacarry might be suitable SOE material.

Lassen's ironic, understated manner impressed the Danes. They noted his upper-class language and corresponding self-assurance, but also that he spoke to them as equals and understood their difficulties with the British authorities – in particular, with Captain Iversen.

Lassen encouraged the sixteen Danes to sign up for 62 Commando. The head of the Achnacarry School, Lieutenant Colonel Charles T. Vaughan, the legendary 'Laird of Achnacarry', warned the Danes strongly against signing up. Even Lassen himself promised them no more than a 50/50 chance of surviving service in 62 Commando. All sixteen volunteered.

When Lassen visited the same group at Wraxall Manor (STS62c) in Dorchester, where they were now quartered, he made a less favourable impression. As the Danes were walking through the village, Lassen suddenly shouted 'Look!', drew his pistol and fired four shots, two of them at the church tower clock face. An elderly woman fled screaming and fell head over heels. To the Danish SOE recruits, Lassen appeared to be a brave and likeable man with lots of energy, but also possessed of a juvenile desire to show off.[227]

* * *

Around mid-November 1942, Lassen, Ian Warren and two half-English, half-French officers under the command of Peter Kemp (who was still plagued by nightmares in which he heard the German sentries' terrible screams), were sent to the parachute school in Ringway to prepare for an intelligence operation in France. The operation was to be led by Major John Gwynne. He had been in the SSRF from the beginning, but had mainly been responsible for planning. He expressed frustration with this sedentary work by devising one dangerous operation behind enemy lines after another, always with him in command.[228] None of his plans ever came to fruition, but it now looked as if his time had come. The impending operation was so secret that no one on the team was told anything other than it was not planned by Bill Stirling and had nothing to do with Combined Operations.

It was ultimately decided that Gwynne's group would not be parachuted in but would be sailed over to Brittany by the SSRF, which would also provide combat support if the agents encountered difficulties during the landing. Once Gwynne's group was safely ashore, the other SSRF men were to sail back to England and leave their comrades to their fate in France.

In early December, Lassen, along with a group including Kemp, Warren, Appleyard and Ogden-Smith, spent a week in the seaside resort of Paignton on the Devon coast, where they waited for weather that would allow a landing in Brittany. But the weather did not improve, the operation was eventually abandoned and the team returned, disappointed, to Anderson Manor.[229]

* * *

At the end of November 1942, Frants Lassen finally arrived in Scotland from Stockholm, where he had been waiting since August for a visa and a seat on a flight. From there he proceeded to the Royal Victoria Patriotic School in Wandsworth, where he had to undergo the usual security clearance that served as a precursor to being released into British society or the military system.[230]

Chapter Twenty-Five

SAS/SBS – Jellicoe[231]

The Germans have received back again that measure of fire and steel which they have so often meted out to others. Now this is not the end. It is not even the beginning of the end. But it is, perhaps, the end of the beginning.
(Winston Churchill at the Lord Mayor's Luncheon, Mansion House, following victory at El Alamein – London, 10 November 1942)

When Layforce was disbanded at the end of May 1941, George Jellicoe was transferred back to his old regiment, the Coldstream Guards. While awaiting new orders, he sailed with David Carol MacDonnell Mather – a friend from Cambridge, the Snowballers and Layforce – to the besieged Libyan port city of Tobruk, where a British, Indian and South African garrison had been holding out against superior German and Italian forces since early April.

From Tobruk, the two daredevils made two or three fruitless attempts to land behind German lines and attack the airfield at Gazala. Jellicoe and Mather returned to Alexandria shortly before the Germans captured Tobruk following a surprise attack on 21 June.

On 21 January 1942, Jellicoe was wounded while serving in the Libyan Desert. He spent part of his sick leave at the famous long bar in Cairo's Shepheard's Hotel, where he ran into David Stirling, head of the so-called L Detachment, Special Air Service Brigade, which had begun operations behind enemy lines a few months earlier.

Stirling was in need of a second-in-command for his force, which had also swallowed up Roger Courtney's Special Boat Section. He offered Jellicoe the job. In April 1942, Jellicoe reported for duty to L detachment's HQ at Great Bitter Lake in Kabrit, north-east of Suez. The headquarters consisted of a camp with tents and other inventory, including vehicles and training equipment, 'borrowed' from other units. Here Jellicoe met Carol Mather and other comrades from Layforce who had found their way to L Detachment, including the Scot Captain David Sutherland and the prime minister's son, Randolph Churchill. The latter, overweight and rather fond of the booze, was not obvious SAS material, but Stirling understood the usefulness of a direct link to the Prime Minister. Churchill had been a journalist before the war, and so was put in charge of the SAS's contacts with the press.

Jellicoe was put in charge of L detachment's administration – to the extent that such a thing existed. He also trained a group of Free French paratroopers who were to join the SBS. Jellicoe found the Free French 'very very free and very very French', but his knowledge of French and his diplomacy meant that they were successfully integrated. Sutherland was responsible for the training of the SBS as a whole.

* * *

On 10 June 1942, a submarine and a patrol boat landed four SBS patrols on Crete to attack four German airfields: Maleme at the western end of the 160-mile-long and 65-mile-wide island, Heraklion in the east, Kastelli Pediada in the middle and Tymbaki to the south. The attacks were to coincide with SAS attacks on five airfields in Libya and destroy aircraft that would otherwise pose a threat to an important Allied convoy departing on 11 June from Haifa and Port Said (Operation Vigorous), together with a second convoy from Gibraltar (Operation Harpoon) bringing vital supplies to Malta.

David Sutherland.

The Tymbaki airfield turned out to have been abandoned, so the patrol leader, David Sutherland, decided to return to the beach and wait to be picked up. Maleme, on the other hand, was so heavily defended that the operation had to be abandoned. At Kastelli Pediada, eight aircraft and 200 tons of fuel were destroyed. At Heraklion, the raiders destroyed thirteen Junkers Ju 88 bombers and other aircraft. The patrols were evacuated by the submarine *Porcupine* on 23 June 1942.

Of the four Free French soldiers who took part in the attack on Heraklion, one was killed and the other three were captured. George Jellicoe was the only member of the Heraklion team to return. The Germans executed fifty Cretan hostages in retaliation.

Although the SBS took out sixteen or eighteen German planes on Crete, and the SAS thirty-two in Libya, the Vigorous convoy was still attacked for four straight days on end by powerful German/Italian air and submarine forces. When a large Italian fleet approached, Vigorous sought shelter in Alexandria. Two of the transport ships and four of the warships accompanying the convoy were sunk. The Harpoon convoy from Gibraltar lost four out of six merchant ships and two destroyers, but the two surviving supply ships made it to Malta.

* * *

On Wednesday, 1 July, Rommel's forces reached the last British defence position before the Nile delta – the narrow passage at the small railway station El Alamein. Here, after three days of fighting, the 8th Army halted the advance of the now spent and exhausted German and Italian forces.

During the fighting at El Alamein, the SAS carried out ten attacks on enemy airfields in Egypt and Libya. Three failed because the raiders could not penetrate the defences or were repelled by guards. The others resulted in the destruction of a large number of aircraft and great quantities of fuel.

After suffering a knee injury that required surgery, Jellicoe was sent to hospital in Cairo, and then, in late November, to England to recuperate. While home, he made the most of the opportunity to reconnect with old friends, including Stirling's older brother Bill, who since mid-October 1942 had been commander of the SSRF/62 Commando.

Chapter Twenty-Six

The SSRF – The End

Every single little operation you go on helps. Every time you get that tight feeling round your heart and the empty feeling in your tummy, you are mentally and nervously tougher than the time before and so are better fitted for real continuous military action.

(Geoffrey Appleyard)

Frants and Anders

Anders Lassen's first meeting with Frants after the latter left the Royal Patriotic School was at a lunch in the Danish legation on Christmas Eve 1942. They had not seen each other for three years, but Frants found his brother little changed, except perhaps a bit older and more mature.

On 20 November, Anders had been promoted to lieutenant.[232*] On 7 December he was awarded the Military Cross. All names were carefully redacted from the commendation, but it alluded in enigmatic terms to his role in the operations Postmaster, Branford, Barricade and Basalt, and stressed his great courage, inspiring leadership, brilliant seamanship, good judgement, determination, resourcefulness, ingenuity and cool head.

Frants Lassen.

* * *

Receiving the Military Cross marked the end of Lassen's time with the SSRF. The old disputes between the SOE, the intelligence service SIS (MI6) and Combined Operations erupted again during the winter. On 4 January 1943, the Chiefs of Staff Committee decided that further small-scale raids would primarily be under the SIS, and that Combined Operations was not to launch raids west of the Cherbourg peninsula.[233] It was also decided that, following the success of Operation Torch on 8 November 1942, there was no longer a need for decoy operations in northern France.

However, the SSRF did not stop there. In early 1943 a whole series of attempted raids were made, including on Guernsey and the small neighbouring island of Herm. Most of them had to be abandoned due to poor weather – and none resulted in contact with the Germans or civilians. Frants took part in one of the aborted Herm raids, Operation Pussyfoot, on the night of 3/4 April.[234] Later that same month, the SSRF/62 Commando was disbanded and several of its members, including Peter Kemp[235]* and Frants Lassen, were transferred to the SOE.[236]*

Casablanca

On 14 January 1943, Winston Churchill and President Roosevelt attended a summit in Casablanca. Once again Churchill and Brooke succeeded in having the landing in Western Europe postponed, this time until 1944. In the meantime, the war in North Africa and the Mediterranean would continue, to open up the sea route through the Mediterranean, force Italy out of the

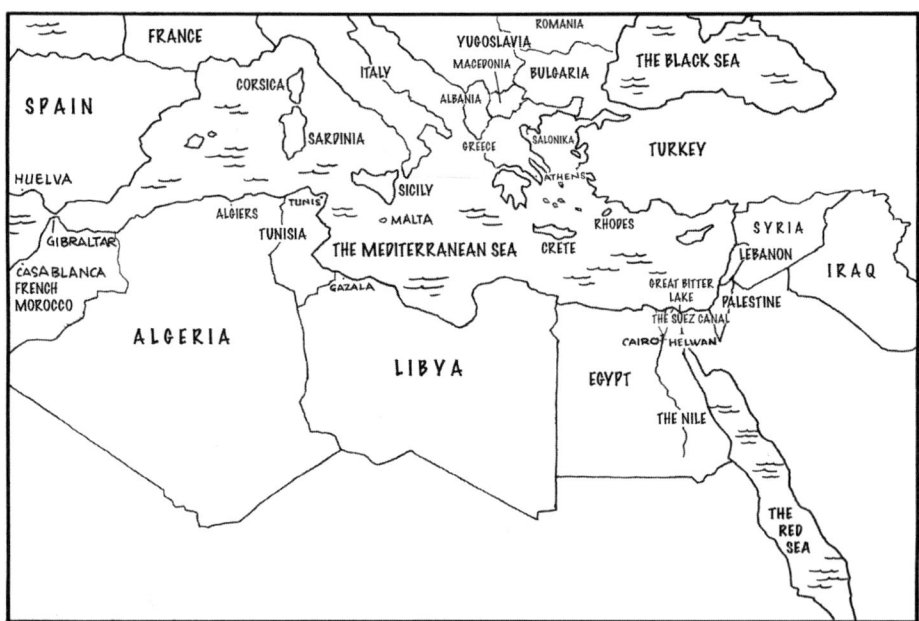

war, compel Germany to spread out its forces, and draw neutral Turkey into the war on the Allied side. The plan was to conquer Tunisia and invade Sicily in July 1943.[237]

Lord Mountbatten was part of the British delegation. He used the occasion to persuade the commander of the Allied forces in North Africa, US General Dwight D. Eisenhower, to set up a Mediterranean SSRF to carry out raids in Tunisia and along the western part of the Mediterranean coast, just as the SAS, the Long Range Desert Group and Popski's Private Army (PPA)[238*] were doing in the east. The SSRF, no longer with any real role to play in England, would form the core of the new force under the command of Bill Stirling. On 2 February, Stirling handed command of the remnants of the SSRF over to Peter Kemp. Two days later, he flew to Algiers with four other SSRF officers. Geoffrey Appleyard and a dozen other SSRF veterans joined them several days later, and the rest of the force followed after a few weeks' rest. In May 1943, 2 SAS Regiment was set up under Stirling's command in Tunisia. (David Stirling's 'L Detachment' had been 'promoted' to '1 SAS Regiment'.)

* * *

Lassen had only just renewed his membership of the Danish Club and the Wellington Club in Knightsbridge when, on 25 January, he was ordered to go to Egypt.

David Stirling had been asked to put a handful of men at the disposal of their new SAS colleagues for their first desert operations. In return, Combined Operations HQ would send two officers with experience in amphibious raids to Cairo to train Stirling's men and later join his SBS.[239] Stirling chose Lassen, who had just been awarded his Military Cross, and Philip Pinckney, who was known as a skilled and courageous officer with a good relationship with his men. Lassen travelled as a British citizen under the name 'Andrew Lawson', and gave his address as '44 Ashley Court, London SW1'. The false name was part of the new unit's cover, but the address belonged to Esther Molloy, whom Lassen knew well enough to give her name as next of kin for personal matters – a role previously assigned to Eduard Reventlow.[240] However close his relationship with Esther, it did not stop him from having dinner and going to the pictures with Ellen Karsten before he left.[241]

Before leaving, Lassen gave his hunting journal to Lady Hambleden for safekeeping. British officers were not allowed to keep diaries in the field. Lassen himself wrote: 'I do not like to write too much down in case some swine or other would go and get hold of this book.' He also knew that if he were killed, the journal would be returned to his parents. He did take with him the letters from home and one of Suzanne Lassen's children's books given to him by Ellen Karsten, which he would often reread in the months and years to come.[242]

On 8 February, Lassen flew from England to Egypt on board a B24 Liberator bomber. He arrived at the SAS camp in Kabrit fourteen days later. On 6 March he wrote to Leslie Prout, 'I have arrived safely after a quick passage and am now again finding myself surrounded by numerous Nigger pigs of all coulours [sic!] and designs.'[243]

Pinckney travelled on a later plane and did not arrive in Kabrit until 8 March.[244]

Anders Lassen's shoulder flashes worn during his training with the SOE (Danish flag and 'DENMARK', and cap badge (SAS winged dagger) and shoulder flash (parachutist's wings) from his SBS uniform.

Chapter Twenty-Seven

Special Boat Squadron

The little I knew of [SAS] appealed to ... my latent Red-Indianism.
(John Verney: *Going to the Wars*)

Break-up

George Jellicoe.

When Lassen arrived in Kabrit, 1 SAS Regiment was in a state of considerable flux, if not outright chaos. The unit's founder and commander, David Stirling, had vanished during a raid in the Libyan Desert on 24 January 1943. On 14 February the camp heard that Stirling had probably been taken prisoner by the Germans, which triggered a crisis in 1 SAS. Despite Jellicoe's efforts as second-in-command, Stirling was the only one who knew everything that was going on in his private army.

When Stirling disappeared, 1 SAS had 570 men (out of a potential maximum of around 850), divided between the SAS Squadrons, the SBS, the Fighting French Squadron and the Greek Sacred Squadron (in Greek: *Hieròs Lókhos*).²⁴⁵ The latter consisted of Greek officers and cadets who had fled their homeland to fight for its freedom. It was named after a Theban elite corps that defeated a much larger Spartan army around 330 BC, and also a corps of revolutionary nationalist volunteers who fought the Turks in 1821. The commander was Colonel Kristododoulus Tsigantes, a large, bearded man who, despite his relatively advanced age, had taken the SAS parachute course and now served as a rallying point for the Greeks fighting alongside the British.

Following Stirling's disappearance, the head of 1 SAS B Squadron, Major Vivian Street, took command. On 9 March he was replaced by the former head of 51 commando, Lieutenant Colonel H.J. Cator. Under Street and Cator, the adjutant Captain Blyth and his beleaguered staff spent two months trying to get the regiment running smoothly.

Meanwhile, life went on in Kabrit. Aside from the routine training in and around the camp, patrols returned from desert operations, Cator and Jellicoe travelled to Palestine to scout locations for a new training base, while Captain Sutherland and three of his men returned from training in Syria and went to Alexandria to fetch supplies for SBS. The day after Lassen arrived in Kabrit, C Squadron and a Free French unit were despatched to deal with local gangsters posing a threat on the road between Cairo and Suez. They were believed to be under the command of a notorious German agent, Johannes Behl, who – according to the Army's Field Security Section – had been absent from his usual place at the bar of the Shepheard's Hotel for weeks. 'A suspicious coincidence,' according to SAS intelligence officer (and later children's book author and illustrator) Captain John Verney.[246]

Without Stirling to hold it all together, the disparate organization that was the SAS started to fall apart. Jellicoe's SBS broke free, the Free French Squadron sought status as a separate regiment, and the Greek Sacred Squadron went its own way too.[247] On 19 March, 1 SAS Regiment was dissolved and reorganized. What remained of the unit that Stirling had extracted from Layforce was renamed the Special Raiding Squadron (SRS), under the command of one of Stirling's first recruits, the 28-year-old Northern Irish rugby star and marksman Major Robert Blair 'Paddy' Mayne. The SBS was renamed the Special Boat *Squadron*, while the 'Sacred Greeks', as their British comrades sometimes called them, became the Greek Squadron. The three squadrons were subordinate to a new HQ Raiding Forces, under Col. D.J.T. Turnbull in Azzib, on the coast north of Haifa in Palestine.

SRS, which was later given its old name back (1 SAS Regiment), was sent west as an advance party for the 8th Army and later served in Italy. The SBS and Greek Squadron remained at the eastern end of the Mediterranean.

The SBS grew to a regulation size of 230 men, including approximately 50 in various staff and support functions. The fighting force comprised approx. 180 men in three detachments, each consisting of five patrols of ten, plus a staff and signalling unit. The three detachments were called L, M and S, after their first commanders: captains Tom Langton, Fitzroy Maclean and David Sutherland.

Immediately after the reorganization, the SBS began the process of relocating from Kabrit to its new base at Atlit Bay, 6–10 miles south of Haifa. Here Jellicoe established a camp above the beautiful crescent-shaped bay, with the ruins of a Crusader castle at one end and the steep Carmel

Mountain behind. The SBS was in place – and more or less in order – by April Fools Day 1943. 'As good a day as any,' said Jellicoe as he assumed command of his new men.[248]

Lassen and Philip Pinckney, like several of their new comrades, were sent to Holding Unit Special Forces until they joined the SBS in Atlit in April.

Atlit

In his memoir, *A Dinner of Herbs*, Verney described life in Atlit as free, independent, formless and characterised by equality between officers and men. For him and many other SBS men, this was a bit of a paradise compared to the regular army's rigidity and formality.

> In our pirate camp the usual tensions of army life, and of any organized communal life, were reduced to a minimum, we were there at all by our own fervent wish, and were free to leave any time we chose. No one tried to parade his authority – there was very little of that sort of authority to parade. Nor was there much place for the detestable concept of one-upmanship. There was no point in pretending, for example, that you could swim better than you did, when your capacity was daily tested and exposed, and when – the vital point – there was no advantage to be gained by that or any other similar pretence. We pretty soon came to know one another's physical and mental capacities, and with them our own. Strength and

skill were respected, and a fair degree of both were essential, but everyone recognised that there were other qualities, such as a cool head, or a good temper, that might well prove more valuable. On our type of operation the man who could make you laugh was more worth having than the bore who could only shoot straight. … Life in the camp itself was such fun, and my fellow pirates so amusing and delightful. An atmosphere of Bohemian sociability reigned in our mess where high spirits and a conversational free-for-all usually made up for what the cooking lacked.[249]

The credit for this jolly atmosphere was mainly Jellicoe's:

In the best piratical tradition, he held the appointment by right of being the most experienced officer at small-scale raiding, and probably the most daring. Physically he was about as tough as the herculean sergeant, intellectually he could more than hold his own with the don or the M.P., and his vitality exhausted even mine. His title, too, was an undeniable advantage in wresting concessions from military and naval senior officers. [Like] most dynamic personalities, he was an ardent burner of the candle at both ends. He was young, gallant, gay and, in things that really mattered, extremely efficient, and we all loved him.[250]

Lassen was also young and brave – and effective when it mattered. Like Jellicoe, he too had a well-developed sense of fun and burned the candle at both ends. He also had a heated disposition, precious little respect for authority, and a tendency to want to fight, especially when drinking. His commander found this out during a night out in Tel Aviv. The city was a 45-minute drive from Atlit, and its bars and nightclubs made it a popular destination for the SBS men. After sampling the nightlife, Lassen and Jellicoe ended up in a bar late at night. Jellicoe said something Lassen did not like, at which point the Dane punched his superior. Not wanting to lose a good man, Jellicoe chose to ignore the incident. They buried the hatchet and drove through the night along the winding coastal road back to camp.[251]

At one point in June, there was an attempted coup in the camp. Fitzroy Maclean and other representatives of the more 'military-minded' wing among the officers decided they had had enough of Jellicoe's loose discipline and, as they saw it, slapdash administration. The coup was foiled by Verney volunteering as adjutant with responsibility for ensuring more orderly and satisfactory paperwork, and a series of compromises were reached:

Webbing need not be blancoed, but we would indent for a bugle, and someone to blow it. There would be no drill on the beach, but the contractor would be bullied into finishing off the latrines properly. And never never again would Palestine Soup be served in the officers' mess.[252]

'Palestine soup' was one of Philip Pinckney's experiments with alternative foodstuffs, and consisted of different kinds of grass, clover, dandelions, snails, etc. The concoction had forced his involuntary guinea pigs to spend most of the night and the following day in the unshielded hilltop latrines that resembled columns in an ancient Greek temple when silhouetted against the sky – at least according to Verney.

* * *

Fitzroy Maclean, the rebellious MP, had stood for election for the Tories because a seat in the Commons was incompatible with employment in the Foreign Office, which had refused him leave to join the army. Immediately after leaving the Foreign Office, Maclean, who was of aristocratic stock from the Isle of Mull, signed up for the Cameron Highlanders and then the SAS, taking part in David Stirling's attacks on German airfields. Before Maclean came to the SBS in Atlit, he had been to German- and Italian-friendly Iraq, where he had abducted the German consul, and Persia, where he abducted General Fazlollah Zahedi, whose Nazi sympathies were considered a threat to British interests.

> The soldiers he used for his amusing and important task, many of them Highlanders, were, in his view, just the right men for the SBS. They became the notorious 'M Detachment'.[253]

Maclean left the SBS during the summer of 1943, when he was sent as the British government's (and Winston Churchill's personal) representative to the Yugoslavian partisan leader Tito.[254] Command of M Detachment passed to another Scot, also with a past in the Cameron Highlanders, John Neilson 'Ian' Lapraik.

During the summer, Langton fell ill and was shipped back to England. John Verney took over command of L Detachment.

* * *

Training in Atlit consisted of gymnastics, team sports, swimming, marches in the mountains, fieldcraft, map reading, British and foreign firearms, sabotage and explosives, landing exercises and sailing in the caiques (Greek schooners) that were to become the SBS's most important means of transport. The men also listened to lectures about enemy military matters, etc, and did parachute training and practised skiing at the British Army ski school at the Cedars in the Lebanese mountains. The purpose of the parachute training, which

Lassen did not like at all, was to enable drops behind enemy lines and boost the raiders' self-confidence.[255] The skiing was to prepare the raiders to fight alongside the Russians in the Caucasus mountains if the Germans broke through on the southern front, or perhaps carry out an operation against the railway tunnel at Brenner Pass, between Italy and Austria. The rank-and-file SBS men found it difficult to see the point of the mountain and ski training, and left the ski school in disgrace after raiding and plundering the staff canteen. 'I do not see how this unit can ever be put into action against the enemy,' wrote the school's commanding officer about the SBS.[256]

Among the students at the school was a young SAS officer, Stephen Hastings, who had joined the school hoping for a 'free skiing holiday'. After a couple of days of abortive attempts at learning to ski, he hitched a lift back to Beirut with Anders Lassen. Hastings had seen action with the Scots Guards in the Western Desert and had participated in a couple of raids with the SAS, in one of which he earned a Mention in Despatches, but the roadtrip with Lassen was something else again:

> The road was a precipitous track round hairpin bends. I have never been more terrified and well understood later how Andy got so many medals, we hurtled down to sea level on two wheels. Fear was simply left out of his disposition.[257]

* * *

The heads of the three detachments were, to a large extent, responsible for training their own men. Sutherland, based on his experience in Crete in June 1942, placed great emphasis on the ability to survive at sea and in the mountains. After a month of training in Lebanon, all of his men could handle a 10-ton caique in moderate weather, march over rough terrain with a 50-pound backpack, and disappear into the landscape.

Lassen's first exercise as a member of Sutherland's S Detachment was a 90-mile march with packs, moving at night, hiding by day and 'attacking' various targets along the way.

> Lassen … floated effortlessly over the ground carrying a 50 lb Bergen. He memorized the map and arrived at the RV early.[258]

During another exercise south of Beirut, Lassen and his patrol were delayed. To avoid arriving back late, Lassen hijacked a French military truck, threw the Senegalese driver in a ditch, and his men drove the rest of the way, arriving on time. Lassen's practical mind and disregard for rules was completely in line with SBS's ethos, but appeasing the French military authorities required considerable diplomatic finesse on the part of Jellicoe.

Plan Barclay

On 7 May 1943, while the SBS was training in Atlit, the remnants of the German and Italian Army Group Africa surrendered to the Allies.

The next step in the Allied strategy was so obvious that Churchill said that '[e]veryone but a bloody fool would *know*' that their target was Sicily. Nevertheless, the Allies started the large-scale 'Plan Barclay', the objective of which was to deceive the Germans into thinking that the next attacks would be on Sardinia and Greece.[259]

Plan Barclay, which was coordinated by Lieutenant Colonel Dudley Clarke's 'A' Force in Cairo, involved a number of different elements. The most original was Operation Mincemeat, in which the corpse of a destitute was dressed in the uniform of a Royal Marines major and left to float ashore on the south coast of Spain. Planted on him was a briefcase containing forged documents suggesting the Allies planned to attack Sardinia and Greece, and that the mighty build-up of troops and supplies in North Africa, which the Allies could not possibly conceal, was in fact a ploy to fool the Germans into thinking that they planned to attack Sicily. The Spanish authorities believed the documents were authentic and passed them on to the Germans, who also believed them and redeployed their forces accordingly. The SS Sturmbrigade Reichsführer SS was sent to Sardinia, and the brand-new 90th Panzergrenadier Division was created on the island on 6 July 1943.[260]* The Axis forces in the Balkans were also significantly reinforced. The Italians had thirty-three divisions in Greece, Yugoslavia and Albania, while the German forces in Greece and Yugoslavia on 1 December 1942 consisted of a single army corps made up of six divisions, including the 7th SS Volunteer Mountain Division *Prinz Eugen* in Yugoslavia and an infantry division in the 'fortress' of Crete. Three panzer divisions were moved to Greece – one from France and two from the Eastern Front. One hundred and sixty train cars were required to move a panzer division, and the journeys from France and the Eastern Front took a week and 9½ days respectively. The illusion lasted until well after the landings on Sicily and the Italian mainland. On 30 July *Marinegruppenkommando Süd* (Naval Group Command South) noted that an agent had reported that Allied attacks were imminent on Crete, Rhodes and western Greece.[261]

Plan Barclay also included numerous air strikes against targets in Sardinia,[262] as well as landing agents and saboteurs on both Sardinia and Crete.

Chapter Twenty-Eight

Operation Albumen, Crete, 23 June–11 July[263]

This operation I consider to be one of the most physically exacting ever undertaken by Special Service troops in the Middle East, since distances of well over 100 miles of mountain country were covered by night over a period of three weeks in enemy occupied territory, each man carrying approximately 70 lbs of food and explosives.

(David Sutherland, *Report on Operation Albumen*, 18 July 1943)

Destination unknown

When a mobile cinema visited the camp in Atlit on 18 June 1943, Lassen and his companions in S Detachment were not around to see the show. Earlier that day they had departed for an 'unknown destination', which proved to be the port city of Mersa Matruh, 170 miles west of Alexandria. 'Andy and Ken [Lamonby] left with their boys leaving a feeling of emptiness behind,' wrote Jellicoe's second in command, Walter Milner-Barry, in his diary.[264]

Just as the SSRF operations in the Channel Islands and along the north coast of France had been used to conceal Allied plans, the SBS (unbeknownst to the raiders themselves) was now a pawn in a great game of deception as well. On 12 June, Captain Sutherland received orders to land on Crete again with S Detachment and attack the airfields at Heraklion, Kastelli Pediada and Tymbaki, which served as forward bases for the larger German airfields on the Greek mainland. The attacks, codenamed Albumen, were to take place on the night of 4/5 July 1943. At the other end of the Mediterranean, John Verney's L Detachment was to attack a handful of airfields in Sardinia at the

Kenneth Lamonby.

same time. Although the orders did not specify any reason for the attacks, the idea was partly to reduce German attacks on Allied convoys on their way to Sicily, where the invasion (Operation Husky) had been fixed for 10 July, and partly – probably mainly – to bolster German suspicions that the next targets for invasion would be Crete and Sardinia, not Sicily.

* * *

In Mersa Matruh, Sutherland, Lassen and his good friend, the eternally pipe-smoking Lieutenant Ken Lamonby, along with fourteen SBS men and two Greek SOE men, boarded the patrol boat *ML361*. The two Greeks were Kimon Zografakis, who was to accompany Lassen's C Patrol to Kastelli Pediada in the middle of Crete, and Giannis Androulakis, who was to lead Lamonby's B Patrol to Heraklion on the north coast of the island. Zografakis had been involved in Sutherland's sabotage raid on the German airbases on Crete in June 1942, and Androulakis had been an intelligence operative in Heraklion.

In addition to Lassen, C patrol comprised Sergeant Nicholson, Corporal Sidney Greaves and Private Ray Jones. Before leaving for Crete, Sutherland, who was concerned by the stories of Lassen's killing of a German prisoner on Sark, asked Nicholson to 'Keep an eye on him. Restrain him!'[265]

ML361 sailed first to Bardia, approx. 140 miles further west, where the raiders spent three days. From there they sailed directly to Crete, approx. 200

miles to the north. They then sailed from Bardia at 05:00 on the morning of 22 June. Despite heavy seas, the whole force was safely ashore on Tripiti Beach, on the south coast of Crete, at 01.15 the next morning. Lieutenant Rowe's D Patrol, which was to attack Tymbaki near Tripiti, would join them four days later.

Two Greek SOE-men, Manolis Vrellianakis and Nikos Souris, welcomed Sutherland's men on the beach and acted as their guides. Any equipment not immediately needed was hidden behind some rocks. The whole force then made its way through a narrow, steep ravine, the only route off Tripiti Beach, which led up to the small church of Agios Savvas. From there they proceeded inland towards the village of Koumasa, and spent the first day in hiding nearby. The rough terrain and heavy packs – 65–90 lbs each and 110 lbs for the three radio operators – slowed them down, and it was light by the time they reached Koumasa. Sutherland set up base camp in some caves in a dry riverbed while Lassen and Lamonby hid their men a few hundred yards away.

Kimon Zografakis.

While they were in hiding, Zografakis spotted a young man and shouted to him. The young man, Lefteris Tsiknakis, was from Koumasa. Zografakis asked him to fetch some food to supplement the raiders' rations of salted beef, dried fruit and nuts. Tsiknakis soon returned with bread, cheese and water, having been told by his father to take good care of the British.

Concerned about the difficult terrain and long distances, Sutherland decided not to wait for dark and sent the two patrols off at 18:30. The young Tsiknakis showed the way to the Katsounas family home in the village of Panagia. Androulakis had with him a letter from SOE headquarters in Egypt to Mr Katsounas, who was a generous host. During the night, the group was joined by another local, Miron Maris, who led the raiders on to Apoini. Here they were put up in the Valavani family's hut, which Zografakis knew from Sutherland's first Crete expedition in June 1942.

The locals were taking a huge risk helping the SBS, but the raiders were almost constantly surrounded by helpful Cretans throughout their almost three-week stay on the island. However, the patrols' dependence on local guides, informants and hosts was also a significant safety risk. The more locals who were aware of their presence, the greater the probability that the

Germans would get wind of it too. Indeed, this appears to have been the case. On 3 July, the Germans beefed up the already strict security measures around the airfields.[266]

Lassen, Lamonby, their men and Greek companions spent a day and a half in Apoini. They were waiting for a second guide, Giorgi Tzouanakis, also called 'Kokkinos' ('Red') from Heraklion, who was to join Lamonby's group. On 25 June, Kokkinos finally appeared bearing a sack of medlars, a type of fruit grown locally, for the visitors, and the march could resume.

Lamonby's B Patrol went north-west to Heraklion, while Lassen's C Patrol continued north-east towards Kastelli Pediada. Both patrols left their radio operators, along with one of the radio transmitters, in Apoini. The village was more or less equidistant from the two targets. Instead of lugging the heavy MK2 sets and the even heavier batteries, etc, Lassen and Lamonby elected to use runners to pass messages between the patrols and the improvised radio station.

The second set was left in the village of Apayina, where it was picked up by Captain Patrick Leigh Fermor, head of the local SOE mission.[267*]

The march through the mountains

The raiders continued their progress through the mountains. Zografakis noted and admired Lassen's pace and apparently endless stamina in spite of an average temperature of 30ºC in the shade.[268]

There were still a couple of stages to go – the villages of Poulies and Nipiditos[269] – where Zografakis' friends, or friends of friends, showed the way, provided food and drink and helped carry the men's packs.

German soldiers were based in every village the patrol passed through, and it was not always possible to avoid them. Lassen and his guide, Giannis Androulakis, led the way, singing or softly whistling German marching tunes. The darkness made it difficult to differentiate the British khaki and the German tropical uniform – and on several nerve-wracking occasions they had to fool both the Germans and the locals into thinking that they were a German patrol on the lookout for partisans or British saboteurs.[270]

In Poulies, the group stopped to rest in the hut of Nikolaos Aslanis. He placed a bottle of the local brandy, *raki*, on the table. 'Lassen hadn't tried it before. I told him it's a drink we make in Crete. He emptied the bottle and Aslanis had to go out and fetch another one.'[271]

Aslanis' son Giannis found Lassen to be tense and uneasy around the locals:

> A lot of curious people from the village came to look at them, and that really annoyed one of the Englishmen (Lassen). He was a little strange and nervous. One evening, I came with food for them with Charis Karfopoulos from Pano Poulies. [Lassen] heard us and shouted at us:
>
> 'Stop!!!'
>
> We ignored him but heard him load his weapon right away. He nearly killed us, he told us afterwards.[272]

On 2 July, another local helper, Manolis Alexakis, led Lassen and his men to the Chostos cave above Nipiditos, which afforded a view of the airfield, about half a mile south-west of Kastelli Pediadas. The eastern end of the airfield featured taxiways and woodland where aircraft could be hidden in concrete shelters, as well as a narrow-gauge railway to bring supplies out to them. To the west were more taxiways and shelters. The runway itself was just over 5,500 feet long and more than 850 feet wide.

On 19 April, British aerial photoreconnaissance had identified five aircraft. From his hiding place, Lassen now counted eight Stuka dive bombers, five long-range Junkers Ju 88 bombers and a couple of fighters and older aircraft. He saw the Stukas as the main target. They were at the south-western end of the airfield and, according to the locals, heavily guarded.

In early 1943, the SOE mission on Crete had instructed the local resistance fighter Dimitri Eliotis to find work at the base and garner information about its layout and defences. Eliotis succeeded in this dangerous task and drew up

The cave where the raiders spent their first night on Crete.

a detailed map, which his contact took to Cairo. In June 1943, Lassen – or Captain Giannis Bandouvas, who accompanied him throughout most of the operation – asked Eliotis to procure fresh intelligence. Eliotis drew up a new map that, among other things, showed the actual number of planes.

The guide, Manolis Alexakis, sent his son Andonis up to the cave with boiled potatoes, wine and rusks, telling him to leave it outside because the British did not want anybody to enter. The village policeman Manolis Mourtzakis brought a pitcher of water and fourteen eggs. Later Alexakis had his wife cook a freshly slaughtered goat kid whose owner refused to accept payment for it. Andonis asked his father

> if I could go with him in and see the English. 'Wait,' he said. He took them the pot of food and asked if I could come in, and I did.
>
> At the entrance to the cave I saw two men studying a map spread out on the ground. The others were in sleeping bags reading books. Nobody said anything. …
>
> The next day I went up to fetch the things we had taken them. I found the pitcher and the pot and everything else. In a corner of the cave, I also found a full box of English cigarettes.[273]

The attack

According to the intelligence reports that Sutherland and his officers had received before leaving for Crete, the airfield at Kastelli was surrounded by some not very impressive barbed wire fencing. There were believed to be about 3,000 German and Italian troops in the area, most of whom were stationed in the village of Kastelli Pediada, north of the airfield. Around 300 Germans and 100 Italians were billeted in the village of Moukhtari (Evangelismos) to the south-west. The Greeks did not know exactly how many Germans and Italians were inside the airbase, but they were in no doubt that the aircraft were heavily guarded. Each plane was guarded by three men who camped beside it and took turns sleeping and keeping watch. Sentry posts had been set up every thirty feet around the concrete shelters. This was entirely in line with German guidelines for the ground defence of airfields and the training of ground personnel in the neutralisation of bombs – a defence strategy partly inspired by Sutherland's attack in June 1942 and by the SAS, LRDG and Popski's Private Army's activities in North Africa.[274] However, Lassen considered the Greeks' reports 'exaggerated'. He and Zografakis disagreed vehemently about what to do. Zografakis thought it would be possible to penetrate the defences from the east, towards Drozitis, where the planes were hidden among olive trees, but not from the more open west where most of the Stukas were parked, as the Germans there were too active and alert. Lassen insisted on attacking the Stukas. Zografakis tried to dissuade him, but finally relented.[275]

Lassen decided to split his group in two. Sergeant Nicholson and Corporal Greaves, with Zografakis as guide, were to make their way in from the east, Lassen and Gunner Jones from the more difficult west side.

A couple of new local guides, Manolis Kritsotakis and Michalis Petougakis,[276] led Lassen and Jones to Moukhtari, about half a mile west of the airfield. The two raiders intended to spend the whole of 4 July hiding in a field observing their target. Activity in the base was heavy all day.

Meanwhile Sergeant Nicholson and Corporal Greaves, accompanied by Zografakis, Bandouvas and Kokkinos, went the other way around the airfield. At 04:00 on 4 July they took up positions on a hill overlooking the east side. They too spent all day studying access routes and the guards' movements, and counting the aircraft taking off and landing. As dusk fell, there were only seven planes on the field, all parked in concrete shelters. At 22:00 another one landed. Nicholson, Greaves and the three Greeks began to advance towards the barbed wire fence, which was around a quarter of a mile from the nearest plane. When they reached the fence, Nicholson and Greaves took off their wristwatches and gave them to Bandouvas, along with £5 sterling in gold – the remainder of the funds they had brought to buy help and provisions along the way: 'In case we do not return alive,' they explained. But the Greek refused, telling the two Englishmen to do what they had come to do and come back in one piece. At 23:45 the raiders started cutting a hole in the fence with the foldable wirecutters they had brought with them (a special piece of light equipment introduced on David Sutherland's recommendation, based on his experiences from raids on two enemy airbases on Rhodes in September 1942).[277] At that very moment, shots were heard from the opposite end of the airfield. The gunshots continued for about five minutes while Nicholson and Greaves continued to cut through the barbed wire.

Once the hole was big enough, Nicholson, Greaves and Zografakis sneaked through. Bandouvas and Kokkinos waited outside, armed with a sub-machine gun and a pistol, respectively.

At midnight Nicholson and Greaves activated their time pencils, which acted as delayed fuses and gave them half an hour to place their bombs and get away. The 'Lewes bombs' consisted of a mixture of diesel oil, thermite and plastic explosives. They combined explosive force with an incendiary effect, and as little as 1 lb was enough to destroy an aeroplane. Standard SAS practice was to place bombs on the same wing (the left), to make it harder for the enemy to repair the damage with cannibalised spare parts from other sabotaged planes.²⁷⁸

Zografakis ran straight to the fuel and oil tanks beside the small church of Agios Giannis and placed his explosives there. Nicholson and Greaves placed a bomb on the nearest plane, a light two-seater reconnaissance aircraft. The next plane was guarded by three soldiers. The saboteurs crept around it and moved on to a Junkers Ju 88 instead, placing a couple of bombs without the guards noticing anything. At this point they again heard shots from the opposite end of the airfield. Star shells were launched, forcing Nicholson and Greaves into hiding for about ten minutes. Once the commotion died down, they sneaked up on a Stuka, placing another bomb before returning to the plane they had previously given up on. The guards had been instructed not to leave their aeroplanes under any circumstances, and were still patrolling back and forth at their posts. This time, however, the saboteurs managed to sneak behind the concrete shelter and place a bomb on the plane's tail.

Just then a truck pulled up. A dozen Germans jumped out and scattered in all directions. Nicholson and Greaves retreated to the olive trees. Explosions were heard in the distance, then a siren started to wail. After placing their remaining bombs on a Stuka that they had initially overlooked, the saboteurs rushed back through the hole in the barbed wire fence, and left the airfield with Zografakis and their two guides. It was now 01:30 and the whole airfield was lit up by spotlights sweeping the fence. Other spotlights searched the surrounding terrain from two hilltops outside the base. Approximately five minutes after Nicholson and Greaves had disappeared through the hole in the fence, the first of their bombs exploded, and a further five explosions were heard in as many minutes. The two Englishmen and their Greek companions had hidden at the bottom of a small valley and could see nothing but a shower of sparks and a huge, fiery glow. The darkness, the terrain and the need to keep hidden meant that it took them two hours to cover the mile-and-a-half to the point below Sarakino Mountain where they had arranged to meet with another Greek who was to convey news of the operation to the radio station in Apoini. When they finally arrived, the messenger had left.

The shooting and explosions that Nicholson, Greaves and Zografakis heard from the opposite end of the airfield came from the clash between Lassen and Jones and the German and Italian sentries. They left their Greek guide about 200 yards from the fence, and started to cut through the barbed wire at 22:30. Once through, they followed the taxiway that stretched in a semicircle around the Stukas' concrete shelters. Every now and again they stopped and looked around before continuing.²⁷⁹* Some 60 to 70 feet away, 20 to 30 Italians were sitting and talking around a bonfire. As Lassen and Jones left the taxiway, they were hailed by an Italian sentry who had been hidden in the shadows. Lassen spoke German to him and the Italian was fooled. Fifty feet later, Lassen was hailed again, and once more bluffed his way past the sentry. But his luck eventually ran out. As he was passing a fourth sentry post, the three soldiers he had just passed opened fire. The fourth, just six feet away, adopted an 'on guard position'. Lassen pointed at the muzzle flashes behind him, distracted the guard, took advantage of this momentary lapse and shot him in the stomach at close range with his Colt .45 – twice in quick succession, the way he had been taught at Arisaig House. The siren started to wail, and 10 to 15 men opened fire on Lassen and Jones, who had to beat a hasty retreat. It was presumably this firefight that forced Nicholson and Greaves into hiding the first time.

Lassen, Jones and their two guides wanted to hide in a vineyard where they had stopped on their way to the airfield. Just as the four of them were crossing a small viaduct, they spotted a German truck approaching. They were seconds from being caught in its headlights, but reached the bridge just in time to plunge into the darkness on either side of the road. The vehicle stopped a short distance from their hiding place. For a moment it appeared as if the soldiers would jump out and start looking for the saboteurs and their helpers. Instead, the driver opened the door and looked up at the flares that were lighting up the sky. Just then, the base turned on its spotlights and swept the surrounding countryside. 'Bloody Italians,' the German driver cursed before slamming the door shut and driving off again.

In the confusion, Lassen and Jones had been separated from their two guides. The Greeks stood waiting by the roadside for some time. Lassen and Jones headed back towards the airfield, but strayed into more barbed wire surrounding an anti-aircraft battery at Agios Nektarios, near the village of Moukhtari, on the edge of the base. The Germans had hung empty cans on the wire, and when the two raiders touched the fence, the noise was heard far and wide.

Lassen and Jones were immediately challenged by a German sentry and responded with a hand grenade.[280] More Germans quickly arrived and the two saboteurs came close to being caught between the barbed wire and the soldiers trying to cut off their retreat. Despite heavy fire, Lassen and Jones extracted themselves. They then made their way towards a part of the airfield they thought looked quieter, but enemy troops were posted there too. A German guard challenged Lassen from just a few yards away. Lassen immediately despatched him with his pistol. The Germans set off more star shells. Lassen and Jones found themselves in the open and brightly lit terrain, with yet more guards arriving fast and firing on them. Lassen managed to take cover behind a big tractor, where he placed his bombs. Under heavy but inaccurate fire from the guards, he disappeared into the darkness and fled the airfield.[281*]

Lassen and Jones had now become separated, but while sneaking around in the dark, in almost unknown terrain that would soon be overrun by enemy patrols, they were both found by locals. They led the two men to the Spanoyannis family's sheepfold, which served as a meeting place for the local resistance. The family's children, who were guarding the sheep, were frightened by the night-time visitors. They only calmed down once a local resistance fighter, Grigoris Chnarakis, who had taken part in several operations with British agents and could speak some English, assured them that Lassen and Jones were not Germans. Chnarakis found them a couple of guides and sent the pair off to Apoini.[282]

On 5 July, at approximately 16:00, Sutherland and the Middle East Command radio station in Cairo received a message from the radio station in Apoini. Lassen reported that C Patrol's attack on Kastelli had been a success. A phone line had been cut, eight aircraft (four Stukas and four bombers) had been destroyed, and thousands of gallons of fuel had gone up in smoke.

Nicholson and Greaves had taken a route north from Kastelli to circumvent the areas between Kastelli and the south coast where the Germans were thought to be most active. They did not pass through Apoini, where the radio transmitter was located, and they had no contact with Lassen and Jones before they met up again at Sutherland's base camp several days later. Lassen's assessment of the number of destroyed aircraft (which, incidentally, exceeded the number of machines – five – that Nicholson and Greaves had sabotaged) was based either on what he and Jones believed they saw as they were heading away from the airfield, on what local people told them about the number of explosions, or perhaps on rumours circulating the next day. Lassen's account of the damage certainly did not accord with that of the Germans:

> 3 incendiaries set off in aircraft shelters, 1 Klemm 35 [the reconnaissance aircraft Nicholson and Greaves sabotaged first] destroyed, 1 anti-aircraft gunner killed. Other charges removed in time ... Further damage prevented by rapid reaction.

Another report stated:

> New attack on Kastelli averted due to vigilance of sentries.[283]

And according to the war diary of the 22nd Infantry Division the material losses amounted to the Kl 35 aircraft, a barrel containing 30 litres of petrol that had been standing close to the aircraft, and 34 barrels each containing 300 litres of aircraft fuel. The bomb placed by Lassen on the tractor was dismantled.[284]

It is unclear how the gunner was killed. Perhaps he was a victim of the grenade Lassen or Jones threw when confronted near the anti-aircraft battery. Or maybe he was one of the two guards Lassen reported killing earlier in the attack. Nevertheless, one German report only talks of a single casualty, while another mentions one dead German and one wounded Italian.[285] Lassen reported shooting two men, and his Greek guides saw him or Jones throw a hand grenade at an anti-aircraft battery and perhaps kill somebody.

For their part, Lieutenant Lamonby's B Patrol reported that they had not found a single aircraft to attack on the airfield at Heraklion. Instead, they had attacked a nearby fuel store at Peza (which according to German records destroyed a 2,000-gallon tank of petrol). Lieutenant Rowe's D Patrol had not found any targets on the airfield at Tymbaki and returned to base without inflicting any damage or casualties.

When Lassen and Jones left Apoini, they were, according to Lassen's report to Sutherland, 'however, given away by the local inhabitants and chased up into the mountains by a German patrol. Here we laid up for 3½ days without food.'[286] Lassen did not specify, and most likely had no way of knowing, whether he and Jones had been betrayed by collaborators, whether one of the many helpful Cretans who worked with the raiders talked too

Anders Lassen (far left) with a group of Greek helpers after the Kastelli attack.

much, or whether the Germans, or the Greek police who collaborated with them, had perhaps observed unusual movements at unusual times.

On the night of 7/8 July, Lassen and Jones met Lieutenant Lamonby and his patrol. Together, they continued south towards Tripiti Beach, still with locals as guides.

Reprisals

Neither the British nor their Greek allies could have been in any doubt that Operation Albumen would trigger German reprisals against the civilian population. In the weeks after they invaded Crete in May 1941, German forces, on the orders of the commander of XI Flying Corps, General Kurt Student, executed more than 1,000 Cretans as punishment for helping the British, for attacking Germans, mistreating the wounded and desecrating corpses. After Sutherland's attack on the airfields at Kastelli, Tymbaki and Maleme in June 1942, the Germans executed fifty Cretans.[287] At the beginning of the German occupation of Greece, Wehrmacht High Command (OKW) had issued a directive on 'retaliation ratios' in the event of attacks on German soldiers by the resistance, partisans or civilians. For every dead German, 50 to 100 hostages were to be executed, and 10 for each wounded German. For practical reasons, the local commanders often 'only' executed 10–20 Greeks per dead German. Doctors, chemists, clergy, lawyers, schoolteachers and other prominent members of the community were taken hostage to deter resistance. On 1 July 1943 the German Commander-in-Chief Southern Greece, General Hellmuth Felmy, issued an order stating that 'Any softness will be seen as weakness and cost German blood!'[288]

The SBS men did what they could to prevent reprisals against the civilian population. Nicholson and Greaves left their barbed wire cutters hanging on a fence to let the Germans know that it was British soldiers, not local resistance fighters, who had attacked the airfield. They also left a parachute nearby to make it look as if they had arrived by air, rather than landing on the coast and making it to the base with the help of local people. This latter manoeuvre was not particularly convincing, as it was some time since the British had flown over the area.

Shortly after dawn, 13-year-old Spyridon Karyotakis found the barbed wire cutters hanging on the fence as he drove his donkey, loaded with freshly cut barley, to the threshing place at Loutra in Kastelli. As soon as he spotted the cutters, he looked around to make sure no one was watching, ran over to the fence, snatched them, folded them up and hid them in the sacks of grain. There is no reason to believe that his souvenir hunting made any difference to the Germans' response to the civilian population – they did not need the clippers to know that British saboteurs had been at work.[289]

On 5 July, the British authorities issued a statement in which they pointed out that:

> the Allied Governments have signed a joint declaration to the effect that the punishment of war crimes is one of their principal aims, and furthermore that steps are being taken to put these decisions into practice.[290]

At dawn on 6 July, the BBC announced that British forces had attacked German airfields in Crete, where they had destroyed several aircraft. There followed a 'Special message to the people of Crete', including the words:

> You know that these forces neither asked nor received any assistance from local inhabitants. The Germans know this too. …
>
> The Germans will commit their usual crimes and you may expect their so-called reprisals on innocent persons. If this happens, you must bear it, knowing that the victims by their suffering and sacrifice contribute to the longed-for purpose of the common struggle. Furthermore, the Germans know that you have no responsibility for these raids. If they take any action against you they are committing a breach of international law. They know well that they will be punished for any outrage they commit. The day is coming when they will pay for all their crimes.[291]

As the BBC was broadcasting this message about the attacks, 19 or 20 civilian Greek men were being put to death in a field at Xeropotamos near Heraklion. On 5 July, the day after the attack on Kastelli, the Germans had taken 190 hostages. At 05:25 the following morning they executed every tenth one. During the day, another 30 or 31 Greek hostages were shot. The German authorities threatened further executions if the saboteurs were not found with the help of the local population within seven days. A curfew was also imposed across the island between the hours of 21:00 and 04:30. Restaurants, pubs etc were ordered to close at 20:00, cinemas were shut down completely, and all Greeks who worked for the Wehrmacht had their leave cancelled.[292]*

The rumours of German reprisals spread quickly and grew legs along the way. On 7 July, Lamonby reported to Cairo and Sutherland that the Germans had shot 50 Greeks, including 'Lassen's guide'. The next day, when Lassen and Lamonby were reunited, they announced that the Germans had shot at least 62 Greeks, imprisoned women and children, and threatened to shoot a further ten hostages a day until the saboteurs were caught, but the locals still helped the SBS men. The two officers stressed that the Greeks 'need a morale boost after the misery caused by British troops' and suggested a heavy air attack on the German barracks and strafing from the air by daylight. The request was not granted.

On 11 July, when the Allied landing in Sicily was in full swing, the SOE officer Patrick Leigh Fermor wrote a letter to his 'Dear friends and allies'. He knew that the German reprisals had made a deep impression on the Cretans, and feared that they might turn their backs on the British and try to come to terms with the occupiers. He wanted to explain to the locals that their suffering had served a higher purpose:

> thanks to the destruction of bombers and fuel depots, hundreds and hundreds of Allied soldiers have escaped death and reached their destination unharmed to fight the first battle for the liberation of Europe. Although it is not always easy for us to understand the reasons for the actions that have such tragic consequences for us, I assure you that there is always one. Such is war, unfortunately. Each air strike has innocent victims, almost every artillery bombardment kills some men in the vanguard of the force that will press home the attack later on. Every soldier knows this.
>
> Today Crete is in the front line. Sacrifices have been made and they will undoubtedly not be the last. We must prepare ourselves to face them bravely and calmly. If we let fear rob us of our fighting spirit, it means that the barbaric acts of our dishonourable enemies have defeated us. If we remain steadfast and determined to continue the fight, it means that the enemy has failed. That will be a major defeat for him…
>
> Every act of resistance is a step forward that helps us to realise our goal of victory and freedom.
>
> If it becomes unbearable to live under the yoke, the mountains are still free and hospitable.
>
> We must try to see the war in a wider perspective… Victory and liberty deserve every sacrifice.[293*]

Evacuation

On the night of 10 July, after marching for three nights and hiding for two days, Lassen, Jones, Lamonby and B patrol, along with about twenty-five Greeks, arrived at the ravine above Tripiti Beach. The SBS men's Greek companions had compromised themselves by helping the raiders. If they returned to their villages they would be arrested by the Germans. During the night they were joined in their hiding place in the ravine by Nicholson and Greaves, who had been led there from Kastelli by other local people. Nicholson and Greaves continued down to Sutherland's camp. They arrived at dawn and announced that Lassen, Lamonby and the others were in hiding in the mountains, a two-hour march from the beach. Rowe's D patrol was nearby. As the whole force was now almost gathered, Sutherland decided to send a request to Cairo that they be picked up on the evening of 11 July, instead of during the night of 12/13 July as planned. Sutherland knew from the previous incursion in June 1942 that the Germans would not take long to find his group. Sutherland's radio operator, Sergeant Beagley, started transmitting at 11:00. Halfway through, the battery in his radio ran out. Sutherland sent two groups of two men out to D and B + C patrols to pick up batteries. It was a dangerous venture in daylight, but the runners returned at 14:50. Even the combined batteries barely produced enough power, but Beagley managed to send the rest of the message at 15:00. Four hours later, Cairo finally responded: 'Confirmed all arrangements will be OK'. At 21:00 the same evening, Sutherland sent a runner up to Lamonby with orders to bring the two patrols and the Greeks down to the beach. The two patrols arrived shortly before midnight and took up position in the wooded ravine just below Sutherland's camp. Sutherland spent an hour listening to Lassen and Lamonby's accounts of the events of the last two weeks before all three settled down for the night.

Shortly before dawn, the lookouts Sutherland had posted announced that Lt. Rowe and D Patrol were on their way. They took up positions in the ravine along with the two other patrols. Rowe had left his camp a little further inland when his men spotted three Greek police officers and a German soldier nearby. This added to Rowe's concern that one of the Greeks, who had joined his men to be evacuated from Crete, had slipped away from the camp during the night after stealing a large sum of money from the SOE agent who was acting as guide.

Sutherland sent out lookouts, but no activity was spotted. At 15:00, Cairo confirmed that the boat that would pick up Sutherland and his men had sailed from Mersa Matruh at 05:00. It was expected to reach them as planned, although the weather might cause a slight delay. Sutherland began making ready to depart, possibly under fire, when the boat arrived.

It was a scorching hot day and there was no access to water in the camp. The SBS men had to physically prevent the thirsty Cretans from fetching water from surrounding springs and brooks. There was nothing to do but lie in the shade, wait for the sun to go down, a little after 20:30, and hope that no German patrols turned up before Lieutenant Young and *ML361* were ready to sail them to safety.

Around 20:00, while Sutherland was asleep, and the others were busy eating the last of the supplies, the lookouts spotted two German soldiers approaching the camp. Lassen's and Rowe's C and D patrols spread out while Lamonby's B Patrol made sure that the Cretans, who were itching for a fight, stayed put. The two Germans were at first allowed to continue undisturbed. All of a sudden, they were surrounded by SBS men and surrendered without a shot being fired.

While the two prisoners were being searched, the Greeks spotted another two Germans in the riverbed. They opened fire, and the Germans retreated in the direction of the sea, closely followed by fifteen Cretans – who were now utterly beyond any SBS control. While the Greeks heavily outnumbered the Germans, they were disorganized and their weapons old. The two Germans, who had taken up positions behind some rocks with their backs to the sea, knew how to exploit the terrain and use their superior weapons to keep the Greeks at bay. A fierce firefight ensued, lasting nearly 45 minutes. Several SBS men came to the Greeks' aid. One of them, Corporal Dick Holmes, climbed atop a rock shelf above the German position, intent on lobbing a grenade in if they refused to surrender. Before he got that far, Lassen waved him down and asked, somewhat heatedly, *what the fuck* Holmes was doing up there, and how he could 'be so stupid' as to even consider using a grenade in the narrow space between the rocky cliffs. Holmes and Lassen had already had a heated exchange earlier that day, when both of them were on edge because of the temperature and the tension. They also shared a tumultuous history, each fiercely competing to be the fastest and most indefatigable during the training marches from Atlit. Holmes now responded to his superior's dressing down by asking him *what the fuck* Lassen 'was doing down here' and added that he himself was at least *fucking* doing something.[294]

Sutherland feared that the shots, which could be heard far and wide, would raise the alarm. To compound matters, a strong north wind had been blowing all day, which might mean the patrol boat could be delayed until around 02:00. He sent Lieutenant Lamonby and four men down to the ravine to put an end to the firefight, but it stopped more or less of its own accord when darkness fell and the Germans slipped away. Two Greeks were put on guard to keep the Germans away from the disembarkation point, while Lamonby and his men pursued them inland. After a while he sent his men back on their own. Sutherland assumed that Lamonby had gone directly down to the beach to wait for the boat.

At 21:20, Sutherland led the whole force, with the Greeks bringing up the rear, down to the beach. The two prisoners were under heavy guard – not only to prevent them from escaping, but also to protect them from the wrath of the Cretans. The Cretans had risked their lives to help the SBS, but they were also so undisciplined, noisy and vengeful that they might put everybody at risk. As far as possible they had to be treated in a tactful and friendly manner, but Sutherland opted to prioritise safety above diplomacy. After demanding that they hand over all of their knives and sticks, he placed the Cretans at the top of the beach, guarded by two SBS men armed with Beretta sub-machine guns. Further down the beach, as close to the water's edge as possible, Sutherland placed the radio transmitters and other equipment in six parallel rows so that everything was ready to carry on board once the boat appeared. The prisoners and anybody not on some other duty took cover in the shade beneath a cliff at the western end of the beach, while B Patrol and the crew from Sutherland's base camp secured the northern and north-eastern exits – respectively. Lamonby had still not returned. Sutherland sent Lassen and the rest of C Patrol into the ravine where he was last seen. Despite expecting that the two escaped Germans would summon reinforcements quickly, Sutherland ordered Lassen and his men to call out Lamonby's name at regular intervals. At 23:45, Lassen and C Patrol returned to the beach and announced that he had vanished without a trace.

While Lassen and his men were out looking for Lamonby, the mood among their comrades had become increasingly tense. It was only a matter of time before the Germans returned in superior numbers. If the boat did not reach them before dawn, the raiders and resistance fighters would have little chance of avoiding death or capture. Sutherland and the Greek SOE

Lassen (left) and Kenneth Lamonby.

men talked about sending the civilian Greeks away, killing the two prisoners, taking the life jackets and walking along the beach towards the fishing village of Tsoutsouras, about seven miles further east.[295*] While they were considering this plan, Sutherland had one of his men send the agreed light signal – 'DS' – out to sea, first at 23:59 and then at five-minute intervals. Just as the raiders and SOE men were about to kill the prisoners and flee on foot without the Greek civilians, they heard engine noise in the dark. At 00:15, *ML361* lay off the coast. Five minutes later they began to board. By 01:05, 22 British soldiers, 25 Greeks, two German PoWs and about 1,000 lbs of equipment had all been loaded. Sutherland had the boat sail in an arc around the point and lay off the mouth of the river valley. When there was still no trace of Lamonby, Lieutenant Young set course for Mersa Matruh at 01:30.

After sailing from Tripiti, Sutherland asked Lassen, the most experienced raider in the company, what he thought had happened to Lamonby. Lassen thought he had been wounded and taken prisoner by the Germans. Later intelligence confirmed his pessimistic assessment. Lamonby had indeed been wounded and taken to hospital in Heraklion, where he died, aged 22.[296]

Home again, 12–14 July 1943

ML361 docked in Mersa Matruh at 18:45 on Monday, 12 July. The twenty-five Greeks were met by the SOE and driven away in trucks. The SBS men moved into a Royal Navy camp near the port. They spent the whole of the next day sleeping, bathing, shaving and talking about the past three weeks. While there was great relief at having made it out of Crete alive, the operation had, as Sutherland dryly remarked 'lasted too long'.[297]

On 14 July, Sutherland and his men enjoyed a hearty breakfast and then drove five hours by jeep to Cairo. Their first stop was the famous Groppi's Restaurant. The raiders and their two prisoners occupied a handful of pavement tables and consumed 'large quantities of everything on offer: coffee, tea, cakes, fruit, ice-cream sodas'. The raiders – and especially Lassen, wearing his Military Cross ribbon on his left breast – were extremely popular among the 'countless pretty girls sitting around waiting for something to happen'. The prisoners had removed their distinctive Afrika Korps hats, and the rest of their khaki get-up looked British enough not to cause a stir. In any case, Cairo in general – and Groppi's in particular – was swarming with all sorts of exotic uniforms, languages and accents, so nobody took any notice of the two somewhat special guests. At 18:00 it was time to say goodbye to the two prisoners, who were handed over to the Combined Services Detailed Interrogation Centre (CSDIC). The men and officers then went their separate ways. Sutherland, Lassen and Rowe to the famous Long Bar at the posh Shepheard's Hotel.

The next morning, Sutherland received a call from the head of the local CSDIC unit, furious that he had violated the ban on fraternising with prisoners. Sutherland's response was characteristic of the self-perception – and high self-esteem – that prevailed in the SBS:

> Brigadier, it is rare for the SBS to take prisoners on operations in enemy territory. In this case we were obliged to treat them as normal human beings since we did not know if we were going to be re-embarked safely with them or not. This is why they participated in the Groppi's celebratory event, where we could keep a close eye on them. Also we handed them over in a positive co-operative frame of mind for your interrogators to work on. You must appreciate, sir, that we in the SBS, due to our role have a different code of conduct in these matters.[298]

Sutherland did not mention that the two Germans, whom he and his men had so jovially plied with ice cream and other treats, had been only minutes from being killed on the beach at Tripiti.

Sutherland heard no more from the angry brigadier, but was later told that the two Germans had provided much useful information about the conditions on Crete, and that their semi-automatic rifles were technically more advanced than those used by the British at the time.[299]

* * *

Operation Albumen led to both Sutherland and Lassen receiving their second Military Cross. The three raiders who had attacked Kastelli along with Lassen – Ray Jones, Sidney Greaves and Jack Nicholson – were all decorated with the Military Medal, as was Dick Holmes from B Patrol who had placed the bombs on the fuel depots at Heraklion.

Meanwhile on Sardinia: Operation Hawthorn, 30 June–16 July

While Sutherland's men fought their way through the mountains of Crete, six patrols from the SBS's L Detachment, a total of thirty men under Captain John Verney, landed on Sardinia (Operation Hawthorn). Four of the patrols – *Bluebell*, *Jasmine*, *Hyacinth* and *Daffodil* – were ferried to the island by submarine on 30 June. *Periwinkle* and *Mistletoe* were dropped by parachute on 7 July. Like Albumen, one objective of Operation Hawthorn was to destroy aircraft – at eight different airfields – to prevent them from attacking the *Husky* convoys. However, the main point was to reinforce the impression that Sardinia and Greece, not Sicily, were about to be invaded.

* * *

Hawthorn was the third, and by far the most comprehensive and complicated, of a series of landing operations (collectively referred to as Operation Marigold) launched by the Allies in Sardinia in May–July 1943 to support Dudley Clarke's large-scale decoy manoeuvre. On the night of 30 June, four men from SBS's Z Group, under the command of Captain Geoffrey Courtney (brother of Roger Courtney who founded the original Special Boat Section), landed at Muravera on the south-east coast. The raiders left behind a pad full of notes about the area near the Italian coastal defences. The following night, eight men from 2 SAS, under the command of Captain Patrick Dudgeon, landed at the fishing and resort town of Cala Gonone. They were supposed to abduct a German or Italian soldier, but one of the raiders stumbled and his machine gun went off. Alerted by the noise, the Italians stormed out of their barracks, taking one SAS man prisoner and forcing the rest to beat a hasty retreat.[300*]

The Americans were also active on Sardinia. On the night of 1 July 1943, five agents from the intelligence service OSS, which along with the SOE made up No. 1 Special Force, were landed by torpedo boat at Punta Furana on the west side of the Stintino Peninsula in the north-western corner of the island. The five men, two of whom were born on Sardinia, were to gather intelligence and make contact with local anti-fascists identified by the Sardinian exile politician Emilio Lussu who was working with the SOE. All five were taken prisoner by Italian soldiers on 2 July.[301*]

* * *

Unlike the Albumen troops, Verney and his men had no local help, and had to find their way and obtain supplies on their own. The operation was also hampered by inadequate intelligence. Just as in Crete, one of the airfields turned out to be empty because it was only used during daylight hours, and another was far more strongly defended than anticipated. Some of the raiders were weakened by malaria, which they had contracted in Algeria while preparing for the operation – indeed, three men died of the disease after arriving on the island. To compound matters, the freeze-dried rations that the raiders brought with them required large amounts of water, which was hard to find in the Sardinian mountains. On top of all that, some of the money that they used to buy food and other help from the locals consisted of 500 lire banknotes from Italian East Africa, which aroused suspicion right away. On the night of 7 July, the patrols *Periwinkle* and *Mistletoe*, which were under Verney's direct command, destroyed four German aircraft at the aerodrome at Ottana. *Bluebell* Patrol blew up a railway track. And that was it. In the 16 days after the first *Hawthorn* patrols landed on Sardinia, all 27 surviving SBS men were captured by Italian police and military forces, who had been alerted by suspicious locals.

* * *

The Italians interrogated the captured raiders. One of them gave very accurate information about the SBS's missions, training, weapons and equipment, but included a lot of false information about the unit's history, commander, organization, etc. For example, he told the Italians that Roger Courtney was still in command, that the force was only around 100 strong, that the SBS always operated in fixed pairs consisting of men of about the same height, build and type, and that the SBS operated from a central base in Scarborough, from where ad hoc groups of 4–12 men set out on special projects at the request of other units, and to where they returned afterwards. It is not known why the anonymous prisoner chose to select Scarborough in North Yorkshire as the SBS's home base, but his curious deception perhaps reflects Verney's sense of humour.[302]

* * *

The Allied invasion of Sicily commenced at 02:45 on 10 July 1943. It was unexpected. The Allied forces established solid bridgeheads and advanced along the coast to the east and south before the Germans had time to reinforce the weak Italian forces on the island.

On 8 August, the German Commander-in-Chief Italy, Field Marshal Kesselring, ordered the commander of the German forces on Sicily, General Hube, to evacuate the island. At 06:35 on 17 August, Hube reported that the last German and Italian troops had withdrawn to the mainland.

Chapter Twenty-Nine

The Battle for the Aegean Sea – 1

A difficult COS at which we discussed the desirability or otherwise of vacating Leros. A very nasty problem. Middle East [Command] have not been either wise or cunning and have now got themselves into the difficult situation that they can neither hold nor evacuate Leros. Our only hope would be assistance from Turkey, the provision of airfields from which the required air cover could be provided.
(Field Marshal Lord Alanbrooke, War Diaries, 28 October 1943)

The fall of Mussolini, 25 July 1943

On the night of 24/25 July 1943, the Grand Council of the fascist party ousted Benito Mussolini as commander of the Italian military. The following day, King Vittorio Emanuele III ordered his arrest and appointed Marshal Pietro Badoglio as his successor. The former dictator was transported to the small island of Ponza, where many of his opponents had been interned. To prevent the Germans from finding and freeing him, he was moved to the island of La Maddalena, north of Sardinia, on 7 August. On 27 August, Mussolini was transferred to the winter sports hotel Campo Imperatore on top of Gran Sasso mountain in central Italy.

On 3 August, Italian diplomats told the British Ambassador in Lisbon and the British consul in Tangier that Italy wanted to negotiate. The contact was made in secret to avoid provoking the Germans, who were de facto occupiers of the country.

Allied disagreement

In April 1943, Britain and Turkey agreed on a plan codenamed Hardihood, which entailed the Allies moving two British armoured divisions to Turkey. The British troops and their equipment were to land in the Turkish port city of Izmir. This would necessitate the removal of German and Italian forces from the Dodecanese Islands to open up the sea route through the Aegean. To pave the way for Hardihood, the Middle East Command's planning staff,

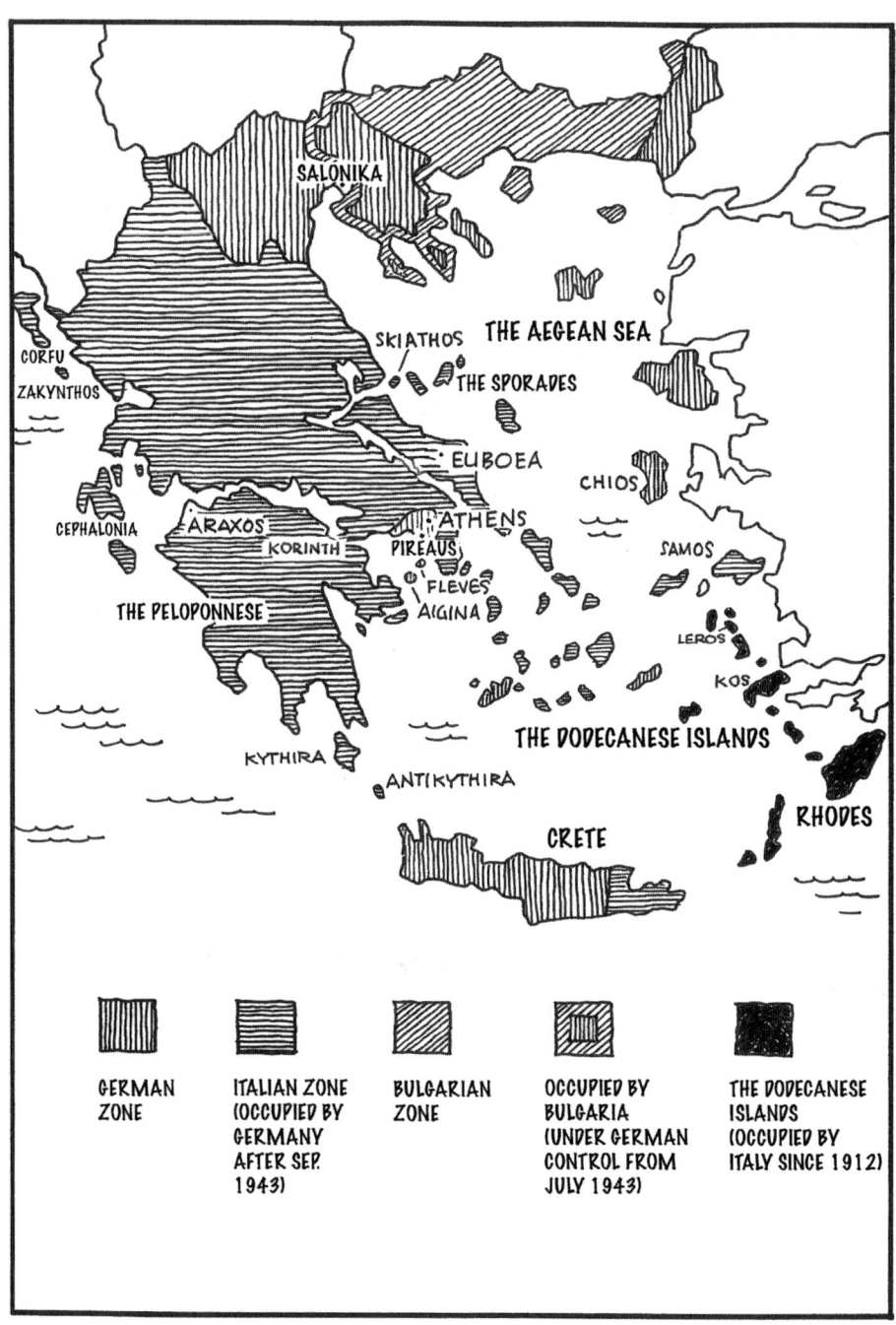

Occupied Greece.

Force 292, had drawn up another plan (Accolade), under which British forces would occupy the southernmost islands, including Rhodes. The Turks would then occupy the northern islands, bolstered by Allied air support from bases in Turkey.

As long as war continued to rage in North Africa and Sicily, resources could not be diverted to operations in the Aegean. Victory in North Africa, the invasion of Sicily and the fall of Mussolini changed matters. In a memorandum on 27 July, Churchill asked the Chiefs of Staff Committee how plans to occupy Rhodes were progressing: 'we ought to get there quickly if it is humanly possible, as I need this place as part of the diplomatic approach to Turkey.'[303]

The British also had other reasons to be interested in the Dodecanese Islands. Rhodes had two airfields and a major port; Karpathos and Kos each had an airfield suitable for single-engine fighters; and Leros had both a seaplane base and a port from which light warships and submarines could operate. Whoever controlled theses bases controlled the waters between the Greek Aegean islands and Turkey. From these islands it would be possible to supply the Yugoslav partisans and bomb German lines of communication in the Balkans and the Romanian oil fields until bases in Italy became available. Moreover, dominion over the Aegean (and Turkish goodwill) would make it possible to send supplies to the Soviet Union through the Black Sea, rather than having to choose between risky Arctic convoys and the long voyage via the Persian Gulf. Churchill and the British also wanted to establish a military presence in Greece and the Balkans to prevent Greece and Turkey falling under the Soviet sphere of influence.[304]

In the week after the fall of Mussolini, reports came in from the Balkans, Crete and the Dodecanese of a marked deterioration in relations between the Germans and the Italians in Italian-occupied areas. Middle East Command recommended preparing an attack force as soon as possible to exploit the emerging rift between the two Axis powers. The Command only had one fully equipped and trained division available: the 8th Indian. The German forces were not much bigger and were scattered over a wide area, with one division on Crete and another spread out over the Dodecanese. The Italians also had a division on Crete and two on the islands. If the Italians remained passive, the 8th Indian Division could probably take Rhodes. Middle East Command also had eight landing craft at its disposal. Five of these were supposed to be leaving for India but were temporarily held back in the Mediterranean. The flow of British supplies to Turkey, which began in January 1943, was put on hold and resources diverted to Accolade. General Eisenhower was asked to make available two landing ships, six supply ships, four squadrons of long-range fighters and a battalion of paratroopers with the requisite transport aircraft. The attack on Rhodes would then go ahead on 18 August.

However, while Churchill was negotiating with President Roosevelt in Quebec, 17–24 August, Eisenhower and his Anglo-American staff announced that no ships or aircraft could be spared for use in the eastern Mediterranean. The five landing ships that had been held back were then sent to India. On 26 August the 8th Indian Division was reassigned to the force that would land in Italy.

Middle East Command now only had five infantry battalions from the British 234th Infantry Brigade – straight from garrison duty in Malta and almost completely devoid of combat experience – as well as SAS and SBS units. With such modest forces at their disposal, the plan to invade Rhodes would have to be abandoned – unless, of course, the 35,000 Italian troops on Rhodes could be persuaded to play an active role in defeating the 7,000 Germans on the island. The small British force could also be used to shore up Italian garrisons on the other islands should they take up arms against the Germans.

To transport and support these forces, the British had eight destroyers, a handful of submarines, and a mixed bag of small vessels belonging to the Levant Schooner Flotilla (LSF), a transport unit formed in summer 1943. LSF grew out of a small fleet of caiques that the SOE had been using to sail agents to and from the Greek islands since the battle for Crete in 1941. It was commanded by yachtsman, adventurer and author Adrian Seligman, and crewed by British service personnel from all three armed forces and by Greeks. LSF operated from Beirut, but also had a repair base in Haifa.[305]

The eight destroyers operated from Alexandria, about 400 miles from Kos in the Aegean. German air superiority forced the destroyers to operate mainly by night and hide in Turkish territorial waters by day. The vessels carried only relatively modest amounts of fuel and supplies, which meant that their staying power – and usefulness – was limited.

The RAF had 280 bombers and fighters available for operations in the Aegean, but the nearest British airfield was in Cyprus, some 250 miles from Rhodes. Single-engine fighter aircraft could not operate over such great distances. Twin-engined Beaufighters could, but they were no match for the Messerschmitt 109s, which flew from bases on Karpathos, only about 45 miles from Rhodes, Crete and southern Greece. If the British had been able to operate from airbases in Turkey, they could have played a significant role, but the Turkish government considered the risk too great.[306] To break the German air superiority, the British needed to either secure the airfields on Rhodes or conquer Kos and build enough runways good enough to serve four fighter squadrons with the utmost haste.

The most important islands in the Aegean Sea

Italian name	English name	German name	Area [1]	Population [2]
Stampalia	Astypalaia	Astypalea		
Calchi	Halki	Chalki	30.3	800
Calino	Kalymnos	Kalymnos	128.2	15,500
Scarpanto	Karpathos	Karpathos	306	6,750
Caso	Kasos	Kasos	69.4	1,250
Castelrosso	Kastellórizo	Megisti	19.6	1,250
Coo	Kos	Kos	296	17,000
Lero	Leros	Leros	71.5	9,500
Lisso	Lipsi	Lipsi	17.4	750
Nisiro	Nisyros	Nisyros	48	2,500
Patmo	Patmos	Patmos	57.1	2,000
Rodi	Rhodes	Rhodos	1,412	57,000
Simi	Symi	Symi	63.6	4,750
Piscopi	Tilos	Tilos	64.3	1,000

(1) Including adjacent small islands; areas given in km².
(2) Approx. civilian population 1940.
(Source: Sirotti, *Il postalista*)

'I've never been so happy in my life…'

During the summer of 1943, unrest and sabotage were rife in Denmark. In late August the Germans demanded special courts and the imposition of the death penalty. On 28 August, the Danish government, which had previously worked with the occupiers, rejected the German demands. The Germans moved against the Danish armed forces the very next day. Army barracks were attacked and disarmed after brief skirmishes, but attempts to capture naval vessels were thwarted. Most of the ships were scuppered by their own crews, while a few sailed to safety in Sweden. The Germans introduced martial law and effectively became the executive power in the country. The royal family and government ceased to function. To a much greater extent than at any other time during the three years of occupation, Denmark could now be considered a nation at war with Germany.

Lassen welcomed the news, as he finally felt that his countrymen were standing with him against Nazi tyranny. On 1 September 1943 he wrote to Count Reventlow:

Dear Count Reventlow,
When I last saw you we talked about whether Denmark would get a chance to show the world what it is really made of, and perhaps the Count will remember that I had my doubts.

On the other hand, I did not doubt for a second that the Danes would fight and die for their country when the day came, and you were totally convinced that the day would come. It came, and I have never been so happy in my life, and I have never had nor hoped to receive as much reward for what little good I have done in this war, because now I know for the first time that I really have been fighting for Denmark and each German pig I have killed has been my country's enemy. I hope that the Countess is well and look forward to seeing you again, hopefully before too long.

I have recently received a 'Bar' for my M.C. Otherwise, I have nothing particularly new to tell. Greet the Countess for me. Your
Anders[307]

Lassen was in no doubt that it was both his right and his duty to kill Germans in battle. Nevertheless, the wording 'I know for the first time that I really have been fighting for Denmark and each German pig I have killed has been my country's enemy' hints at his – perhaps unacknowledged – relief at feeling a greater sense of moral authority, knowing that he 'really [was] fighting for Denmark' and in a sense the rest of the people of Denmark now shared the responsibility for his actions.[308]

* * *

During August and September, Lassen was hospitalised at least twice – on one occasion with jaundice. While in the military hospital in Nazareth, he shared a ward with Arthur R. Walter, a chaplain from a British parachute regiment. The two men spoke a great deal. Walter noted Lassen's incessant recalcitrance about hospital rules and regulations, and was amused by his tenacious pursuit of the nurses. However, what really made an impression on the chaplain was the Dane's restless energy, nervousness and mixture of determination and doubt.

> He had yellow fever, hepatitis – and at times he was raving, out of his mind. He had bad dreams with a certain amount of hysterical talk to which I lent a sympathetic ear although I can't remember the details. He was very tense, tightly coiled – a wild young boy. Very often, in my impression, he was not aware of all that he was doing.

Without denigrating the bravery, I think he was one of those people who act without foreseeing the consequences. Something had to be done, so they go and do it regardless of their own safety. I acted, more or less, as father confessor while he lay naked on the bed and poured out his inner pressures. In action, he would be physically alert but mentally relaxed; afterwards, it would be the complete reverse.

He would be fatigued but as taut as a spring, and then he would have to find someone with whom he could unwind as he talked over the men he'd killed. I don't know if the tension clarified the action as he tried to find faults in it; certainly, it didn't stem from guilt. A guilt complex was the last thing Andy had; his deep feelings were about getting one back at the Germans. He was very restive in hospital and wanted to be out doing something.[309]

Most of all Lassen would have liked to have been 'out doing something' in the Danish Resistance, but he was too valuable a member of the SBS for Jellicoe to let him go.[310]

The Italian capitulation, 8 September 1943

At 04:30 on 3 September 1943, the British 8th Army crossed the Messina Strait and, virtually unopposed, established a bridgehead on the tip of the Italian peninsula. The objectives were to open the Strait of Messina for Allied shipping and to draw German forces to the south of Italy, to facilitate the imminent landing in Salerno, about thirty miles south of Naples. At 17:00 the same day, the Italian negotiators signed the nation's capitulation at Eisenhower's headquarters in Sicily. At 18:30 on 8 September, Eisenhower announced the news on Radio Algiers. The following morning, US General Mark Clark's Fifth Army landed in Salerno.

* * *

The German response was hard and fast. All over Italy and the Mediterranean, Italian barracks were attacked and disarmed by German forces, and the whole of Italy north of the front line was occupied. Some 600,000 Italian soldiers were shipped off to prison camps in Germany.

In the early hours of 9 September, the Italian royal family left Rome. The royals and their entourage, including senior military leaders, fled to the coastal town of Ortona a Mare. From here a warship ferried them to Brindisi, behind Allied lines.

Badoglio's government, along with the royal court, relocated to the southern Italian port city of Bari, and declared war on Germany on 13 October. Despite this move, the Kingdom of Italy was not accorded the status of Allied nation, only of 'co-belligerent'.

* * *

On 12 September, German airborne troops freed Mussolini and transported him first to Rome and then on to safety in Germany. On 23 September 1944, the 'Social Republic of Italy' (RSI) was proclaimed, with Mussolini as *Duce*. Mussolini's Republic, the government of which was scattered among small towns around Lake Garda, covered the whole of northern and central Italy. RSI was little more than a German vassal state. Often German officers and officials bypassed Mussolini and the RSI's authorities, and Rome was completely outside *Il Duce*'s control.

Crisis on Rhodes, 8–11 September 1943[311]

On the evening of 7 September, George Jellicoe dined with Captain Lapraik, head of M Detachment, at the elegant Hotel Saint Georges in Beirut. As their meal was drawing to a close, a military policeman brought Jellicoe an order that he was to report to Raiding Forces HQ immediately. Jellicoe somewhat reluctantly had his driver take him to the HQ in Azzib. From there he was sent to Haifa, where a plane was waiting to take him to Cairo. At 10:00 he was to attend a meeting with Brigadier Heyman at Middle East Command HQ. When Jellicoe arrived for the meeting, he was surprised to hear that Italy had capitulated. A mission led by the CO Raiding Forces, Colonel Turnbull, was to sail to Rhodes to ensure that the island's commandant, Admiral Campioni, who also commanded the Italian forces in the whole Aegean Sea, would resist the Germans long enough for Allied forces to land on the island. Jellicoe spotted several weaknesses in the plan, including that Turnbull would not arrive on Rhodes until 11 September, and that Admiral Campioni did not know he was on his way. Jellicoe was also unhappy that he and the SBS were informed of the plans at such a late stage. He suggested instead that a small group be sent by air in advance to make contact with Campioni, without having to wait for Turnbull and his staff to arrive by sea. His proposal was approved. The airborne delegation was to consist of Jellicoe, the Italian-speaking SOE man 'Major Dolbey' (aka the Polish/Italian Count Julian Dobrski), and a radio operator, Sergeant Kesterton. Their mission was codenamed Rodell.

Vice Admiral Inigo Campioni (front, right).

The first attempt to parachute Jellicoe, Dolbey and Kesterton into Rhodes failed due to thick cloud cover. However, at 22:50 on 9 September, they succeeded – albeit not without incident. Dolbey broke his right thighbone on landing.

After an hour Dolbey was found by an Italian patrol and taken to Admiral Campioni's HQ in the Knights Templars' mighty fortress in Rhodes City, where he arrived at 01:15. Dolbey explained the purpose of his visit to the Admiral and had him send out patrols to search for Jellicoe and Kesterton. Jellicoe and the wireless operator were found shortly and arrived at Campioni's HQ at 02:45. Dolbey remarked that Jellicoe looked 'fit and … wellfed'. Fearing to be captured by the Germans he had eaten the letter from the British Commander-in-Chief Middle East, General Maitland Wilson, which he had been supposed to deliver to Admiral Campioni. It had taken him an hour to chew his way through this 'surprisingly tough and indigestible' letter 'which occasioned me acute thirst the next morning.' Campioni, nevertheless, was convinced that his three visitors were really who they claimed to be.[312]

Jellicoe and Dolbey entered into negotiations with Campioni – who, like the other Italian military commanders in Greece and the Balkans, had received a series of unclear and in some cases contradictory orders from Italian High Command that essentially left them fending for themselves.

On 9 September, sporadic clashes had flared up around the island, and the Germans (Lieutenant General Ulrich Kleemann's 6 to 8,000-strong Sturm-Division Rhodos) seized the island's airfields.

Campioni told Jellicoe and Dolbey that his forces would probably be able to secure the port of Rhodes for the time being, but that he would require immediate reinforcement to stop the Germans conquering the whole island. Dolbey and Jellicoe explained that the British would be able to supply a single brigade on 15 September, but it would only be able to land if the Italians were able to secure the port. Another 200 men from the special forces could be landed in a couple of days. Campioni found the information deeply dispiriting. His position was already precarious and he was in regular contact with Kleemann and his people. He was terrified that the Germans would find out that he was conspiring with the British.[313*]

On the afternoon of 10 September, the injured Dolbey was evacuated on an Italian motor torpedo boat. Also on board was Captain Giannotti from Italian military intelligence (SIM). Dolbey and Giannotti were first transported to Symi. On the morning of 11 September they met with Turnbull, who had flown via the small island of Kastellorizo in the far-east end of the Aegean Sea and was now waiting to sail to Rhodes. After a short meeting, Dolbey was sent by plane to Limassol in Cyprus, and from there to a military hospital in Cairo. Giannotti flew directly to Cairo to meet with the British commander-in-chief in the Middle East, General Wilson. He handed him a letter from Campioni in which the admiral stressed the need for reinforcements and asked that Allied air and naval forces made their presence visible along the south coast of Rhodes to draw German forces away from the the main town on the island.

Back on the island, the Germans continued their attacks during the afternoon and advanced towards the main town (also called Rhodes). Campioni had his British guests inform Turnbull that he should not sail to Rhodes but instead stay on Symi or return to Kastellorizo. At 19:45 he sent Jellicoe and Kesterton off to Kastellorizo on board an Italian motor torpedo boat. Also on board were Italian officers, including Campioni's deputy chief of staff, Lieutenant Colonel Fanizza, who was to explain to the British the situation on Rhodes and the urgent need for reinforcements. As a sign of Campioni's goodwill, Jellicoe was given a map of the defence installations on Rhodes and the Italian minefields in the Aegean to take with him to Kastellorizo. The group arrived in the early hours of 11 September. They were immediately offered a large gin and tonic by David Sutherland, who had arrived shortly before with a small group of SBS men and established a good relationship with the island's Italian commandant and his 300 men.[314*]

* * *

On 11 September at 07:00, German planes attacked an Italian coastal battery on Rhodes, cutting off the naval radio station. Just over an hour later, an emissary from the CO of the Italian forces in the southern part of the island approached Campioni and asked for permission to cease fire. Campioni ordered him to keep fighting until he had held another meeting with General Kleemann. At 10:30 two German officers presented the terms of surrender: all Italian troops on the island were to surrender unconditionally, and all German prisoners were to be released. Campioni was given half an hour to consider, after which German planes would attack the town of Rhodes. With no prospect of help from the British any time soon, the admiral entered negotiations with Kleemann – and at 15:30 the German and Italian commanders met and agreed the terms.

The Italian officers and their men around the island did not welcome the news, and sporadic fighting continued for a few days. During the period 9–13 September, German losses amounted to 91 killed, 212 wounded and 2 missing,[315] while 143 Italians were killed and over 300 wounded. Ninety Italian prisoners were executed by the Germans as 'traitors' or 'irregulars', forty of them summarily.

Most of the Italian ships in Rhodes harbour managed to slip away under cover of darkness and sail to Kos, Leros or Kastellorizo, taking with them a large number of soldiers who wanted to keep fighting the Germans. Other Italians made for the mountains and the forests to fight alongside the Greek partisans, and many more fled to Kos, Leros and Turkey. In total, around 1,580 Italians escaped from Rhodes. As they had done on the other islands they occupied, the Germans gave the Italian prisoners the choice to pledge an oath of allegiance to Hitler, sign up to work in Germany, or be interned. On Rhodes, 250 members of the fascist militia and fifty men from the harbour police opted to serve the Germans, but most opted for internment. Across the Aegean islands as a whole, approximately 1,900 Italians joined the German armed forces, while 4,330 opted to work in Germany.

Chapter Thirty

The Battle for the Aegean Sea – 2

We were watched by a crowd of the inhabitants. The men and women kept to their houses and looked from the windows but the children crowded round and were soon begging for food and cigarettes. They looked starved and their sunken cheeks and eyes which seemed to have known no childhood told a pitiful story of the suffering of the war and were a strange contrast to the background of a beautiful island.

(Searle: *At Sea Level*)

Kos, Leros, Samos, Kalymnos, September–October 1943[316]

On 11 September, Turnbull, Jellicoe and Sutherland discussed what to do now that Rhodes had fallen. As neither Rhodes nor Crete could be occupied with the forces available, Middle East Command suggested that attempts be made to capture as many of the Aegean islands as possible before the Germans did: in particular Kos and Leros, where the

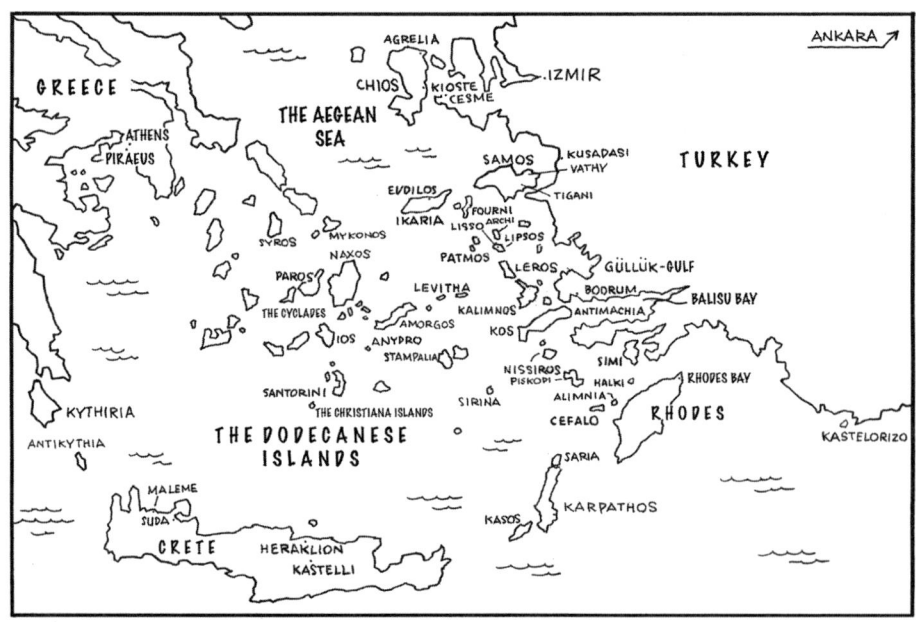

Italians had an airfield and a naval base, respectively. For this purpose, Turnbull's Raiding Forces HQ had at its disposal the British 42nd Motor Launch Flotilla, consisting of eight fast 115-foot motor gunboats. General Wilson's Middle East Command approved the idea, which was consistent with both Churchill and General Wilson's own strategic thinking. Jellicoe and Sutherland sailed from Kastellorizo to Kos, further up the Turkish coast, landing on the island in the early hours of 14 September. They were received enthusiastically by the island's Greek population, but somewhat less so by the Italians. Nonetheless, the Italian commander was cooperative and warmly welcomed the British officers and their men, who were assigned temporary quarters around the Antimachia airbase in the middle of the island.

Rear Admiral Luigi Mascherpa.

After lunch, Jellicoe sailed in an Italian motor torpedo boat to Leros to seek out the Italian commander, Admiral Mascherpa, who was also friendly to the British.

As soon as Middle East Command learned that there were no German forces on Kos and Leros, and that their Italian commanders would cooperate, British reinforcements were sent to the two islands. Sutherland made his way to Samos with twenty-five men. The Italian garrison on Samos, under the command of General Mario Soldarelli, was approximately 2,500 strong. There was also a legion of fascist militia (24. Legione MVSN). The fascist legionnaires posed a potential risk, but the officers in the regular Italian units accorded Sutherland and his men a friendly welcome until, shortly afterwards, they were relieved by an infantry battalion of the Royal West Kent regiment.[317]

On 14 September, General Wilson wrote to the Chairman of the COS, General Brooke:

> We have occupied Castelrosso island, and have missions in Kos, Leros, and Samos. A flight [3–4 aircraft] of Spitfires will be established in Kos today, and an infantry garrison to-night by parachute. An infantry detachment is also proceeding to Leros. Thereafter I propose to carry out piratical war on enemy communications in the Aegean.[318]

The 'piratical war' would be waged from the small volcanic island of Kalymnos between Leros and Samos, which Sutherland occupied after Samos had been secured. On 1 October a base was set up here for all of the raider forces in the area, i.e. SBS and a force from the Long Range Desert Group that had been retrained for island warfare after the end of the desert war. Colonel Turnbull set up his Raiding Forces HQ on Leros. The 42nd ML Flotilla was based in Paphos, on the west coast of Cyprus.

Symi, 7 September–2 November 1943

On Tuesday 7 September 1943, Lassen was discharged from hospital. On 12 September, along with the rest of Captain Lapraik's M Detachment, app. 22 men in all,[319*] he boarded one of Levant Schooner Flotilla's ships leaving Haifa at 20:00 for Kastellorizo, where they arrived at 22.30 the following evening. On Kastellorizo Lapraik was to set up a base for raids and intelligence activities. While M Detachment was waiting for orders, the caique's radio station received a signal – from a British spy, an SOE agent, a forward patrol, an Italian source? – warning that the Germans were probably preparing an operation against Symi and asking for rapid action to prevent them from taking the island. Lapraik went to his superiors on Kastellorizo, showed them the message and requested permission to proceed to Symi. He was at first ordered to go to Kos, where his Detachment arrived at 05:00 on 17 September. Here he spoke to the CO of III Corps, Lieutenant General Desmond Anderson, who gave him permission to proceed to Symi.[320*]

* * *

On 13 September, Lassen was promoted to acting captain. He was also head of the Irish Patrol, which included three big, heavy-drinking scrappers: Corporal Sean O'Reilly, Corporal D'Arcy and former gymnastics instructor Patsy 'the Brown Body' Henderson, all three of whom had served in the Irish Guards but were none too enamoured of its rigid discipline. O'Reilly became a particularly close friend of Lassen. Assigning the men to patrols with similar backgrounds (the Irish patrol, the Guard's patrol, etc) was an informal means of encouraging solidarity within the patrols and competition between them. When the Englishman Hank Hancock was assigned to the Irish patrol, his comrades didn't speak to him for the first three months.[321] The Irish patrol were, in Lapraik's words, 'an incredible collection of bandits', but they 'worked very well' under Lassen's command. Concerning Lassen's abilities as an officer, Lapraik said:

Some people found him a little bit trying and insubordinate, but I got on with him very well. Most of the officers and pretty well all the sergeants would have followed him anywhere because he knew his job.

However, not all of the officers shared his admiration:

They had the idea that Andy was a pirate, which was very far from the truth. ... Andy ... could have commanded a battalion. ... He didn't need to be told.[322]

* * *

On the evening of Friday 17 September, Lapraik and his men arrived on Symi. The noise of the ship's engine caused great consternation on the island, where people thought it was a plane and that an air raid was imminent. When the ship came into view, as a dark shadow behind the headland off Symi town, the Italian forces on the island fired a warning shot that made the skipper slightly change course. Lapraik put a few boats into the water and sent Lassen and former boxing champion Doug Pomford to the quay to explain to the Italians that they were not Germans. Once that had been cleared up, the newcomers were well received by the Italian officers.[323] The rest of the

SBS raiders on Symi.

force could not come ashore until it was ascertained whether the harbour was deep enough for the ship to dock safely. No one seemed to know exactly how deep the harbour basin was, so Lassen dived in to find out. Once the depth had been measured and deemed adequate, the ship docked and Lapraik and his men landed. The ship set sail again shortly afterwards to avoid being seen in open water in daylight and present an easy target for the Germans, who still ruled the skies.

The Greek inhabitants rejoiced at the arrival of the British. The head of the Italian school system on Symi, Maria Luisa Caporali Cavallari, said that some of the British and the Greeks seemed to know each other from previous nocturnal visits when local families had sheltered British agents. She also noted that the British soldiers were well-armed, well-supplied with provisions, well-disciplined and always preoccupied with their duties:

> …no aimlessly wandering about, no wooing women.
>
> The residents noticed the difference between the discipline of the British and Italian troops.
>
> The Italian officers who had so warmly greeted the British officers, were somewhat ill at ease with their reserved and cool behaviour.
>
> The same applied to our troops, … with whom the English would not enter into any form of comradely relations. The two groups lived side by side, but deeply separated.[324]

The somewhat chilly relationship between the British and Italians did not prevent them working together on the island's defences. Lapraik and the two Italian officers who shared command on Symi, Lieutenant Andrea Occhipinti and Lieutenant Commander Corrado Corradini (a former port commander in Rhodes wanted by the Germans for his anti-German attitude), were willing to do their best to hold the 26-square-mile island. Occhipinti and Corradini had at their disposal a machine-gun company, two 20 mm anti-aircraft guns, some *carabinieri* and members of the military customs corps *Guardia di Finanza*.[325] The Italian Navy also had a lookout post on the island and the harbour commander had his own staff. Symi's Italian garrison numbered approximately 150, bolstered by around the same number of soldiers and sailors who had fled to the island from Rhodes. Occhipinti had been promised 200 men from the Italian naval force on Leros, but they never arrived. Nor did Lapraik's force receive any reinforcements, although he asked for them and stressed that Symi was crucial to operations on Rhodes.[326]

Corradini moved the Italian forces from Panormitis and Dracunda, near Symi town, to various high points from where the most obvious landing places along the coast might be covered. On 13 September, General Mario Soldarelli on Samos, who had assumed command of the Italian forces in the Aegean Sea after the fall of Rhodes, ordered Occhipinti to mount the strongest possible defence of Symi against German attempts to land. By this time the lieutenant had already made great efforts to strengthen his positions and prepare his men.[327]

On 25 September the Levant Schooner LS *Hedgehog* arrived in the port of Symi carrying a party of six men of the LRDG commanded by Captain A.G. Redfern.

* * *

Redfern, who was born in 1906 in Harare, Mashonaland East, Southern Rhodesia, had been a civil servant, hunter and wildlife photographer before the war. When war broke out he volunteered for service and received a commission in the newly formed Rhodesian African Rifles in 1940. At a time when an Axis invasion of Southern Africa was considered a real possibility he was put in charge of training men for commando and guerrilla warfare (much as Lassen had been in Nigeria). Many of his trainees joined the Long Range Desert Group in North Africa, as did Redfern himself; as temporary captain he was appointed OC of the LRDG's S1 Patrol.[328]

* * *

After liaising with Lapraik, Redfern and his men sailed on, this time in a local caique, to the large St. Michael monastery in the village of Panormitis on the west side of the island. After some initial confusion during which the LRDG party was fired on by Italian troops, without sustaining losses, Redfern and his men were received by the monastery's abbot, who had the church bells peal in their honour and placed the monastery at their complete disposal. Redfern also met with the Italian lieutenant whose men had fired on him and who was now 'most apologetic and all out to please'.

The monastery's abbot, Chrysanthos Maroulakis, was a very active member of the local resistance movement. His activities had included helping the SOE smuggle agents into and out of Rhodes and hiding Italian deserters. After the SBS occupied Symi, the abbot had worked with both Lapraik's people and with his SOE contacts, who in turn worked in parallel with and independently of SBS. The abbot hid weapons, radio equipment, food and personnel in his monastery.[329] He now assisted Redfern's party in setting up an observation post with a wireless set on a hill approximately 45 minutes climb from the monastery from where Redfern's men could monitor the narrow strait between Rhodes and Turkey and report on sea and air traffic to and from Rhodes, Kos, and Leros.[330]*

The British were primarily interested in Symi as an observation post and because of its proximity to Rhodes, which they regarded as the key to the Aegean. From Symi it was relatively easy to smuggle agents into and out of Rhodes, where they could spy on the Germans and make contact with local resistance fighters and SOE agents. Had the Germans occupied the island, it would have been more difficult for the British to maintain the link between the Aegean and their bases in the Middle East and Cyprus through Kastellorizo. Symi was also a good starting point for expeditions to the islands of Halki, Alimnia, Nisyros and Tilos between Rhodes and Kos.

Unable to count on reinforcements or air support, Lapraik had to rely on the Germans' lack of interest in Symi or the German forces on Rhodes not having the resources to take on his British/Italian garrison. Despite Corradini and Occhipinti's professions of goodwill, Lapraik did not know how fiercely their men would fight against the Germans if it came to it. He also feared that the Italians' poor relations with the islanders might pose a problem.

Lapraik, a lawyer by profession, took it upon himself to govern Symi. He sought to prevent clashes between the Greek population, emboldened by the British presence, and the deeply unpopular Italians. A couple of incidents arose when Greeks and a few British soldiers refused to stand during the evening ceremony when the Italian flag over the harbour commander's office was lowered. The Italian *carabinieri* arrested four Greeks and complained about the British to Lapraik. Soon around seventy Greeks had congregated in front of the British command post, demanding guns to kill the Italians. Lapraik explained in no uncertain terms to the angry Greeks that their island was still under Italian sovereignty, and as such they had to show respect for the flag and to obey its representatives. At the same time he made it clear to the Italians that they should not insist that civilians solemnly salute their flag. To avoid further incidents, Lapraik ordered that every morning and evening the British flag should be raised and lowered alongside the Italian one, and urged local people to attend the joint ceremony. When a drunken SOE-officer shot at portraits of the Italian royal couple on the wall of a taverna one evening, Lapraik deported the culprit to Kos right away.[331]

Once Lapraik had made it clear to all three parties that trouble would not be tolerated on the small island, a period of relative calm ensued. He left the civilian administration to another officer and focused instead on what he had come to Symi to do.

Dion 'Stud' Stellin.

He had at his disposal six local caiques. On 21 September, he used them to send Lieutenant Dion John 'Stud' Stellin (a New Zealander) and another SBS man to the neighbouring island of Rhodes, along with a couple of agents from Inter Services Liaison Department (ISLD, the codename for the SIS in the Middle and Far East) whom Lieutenant Corradini had briefed on the situation on Rhodes.[332*]

The Germans had extended the Italian minefields along the coast of Rhodes. However, near the village of Villanova (now Paradisi), Michael Lukas, the local Greek Orthodox archpriest, along with two Italian sappers who had gone into hiding after the surrender, had cleared the mines from a narrow strip of beach. This strip and a similar one near Kalithea served as escape routes for Italian soldiers. Members of the espionage and sabotage organization *Erratic*, which the SOE ran on the island, used them too. As often happened when the British went ashore secretly on the Greek islands, rumours of Stellin and his colleague's presence spread rapidly. The Germans chased them from mountain to mountain until they finally escaped back to Symi on 26 September.

* * *

The agents landed on Rhodes by 'Stud' Stellin were part of an extensive network of spies and escape teams controlled by the British businessman Noel Rees from the Turkish port city of Izmir. Rees was a lieutenant commander in the RNVR. At the outbreak of war he was appointed British consul on the Aegean island of Chios, where he ran intelligence operations. When Greece fell in 1941, Rees and his family fled to Turkey, where he was appointed vice consul in Izmir. His home became the centre of the Aegean activities of ISLD and the escape network MI9. (MI9 was responsible for helping escaped Allied prisoners of war, downed pilots and others out of hostile occupied territories.)

Rees had considerable organizational talent and in-depth knowledge of the Aegean, where he had good connections and considerable influence on both sides of the Greek/Turkish border. He was also a man of means, and drew on his own personal wealth whenever there were officials to bribe, or if equipment or supplies were needed.

Rees organized escape and rescue operations on the Greek mainland, placed agents on countless Greek islands and sent caiques on long voyages to watch German fleet movements at the Dardanelles and along the southern periphery of the Aegean. His agents sought help and information from anti-German elements on the islands and paid for them with food – especially potatoes, which were in high demand on these small, barren islands that war had left even more isolated.

Rees's fleet of caiques was manned by fishermen, merchants, smugglers and others from Chios and other Aegean islands, who sailed from the natural ports Kioste and Agrelia, north and south of Çeşme on the Turkish coast. Rees, a noted yachtsman, had rented these ports for 'recreational purposes'. He then added a shipyard, workshops and storage facilities, and set up a small market and cafés for the sailors. A British carrier pigeon trainer provided the caiques with a means of communication that the Germans were unable to find or intercept. His organization not only brought Allied soldiers out of Greece, but also helped thousands of Greeks flee to Turkey. By the summer of 1943, Çeşme was the site of a large camp for refugees, many of whom moved on to Cyprus or Egypt to sign up with the Free Greek forces.[333]

* * *

Symi's beautiful landscapes and picturesque settlements could not hide the fact that most of the Greek population lived in poverty and very primitive conditions. Each of the 3–400 houses in the main town had a filthy, stinking latrine, the sewers were chronically blocked, and there were flies everywhere. Dysentery was rife, and the SBS men caught it too. A few also contracted malaria.[334] Lassen was among those afflicted by diarrhoea, although this did not prevent him going on patrols. To establish a certain degree of hygiene, Lapraik's men dug their own latrine, which they surrounded with a wall of loose stones. Lassen tried to disinfect the latrine by dousing it with petrol and setting a match to it. Needless to say, it blew up. He suffered severe burns to his legs which he covered with makeshift bandages made of mosquito net, running from his socks, up under his shorts and fastened to his belt. It did not stop them becoming infected.[335]

The day after he arrived on Symi, Lassen led a patrol of twelve men to the small islands of Halki, Alimnia and Tilos, all of which were about 25 miles away. The small Italian garrison at Alimnia had left for Leros to join the Italian forces there. Nor were there any Italian soldiers on Tilos or Halki.

Lapraik considered fortifying Halki, but when Lassen returned to Symi on 19 September he said that it would be very difficult to defend: trenches could not be dug in the bedrock and otherwise suitable defence positions were too vulnerable to mortar attack. Halki was home to 820 Greeks, six *carabinieri* and four members of the Italian military customs corps *Guardia di Finanza*. Lassen and his men seized a machine gun and seventy-two hand grenades left behind by the Italian garrison when it moved to Kos in 1941. From Alimnia,

Lassen brought back a slightly damaged 20 mm Breda cannon that the Italians had left behind. After the smith on Symi had repaired the damage, Lassen's cannon was placed outside the school in which his patrol was billeted. The school was partway up a hill, next to an old citadel and a Knights Hospitaller fort – a location that offered clear lines of sight and fire over one side of the harbour in the town.[336]

Shortly after this first visit to Halki, word came that Germans had landed on the island. Lassen's patrol paid another visit to Alimnia and Halki on 28–30 September but found no Germans. On Alimnia they confiscated a store of petrol and some clothing. From Halki they removed the only motor boat in the harbour, two rowing boats and the civilian mail to and from Rhodes, the post office on which handled mail to and from all of the Aegean islands.[337]

Lapraik declined to station British forces on Halki, but Lassen set the Italian *carabinieri* and customs officials to work building a fortified position on the island, threatened them with reprisals if they did not oppose any German landing attempt, and may have put them through a short training programme to motivate them to fight their former allies.[338*]

* * *

Ultimately Lassen's work on Halki bore no fruit. When a German force of sixty-three men under a Captain Rehe arrived on Halki late in the evening on 16 October 1943, they met no resistance. In fact they received nothing but cooperation from the head of the small *carabinieri* force and the island's Greek mayor. The Germans remained on Halki until 18 October. When they sailed back to Rhodes, they gave local members of the fascist party a machine gun and five rifles with which to guard the harbour against any new British incursions.[339]

* * *

During the boat trip back to Symi from Halki, the American medical orderly Porter Jarrell changed the dressings on Lassen's burns. In June 1942, Jarrell had volunteered for an ambulance unit under the 8th Army and had served during the last six months of the desert war. He then volunteered for the SBS, where he served as medical orderly – with a Red Cross armband and a machine gun. Lassen told Jarrell that he was considering applying for leave to go to England. Jarrell strongly advised him to do so, as he needed rest and treatment for his burns. However, upon arrival at Symi it transpired that Lapraik had ordered Stellin back to Rhodes, this time with three companions, among them Captain Redfern's interpreter Bairaman, whom Redfern was to 'miss sadly' during the remainder of his stay on Symi. Lassen insisted on accompanying them to ensure that his comrades made it ashore safely.[340]

The landing went as planned, and Stellin stayed on Rhodes for three weeks, gathering valuable intelligence. He and his men were almost captured when a German patrol surrounded the house in which they were staying. However, the priest in Villanova, Michael Lukas, whose son had just been married, took advantage of the confusion as the wedding guests dispersed. He hid Stellin and his three companions in a hay cart, which drove away under the noses of the Germans.[341]

Kos, 2–4 October 1943

On Kos on 16 September, David Sutherland's SBS force had been replaced by a company of the Durham Light Infantry (DLI). The rest of the DLI battalion arrived on 18 September. The British force also included an Indian unit and anti-aircraft artillery, as well as sappers and RAF men tasked with building a new airfield and repairing the neglected one at Antimachia, where six South African Spitfires were already in place. Overall, the British had about 1,600 men on Kos, the Italians about 4,000.

Despite the South African fighters and four Italian aircraft (but only two pilots), the Germans dominated the skies over Kos. Air raids were a daily occurrence. On the night of 2/3 October, the attacks escalated. Early in the morning the Germans launched *Unternehmen* [Operation] *Eisbär*. The combined offensive consisted of two infantry battalions, sappers, artillery and light tanks from the experienced 22nd Infantry Division stationed on Crete, which landed at three locations along the coast, as well as a company of paratroopers from the elite Brandenburg Division – the closest German equivalent of the SAS/SBS – which landed at Antimachia airfield. The landings were supported by massive air raids, especially by Stuka dive bombers. During the day the Germans landed additional forces with heavy weapons. The fighting raged over the whole island, and in the afternoon and the evening the British forces started to fall into disarray. At 20:00, their commander, Colonel Kenyon, ordered his men to split into small groups and retreat into the mountains. At this point organized British resistance effectively ceased – although as late as 06:00 the following morning Kenyon announced that he intended to fight on. The British collapse had a strongly demoralising effect on the Italians who had tried to defend Antimachia. Nevertheless some 200 Italians continued to hold out on the peninsula of

Kefalos, only surrendering when they ran out of ammunition. By the evening of 4 October, the Germans had taken over the whole island.

The number of British, Indian and South African dead on Kos is not known, but the Germans took around 900 prisoners. Eleven officers and around 100 men from the Durham Light Infantry were rescued by a patrol from Sutherland's S Detachment under the command of Walter Milner-Barry. Every night for a whole week, S Detachment caiques ferried men between Kos and one of the neighbouring islands. Noel Rees's organization also played a major role in the rescue efforts. The number of Italian dead is not known either, but about 2,100 were taken prisoner by the Germans. One hundred and one Italian officers were forced to dig their own graves and then executed by the Germans. One hundred and seventy-one Italians escaped to Turkey, while several hundred hid on Kos along with the remaining British troops. Some of them were given food and shelter by nuns at an Italian convent on the island, the mother superior of which also actively helped to smuggle refugees from Kos.

German losses amounted to 15 dead and 70 wounded and missing. They left a small garrison on the island, but the main force left Kos again right away on 5 October.[342]

Symi, 7 October–2 November 1943

On 6 October, a contingent of forty-five men – ground personnel, medical orderlies, an RAF doctor and reserve pilots from the South African Air Force (SAAF) – arrived on Symi. The doctor, Lieutenant Leslie Ferris, and his assistants took over a house near Lapraik's command post in the middle of the town and set up a makeshift infirmary to receive people injured and wounded in fighting or air raids. Ferris immediately began examining two SBS men who appeared to be suffering from malaria, and Lassen's extensive burns.[343]

The newcomers were placed on sentry duty that night. Lassen and his patrol seized the opportunity to get a proper night's sleep before they were to embark on an expedition to Rhodes the next day.

The SBS was not the only force to conduct raids in the Aegean. The same morning, at 02:30, the German Sturm-Division Rhodos received a telephone call from Army Group E's headquarters in Thessaloniki. The commander of the Army Group, Colonel General Löhr, who was in command of German, Bulgarian and Mussolini-faithful Italian forces throughout Greece, ordered 'immediate clarification of the situation on Symi', which the Germans knew was a base for spying on Rhodes. At 08:00 the commander of Sturm-Division

Rhodos, Lieutenant General Kleemann, met with half a dozen key officers from his division and the *Kriegsmarine*. Half an hour later he gave the order to launch *Unternehmen Trianda*.

The operation involved landing a 'pirate detachment' on Symi to locate and destroy a radio station the Germans suspected was on the island (this may have been the transmitter that Redfern had established in the Panormitis Monastery, another that Lapraik used to communicate with Kastellorizo, or perhaps one that the SOE had set up on the island before Lapraik arrived). Any enemy combatants they encountered were to be captured or killed. The whole operation was to last no more than three hours. When it was finished the force was to withdraw, continue to Nisyros, thirty miles due west of Symi, and carry out a similar operation there.[344]

At 04:00 on Thursday 7 October, the 120-ton caique *Esperia*, with the motorboat *Parma* in tow, sailed into the long, narrow Pedi Bay, approximately one mile east of Symi town. On board were 59 men (of which 17 were sailors, wireless operators, interpreters and other more or less non-combatants) some of whom had volunteered for an operation with an unknown target and purpose, under the command of First Lieutenant Fresemann from Grenadier Regiment Rhodos. Fresemann and his men had set sail from Rhodes at 21:45 on Wednesday evening. They now sailed unchallenged into the bay. *Esperia* dropped anchor about 200 feet from shore. At 04:25, *Parma* brought the first group ashore at a small fishing village at the westernmost end of the bay. It was already light, the sky was clear and it promised to be a hot day.

Pedi Bay opened up to the sea to the east. North and south of the bay were steep, barren hillsides. However, to the west, the landscape was relatively flat and open, rising gradually up towards Symi town, the highest points of which were 2–300 feet above sea level. A dirt road ran from the fishing village up towards Symi, passing through vineyards and scattered houses.

As the Germans came ashore, curious locals greeted them with a surprisingly cheery English 'Good morning!' They told them that all of the soldiers had left Symi (in recent days, there had been a lot of traffic back and forth with men and supplies, which had given many locals the impression that the British and Italian forces were evacuating)[345] and they knew nothing of any radio transmitter. However, the Germans had caught sight of a tall mast on top of a citadel-like building on the outskirts of the town, which they thought might be the antenna.[346*] With a Greek as a reluctant guide, the Germans headed towards the town. At 05:20, the two German groups at the front – each comprising approximately ten men – came under heavy fire from (as far as Lieutenant Fresemann could make out) four 20 mm anti-aircraft guns and ten light and heavy machine guns located in a row of old windmills on a ridge at the edge of the town. Part of the Italian garrison had taken up position there.

The Germans returned fire immediately. Fresemann sent a runner back to the main body with an order to send a group north of the windmills to attack from the rear. The runner never arrived, but a dynamic NCO, on his own initiative, launched the attack anyway. This forced the Italians to retreat westward, into Symi and upward into the high part of the terraced town.

The battle raged from house to house and from gateway to courtyard. The labyrinth of narrow, steep streets made it difficult to maintain an overview of the whole battlefield. The fighting dissolved into a series of clashes between small groups of often only two or three men. The Germans almost reached the citadel on the city's eastern edge, but could not make it past the 50 to 60-foot-high walls and were driven back by machine-gun fire and hand grenades.

Just after 08:00, as fighting raged in the town, the 20 mm guns around Symi – especially from the tall citadel, and most likely Lassen's cannon – opened fire on *Esperia*. The caique was forced to leave Pedi Bay and wait in open water, hidden behind the foothills along the mouth of the bay.

At 11:15 – after six hours of continuous combat – Lieutenant Fresemann pulled his men out of the town. They were exhausted, weakened by heat and thirst (although the locals gave them water after they banged for long enough on the closed doors and shutters), and running out of ammunition. Fresemann had no more reserves to deploy, and had lost faith in the reinforcements and air support promised to him from Rhodes. He feared that his retreat would be cut off by British and Italian forces advancing from other parts of the island. He ordered his men to retreat to a bridgehead at Pedi Bay and Muglia mountain, which formed a peninsula along the north side of the bay.

The SBS and Italians harried the Germans as they withdrew. Some of the Italians fought under Lassen, who had seized command from the Italian lieutenant – who in his opinion showed insufficient gumption. Lassen led the attack, and his example encouraged the faltering Italian soldiers to follow.[347]

Despite his dysentery and burns, Lassen's lead made an impression on his companions. They later described his inexhaustible energy and ability to 'be everywhere', instinctively 'read' his surroundings, sense where danger lurked, and move quickly and quietly. Lapraik said of him:

> He had a natural eye for ground, for fire, for movement. … He was what he was fortuitously. All the elements of a first-class soldier and very quick-thinking … I'd never known Andy hold fire. It could be said he was a killing-machine; you stayed alive if you became that.[348]

Lassen's actions on Symi earned him his third Military Cross. The citation gave him much of the credit for the fact that the Germans were driven back – the British did not know that the Germans were not there to occupy the island – and stated that he *stalked* at least three Germans and killed them 'at the closest range' – which may be a euphemistic way of saying 'with his knife'. Several of Lassen's comrades spoke of his love of this weapon, and of the way in which he put himself 'in a trance, so that he saw no danger in anything' during the fighting in Symi, and how 'once he got going he'd kill anyone'.[349] It cannot be ruled out that Lassen used his knife on Symi, but eyewitness accounts concentrate on the ferocity of the firefights.

Several of Lassen's comrades, who were not particularly squeamish otherwise, found his eagerness to 'slaughter bastards' somewhat alien. Some attributed it to a particularly bloodthirsty nature, others likened his hatred of the Germans to that of the Greek resistance. Both he and the Greeks fought against an enemy that had occupied their homeland. The eyewitnesses on Symi – like other places where he saw combat – agreed that Lassen showed extraordinary bravery and cold-bloodedness, even by SBS standards.

* * *

Around noon, First Lieutenant Fresemann was informed by radio that he could not count on air support as the Stukas were busy elsewhere. Shortly after, he found out that his men at the bridgehead on Muglia were running out of ammunition. At the same time, *Esperia* was being fired on by a 20 mm gun mounted on a British caique off the mouth of Pedi Bay. The Germans returned fire with a 28 mm anti-tank gun. After a ten-minute firefight, the British vessel pulled back, but the Germans were now under fire from both ends of the bay. At 13:00, Fresemann gave the order to withdraw. The last man was on board *Esperia* by 13:30, and Fresemann immediately gave orders for departure. During the embarkation, the motorboat *Parma* and the confiscated rowing boats that ferried the Germans from the beach out to *Esperia* came under fire from a 20 mm cannon in the town. No one was hit, but the shelling made it abundantly clear that the time had come to leave Symi. Just as the last Germans climbed aboard *Esperia*, three Stukas flew over the coast and bombed the town. At 16:30, Fresemann received instructions by radio to resume the attack, with a promise that reinforcements were en route from Rhodes. Before he had time to so much as think about obeying the order, the sailor responsible for *Esperia* informed him that there was only one vessel in the harbour at Rhodes ready to sail, and it could take a maximum of ten men. Fresemann continued to Rhodes, arriving at 19:00.

It perhaps says something about the severity of the fighting that both sides dramatically overestimated the enemy's strength. In his report, Fresemann estimated an enemy force of about 100 British (all 'big and powerful figures') and 2–300 Italians. According to a British report, the Germans landed 120 men.[350] While the German estimate of the number of Italians was fairly acurate, the number of Britons (even including the forty-five RAF and SAAF men) was unlikely to have been 100, and the German landing force, as mentioned previously, consisted of only fifty-four men. When the reports about the abortive landing on Symi reached *Marinegruppenkommando Süd*, the number of British troops on the island had risen to 300 men 'in bunkers'. The very next day, the Germans started to plan a new raid on Symi, with a larger force from Division Rhodos.[351]

British losses amounted to one dead (hit by several shots to the head and chest, according to Dr Ferris) and a handful of wounded. Five Italians were wounded. Among the British wounded were Lt Charles Bimrose, who was hit in the right upper arm but insisted on fighting on. When he later underwent surgery at a hospital in Cairo, two 9 mm bullets were found side by side in his arm. Seven Greeks were killed and several wounded. German losses amounted to two dead and four badly wounded (one of whom later died in the field hospital), plus one slightly wounded and nine missing. Six of the missing Germans had been taken prisoner, the other three were probably killed – either during the fighting or perhaps later by Greek civilians when they tried to hide in the mountains.[352*] If the information that Lassen killed at least three Germans is to be believed, he alone was responsible for over half of the German casualties.

* * *

According to the Italian head teacher in Symi, the locals were impressed that the Germans managed to get away from the island under the noses of the British and the Italians: 'What devils, the Germans!' Nevertheless, the raid on Symi was a rather costly defeat, and the Germans did not attempt to land again right away. Instead, the island became the target of a series of massive air strikes. On 8 October, Stukas attacked the town five times. Four British troops were killed when Lapraik's command post was hit. The Italian *carabinieri* barracks were destroyed, the port commander was injured, many homes were destroyed, and Dr Ferris's infirmary was razed to the ground, killing two nurses and six civilian patients. In total more than forty Greek civilians were killed during the first attack. The air raids continued for three days and destroyed most of the town. The bombing was so violent that Lapraik and his Italian colleagues assumed that it was the prelude to a new German landing, and had their men take up defensive positions. However, around 22:00 on 11 October, Lapraik received orders to evacuate Symi immediately. At 23:00 the British sailed for Kastellorizo, and at midnight the Italians followed with all of the garrison's weapons, food, etc. The evacuation was completed by 01:00 on 12 October. Before leaving, the British set fire to the Italian ammunition and fuel depots, resulting in a fire that destroyed all of the homes in the town's Murajo district. Lapraik's men also burnt some caiques that were being repaired, while seventeen seaworthy vessels, along with their crews and their families, were taken to Kastellorizo. Captain Redfern wrote about the evacuation:

> Petrol and Naphta dumps were destroyed but all other stores loaded in caiques. Some drunken Italians were not helping matters by firing at the working parties and throwing grenades at them under the impression that they were Germans. So ended the occupation of Simi. We left behind 4,500 unfortunate people, terrified, homeless and foodless. Their town gutted and on fire, and smelling from dead bodies in the wreckage. We also evacuated all caiques to prevent enemy from getting hold of them, so there is little they can do about it.[353]

Many young Greeks left the island with the British to sign up for the Free Greek forces in Cyprus.[354]

The Germans did not notice that their enemies had left the island, so the air strikes continued until 22 October.[355]

* * *

Captain Redfern's report gives a vivid impression of conditions on the tiny island of Kastellorizo and some information on Lassen's activities after the evacuation of Symi:

> 14 Oct. 1030 – Reached CASTELROSSO. About 50 caiques of various sorts followed us. SBS kept 6 good vessels and dispersed the good ones remaining (about 10) to CYPRUS and balance to TURKEY or whither they pleased.
>
> Caique crews were fed and promised sums of Lire 3000 to 5000 a month for their services. Actually they asked for no fee, stating their only wish was to serve GREECE.
>
> We got billets in the EAST corner, adjoining 4 M.Ls, 3 M.T.B.s, and 2 gun positions and with no protection from Air Raid. When we

questioned this we were told patronisingly that there was no possibility of bombing. A cruiser and 3 destroyers did nothing to allay our fears.

Beaufighters shot down one RAF seaplane in the harbour. Capt. LAPRAIK decided to visit CAIRO to clarify situation.

15 Oct. – Sanitary conditions beggar description. Lt. LASSEN went off on L.S. 7 to evacuate CLARKE and MACBETH and if possible STALLEN's [Stellin's] party [who had been left behind on Rhodes when Symi was evacuated]

16 Oct. – Capt. MILNER BARRY, Major BLAGDON and some 40 others who escaped from COS after 10 days privations in the hills arrived here with McLEOD RN. …

17 Oct. – 1200: Six Stukas and 2 M.E. 109s! The first blast took the roof and a wall off our billets leaving us open to public gaze but unhurt. Most of LRDG were out at the time.

There were some ugly scenes among the civilian population and about 6 killed and 12 injured among the Garrison Troops. One M.T.B. badly damaged.

18 Oct. – 1030: JU 88s bombed us harmlessly. We had now moved to outskirts of town and felt better. … Civil population evacuated to CYPRUS. Lt. STALLEN and BAIRAMIAN [previously spelled Bairaman, Redfern's interpreter on Symi] got back, after fantastic experiences.

Lt. LASSEN back with MACBETH and CLARKE, whom he picked up in TURKEY and parties complete. …

1500: Loaded up L.S. 7 with 4 tons H.E. 1 ton Petrol, 7 LRDG 8 SBS, and sailed for Leros.[356*]

* * *

In the weeks after the evacuation, the SBS returned to Symi several times. On the night of 18 October, a caique sailed into the town's harbour, and the two British officers on board met with the Italian harbour commander for two hours. Over the following week, the British paid two more night-time visits to deliver food to the locals. The food was of Italian origin, and the final shipment, which came from Leros, consisted entirely of canned goods. The locals concluded that the British were clearing out stocks ahead of an evacuation of Leros.

A British sergeant inspecting a 20 mm gun after the British recaptured Symi in July 1944.

Around the same time that the two British officers were visiting the port commander, Lassen and his patrol – perhaps while searching for Clarke, Macbeth and Stellin's party – went ashore at Panormitis, on the opposite side of the island. Here, they blew up the Italian radio station and took eight Italians prisoner.[357]

On 24 October, a German reconnaissance mission to Symi was postponed due to engine trouble. It was not until 2 November, after a spy had informed the Germans that the British and Italians had evacuated, that a new German force arrived on the island. It was set ashore from a motorised vessel accompanied by two patrol boats, two motor boats and fighter planes. According to the *Marinegruppenkommando Süd* war diary, the force only met 'resistance from light anti-aircraft guns, which were silenced by Junker Ju 88s'. Unfortunately the diary does not say anything about who was manning this battery two weeks after the British evacuation. This time the Germans installed a small garrison consisting of two officers and fifty Italians who remained loyal to the Axis. Its primary task was to staff and protect a telephone exchange that secured the connection to Rhodes via an underwater cable, and a radio station that connected Symi town with Panormitis.[358]

Leros, October–17 November 1943[359]

The German takeover of Kos ruined a British plan to use both Kos and Leros as springboards for an attack on Rhodes. Churchill then asked the Americans to reconsider the entire Allied strategy in the Mediterranean. He wanted to prioritise taking Rhodes and the other Dodecanese Islands so that they could serve as bases for Allied air power in the eastern Mediterranean. This would, in Churchill's eyes, give the Germans no option but to spread their forces far more thinly than the Allies, and wear down the Luftwaffe. However, Roosevelt did not want to redeploy forces from Italy or Britain to the Aegean. Churchill and the British military leaders in the Middle East had to find alternatives for the forces already deployed in the Aegean. Kos could not be recaptured with the forces available, but Middle East Command believed that if Leros and Samos could be supplied by submarines, planes and ships operating from Turkish waters, it would be possible to keep control of the two islands as forward bases.

The British planners' faith in the ability to hold Samos and Leros was reinforced by the arrival in the Aegean of four cruisers and five destroyers from Malta, along with a squadron of long-range RAF Beaufighters and several US bomber squadrons. Six other American squadrons also arrived, equipped with long-range and well armed P-38 Lightning fighters which were on loan to the Aegean from the central Mediterranean – albeit only for five days.

The British warships attacked German troop transports, sailed supplies to Leros and Samos, and attacked the ports on Kos and other German-occupied islands to give the impression that the Royal Navy had greater capacity in the area than was actually the case. However, the Germans still enjoyed air superiority, which greatly limited the Royal Navy's options.

As part of their routine interception and deciphering of German radio signals, the British learned that the Germans would very shortly launch an operation codenamed Leopard. It appeared to be an attack similar to the one on Kos, and the targets had to be Leros and Samos.[360]

Since Jellicoe and Turnbull's first visit to Leros on 13–14 September 1943, the British had landed nearly 4,000 men on the island, mainly from the 234th Infantry Brigade. Also on the island were some 7,000 Italian military personnel of various kinds, but only around 1,200 were actual soldiers or members of the military police *carabinieri* or *Guardia di Finanza*.[361] Their equipment was inadequate and some of it outdated. The RAF had 400 men to defend the airfield, and the Navy manned about 100 artillery pieces, ranging from 20 mm to 150 mm. These were old weapons, mostly in fixed positions that were poorly fortified, if at all, and lacking in fire-control systems and

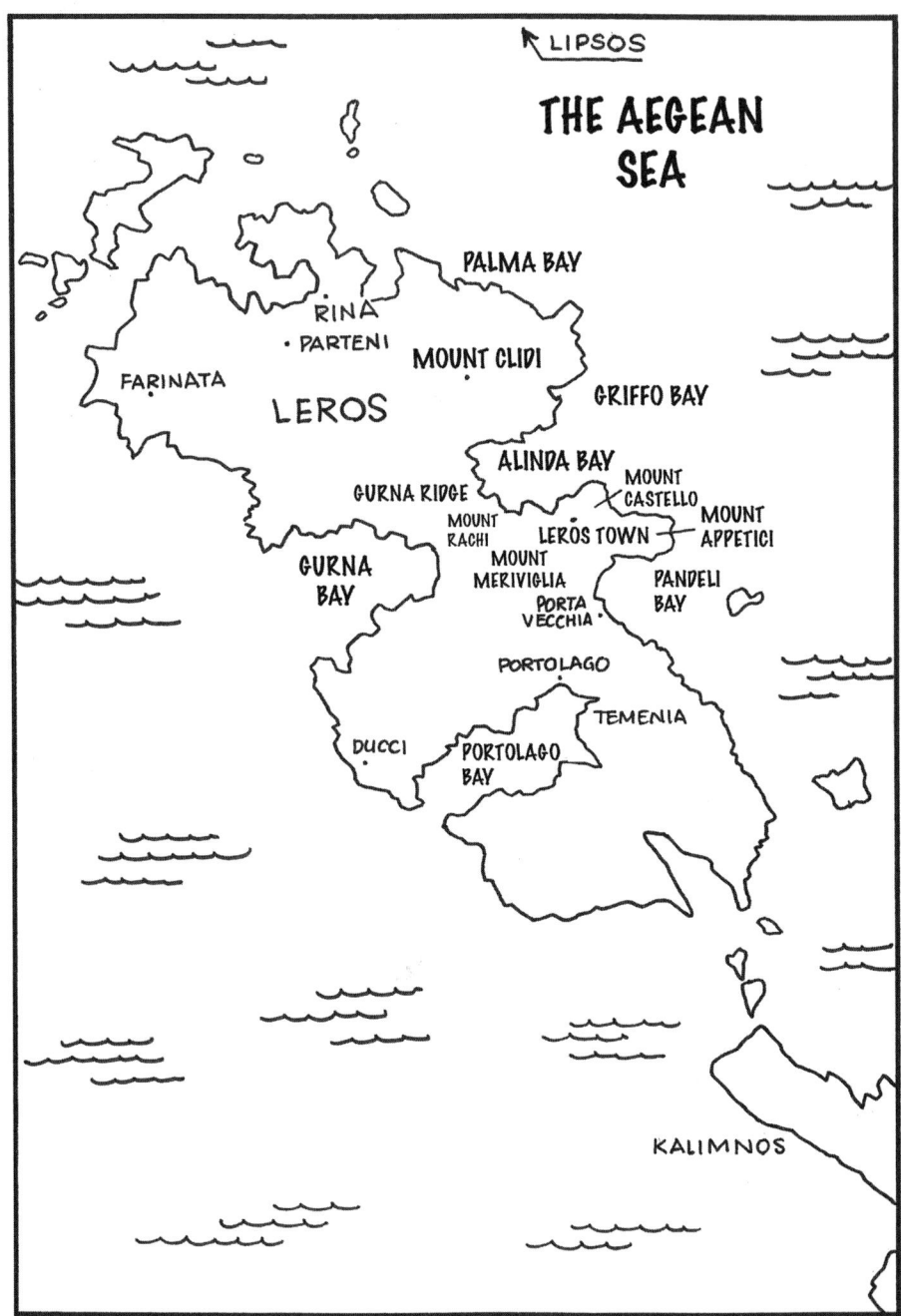

communications equipment. The Italian commander on Leros, Rear Admiral Luigi Mascherpa, favoured cooperation with the British. His men felt the same, but after a long period of uneventful garrison duty, they were not exactly keen to fight.[362]

On 26 September, the Luftwaffe bombed targets on Leros. The air raids continued, with great regularity, every morning and every evening, for the next fifty days. In October alone, there were 140 attacks.

On 10 November 1943, the Germans occupied Lipsos, Patmos, Fourni and Icaria. The net was tightening on the few remaining British bases in the Aegean.

* * *

Anders Lassen and his 'Irish patrol', which had been loaned to Lapraik during the operation on Symi, was reunited with David Sutherland's S Detachment on Leros. Sutherland and the rest of his men had arrived on Leros from the neighbouring island of Kalymnos (between Leros and Kos), which they had evacuated, along with patrols from LRDG and a commando force, when the Germans attacked Kos.[363] Lassen and his men came to Leros from Turkey, where they had spent quite some time anchored in one of the bays that served as a base for SBS activities. They had to abandon their first attempt to leave for Leros when a spy who lived on an island in the bay informed on them to the Germans, who sent out patrol boats to intercept their caique. The next attempt was made by night, under the Turkish flag, and went smoothly. Lassen and his men arrived safely in Alinda Bay on the east side of Leros. Sometime later, Lassen and the Greek skipper Marcos went back to the Turkish bay and picked up the German spy.[364]

David Sutherland saw Leros as

> an advanced form of hell. There were deep lines of exhaustion and defeat on all our faces, and the whiff of disaster lying just ahead. We were all demoralized by the ceaseless bombing and the fact that the enemy called all the shots. It was like Dunkirk and Tobruk all over again. I longed to get away.[365]

However, Sutherland saw one bright spot 'amid this Stygian gloom' when his radio operator brought news that Lassen had been awarded a third Military Cross for his actions on Symi. Sutherland had the dexterous radio operator produce a copy of the ribbon for the Military Cross, using white paper and Gentian blue paint, on which he placed two rosettes that he had made from the foil in a pack of cigarettes. Later that evening, he requested that the whole of S Detachment on Leros gather 'for an interesting event'.

> About fifteen were there, including Digger Rice, the Australian, Hancock, Cree, some of the Irish patrol and of course Lassen. I said,

'We can forget our Leros woes because I have just had a message from RFHQ that Anders Lassen has been awarded his third Military Cross for gallantry on Simi, and I am going to pin the ribbon on his chest now.' The roar of approval echoed around the bare hills above as I walked forward to shake his hand. Our eyes met: for once in his life he was nonplussed and mumbled an incoherent reply. But knowing him so well, I knew how touched and proud he was and we of him. We drank everything in sight long into the night and slept like babes.[366]

* * *

Lassen briefly escaped the depressingly passive waiting and the exhausting air raids. As an experienced seaman and amphibious raider, he was given responsibility for one of the numerous evacuations carried out by SBS and MI9 during the British collapse in the Aegean Sea in autumn 1943. A message had been received that an LRDG man – perhaps a survivor of the fighting on Kos or Levitha, where forty-one LRDG men out of a force of fifty had been killed – was hiding on Kalymnos, a German-occupied neighbouring island to Leros. Lassen was given command of the caique *LS7*, whose skipper was busy with another operation. He and a Greek familiar with the area departed from Leros at 19:00. At midnight he dropped the Greek off on Kalymnos to find the missing man and bring him to the agreed location at the beach in 48 hours. Lassen repeated his nocturnal voyage two days later, and everything went according to plan. The Greek and the LRDG man were taken on board and transported safely to Alinda Bay on Leros.[367*]

LRDG's severe losses on Levitha weakened the force so badly that it was largely sidelined for the rest of the war in the Aegean, where the SBS and Greek Sacred Squadron were the only remaining raiders on the Allied side.[368]

* * *

The Greek Sacred Squadron, which like the SBS belonged to Raiding Forces, was part of the Leros garrison. Tsigantes was a good friend of both Jellicoe and Sutherland, who admired the Greek's courage and patriotism and considered him a great military talent. Tsigantes and Lassen came to appreciate each other too, and Lassen went on to spend periods of his leave on raids with Tsigantes and his 'Sacred Greeks'.[369]

* * *

Lassen decided to lift the pessimistic mood on the island. A handful of caiques had docked at Leros to deliver food to the garrison, and Lassen arbitrarily ordered them to depart again and take supplies to other islands, where they would benefit the local population.[370]

* * *

On 11 November 1943, intercepted radio messages revealed that the German attack was planned for the following day. The information provoked Major General Hall, commander of the combined British forces in the Aegean, to move his headquarters from Leros to Samos, which did nothing for the garrison's already threadbare morale. Jellicoe shared Hall's pessimism about the chances of holding on to Leros, and he ordered Sutherland to go to Turkey that night. Sutherland did not have to be told twice. He got his hands on a small caique lying in Pandeli Bay on the east side of Leros, and sailed at midnight to the small Turkish port of Gümüslük, accompanied by lieutenants Harold Gordon Chevalier and Stefan M. Kasoulis, as well as eight other ranks. On the way, Sutherland's caique passed close to the German Battlegroup Müller, which was heading in the opposite direction to land on the north of Leros in the early morning of 12 November.[371*]

* * *

Lassen and the other SBS men on Leros took part in fierce fighting with the 700 German parachutists who landed on the narrow Gurna ridge that links the north of Leros with the rest of the island. The British opened fire while the Germans were still in the air, killing or wounding 280 before they fired a shot. RAF officer Tony Grech, who was with Lassen in the British command post, was surprised when Lassen stopped him just as he was about to lift his rifle to participate in 'the clay pigeon shoot'. 'Don't. It will just tell them where the command post is,' said Lassen. Grech noted that it was 'a strange comment from someone who was supposed to be a killing machine'.

Lassen did not take part in the final battle on Leros because Jellicoe sent him to Samos with a patrol including sergeants Roger Wright and Jack Nicholson, corporal Dick Holmes and the medical orderly Porter Jarrell.[372]

Officially the Battle of Leros ended at 17:00 on 16 November when the commander of the British forces on the island, Brigadier Tilney, capitulated and ordered the head of the Italian forces, Rear Admiral Mascherpa, to do the same. The fierce fighting resulted in British losses of about 600 dead (among them Captain Redfern of the LRDG who was killed in action on

12 November) and 3,200 PoWs, many of them wounded. Of the Italian forces, only some of whom had been deployed in the fighting, 87 were killed and about 5,350 were taken prisoner. German losses – dead, wounded and missing – totalled 520 men.

* * *

While Tilney was negotiating the terms of surrender with the Germans, he was suddenly joined by Jellicoe, who had heard nothing from the command post for over twelve hours and had made his own way there to request orders for his SBS men. Jellicoe was taken prisoner, but released again under the pretext that he would find his men and order them to surrender. The Germans failed to ask him for his word of honour that he would return – so he made his escape. His men had not been involved in the final bloody battle, but had acquitted themselves well against the German paratroopers. They retained some of the fighting spirit that the other British troops had lost. Around forty SBS men continued to fight, alongside scattered groups of others (approximately 200 in total). Eventually, on the night of 17 November, they were evacuated to Lipsos, about five miles north of Leros. A few days later they continued on to Turkey. The SBS lost only seven men on Leros and departed with its weapons and equipment intact.

* * *

On the afternoon of 16 November, Middle East Command had ordered that Leros be evacuated that night. Small groups of British soldiers sifted their way out to the coast at Portolago Bay, where a small fleet of caiques and other craft waited to take them on board after dark. Over the next four nights, British soldiers were evacuated on vessels manned by the SBS and others, operating from Turkey or the surrounding islands that were still in British hands. However, they only managed to rescue about 100 British soldiers from Leros.

Samos, 17 November–December 1943

On 17 November 1943, the Luftwaffe, which had frequently bombed Samos, launched the fiercest attack yet on the island's two main towns: Vathy and Tigani.[373] In Vathy a fifth of the houses were razed to the ground, while Tigani was almost completely wiped off the map. Many soldiers and civilians were killed, and the already pessimistic mood on the island plummeted even further. The following day, Middle East Command ordered the island's commander, Brigadier Baird, to evacuate all British forces. Baird was also tasked with evacuating the Greek Sacred Squadron and the Greek partisans – who, while Samos was under British control, had acted as a kind of militia under the command of the Greek-speaking Major Dennis Hamson.[374*] The Italian General Soldarelli felt that the 2,500 Italian soldiers on the island would be unable to withstand a German attack on their own – especially since a significant proportion of his men were members of the fascist militia (24. Legione MVSN), who it was feared might prefer to fight on the German side against the regular Italian soldiers from the infantry division Cuneo. There were other problems too: food and drinking water were in short supply on the island, and the locals were convinced that the Italian presence was attracting the German air raids. On 19 November, Soldarelli informed Italian High Command that he intended to evacuate Samos. Baird and Soldarelli sailed to Kusadasi, on the coast of Turkey, to negotiate with the Turkish authorities on passage for the British and Italian troops. The German success on Leros had made an impression on the Turks,[375] and the negotiations were protracted and difficult. However, thanks to, among others, the British military attaché in Ankara, the Turks eventually agreed to give the evacuees permission to pass through Turkey to Syria. Along with MI9 in Cairo, Rees and his colleague Commander Wolfson, who was consul in

Anders Lassen (left) on Samos.

Istanbul, immediately started to organize a fleet of caiques and launch an operation that would develop into a miniature Dunkirk. Although the first departures were to be from the port of Vathy, every effort was made to give the impression that the evacuation would be from Tigani.[376]

The evacuation of the British and 'important Greek' personnel began on the night of 20 November. It continued the following night, now including the Italians.[377] Lassen participated actively in the difficult work of organizing the embarkation. He had to coordinate – in the dark, and in English, Greek and Italian – the many caiques sailing in and out of the small harbour, the quays of which were swarming with British and Italian soldiers and Greek partisans and civilians. This required a talent for improvisation and the ability to maintain an overview, as well as diplomatic skills and an air of authority. Major Hamson later described Lassen's performance as an 'example' and an 'inspiration':

> He was a wonderful man to be with in a tight corner. His coolness and courage in action were outstanding and were gradually coming to be considered a matter of course.[378]

It is not known exactly how many were evacuated from Samos. According to an official British report, the total number up to and including 23 November was 222 British, 358 members of the Greek Sacred Squadron, 400 Greek guerrillas and 2,978 Italians.[379]*

On the afternoon of 22 November, Jäger Regiment 1 'Brandenburg' occupied the island without meeting resistance. The evacuation continued over the next couple of nights. The members of the island's fascist militia joined the Germans, while the soldiers of Divisione Cuneo, who had not had time to leave Samos before the rescue operation stopped, headed for the mountains.

Lassen and his men had also remained on Samos. Like some of the Italians who were left behind, and some Greek partisans who did not make it off the island in the first wave, the SBS men hid in the mountains, from where they planned to wage a guerrilla war against the German occupying force. Somewhat against their wishes, Lassen led his men out of their hiding place and down to Vathy, to show the Greeks that there were still British forces on the island and give the impression that there were many more than was actually the case. The raiders took the opportunity to boost their supplies with food that the evacuees had left behind.[380] Lassen and his patrol remained on Samos for a couple of weeks after the Germans had landed.

On 29 November, the chief of staff of Divisione Cuneo went to Izmir, where he secured Rees's help to evacuate the approximately 2,000 Italian soldiers still on Samos. The new series of nightly evacuations lasted a week, and Lassen played an important role as organizer and driving force. The evacuation again made use of MI9's fleet of caiques and small vessels that had been acquired by other means. However, the short distance between Samos and the Turkish coast also invited more imaginative solutions.

It may or may not have been Lassen who thought of gathering all the rope that could be found in Vathy and the surrounding fishing villages and military stores, and tying together a number of small boats and empty water bottles to make a mile-long lifeline that would keep non-swimmers among the evacuees afloat as they crossed the strait under their own power.

> We fixed the rope at both ends despite being told by one of our Marine members that we were using the wrong sort of rope. As soon as it was dark we sent the first Italian along the rope. He disappeared but soon reappeared, swearing (we assumed) in Italian. When Andy asked our interpreter, a signaller named Shohet who spoke several languages, what he had said Shohet was at first reluctant to tell him but was finally persuaded to do so. 'He said, "Stick your rope up your arse!"' Viv Shohet replied. Andy was very embarrassed. … As we laughed, Andy threw one of his notorious temper tantrums.[381*]

After this last major evacuation, Lassen and his patrol left Samos too – he and Sergeant Jack Nicholson were the very last to leave. For some time, however, Lassen and the other SBS and MI9 men continued to make nightly trips to Samos to pick up evacuees. In the weeks following Middle East Command's order to evacuate, thousands were rescued from the island. The Germans took some 4,000 prisoners on Samos.[382*]

* * *

On 27 November, the Germans occupied Santorini, where there had been no British troops, and Kastellorizo, which the British had evacuated before the enemy arrived. The fall of Kastellorizo meant that the British had lost their final stronghold in the Aegean.

Back to Atlit, December 1943

Despite vigorous efforts by British and Italian diplomats and agents, there were limits to the Turks' good will. The refugees from Samos were interned on a narrow, sandy strip off Kusadasi. Boredom was great, the frustrations many, and the men's nerves were frayed after the events of recent weeks. A brawl between two members of the Irish Patrol led to an intervention by an officer from another unit, who outranked Lassen. For his trouble, he received a torrent of abuse from the Dane, who then let the patrol's champion boxer restore calm by knocking out the two brawlers.[383]

After a few weeks of involuntary beach life, the evacuees were put on a livestock train that took them from Kusadasi to Aleppo in Syria – a three-day journey of around 600 miles. Lassen brought with him a dog, Pipo, which he had found on Leros. Pipo would prove useful when it came to meeting women, but was less popular with his fellow passengers on the journey through Turkey. One of those who absolutely did not appreciate Pipo's company was corporal Dick Holmes.

> Unfortunately, I found myself in the same truck as Lassen and his bloody dog, Pepo. During the journey, this animal urinated over the sleeping bags of several occupants of the compartment but when he approached my sleeping space, I left Andy in no doubt as to the fate of his cherished pet if he committed the same indiscretion on my property. Not sure of his ability to put me in my place physically and being unarmed, Andy was forced to swallow his pride.[384]

In Aleppo, the British were issued with new kit and spent the night in a camp before heading south to Haifa and Atlit.[385]* The time spent in the camp gave rise to one of many clashes between the SBS men and the more traditionally minded members of the British officer corps:

> We had just packed our kit prior to our departure when the door of the hut opened and an elderly colonel and a sergeant entered. The officer congratulated us for our efforts for which we were very grateful but then he went on about his adventures in the previous war. We suffered his waffling for some time then some of us began to edge towards the door. The old boy was on a roll, however, and he rambled on despite the hint that we were giving him. Finally, we began to hoist our rucksacks on to our shoulders and he got the message. Then he handed a fistful of banknotes to his aide, who handed us one each. Now most of us had secreted some valuables on our person or in our packs and this silly old bastard was giving us a Syrian pound note – value 2 shillings. My friend and I had liberated a number of gold sovereigns from a MI5 officer who had attached himself to us on Samos, each of which was worth 5 pounds sterling on the open market. We had been away from base for over three months. Hounded from island to island, we had survived an attack by German paratroops on Leros, been divebombed for about an hour on

Samos where we had lost two of our number (another had lost his life in the crossing to Turkey), been interned for a couple of weeks by the Turks, then loaded into cattle cars on the Turkish railway and issued meagre rations during the journey across the country into Syria and this silly old sod rewards us with 2 shillings! My friend was the first to the door and he bent over and wiped his arse on the note and dropped it on the floor! We all followed his example.[386]

Anders Lassen skiing in the mountains of Lebanon.

After a period on leave in Cairo, the SBS returned to the camp in Atlit and Raiding Forces' headquarters in Azzib to spend a few months resting, training and reorganizing. The loss of the Aegean was a searing defeat – but for the raiders it was also a liberation. After months of transporting and escorting others, and doing infantry work for which they were neither trained nor equipped, they were at last able to concentrate on their original purpose again.

Chapter Thirty-One

Raiders in the Aegean, 1944

You can't conceive how hard it is to move and fight at night. The country is rugged, the ground rough. Everything is new and strange. The nights are pitch black, you grope with your feet. You step into holes, and fall sprawling in little gullies and creeks. You trudge over ploughed ground and push through waist-high shrubs. You go as a man blindfolded, feeling unsure and off balance, but you keep on going.

(Ernie Pyle, *An Inconceivable Life*, 1 May 1943)

Raiding Forces HQ

Following the reorganization, Brigadier Turnbull's Raiding Forces HQ in Azzib commanded not only the SBS but also the Long Range Desert Group (which, after the disaster on Levitha in October 1943, mainly sent very small groups out to islands, where they went into hiding and reported German naval movements and other marine traffic by radio), the Greek Sacred Squadron (which shared raider functions with SBS) and Holding Unit Special Forces, which was a sort of depot from which officers and men were allocated to other units. Turnbull's command also included the Raiding Support Regiment, which had been established in October 1943 to support the other raider units with heavier weapons and equipment, as well as a section of the Royal Marine Boom Patrol Detachment, who were trained to carry out sabotage and reconnaissance on targets that could only be reached by canoe. Also under Raiding Forces HQ were men from the Royal Electrical and Mechanical Engineers (REME), the Royal Army Medical Corp (RAMC) and the Royal Corps of Signals (RCS). In addition there was the small force known as the Kalpaks, consisting of perhaps a dozen anti-Turkish Kurds and/or Armenians, which had been established in 1941 and were to be activated in the event that Turkey renounced its neutrality in favour of Germany. They were commanded by archaeologist and philologist Captain Terence Bruce Mitford, who later transferred to the SBS. The Kalpaks were to operate as guides and scouts along with other units of the Raiding Forces, but individual members could be used for special reconnaissance missions or to kill or abduct important officers.[387]

Operation Zeppelin

As the SSRF had done in the English Channel in 1942, and the SBS had done in Crete and Sardinia in July 1943, Turnbull's Raiding Forces served as important decoys in 1944. Raids in the eastern Mediterranean were designed to divert German attention away from Operation Overlord, the D-Day landing in Normandy that the British and Americans had finally agreed would take place in June 1944. Once again, those doing the work were unaware of the bigger picture.

To keep Overlord a secret, the Allies drew up a diversionary strategy codenamed Bodyguard. It had two aims: to make the Germans spread their forces across the whole of Europe, from northern Norway to the Turkish border, so they would lack the capacity to fend off the invasion of Normandy; and to give them the impression that no invasion would be launched before July 1944. Bodyguard involved no fewer than thirty-six different plans and dozens of associated operations and decoy manoeuvres – many of which, under the codename Zeppelin, took place in south and south-east Europe.

The overall objective of Zeppelin was to fool the Germans into thinking that the Allies, since they could not attack in north-west Europe before late summer 1944, would launch a large-scale spring attack in the Balkans – specifically, a US/British landing on the coast around Trieste, a British attack on Greece, and a British/Soviet incursion on the Romanian coast. Zeppelin was also designed to give the impression that the Allies wanted to encourage Turkey to join in an attack on the Aegean Islands and then continue up through Greece towards central Europe, and that the Allies planned new large-scale landings behind German lines in the north of Italy, from both the Mediterranean and the Adriatic. From here they would supposedly advance north through the Ljubljana Pass to attack Munich and Vienna.

The Germans in the Aegean

After the British withdrawal, the German front line in the Aegean consisted of the 'iron ring' of Crete, Karpathos and Rhodes in the south, and behind them, to the east, Leros, Kos and Samos. It was far from a watertight and impenetrable line of defence though. The Aegean Sea, with its hundreds of islands behind the front, was an ongoing problem for German military commanders.

In January 1944 the Germans had two divisions on Crete, almost one full division on Rhodes, a total of 800 men on Karpathos, Kasos and Saria, 4,000 men on Leros, 2,000 on Kos, 200 on Astypalaia and 150 each on Symi and Tilos.

As for the other islands, the Germans initially tried to station garrisons – albeit often very small, almost symbolic ones – on as many of them as possible. This turned out to be too much of a logistical burden, partly due to a lack of transport ships. Instead they began moving large forces between the islands, spending short periods on each in turn.

The Germans continued to enjoy air superiority over the Aegean. Most of the naval forces had been transferred to the Black Sea, but the 9th Torpedo Boat Flotilla and 21st Anti-Submarine Flotilla were still in the Aegean, based on Leros. They had fast and heavily armed ships manned by skilled officers, and would be an effective counter against raids, even at short notice and over long distances. They also had a number of caiques, some sailing under the German flag and some armed with guns, while others were chartered on demand from Greek skippers.[388]

Operation Fireeater, LSF and Tewfik

After the defeat in the Aegean, the British Middle East Command mapped out a new strategy for operations in the Eastern Mediterranean. Turnbull's Raiding Forces were to draw as many enemy forces as possible to the islands and then work with the RAF and Royal Navy to keep them there. To achieve these objectives, the SBS and Greek Sacred Squadron were to attack small isolated German units. The idea was to provoke the German command into sending reinforcements to as many small islands as possible, generally harass the garrisons, and

D.J.T. Turnbull, CO Raiding Forces HQ.

above all destroy enemy ships (including Greek caiques that sailed for the Germans or would be likely to fall into their hands) and telephone, radio and radar installations, as well as stores of ammunition, fuel and other supplies. In other words, precisely the kind of guerrilla warfare for which the SBS had been set up. The SBS patrols were also to send daily observation reports to headquarters in Cairo about any German ships, etc, that they could not attack themselves, so that the Royal Navy's submarines and surface ships and RAF's long-range Beaufighters could take care of them. Some of the attacks would be ordered from above, in consultation with the RAF and Royal Navy, others

One of the patrol boats that provided transportation for the raiders.

would be based on suggestions from the raiders themselves, 'as opportunity offers'.[389] The Aegean was divided in two: the Greek Sacred Squadron worked north of Leros, the SBS took care of the southern islands.[390] The plan was originally given the codename 'Bullfrog' but this was soon changed to the more dramatic 'Fireeater'.[391]

The raids were to be launched from large schooners moored along the Turkish coast, where the raiders would wait, store their supplies, etc, and from where they could sail to the islands aboard caiques belonging to Adrian Seligman's Levant Schooner Flotilla (LSF). The caiques, manned by volunteers and commanded by reserve officers aged between 19 and 23, had diesel engines originally built for Matilda tanks. They gave the vessels a top speed of about seven knots, which was only slightly faster than a conventional engine due to the shape of the caiques' hulls. On the other hand, Matilda engines were far more powerful, so they managed the same speed at half the power, making them much quieter. When Seligman commenced operations in the Aegean in summer 1943, the caiques' radius was limited by the fact that, to avoid attacks by German aircraft, they could only sail at night and had to be back in hiding before dawn. This changed after a chance encounter with one of Seligman's old school friends, Major Maurice Green, which opened up a slew of new opportunities for the LSF. Green, who had exhibited an artistic bent at school, and was now head of the 9th Army camouflage unit, made Seligman's caiques invisible. The masts were in loose mountings, and could be dismounted and laid flat on the deck. The vessels also had huge camouflage nets that stretched across a series of long bamboo sticks. The results were so effective that the camouflaged caiques could lie in hiding almost anywhere during the day and set sail again the next night. This meant that their range was only limited by supplies of fuel, food and water.[392] The crews of the LSF ships would hide their uniforms and sail under the Turkish flag when they were in Turkish waters, and under a German flag when they were in waters under German control.[393]

During the Aegean operations, the SBS's home was the 180-grt schooner *Tewfik*. Each of the three detachments (L, M and S) would take turns on active duty, which involved being stationed on *Tewfik* for about a month at a time. The other two detachments spent their time on leave and training, including skiing in the Lebanese mountains.

* * *

On 28 November 1943, shortly after Lassen had returned to Azzib following the evacuation of Samos and the train ride across Turkey, he was again in hospital for a prolonged period. It is not known whether it was to have the burns from Symi treated, because of his old kidney disease, or because of dysentery, jaundice, malaria or one of the other ills that plagued the British and Germans alike in Greece – ailments not ameliorated by a way of life in which poor hygiene, chain smoking, canned food, chronic tension and lack of sleep were the rule rather than the exception.[394]

In the bed next to Lassen in 64 British General Hospital in Alexandria was Hugh Stowell, who had met Lassen on Leros.

> Pipo was with him. When the doctors came around, the dog was shoved into my bed and I had to keep him quiet. …. [He] was still on – and very understandably – about wanting to kill as many Germans as he could. He was a tense fellow, very highly strung. Not raving, but in very good form.[395]

Lassen was discharged from hospital on 10 January 1944. The next day, he travelled from Alexandria to Beirut to help prepare the SBS for life on *Tewfik*. L Squadron was to take the first stint in the Aegean, but the experienced Lassen, who actually belonged to S Squadron, was chosen for the difficult trip from Beirut to the Turkish coast to set up the floating base.[396]* At dawn on 24 January, *Tewfik* set sail along with *LS9*, which served as Seligman's flagship, and the LSF caiques *LS3*, *LS5* and *LS10*. Lassen had command of *Tewfik*'s Greek crew. LSF's intelligence officer, W.E. Benyon-Tinker, who was to have much contact with Lassen in the months to come, described him as a gentle-voiced, very youthful-seeming person. His looks belied him! He was, I consider, one of the toughest and bravest men I have ever had the pleasure of meeting. In the S.B.S. – themselves a lot of hand-picked men – who savaged the Germans on every possible opportunity and with every possible weapon – he even managed to stand out. I could praise him no higher than this![397]

Almost immediately, the convoy ran into a storm, which only abated on the morning of 25 January as they approached Famagusta on Cyprus – the first port of call on the way to Kos Bay. The two big schooners, *Tewfik* and *LS9*, rode the storm without major difficulties. However, the smaller *LS5* struggled in the high waves, though fortunately not before *LS9* had attached a tow rope and taken its crew on board, saving them from a perilous, stormy night aboard a small vessel that sat low in the water and offered no shelter from the elements.

Tewfik's cargo had shifted in the harsh weather, and there were problems with the engine. The stop in Famagusta was extended to 24 hours to repair the damage. In the evening, the sailors and the SBS other ranks were granted shore leave, and became embroiled in a fight with men from other corps – a fairly common occurrence that reinforced the raiders' sense of solidarity and 'otherness'. Once the cabaret in which hostilities broke out had been totally wrecked, the fight spilled out onto the street. The brawlers made it back to their ships without serious injury, but the port commander forbade the LSF men from setting foot in Famagusta for the next month. This punishment was felt particularly keenly when an engine failure forced *LS9* to spend three days in port and the crew were not permitted to set foot on dry land.[398]

While *LS9* languished in Famagusta, *Tewfik* and *LS3* sailed on to Kastellorizo, which the British had retaken a week after the rapid evacuation, and which would act as the gateway to the Aegean and a supply station for Raiding Forces for the rest of the war.[399] Jellicoe joined them on Kastellorizo and they sailed further up the Turkish coast. For the next nine months, *Tewfik* and *LS9* would sail between various deep bays (Gulluk, Türkbükü, Deremen, Comce, Kiervasili, Yedi Atdullah and others) on the coast, close to Leros and Kos. From time to time a Turkish official had to be bribed – e.g. with a pair of boots, a commodity apparently not to be had for love nor money in Turkey – and senior Turkish officials were, of course, well aware of what was going on. However, despite recent German successes in the Aegean that heightened concerns in Ankara, they turned a blind eye to the British activities as long as they remained fairly discreet. The Germans too were aware that the British were abusing Turkish neutrality, but were unable to persuade the Turks to do anything about it, and did not want to damage relations with them by

Tewfik in Deremen Bay on the coast of Turkey.

attacking targets in Turkish territory.[400] Besides, the German *Küstenjäger* from the Brandenburg Regiment also used the Turkish coast as a hideout and base from time to time.

Spies on the Turkish coast kept an eye on British movements and warned the Germans of impending raids. When one highly active German agent in Bodrum was 'removed' by Lapraik's men, it was a step too far for the Turks, who arrested him the next time he set foot on land. After three weeks in custody Lapraik was released due to a combination of diplomatic pressure from the British military attaché in Ankara and threats that his men would attack the prison. His case was also strengthened by the fact that the spy had been 'removed' so thoroughly that the authorities were unable to produce a corpse.[401]

* * *

In early March 1944, S Squadron replaced L Squadron on *Tewfik*. To guarantee continuity, it was a three-stage process as the L Squadron patrols returned from operations.[402] The commander of S Squadron, David Sutherland, was in hospital with jaundice when his men sailed for Turkey. He only arrived on *Tewfik* on 26 March, by which time life on board had fallen into more or less fixed routines. He was accompanied by an American war correspondent, who 'had characteristically heard of the ops. From a Greek wife in Alex and then through the American M.L.O. [Military Liaison Officer] had got permission from the Admiralty to come up.'[403]

Sutherland later described his first impression of *Tewfik:*

> I felt excited, interested and a bit apprehensive as to how my task would develop when I first saw the RN ship *Tewfik* moored deep in the wooded inlet Yeti Atdullah. The familiar, friendly faces of Milner-Barry, Lassen, Casulli, Nicholson, Conby, Darcy, Henderson and others crowded around the ship's railing asking if I had mail from home or newspapers. I had both. Climbing aboard *Tewfik*, in which I was to spend the next six weeks, I was reminded of some piratical scene from *Treasure Island*, with contemporary arms, ammunition, equipment and noises for good measure. There was the homely smell of unwashed bodies, mixed with a whiff of garlic cooking in the galley, the quiet background noise of the ship's activities was overlaid by the raucous din from the petrol-driven patrol radio battery-chargers. The ship's large hold was filled with masses of men sleeping in hammocks and bunks. Forward of the hold was a large office used as an operation planning room, table in the middle, chairs around, walls covered with maps. There too, was the terminal of our radio link with RFHQ at Azzib and the outside world. I pinched for myself a small panelled cabin with a comfortable bunk and fitted writing desk. It was two flights of wooden stairs above the Ops Room.[404]

Halki, January–February 1944

While the Allies started transferring troops and landing craft from the Mediterranean to Britain ahead of Operation Overlord, Lassen carried out the first raid of the new campaign by the SBS in the Aegean Sea.

On 31 January, he once again landed on Halki, this time from one of the motor gunboats (*HDML1083*) that had been added to Raiding Forces to increase their range. Lassen's force consisted of four men, including his faithful companion Sean O'Reilly, the 42-year old Irish Corporal, and Katsikas, the Greek lieutenant, who acted as interpreter. First, Lassen and Katsikas visited the mayor. The mayor, who in October had been very accommodating to the German captain Rehe and his men, said that the island's garrison now consisted of six members of the Italian fascist police. To Lassen this 'hardly seemed … to be worth the voyage',[405]* but he went to the police station anyway. After breaking down the doors, he took the Italians prisoner and seized a typewriter, a shotgun, six rifles, a radio receiver, two Beretta machine guns and a telephone. 'I could not find any money, but

I noticed a safe.' Wherever they went, the SBS men were very interested in vaults and safes, and not only because they might contain documents of intelligence value.

Lassen was about to blow open the safe when he was interrupted by the sound of a motor-boat engine. It turned out to be a German 'launch of respectable tonnage' from Rhodes entering the harbour. Lassen left a corporal Smart behind with five of the Italians, and took the sixth down to the harbour, where he and his men hid behind a corner, around sixty feet from the quay. Under threat, the Italian welcomed the Germans – but when the patrol boat docked at the quay the raiders opened fire. Two of the six Germans on board were injured and the others surrendered without resistance. The patrol boat was found to be carrying plentiful supplies, including four live piglets. The cargo was possibly intended for the people of Halki (the Germans, like the British, were aware that food and other daily necessities were a useful means of securing the islanders' help), or perhaps the Germans were on the way to another island and just docked in Halki to show the flag and check out the lie of the land. Lassen towed the boat and its cargo back to *Tewfik* in Deremen Bay where the prisoners were interrogated.

The only casualty among the raiders was Lassen himself, who had been hit in the foot or leg by a bullet from O'Reilly's submachine gun. He was furious at first, but as they headed back to the Turkish coast he forgave the older man, who was hiding from the expected wrath of his superior in the stern of the boat. The Irishman's mood improved when Lassen handed him a bottle of rum. In the following days, Lassen made little fuss about the wound – and to save O'Reilly from getting into trouble, he skated over the details of how it had happened.[406]

A breather and celebrity status

Failing to take care of the wound landed Lassen another spell in the hospital in Alexandria, where Milner-Barry visited him. Despite Lassen's attempt to cover up what O'Reilly had done, Milner-Barry had heard how Lassen was 'accidentally shot by that splendid Irishman'.[407] Like the last time, Lassen had company in the hospital in the form of Pipo. This time the dog was exiled from the ward by a head nurse and sent to board with Lassen's wardmate Lieutenant Cole who lived in Alexandria with his wife. This was the beginning of a firm friendship, and Lassen often stayed with the Coles when he was on leave in Alexandria.

He also found sanctuary with the Danish couple Vagn and Else Hoffmann, who lived in Helwan, just south of Cairo, where Vagn managed a cement plant. The Hoffmanns were generous hosts to all Danish and Norwegian volunteers who passed through Cairo. This was how Lassen met Jørgen Halck, a fellow Dane but a lieutenant and intelligence officer in the South African Army:

Anders Lassen in the garden of the Hoffmann family in Helwan.

> 'How do you do, sir!' I said and saluted. 'Hello,' he said, 'call me Andy' … He was very eager, leaned forward and rapped his knuckles on the table to underline his words.
>
> 'So, you are heading back to the front,' he said and sent me an encouraging grin. 'We can expect some great battles in the near future, and this time it will be *us* who attack. We *must* win those battles. The result of them is going to mean everything for us Danish volunteers. The bigger the victory, the more the resistance movement in Denmark will grow. It will give them new hope and,' he pounded the table, 'we out here mean nothing without the resistance fighters back home. It must not be the case that we get Denmark back as a gift. It must be returned to us as something we have fought for and deserve!' …
>
> Suddenly he leaned forward again (and reminded … me of a very tightly coiled spring) and looked tougher than you would think possible for such a young man. 'I hate the Germans,' he said slowly, 'because they broke a treaty. The 9th of April was a declaration of war against a defenceless country. The foreigner, whoever he is, who against our desire sets foot one inch over the Danish border, must be our enemy. And enemies are to be fought with all available means!' He pounded the table again, and his voice was measured and deeply serious when he said: 'Since the 9th of April, I have never pardoned an enemy capable of resistance, and I will never ask for it!' … When I took leave of the hosts … Lassen came up to me, slapped me on the shoulder, sent me a boyish smile and added half shyly, as if 10 minutes had not passed since he last had said something: 'But I'm such a poor hater. I think even I could shake the Germans' hands when Denmark is free again.'[408]*

Halck told Lassen that he had recently interrogated a German PoW, Captain von Steinertz, who had mentioned Lassen by name and said there was a price of 20,000 Reichsmark on his head. Halck or his source may have exaggerated the size of the reward (which was 7 to 8 times a German industrial worker's annual wages[409]), but in spring 1944 the Germans dropped leaflets informing the raiders that there was a price on their heads and that they would be executed if captured.[410] It may sound surprising that the Germans knew Lassen by name, but given the number of spies who worked for them in Egypt, Palestine, Lebanon and especially Turkey, it is not completely improbable. While the SBS was cloaked in secrecy, it was also much talked-about – so much so that when L Detachment needed to replenish its ranks after the losses in Sardinia in July 1943, there was almost a queue of applicants who were attracted by the stories that circulated about the raiders' accomplishments and lifestyle.[411] Some of those stories may well have featured Lassen as a named protagonist. Several British officers have described their surprise at meeting such a young, friendly and unobtrusive man, after hearing so much about the wild and bloodthirsty Danish warrior with two bars to his MC. German PoWs, who were terrified at the prospect of meeting the infamous Dane, were astonished at Lassen's subdued demeanour.[412]

* * *

Not all of the time Lassen spent on leave was as quiet as his visits to the homes of the Coles and Hoffmanns. When off duty, he was often thoughtless and excessive, and quickly squandered every penny he had. He liked to drink hard and fight harder in the lower-class establishments he frequented, but he could also be kind and gentle, and had a way with the women. For a while Lassen had a relationship with a beautiful singer and dancer, Aleca, who performed at one of Beirut's semi-fashionable nightclubs. The two were often seen together, but she was far from the only one spotted on his arm.[413] Lassen spent early March 1944 in Alexandria. A British naval officer with whom he struck up a close friendship described the unorthodox appearance and coarse attitude to women of 'our Danish S.B.S. murderer'. Lassen seemed to own just one khaki shirt, which he wore 'attractively unbuttoned' and kept tied together with a boot lace. He thought prostitutes were 'the only genuine women'.[414]

At 'dawnish' on Wednesday 22 March, after a leave full of lunches, dinners and general partying, Lassen and his friend boarded a small Percival Proctor communications plane and flew to Beirut where they attended George Jellicoe's wedding the following day, Lassen in the role of usher.

Jellicoe married Patricia O'Kane, one of the leading lights of Beirut society. The ceremony was followed by a 'lovely stand up luncheon at Olga and Nita's' after which the party grew rather wild, at least for some of the participants. The morning after the wedding, Lassen turned up ashen-faced and trembling at a hospital in Beirut, demanding to be X-rayed. His two false teeth were missing, and he was convinced that he had swallowed them during the night's festivities and that he might choke on them at any moment. The X-rays showed no trace of teeth, nor did it take long for the missing front teeth – depending on which version of the story you believe – to be found under Lassen's pillow or in a young lady's evening bag or to be hand-delivered to him by a discreet Arab servant.[415]

Symi, February 1944

On 11 February 1944 the Germans and the Italian fascist police on Symi succeeded in uncovering the spy ring whose existence they had suspected for months. The abbot of Panormitis monastery, Chrysanthos Maroulakis (who had helped Redfern set up a radio transmitter in the grounds of the monastery), and three other men – including the radio operator – were shot and blown to death by grenades. The following night, the British took revenge for the killing of their agents by allowing an SBS patrol, possibly led by Lassen, to launch a new attack on Symi that left one Italian officer and four soldiers wounded.[416]

The Alimnia Patrol, April 1944

During the spring, SBS activity in the Aegean increased as the capricious weather improved and Operation Overlord moved closer. In March and April, patrols went ashore on Astypalaia, Tilos, Kalymnos, Amorgos, Samos and Nisyros and killed, injured or kidnapped Germans and Italians. Caiques were sabotaged or hijacked, telegraph poles destroyed and cable connections between islands severed. From Astypalaia the raiders brought away the German harbour commander and the captain of a German merchant ship.[417]

The night of 20 to 21 March a British motor torpedo boat landed a dozen or so raiders on Patmos. The official report by Raiding Forces HQ said that the men delivered food supplies to the people of the island, four of whom died of hunger while the raiders were on Patmos. They took with them nine Italian prisoners and three women when they departed again on the night of 30 to 31 March.[418]

A German intelligence report, based on descriptions by three locals, went into more detail:

[The raiders] in English khaki uniforms without badges of rank and with rubber boots forced their way into the Carabinieri barracks; each was armed with sub-machine gun and pistol. The Carabinieri and Finanzieri, in spite of previous warning, were disarmed without resistance and their weapons were thrown into the sea. After the Carabinieri had packed their bags the English [raiders] retired into the hills with 3 brothel girls. Only 2 men of the party could have been from GREAT BRITAIN, the others did not look typically English. On 30/3 the English are said to have left PATMOS by M.T.B. with Italians and girls as prisoners. For the 5 or 6 days following the capture of the Carabinieri and Finanzieri the Mayor forbade the sailing of any ships. The English left behind about 1 ton of food.[419*]

The sources say nothing about whether or how the raiders paid the three prostitutes for their services, but it is tempting to assume that Raiding Forces' food supplies played a role in the transactions. Nor do the sources relate how the women's presence on the boat along with Italian PoWs was explained upon returning to base. Perhaps the women risked reprisals from the Fascists and the Germans for 'collaborating' with the British.

The same patrol also visited Lipsi and Arkoi, but without encountering any enemy troops.

Most of these operations were carried out by L Detachment. Lassen was in S Detachment and may have been on leave or training at the time. On the other hand, the SBS war diary says that on 30 March he returned 'from unknown destination', and that on 4 April he departed for an equally 'unknown destination'.[420]

* * *

None of the many SBS operations in February and March 1944 resulted in significant losses for the raiders. But in early April their luck ran out. As part of a coordinated attack on a number of German radar stations, Sutherland's S Detachment was ordered to attack the stations on Karpathos, halfway between Rhodes and Crete. They would not be able to get in, out and back again on the same night, so Sutherland decided that they should camp out on Alimnia, some forty miles northeast of Karpathos, or on the neighbouring island of Halki. Before launching the attack he despatched a patrol of five men, under the command of Captain Bill Blyth, to check out the situation on Karpathos and Halki. The patrol was to spend a maximum of one day on each island before returning to *Tewfik* in Yedi Atala. On 5 April at 16:00

the patrol left from the base on board *LS24*, which had a mixed British and Greek crew of five. The usual skipper, the Greek lieutenant Rigas Rigopoulos, was on Kastellorizo.[421]* In his absence, the vessel was under the command of First Lieutenant Allan Tuckey.

At 07:30 the following day, while *LS24* was moored on the small island of Alimnia, midway between Halki and Rhodes, four German landing craft sailed into the harbour. They carried troops from the Brandenburg *Küstenjäger* and the Pioneer Landing (Pila) Company 780, which was accompanied by two 'sub-hunters'; and the ship *Malona*[422]* had been despatched from Rhodes to occupy Alimnia and Halki because the Germans had been informed by spies that the British would land on Halki some time around Easter.[423] Lieutenant Glaser from Pila Company 780 spotted the carefully camouflaged caique right away. As he approached, Tuckey and his four men took up positions on land. Glaser had his men opened fire with a 20 mm cannon and a machine gun. Two of Tuckey's men were wounded, and the whole group surrendered.

While Tuckey and the crew tried to fight back on land, Blyth and his four SBS men slipped overboard from *LS24*, swam ashore and hid in the mountains. The Germans searched in vain for them. When the search squads withdrew, Blyth found a local fisherman who agreed to sail him and his men over to Rhodes, from where Blyth thought it would be easy to get back to Turkey.

Lieutenant Glaser took the prisoners on board the *Malona* to send them to Rhodes. The skipper, Corporal Timm, was ordered to stop and search every fishing boat along the way. One mile south of Alimnia, the *Malona* encountered the boat carrying Blyth and his crew. After a warning shot was fired, the Greek boat stopped and the crew came on board the *Malona* to show their papers. They pointed silently to their own boat. Timm jumped in and pulled aside the tarp that was stretched out over the hull to reveal Blyth and his four men. They surrendered without a fight.

During the subsequent interrogation, the prisoners tried in vain to convince the Germans that they had sailed from Kastellorizo. Since it was obvious that *LS24* had come from Turkey, Army Group E proposed attacks on British supply points on the Turkish coast. Hitler refused to approve the plan, presumably unwilling to damage German relations with the Turks. Instead the Army Group was instructed to supply documentation as soon as possible to inform the Turks via diplomatic channels that the British had violated their neutrality – or rather that the Germans knew that they had.[424]

Blyth was flown to Athens and from there he was sent to the Stalag VII A PoW camp for officers at Moosburg in Bavaria. He should then have been handed over to the SD after interrogation for 'special treatment as per the Führer's orders', i.e. executed under the 'commando order' of 18 October 1942.

However, the camp commandant, Colonel Otto Burger, chose to ignore the original order as well as a reminder from Army Group E, which seemed then to forget all about Blyth, who spent the rest of the war as a PoW.[425] The other members of his patrol – Lieutentant Tuckey and the four crew members (among them Lassen's buddy from the attack on Kastelli Pediada, Private R.W. Jones) – were executed.

When Blyth failed to make contact over the radio as agreed, and still had not returned after several days, Sutherland ordered Captain Thanos from the Greek Sacred Squadron to land on Halki and Alimnia and try to find out what had happened to the patrol that had vanished. Severe weather stopped Thanos making it ashore and he returned without any information. Meanwhile, on 12 April, German Radio Athens broadcast a communiqué from the OKW announcing that a British commando force trying to land on Rhodes had been wiped out.[426]* Sutherland discussed the matter with Thanos and Lassen. Together, they concluded, correctly, that the Germans must have been tipped off that Blyth and his men were on their way. The suspected spy was later found and shot, possibly by Lassen and two members of his Irish Patrol.[427]*

Santorini, April 1944

Due to the fate of the Alimnia Patrol, combined with uncertainty about what the prisoners might have disclosed – not to mention the codebooks and other documents that had been on board *LS24* and could give the Germans information about SBS operations – Sutherland was ordered, on 9 April 1944, to halt all activities in the Aegean Sea east of the Saria–Icaria line. On 14 April, attacks on radar stations were postponed indefinitely.[428]*

The next day, *Tewfik* moved to Balisu Bay. On 16 April the ban on operations was lifted. Sutherland had submitted a plan to HQ for a major offensive in the Cyclades – a group of around 220 islands in the western part of the Aegean. It would begin with simultaneous attacks on Syros, Ios and Santorini, and continue about two weeks later with attacks on Naxos and Paros. The idea of operating closer to the Greek mainland fitted in nicely with the Zeppelin misdirection, suggesting that the Allies were preparing an attack on the Balkans via Greece. The first phase of the operation was approved, albeit with Mykonos replacing Syros.

On 19 April, two patrols under Lassen (P Patrol directly under him, with his good friend the Greek Lieutenant Kasoulis as deputy commander; and Z Patrol under Lieutenant Keith Balsillie – on board *LS1* and *LS11* respectively) sailed for Santorini. In the days that followed, K Patrol sailed for Mykonos and J Patrol for Ios.

Lassen's mission was to destroy, capture or buy ('entice') ships that sailed for the Germans or might do so, to destroy enemy communications equipment, neutralise soldiers on Santorini, and to attack any other targets that he identified.[429]

For the first purpose, he and his men had 15 gold sovereigns (two years' salary for a private in the British army), 15,000 lire and 400,000 drachma to buy ships, according to a strictly defined tariff based on vessel size: £2.10/- in cash per ton or 10/- in gold upon entering into an agreement, and the same amount when the ship was handed over.[430*] The money could also be used to buy information and other assistance from the islanders, as well as mules to transport arms, equipment and fresh food. The accounts kept of these expenses were often rather cursory, and any excess sovereign coins had a tendency to disappear into the raiders' pockets or in between the double rubber soles in their boots.[431]

Some officers routinely shared any money left over with their men. Some of the raiders preferred to work with the SBS rather than other units specifically because of the prospect of a little extra cash – and also because the food was usually more generous.[432]

For the second part of the job – destroying installations and personnel – the patrols had with them fifty Lewes bombs, ten six-pound explosive charges and ten limpet mines (for attaching to ship hulls), as well as their 'normal' equipment.

'Normal' is in quotes here because it encompasses a variety of weapons that the individual raiders chose for themselves. All had an F-S fighting knife, but otherwise rarely used the British army's standard weapons – the Lee Enfield .303 rifle and the Webley revolver. They preferred the smaller and lighter American M1 carbine and the US Army's Colt .45 pistol, which was popular because of its heavy impact. The raiders used the British Sten sub-machine gun and the Bren light machine gun. They also favoured the American Thompson sub-machine gun, for which they used box magazines of 20 or 30 rounds rather than the distinctive 50-round drum which was prone to malfunction in the field and made the weapon awkward to carry. The raiders also used captured German and Italian pistols – in particular the elegant Luger was in high demand, both as a sidearm and as a souvenir. Anders Lassen used both a Luger and a Colt .45. There was also the Italian Beretta and German MP40 sub-machine guns, the latter of which was considered reliable and easy to use, and its flat design made it easy to carry. As well as the British hand grenade (the 'Mills bomb'), some raiders also used the Italian Army's 'Red Devils', but opinions on them were divided. Some thought they were the best available grenades; others thought they were only useful if you hit the enemy over the head with them. The great breadth of the SBS arsenal reflected the high degree of autonomy the raiders enjoyed. This may have heightened their sense that they were masters of their own destiny, waging war on their own terms, but this same diversity also represented a supply problem as the different weapons used different types of ammunition.[433]

* * *

LS1 and *LS11* left Balisu Bay shortly before dusk on 19 April and sailed for most of the night. No Germans were spotted at sea and the weather was relatively calm. Both caiques sailed with their masts down on the deck to make it easier to mount the camouflage nets the next morning, but this made them roll uncomfortably in the heavy swell from the south. Everyone on board was relieved when the two vessels finally docked, before dawn at the island of Syrna halfway between the southern Dodecanese Islands and the eastern Cyclades. Sentries were posted and some of the crew settled down to sleep. Others headed to the middle of the six-square-mile island to hand over gifts, in the form of canned food, to Syrna's patriarch, Barbaiannis. Uncle John, as he was called by the SBS men who had visited him before, lived alone on the island with his five sons, their wives and children, and a large number of goats. He served his guests warm goat's milk and feta cheese in his stone hut and offered a refreshing bath in the (admittedly quite salty) fresh water from his well, which two small grandchildren poured over the seafarers by the bucket load.

At sunset the crews started to roll up the big, dusty nets and raise the heavy masts. After an hour's work, the caiques left Syrna and sailed out into the calm, moonless Aegean at a speed of 6½ knots. Also on board was a slightly wounded RAF staff sergeant who had taken refuge with Barbaiannis. An hour before dawn, the vessels reached the uninhabited rocky island of Anydros, some twenty miles north-east of Santorini, where they laid up in a 100-foot-wide creek surrounded by steep slopes.

> [A]fter half an hour of fine adjustment (that is, stumbling around in the dark, uttering strong oaths, slipping on the rocks or tripping over soldiers and their gear on board) we were both secure.[434]

The masts were lowered, the nets stretched out, sentries deployed, and the other raiders and crew turned in. Food was cooked over primus stoves. A reconnaissance of the approximately one-square-mile island revealed that it did indeed live up to its name ('without water') – the small amount of water available on the island was only suitable for cattle. In the afternoon the men relaxed in the sun and enjoyed the sight of Santorini, dark purple on the horizon.

From Anydros, they could see the east side of Santorini, an unusual horseshoe-shaped island formed by a volcanic explosion. Santorini was the largest part of an archipelago that included four other small islands: the second-largest, Thirasia; the small and uninhabited Aspronisi, which formed part of the crater rim; and Nea Kameni and Palia Kameni in the lagoon to the west.

A pair of German transport planes, probably on their way from Rhodes to Athens, flew over the island but gave the men in the well-camouflaged caiques no cause for concern.

In the late evening the vessels set sail for Santorini and cast anchor off the Perissa Monastery at the southern end of the island's curved east side – which, as far as they knew, was unguarded. Lassen and Lieutenant Kasoulis landed there at 23:00 to gather intelligence, but without success. After two hours of futile attempts to learn about the German and Italian dispositions on Santorini, Lassen and Kasoulis returned to the caiques. They then sailed in a big arc around the south-west tip of Santorini, where there was thought to be a German machine-gun nest close to the lighthouse, and continued into the bay, where they waited on the west side of Nea Kameni, facing the sea and away from Santorini. The plan was to hide the vessels in a deep and very narrow cove. However, it turned out not to exist – and had not done since 1926 when the last volcanic eruption had radically changed the coastline. The SBS maps did not show this.

Even worse, as the sun came up it revealed that the caiques' camouflage net – a pattern of white and dirty-grey spots that had worked so well on Anydros – did more harm than good against Nea Kameni's black lava cliffs. The only consolation was that the caiques were at least on the outer side of Nea Kameni and invisible from Santorini. The masts had already been lowered, so to break up the vessels' silhouettes it was decided to cover the decks with the dark-brown foresails, which were a slightly better match for the surroundings. The alternative would have been to try to impersonate local boats, but that would have meant raising the masts again – and nobody could be bothered. Sentries were posted and the crew waited for night to fall.

There were no ships in the bay. This was a bit of a disappointment, in the sense that the expedition's main purpose was to sink, capture or entice ships that the Germans might otherwise have used. However, under the circumstances, it was mainly a relief. The caiques were approached by a small Greek fishing boat, whose skipper told them that German patrol boats usually only passed by at dawn or sunset, not during the day. He also reported that the garrison amounted to a maximum of fifty men, and that its HQ was in a cluster of houses just outside Santorini's capital Fira, about 1,000 feet above the port of Skala.

On the afternoon of 22 April, plans were laid for a landing. The raiders were to be put ashore at Vourvoulos beach, on the east coast, just north of Fira. They would be picked up again 48 hours later from one of three embarkation points in the area. In the meantime, the two caiques would hide in the Christiana Islands, about twelve miles south-west of the southern tip of Santorini. While the Greek fishing boat kept watch a little way out to sea, the crew of the two caiques and their passengers grabbed a few hours' shuteye. In the evening the sailors prepared a hearty meal, while the soldiers packed their backpacks, inspected their weapons and prepared their explosives. Once it was completely dark, the caiques sailed out of the bay, heading south around Tharissa, and then over the northern tip of Santorini and down the east coast to a point just off the landing site. It took half an hour to land the eighteen soldiers and their interpreter, 'John'. Once the men were ashore, the two caiques headed for the Christiana Islands, where they arrived just as dawn broke on 23 April.

As soon as they were on dry land, the two patrols made for the village of Vourvoulos, about a mile inland. They hid in a cave there for most of the day, while Kasoulis, 'John' and others tried to gather intelligence from the locals.

Lassen decided to split his men up into three groups. Lassen wanted to take Kasoulis and 12 others and attack the 38 Italians and 10 Germans said to be billeted on the first floor of the Bank of Athens building in Fira. Sergeant Henderson was to take up a position outside the house of the German commander, Lieutenant Hesse, and his adjutant, and either kill them or take them prisoner, when the noise from Lassen's attack lured them outside. The third group, Lieutenant Balsillie and four men from his Z Patrol, were to attack a radio station and outpost in Imerovigli, about half a mile west of Vourvoulos. The attacks were to commence at 00:45 on 24 April.

On the way to Fira, Lassen had each of his men take two Benzedrine tablets – an amphetamine-based stimulant that was part of the raiders' standard kit – and took two himself.

The bank was located in the middle of a maze of steep, narrow streets in the town. As the raiders approached the target, Lassen told Kasoulis to take one route with some of the men while he and the rest took another. After ten minutes the two teams were in place and ready to strike. Despite guards and barking dogs, the whole force managed to get into the bank building unnoticed. With Lassen at the front, the twelve men crept up the stairs and found themselves confronted by five closed doors. Lassen placed two men on each door and the others in the middle of the corridor. They were to kick in the doors on his signal. Lassen blew his whistle. Corporal Sean O'Reilly and Private Sammy Trafford from Z Patrol kicked their doors in. O'Reilly threw a grenade into his room and fired away with his (German) MP40 submachine gun. As Lieutenant Kasoulis kicked in his door he was met with fire from automatic weapons and killed instantly. Private Trafford was then shot in the arm and left leg. Private Jack Harris was hit in the leg and limped out onto the terrace. The medical orderly, Sergeant Kingston, who had persuaded Lassen to take him along on the raid on the condition that he did not enter the bank, took a bullet to the stomach.

The violent resistance and unexpected casualties drove the raiders back onto the terrace in front of the building. Lassen managed to rally his men and led them round to the back. Sergeant Nicholson provided covering fire from his Bren gun to keep the Germans at bay. The raiders forced their way through a French door and found themselves in a dining room with three doors on each side. Lassen's men kicked the doors open and threw hand grenades into the rooms. They were starting to run out of grenades so O'Reilly ran back to the front of the house and took grenades from Kasoulis and Kingston. One of the doors was locked and could not be kicked in. Three men shot at the lock, but to no avail. Finally they managed to kick out the bottom panel and throw hand grenades though the hole. A German or Italian was shot when he tried to save himself by escaping out of a window at the rear of the building. Another was killed in the fall. Lassen was beside himself with grief and rage at losing Kasoulis. He and Sergeant Nicholson went through the dark building room by room. Lassen had a Tommy gun, Nicholson a 20-lb Bren gun. They threw a hand grenade through every door and then each emptied a magazine into the room.

Once Lassen felt confident that all of the enemy were either dead or wounded, he gathered his men on the terrace in front of the bank building. He posted three men, including Nicholson and his Bren gun, along the balustrade and two on the stairs. German voices were heard from the street. Nicholson shouted 'Kommen Sie hier, Kamerad!' (Come here, mate!). The Germans were not fooled, so he opened fire with his machine gun – after which all fell silent.

Although wounded, Kingston tried to throw a hand grenade at five enemy soldiers who had jumped through a window, but he did not have the strength to throw it far enough and the five vanished into the night.

Lassen went back into the house to look for Kasoulis. On ascertaining that he really was dead, he took his dog tag, gold chain and diary.

The raiders withdrew at 02:45. At first, Kingston was carried on a door. His companions managed to manhandle him down from the terrace, but the streets were so narrow and steep that they had to carry him on their backs. About 150 yards from the bank Lassen and his men were hailed in German from a narrow side street. Lassen replied, 'Kommen Sie hier!' (Come here!) The German shouted back 'Kommen *Sie* hier!' (No, you come here!) and fired a burst from an automatic weapon. Lassen threw a hand grenade into the dark alley. There was a scream and the sound of footsteps running away.

Despite severe pain, Kingston did not think his wounds were serious, but his companions had to move very slowly to stop exacerbating it. By the time day started to break, the group had still not reached the cave at Vourvoulos. About half a mile from the village, Corporal O'Reilly stayed behind with Kingston while Lassen and the rest of the group proceeded to the cave. A local told them that the Germans were on their way to Vourvoulos.

When Lassen and his depleted force made it back to the cave, they were met by Lieutenant Balsillie and his four men, who had taken eight Germans prisoner without firing a shot, destroyed their transmitter and seized a number of documents. Seven of the Germans had been surprised in their beds (two of them together) in two different houses. The eighth surrendered when he heard what had happened to his comrades.

Sergeant Henderson had had less luck. The German commander and his aide had left through a garden door while Henderson tried to enter through the front of the house. Henderson had thrown a hand grenade as they escaped, but did not know whether he had hit either of them.

Shortly after Lassen made it back to the cave, a Greek brought them a message that the Germans had taken ten hostages, including the mayor of Vourvoulos. They were threatening to shoot them if the islanders did not reveal the raiders' hideout.

Over the radio, which had links to both Cairo and *Tewfik*, Lassen requested that a fast boat be sent to Santorini right away to evacuate some of the men – most importantly Kingston. Lassen then ordered Lieutenant Balsillie to lead the ten raiders and eight German prisoners down to the coast. He and Sergeant Nicholson then returned to the spot where they had left Kingston with O'Reilly and the two others. They were nowhere to be seen. It was between 08:00 and 09:00 and they were quite close to Fira. Nonetheless they decided to risk walking up and down the road, quietly calling out for Kingston. After a short search, Lassen heard the wounded man groaning, and whistled Nicholson over to him. Kingston was very pale and weak and now thought that he was bleeding internally. He had persuaded his comrades to leave him close to the road where the Germans or Italians would perhaps find him and treat him – if he lived that long. Lassen and Nicholson asked some vineyard workers who were standing nearby to bring them something that could be used as a stretcher. They brought a gate, on which Lassen and Nicholson carried Kingston along the difficult road down to the coast – most of which was plainly visible from Fira. When they finally reached the shore, they walked for about half a mile before meeting the rest of the force.

Balsillie and his men had found a house where the raiders could hide until dark, when the caiques or a patrol boat would be able to come and get them. Lassen placed his men in defensive positions from which they could survey the surroundings all the way to Fira. The local people who came and went between the house and Fira told them that the Germans were preparing an attack, but the raiders would not leave Kingston.

He was restless and in pain and kept saying that his companions should get away and not stay for his sake. He was laid in a bed in the house and a local was sent to fetch a doctor. After first sending his son to ask about the wound, the doctor himself turned up around noon. He confirmed Kingston's diagnosis of internal bleeding and administered a dose of morphine on top of the one the orderly had already taken from his own supply. The doctor recommended leaving Kingston somewhere the Germans could find him and take care of him, but he died before they could do so. The raiders wrapped their dead comrade-in-arms in blankets, placed Nicholson's Bible in his hands and tied him to a stretcher. The doctor made sure that some of the local people carried him away and buried him.

The doctor told them that the German losses probably amounted to three dead and two wounded; for the Italians, nine dead and a similar number of wounded. Lieutenant Balsillie had also taken eight prisoners, bringing Axis losses up to thirty-one men. Lassen had found out that, contrary to his information, there were no more than 35 enemy soldiers in the bank, not 48. Including the commandant and the 8 prisoners from Imerovigli, that suggested a total garrison of about 45 men, of whom 31 had been killed, wounded or taken prisoner.

The German counterattack came to nothing. The German HQ on Milos, 45 miles to the north-west, which was responsible for Santorini, hesitated to send reinforcements to the island, possibly because they thought it had been occupied by a large British force.

During the afternoon, shots were heard from the direction of the cave that the raiders had recently vacated. A local said that the Germans had shot the ten hostages and were threatening to shoot the rest of the inhabitants of Vourvoulos if they did not reveal the British hiding place before darkness fell. Lassen immediately sent Lieutenant Hesse a letter in which he threatened him with prosecution as a war criminal after the war if any more hostages were shot, and promised to return to Santorini with 1,000 men ('and not as this time with only 500') and kill every German on the island. No more hostages were executed and the raiders' hiding place was not given up, even though many locals knew its whereabouts.

When darkness fell, Lassen and Sergeant Nicholson went down to the coast and tried to make contact with the caiques that were due to come and pick them up. Around 03:00 they reached what they thought was the agreed location. They sat against a wall and flashed Morse signals, but received no answer. It was a stormy night and the sea was very rough. The two men were exhausted so decided to take turns to sleep for an hour each. The one who was awake was to continue to send signals every ten minutes. The rest of the night passed without the caiques appearing. Whether Lassen and Nicholson were aware of it or not as they wandered around in the dark, they found themselves not at the agreed embarkation point across from Vourvoulos but much further south – next to the Perissa Monastery, where Lassen and Kasoulis had gone ashore to reconnoitre the night before the landings (they had spent the night up against the monastery's garden wall). As day started to break, they went up to the monastery and sneaked into the courtyard, which led to a row of monks' cells. They found an empty one and lay down to sleep on the floor without waking anybody.

Later on 25 April the rest of the raiders arrived at the monastery, along with the eight prisoners and First Lieutenant Geoffrey Kirk from *LS11*. Kirk had been directed there by locals in the village of Emborio, who knew there were British troops in Perissa. He said that the two caiques had been badly delayed by the weather. They had lost sight of each other and *LS11* had run aground not far from Perissa. He did not know what had become of *LS1* but hoped that the captain had sailed back to the Christiana Islands to try again the next night. The ships had tried in vain to make radio contact with Lassen. Kirk arranged with Lassen that his men would be extracted from the beach by the monastery provided *LS11* could be refloated. He would also make contact with *LS1*. He left the tired and hungry raiders to head back to the spot where *LS11* had run aground. But when he arrived, the vessel was gone. Three Greek women, who were wading in the water gathering supplies that the crew had thrown overboard in their efforts to refloat the caique, told him that it had sailed around dawn. Kirk went back to the monastery to tell Lassen the news. The locals had brought the raiders cheese, tomatoes and fresh fruit, so the atmosphere in the monastery had somewhat improved. It also helped their mood that Kirk was able to tell them that one of the two caiques was probably intact.

A Greek named Niko, who had joined the force, brought regular updates about the Germans' movements. He reported that Arado seaplanes had landed in the harbour and taken off again that morning, and that a German destroyer had been seen lying off the northern tip of Santorini. However, the Germans did not seem to know where the raiders were.

There was nothing for it but to wait for night to fall and the boats to return. To pass the time, Lassen and Kirk, a classical philologist, visited a small Hellenistic shrine a short distance from the monastery. A combination of the afternoon heat and exhaustion overcame the pair's cultural curiosity however, and they fell asleep under a fig tree. They were woken by the noise of four Junkers Ju 88 bombers, which spent five minutes circling the monastery at around 2,000 feet before heading further north. A Messerschmitt Me 109 fighter also flew over the monastery at around 300 feet. The German prisoners ran out onto a terrace, but did not try to send signals, and the pilot did not seem to notice anything.

Early in the evening, the whole force, along with the eight prisoners and a handful of Greeks who had helped the raiders, went to the beach to look for the caiques. While the weather had improved, the sea was still rough and there was no guarantee that the boats would make it.

Towards midnight, not two but three vessels finally turned up. Thanks to a slightly high tide, *LS11* had been refloated and hidden off Anydros. Contact had been established with both *LS1* and the patrol boat *HDML1377*, which had been redirected to Santorini when Lassen called for a rapid evacuation of Kingston. The caiques cast anchor some distance from the coast. Nicholson and a couple of raiders took one of the monastery's rowing boats out to meet it and told the captain that Lassen had studied the coast and guaranteed that the waters were deep enough to approach the beach. In fact he had done no such thing. Nonetheless the captain believed it, sailed in closer, and the waters indeed turned out to be deep enough. The prisoners were loaded first, followed by the rest of the men. It was a wet and difficult business. The sea was still choppy, and a certain amount of confusion reigned due to the numerous Greeks who climbed aboard the boats hoping to be taken to Egypt. The raiders reluctantly threw them overboard to make way for the evacuees. About half of the force boarded the patrol boat, where a medical orderly took care of the wounded. The rest were split between the two caiques.

From Santorini the three vessels sailed to Anydros, where they spent the following day under the camouflage nets while German planes flew back and forth across the island. When darkness fell the patrol boat sailed to a location identified by Lassen in his report as 'Mersinjek'. The caiques sailed to Syrna, over which German planes also flew, and from there back to *Tewfik*, where, in Sergeant Nicholson's words, they 'got drunk (raki and brandy)'. Lassen was, as a Greek crewmember put it, 'drunk two days of sorrow – like a father'.[435]

* * *

In his report on the raid on Santorini, Lassen noted the difference between the veteran SBS men, like Sergeant Nicholson and the corporals O'Reilly and Sibbet, who 'as usual did brilliantly and were calm and efficient during the attack', and the new recruits. However, he did acknowledge that Signaller Reeves and Private Partridge (who both came from the paratroopers) 'although lacking in experience, carry themselves well and proved to be most useful members of the Patrol'. In general, however, the new men were not good enough:

> There is no doubt that shooting up barracks at night requires a great deal of skill and experience, such as only the older men in the S.B.S. have, and which will not be found in re-inforcements.
>
> Lack of experience must be made up by rigid training, especially in Street and House fighting, and they should be generally taught how to look after themselves; not to stand in front of doors, for example. The standard of marching among the recruits was poor, and in many cases not what should have been expected.
>
> As usual, Sgt. NICHOLSON, Cpl. SIBBET and Cpl. O'REILLY did extremely well, and were calm and efficient during the attack.

Lassen also wrote that it had been his intention to take as prisoners the forty-eight enemy personnel he expected to find in the bank building. However, 'This idea had to be abandoned, and will have to be abandoned in similar circumstances in the future, until raiding parties are issued with good torches.' It is uncertain whether torches would have made any significant difference in the chaos that reigned in the bank, nor whether it really was Lassen's plan to take all the Germans prisoner. His instructions from Sutherland – which may well have been influenced by the recent disappearance of the Alimnia Patrol – did not mention prisoners, only that he should 'destroy enemy communications and personnel'. No matter what Lassen may have had in mind when he launched the attack, the reality of the situation did not make it easy to take prisoners. In addition, Kasoulis's death probably drastically reduced any chance the Germans and Italians had of escaping the building alive.

Some forty years after the event, Signaller Billy Reeves told Mike Langley that 'Lassen's motto on prisoners that night seemed to be "Don't take any".' And Sergeant Nicholson said:

> We didn't have torches, we didn't want torches – a man carrying a torch is a target. That was the only time I was in action side-by-side with Lassen and it's one of the reasons why I'm trying to forget the war. It's no fun throwing grenades into rooms and shooting sleeping men. That garrison could have been captured.[436]

Geoffrey Kirk considered Lassen:

> one of those people who are quite fearless and also, at times, quite ruthless, a potential *berserker*. A truly heroic figure in the Iliadic sense, the sheer force of his personality meant that uneducated Greeks could usually understand him, even though he spoke only a few words of their language. This struck me quite strongly during the hours I was with him. He was tall and blond and intrepid-looking, but the Nazi occupation of Denmark had made him a bit unbalanced in certain respects. Thus it was that while he and his sergeant were going through the small rooms of the German and Italian barrack-building outside Phira, a couple of nights before, Lassen had ordered his companion to wake up the sleeping enemy soldiers before cutting their throats, so that they should know what was happening to them. The sergeant had refused. Nothing was said at the time, but when I met up with the party at the Perissa monastery Lassen was insisting on putting his sergeant on a charge for disobeying orders. The other officers had tried to dissuade him without much success. He told me about the incident at some length, during our leisurely afternoon together; naturally I too advised him to calm down, that the sergeant had after all been completely right. Eventually he did calm down, or at least not press the charge, but it reminded one that war was a dirty business.[437*]

* * *

On Mykonos, K Patrol destroyed the German naval radio station and seized all of its documents, code books, etc. One German NCO was killed and seven prisoners taken; one raider was slightly injured. On Ios, J Patrol killed two Germans, took three prisoners, sank a 25-ton caique and delivered 17 tons of food to the islanders. On returning from Ios, J Patrol was sent to Amorgos to attack a German radio station in the port town. It was the night of 1/2 May 1944: J Patrol captured the German transmitter and killed six radio operators. Phase one of Sutherland's campaign in the Cyclades was complete.[438]

The attacks on Santorini and Mykonos triggered a discussion between the German army and navy staffs. Admiral Kurt Fricke, head of *Marinegruppenkommando Süd* in Sofia, asked Vice-Admiral Werner Lange – who as *Admiral Ägäis* had direct responsibility for naval activities in the Aegean Sea and for the radio stations that had been attacked – for an explanation of which posts should be closed or withdrawn. Lange wanted

Army Group E to assume greater responsibility for defending the outlying islands where the *Kriegsmarine* had observation posts, radio stations, etc. Army Group E would rather withdraw from some of the islands than try to hold on to more of them than it had the troops and supplies to defend. Conversely, Lange proposed that Army Group E's troops from the heavily manned islands of Rhodes and Crete should be used to defend the smaller and more vulnerable islands, and that they should take hostages in advance who were to be executed immediately if the locals helped the British with their operations. Meanwhile the *Küstenjäger* of the Brandenburg Division and other German special forces continued their efforts to fight the British raiders and the Greek Sacred Squadron with their own methods. 'Pirate detachments' made surprise landings on unoccupied islands, Greek-speaking 'Makedo-Romanians' masqueraded as Greek partisans to lure the British and real partisans into ambushes, Germans wore British uniforms, and the German intelligence organizations in Greece and Turkey worked flat out.[439]

'Word is Vendetta' – The abduction of General Kreipe and the attack on Paros, April–May 1944.

At 07:05 on 1 May 1944, all Allied commands received the coded message 'Word is Vendetta' – the signal to launch the final phase of the huge campaign to divert attention away from Operation Overlord. Although the main objective was to make the enemy fear an imminent attack on the south of France by Allied forces in North Africa, the Allies also wanted to maintain – and preferably ramp up – the pretence that other parts of occupied Europe were also under threat. Everywhere from Norway to Denmark and France to Yugoslavia and Greece, resistance movements were stepping up their campaigns. Rumours were spread of an impending attack on Petsamo in the Norwegian-Finnish-Soviet border area. In the eastern Mediterranean and the Middle East, the British 9th and 10th Armies, despite mustering only one brigade apiece, were charged with conveying the impression that they were preparing to march into Greece and Bulgaria, and that Turkey was finally about to abandon its policy of neutrality and commit forty divisions to the invasion force.[440]

* * *

On Crete, on 26 April 1944, an SOE team led by Patrick Leigh Fermor abducted the CO of the 22nd Infantry Division, Major General Heinrich Kreipe, who had just replaced Lieutenant General Friedrich-Wilhelm Müller.

(The original plan had been to kidnap Müller, who had been responsible for massacres of Greek civilians and Italian PoWs.)

According to Patrick Leigh Fermor's biographer, Artemis Cooper, Kreipe asked Fermor: 'Tell me, Major, what is the object of this hussar-stunt?' and 'Even Paddy [Leigh Fermor] had to admit that there was no easy answer to that question.'[441]

The idea of a spectacular abduction on Crete was probably conceived by SOE Major Thomas J. Dunbabin who, in a report of May 1942, wrote about the possibility of capturing the crew of a small German observation post somewhere near the coast. The purpose would be to strengthen the morale of the Cretans by exposing the Germans' weakness and to provoke the Germans to retaliate with atrocities that would make the locals hate them even more. Such an operation would also be useful for propaganda purposes, at home as well as abroad, at a time when British successes were all too rare.

The abduction of small garrisons or of a general (Müller was mentioned several times, but so was the commandant of Crete, Major General Bruno Bräuer) was to be a recurring theme in Dunbabin's and his colleague Sean Fielding's reports during the following two years. They generally presented the purpose as making the Germans insecure, undermining the myth of their invincibility, and strengthening the Cretans' will to resist. German reprisals, which would obviously have to be expected, were sometimes described as a desirable objective, sometimes as a risk that should be minimised as far as possible, while at other times they were simply discounted as completely improbable.[442]

In the winter of 1943/4 Leigh Fermor was a frequent guest at a flat shared by some young women who worked for the Desert Air Force in Bari:

> Our flat had an open fire and this was a great attraction. I often worried that there could be a concealed microphone in the chimney that went direct to the enemy! So many secret plans were made round the fire. Patrick Leigh Fermor who I'd known in Cairo, used to be a visitor … He was very keen to kidnap a particularly brutal German general commanding in Crete and the arguments for and against were discussed. Needless to say a decision had to be, and was, taken at a much higher level.[443]

Kreipe's question was a good one. What might have made sense in 1942 did not make equally good sense in 1944. Simple 'subversion', making the Germans feel insecure on Crete or rendering them ridiculous in the eyes of the locals, does not seem like a rational reason so late in the war. Neither does any British interest in interrogating Kreipe. The records of Kreipe's interrogation by the CSDIC show not only that Kreipe (whose superiors considered him to be resolute and cool in times of crisis) said little of importance, but also that the British seem to have had little to ask him about.[444*] The most plausible answer to why the SOE finally decided to undertake such a complicated and dangerous operation with so little impact in an island of limited strategic interest where the Germans had a history of carrying out atrocities in response to sabotage operations etc, would seem to be deception – i.e. drawing the Germans' attention to Greece and away from Normandy.

Kreipe's abduction did not result in immediate German reprisals. On 27 April the commandant of Fortress Crete, General Bruno Bräuer, did threaten harsh retaliatory measures if Kreipe was not immediately released, but he did not carry them out, and his later proclamations were less drastic. It may have contributed to Bräuer's moderate reaction that on 29 April one hundred of 'the best citizens of Heraklion' informed the general that they had set up a committee headed by the mayor, the bishop, the chief of police, and the chief prosecutor, with the purpose of getting the local population to help find Kreipe so that the 'good policy of reconciliation' introduced by Bräuer might continue.[445*]

Bräuer's policy of reconciliation did not prevent the Germans from destroying four villages in early May; however, these atrocities were not connected with the abduction of Kreipe. In August, when Bräuer had been replaced as commandant by Müller, massacres broke loose again. Four villages were burnt down, and hundreds of people were murdered. The Germans gave various reasons for these reprisals, among them the abduction of Kreipe. Dunbabin, who like his SOE colleague Ralph H. Stockbridge had spoken against the abduction, even though it had probably been his idea originally, thought that the killings had nothing to do with Kreipe, but that at least part of their purpose was to make it harder for the German soldiers to desert by involving all of them in war crimes. This seems like a rather farfetched explanation, and no other contemporary sources support it.[446]

* * *

On Rhodes, the Greek Sacred Squadron attacked a radar station, while Raiding Forces stepped up the frequency of its incursions in the Aegean.[447] In the Cyclades, Sutherland's campaign entered its second phase. On 9 May, Lassen and twelve men from P and K patrols sailed for Paros, and on 14 May J and Q patrols departed for Naxos.

Lassen and his men – sergeants Nicholson and Waite, the American medical orderly Porter Jarrell, Hank Hancock, Busty Sibbet, Patsy Henderson, Mick D'Arcy, Williams and other SBS men, accompanied by four members of the

Greek Sacred Squadron – Second Lieutenant Kyriakos Sofoulis, K. Chalkias, Theodor Pyrialas and Stylianos Chrysos – landed on Glyfa Beach near the southern tip of the 75-square-mile island of Paros at 22:00 on 13 May.[448*] They spent the next day in a nearby cave until night fell and then marched about eight miles up to Stroumboula, by the village of Lefkes, not far from the German airfield (which was under construction but already being used by the Luftwaffe) near the villages of Prodromos, Marpissa and Marmara. Here the raiders sought out the Stellas family, whose three sons, Manolis, Christos and Nikolas, were willing to provide them with assistance. Nikolas (23) worked on the building site and was well acquainted with the base and its security measures. Following a few hours' rest and discussing the matter with the family, the raiders, guided by the three brothers, marched to a clifftop approx. 600 feet above the airfield. It was an arduous trip in which they had to climb steep paths barely visible in the dark. Some of the men had a hard time keeping up – especially the radio operator, who had to contend with a 60-lb battery as well as his wireless set. Lassen always carried the bare minimum of kit, and was not exactly renowned for his willingness to help with other people's gear. Nevertheless, on this occasion he took the battery from the radio operator, picked up the pace and reached the top before everyone else. The men had marched for more than seven hours and were exhausted, so Lassen allowed them to rest all morning in a primitive shepherd's hut, before an afternoon reconnoitring the surroundings and observe comings and goings at the base.

The night of 15 May was spent planning the details of the impending operation: Although it turned out that there were more German soldiers on Paros than expected – about 150 men – and that their positions were more scattered and therefore difficult to surprise than originally assumed, Lassen was not to be deterred. He divided his men into smaller groups, each with its own mission: to sabotage equipment on the airfield; destroy the radio stations in Prodromos and on a hilltop near Marmara; cut the phone line between Marpissa and the German observation post on the Kefalos mountain on the east coast; and abduct the commander of the base, Lieutenant Colonel Tabel.

* * *

While Lassen and his raiders continued their preparations, the RAF also tried to put the airfield on Paros out of action. On the morning of 15 May, a British reconnaissance plane photographed the base, just as a German Junkers Ju 52 transport plane was taking off. The same afternoon, at 15:20, four long-range twin-engine Beaufighter TF Mk.X planes set off from the base at Gambut in Libya. They first headed to the island of Tinos, about twenty-five miles north of Paros, where they dive-bombed a 100-ton German ship before heading for Paros. When they tried to investigate the airbase and other facilities, they were met with heavy anti-aircraft fire.

The German gunners shot down one Beaufighter (NE607/Q), which broke in two and exploded in the air before crashing near Lefkes. There were no survivors. The other three Beaufighters had only suffered superficial damage, but now found themselves under attack by four Messerschmitt Me 109 fighters, which downed a second Beaufighter (LZ404/K). Again, both crewmembers were killed. Despite being damaged, the other two Beaufighters made it back to base.

* * *

Lassen and his men went into action at 23:30 on the night of 16 May.

Nikolas Stellas acted as guide for the first group, which was led by Lassen and consisted of eight SBS men and two members of the Greek Sacred Squadron. Its job was to attack a German barracks at the airfield and destroy its fuel depot, and also to destroy a radio station on top of Yalios hill, northwest of Marmara.

The second group consisted of Second Lieutenant Kyriakos Sofoulis and another member of the Greek Sacred Squadron, four SBS men and the local resistance members Giannis Aliprantis and Police Chief Manolis Gryllakis, who was to act as guide. Their goal was to kidnap Lt. Col. Tabel from his quarters in Marmissa and destroy a nearby arms dump and a barracks housing thirty German soldiers.

The third and fourth groups consisted of Antonis Delentas, Panagiotis Emmanuel Tsigonias, Dimitris Perantinos and other resistance fighters from Paros. They were tasked with putting radio and telephone installations in the village of Prodromos out of commission.

The attack on the airfield went awry almost from the beginning. The Greek guide who was supposed to show them the way to the bomb depot in a small church suddenly abandoned Hancock and Sibbet. The pair strayed too close to a German machine-gun position, which opened fire. Within seconds, the airfield reverberated with the sound of barking dogs and was lit up by flares. The two raiders beat a hasty retreat – terrified, they recalled later, at the thought of how Lassen would react when he heard that they had not returned fire. Lassen gave up on the gun position he had selected as his target.

However, not all the Germans in the area had been alerted right away. The Greek partisans managed to sabotage the radio transmitter in Prodromos (killing four Germans in the process), destroy a warehouse and sever the phone line to Kefalos.

Lieutenant Kyriakos Sofoulis and Sergeant Nicholson led their group into Marpissa at 23:40 and struck so suddenly that the Germans had no chance to defend themselves. The Greek guides identified houses where the Germans were billeted, and Lewes bombs were used to clear them out. Three or four Germans were killed instantly, including Tabel's adjutant, but the commander surrendered to Nicholson unscathed. The radio transmitter and weapons store were destroyed. As Nicholson led his prisoner through the village, some of the other raiders reacted to the sound of Tabel's heavy hobnail boots (SBS boots had soft rubber soles) by opening fire on what they presumed was a German patrol. The German commander was hit in the throat but again survived. Nicholson bandaged him and they moved on. Not far from the rendezvous point with the others, a grenade was lobbed at them. The blast blew both men off their feet. Nicholson got back up, but his prisoner remained on the ground, dead or severely wounded, and this time Nicholson opted to leave him behind. Again, the assailants were SBS men who had mistaken them for a German patrol.

After the attack, Lassen, his men and their local Greek helpers (including the police chief Gryllakis, who had been shot and badly wounded) boarded boats from the fishing village of Piso Livadi, a few miles south-east of the airfield. Most of them had reached the rendezvous point on time, but not Jarrell, Henderson, D'Arcy or the young Nikolas Stellas. The pick-up boat could not wait – by dawn it had to be hidden off the coast of Icaria, about forty-four miles north-east of Paros – so the trio were left behind.

Jarrell, Henderson and D'Arcy's target had been the radio station in Marpissa. Following their encounter with the German gun emplacement, the raiders retreated to spend the rest of the night and the whole of the next day in hiding. It was the following night before they managed to sneak down to the rendezvous point. They were a day late, but when they made it to the beach they spotted flashing signals out at sea. The boat had returned to search for the missing men, either – as Nicholson later said – at Lassen's insistence, or because it had been agreed in advance that if anybody failed to make it to the pick-up point on time then an attempt would be made to retrieve them the following day.

All of Lassen's men made it back to *Tewfik* safe and sound. Gryllakis was sent to Cyprus, where doctors saved his life. But Nikolas Stellas was still missing.

The Germans picked him up near Marpissa. He was taken to Athens, interrogated and tortured, but did not give up the names of any other members of the local resistance. On 21 May he was hanged in the square in Marpissa. The Germans forced local people to file past his corpse.

Tabel's successor as head of *Platzkommando Paros*, Major Georg von Merenberg, was ordered by his superiors to execute 125 civilians on the island as punishment for the locals helping the raiders. Von Merenberg, whose career had stalled due to repeatedly and openly demonstrating his aversion to Nazism, thought this was a mistake. At first he saw no alternative but to obey the order, as he risked being executed himself if he refused. However, Philotheos Zervakos, the abbot at the monastery in Longovardas, managed to arrange a meeting with von Merenberg, who was a great-grandchild of Czar Alexander II and his morganatic wife, and had grown up in a family with close ties to the Orthodox Church. The abbot offered to lay down his own life in exchange for the 125 hostages. When the German refused, the abbot asked to be executed along with his countrymen. In the end, von Merenburg agreed to spare the lives of the hostages in return for a guarantee from the abbot that nobody from the island would work with enemies of the Reich in future. This was not just a humane solution to the problem, but a politically wise move, which kept the Germans on Paros safe and stopped the islanders' antipathy towards them growing even stronger.

* * *

While Lassen and his men were on Paros, J and Q Patrols landed on Naxos, where they made contact with a group of local partisans. Following events on Paros, the Germans, who had already established sound defensive positions, were on high alert. The SBS and the partisans attacked temporary German quarters in the town of Naxos, where an officer and seventeen soldiers were billeted. After an hour of street fighting, the raiders and their Greek allies pulled back. They remained in hiding for three days until they were picked up and returned to base. Three men suffered minor wounds and one contracted malaria.[449]

* * *

Most of Sutherland's raiders had now taken part in four operations. Losses had been relatively small, but the exertion had taken its toll. All of the men were starting to show signs of physical and mental exhaustion. Sutherland decided to send J, K, P and Z Patrols back to Palestine. He retained only his staff patrol and Q Patrol on *Tewfik*, which would continue operations until replacements from M Detachment arrived in early June.

In his final report on S Detachment's activities, Sutherland noted that between 26 March and 9 June 1944 his men had carried out 25 landing operations and 17 attacks. They had killed 32 Germans and Italians, wounded 22 and taken 46 prisoners of war. Their own losses amounted to two dead (Kasoulis and Kingston), three injured (two of whom, Harris and Trafford, were wounded on Santorini) and five captured (the Alimnia patrol). During its 2½ months in the Aegean, S Detachment had hijacked three caiques and sunk or damaged twelve, a total tonnage of 500 grt. They had destroyed three radio stations and captured one, and destroyed three cable stations and seven tons of ammunition. At the end of his report, Sutherland wrote,

> What successes the Detachment achieved, I attribute to the keenness and determination of all ranks, and in particular to the outstanding leadership shown by Captain Lassen MC, Captain Clarke and Sgt: Nicholson MM.[450*]

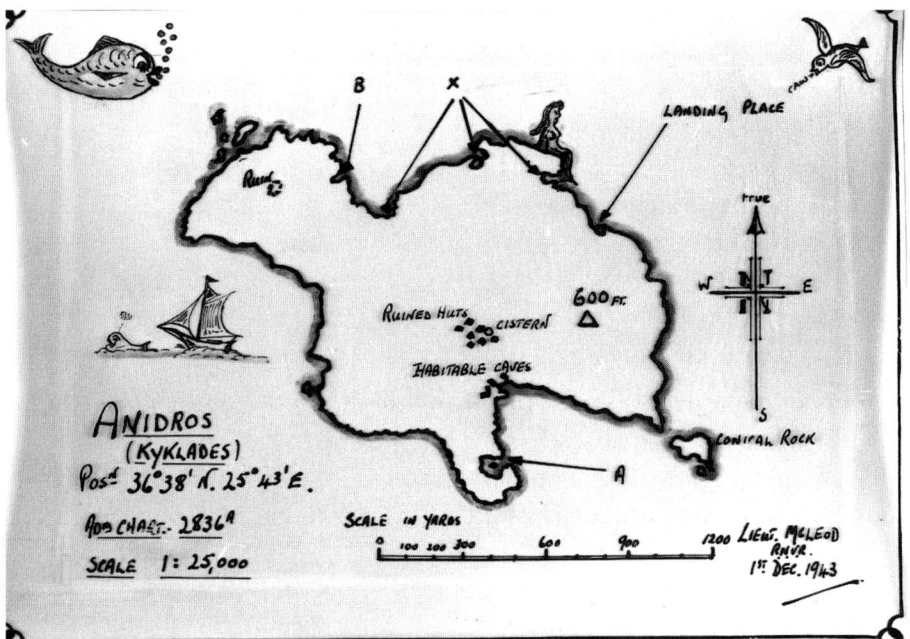

Anders Lassen and his men were not the first British visitors to Anydros. Lieutenant McLeod, RNVR, charted the island and its fauna during a visit on 1 December 1943.

Chapter Thirty-Two

Fatigue and Addiction

It has ever been the way of men to band together to withstand misfortune and outwit fate, and war binds men more tightly together than almost any other branch of human activity.

(Jack Belden: *Still Time to Die*)

On 15 May three SBS men returned to the camp in Atlit from an 'unknown destination' and were RTUed (*Returned to Unit*, i.e. sent back to their original service unit). The SBS war diary does not stipulate whether the trio were guilty of any specific offence, or whether they were simply not cut out for life as raiders. Ever since the very first commando units were set up in 1940, the threat of RTU had been one of the most important means of disciplining and motivating the men in the irregular units. A second and equally important means was the solidarity and mutual dependence that arises among men who live in such close proximity. This comradeship, often described as 'love', a closeness that surpassed that between lovers or spouses, was widespread in all kinds of combat units. The bond was particularly strong among those who spent a long time together in small, isolated groups, with almost no contact with the rest of the military system. In many respects this isolation suited the raiders. They felt as if they were fighting their own war, using means and methods they devised themselves – and when they were not in action they felt that they lived in relative safety, beyond enemy reach. Even on missions they often felt safer behind enemy lines, where they could mount surprise attacks on the enemy from the rear, than they would have in a tank or in a foxhole on the front line, where they might, at any moment, be subjected to hours of artillery bombardment or ordered to storm well-fortified defensive positions.[451] None of them would have traded places with the men in claustrophobic tanks or the *PBI* (Poor Bloody Infantry).

The raiders' hard training, stamina, ability to support themselves, improvise and kill by any means possible made them something special – and they knew it. The strict selection process and training helped boost their self-esteem. They needed to feel that being part of the SBS was particularly important

– otherwise all their exertions and sacrifices would have been in vain. Corporal Dick Holmes described them as 'arrogant bastards' who made a point of cultivating their differences from the rest of the army. (Lassen was perhaps the most arrogant of them all, at least according to Holmes, who regarded himself as a close second.)[452] One obvious difference was the less than rigorous attitude to uniforms, rules and regulations. The conditions in which the raiders lived made it difficult, and perhaps meaningless, to keep uniforms clean, boots polished and webbing blancoed. However, their dirty, seemingly randomly thrown-together uniforms were effectively a 'brand' that underpinned their sense of solidarity and superiority, a show of contempt for the rules that applied to the rest of the army. Similarly the raiders made a point of always having their side-arms with them when they went into town on leave. The atmosphere among the men may well have been informal and in many ways 'democratic', but the men still followed military convention and called the officers 'sir'. On the other hand, officers who were unable to win their men's respect and were too keen on regulations and formalities, or who exhibited signs of excessive self-importance, were ruthlessly taken down – albeit with a 'sir' at the end.

Richard 'Dick' Holmes (left) and Douglas 'Doug' Pomford. Pomford was All England amateur middleweight boxing champion in 1938.

The boots with rubber soles and Dick Holmes' beret (tan, with the SAS winged dagger) are standard kit, but otherwise the two raiders' 'uniforms' are characteristic of the SBS's relaxed style. Pomford's shirt may once have been one of the 'silver-grey' flannel shirts, which the SBS, like the Indian troops, preferred because they absorbed sweat better than normal British khaki shirts or 'bush' shirts. Binoculars, compasses and watches were supplied to officers, sergeants, corporals and signallers, corresponding to approx. one instrument for every two men. (WO 204/8401).

The SBS was unpopular with the rest of the army. The various special forces may well have been admired and romanticised, but their arrogance was a source of envy and irritation as well. There was also a widespread perception that the raiders were pirates or hardened killers who perhaps loved their work too much – a reputation that they to some extent shared with the army's own snipers.[453] Many senior officers, who were initially sceptical about the whole concept, had gradually come to accept that the special forces actually did some good, but still felt that they were overvalued, pampered, too expensive and tied up human resources that could have been put to better use in more orthodox units.

Although life as a raider offered more freedom, and their service was more independent and in many respects perhaps less dangerous than that of the ordinary infantryman, it was no less arduous. Life on board *Tewfik* and the caiques was not the carefree holiday that souvenir photographs might suggest. A larger number of the raiders developed sores from exposure to too much sun and saltwater, and because of their poor diet.[454] The Aegean is a treacherous sea – quite shallow, with countless rocky outcrops, and prone to sudden violent storms. Many of the men in the perpetually pitching and tossing caiques were plagued by seasickness.

In autumn 1943 the raiders were deployed as infantry, even though they were neither trained nor equipped for it, and were caught up in sieges and prolonged air raids. These were, in the clinical sense, stressful experiences. In spring 1944 they were able to play a role that was more independent and in accordance with their training and attitude. But they still faced multiple forms of adversity: physical exhaustion, lack of sleep, poor nutrition, risk of death, danger of mutilation and imprisonment, fear of not living up to expectations and letting colleagues down, the loss of friends, killing, and the frequent necessity of making snap decisions that were a matter of life and death for themselves or their friends. It was hard and exhausting for the men – but even more so for an officer like Lassen. He not only shared the dangers and hardships, but was also responsible for ensuring that the missions were carried out, and that the men, if possible, escaped with life and limbs intact.

His responsibilities as head of P Patrol, and the recognition and autonomy associated with them, had matured Lassen (although he still issued orders in an unpretentious tone, laughed a lot and enjoyed throwing a bucket of water in people's faces). He was no longer so fanatical about weapons or so wild and self-assertive, and he displayed both care and affection for his men. His men also felt confident going into action under him. He had a reputation for being lucky, but above all else for being calm and competent, seeing the bigger picture and always leading from the front in dangerous situations. Dick Holmes regarded him as a manipulator, but also as 'A fantastic soldier, a really determined, strong character'.[455]

Lassen's men did not consider him a typical officer. While he was friendly and approachable, he could also be irascible and throw terrifying tantrums. Something about him kept others at a distance. His most important friendship in the SBS was perhaps with Sean O'Reilly. While he was almost twice as old as Lassen, Corporal O'Reilly looked up to him – and was more than a little afraid of him. For Lassen, O'Reilly was perhaps the last in the series of father figures that had started with 'the bosun' on *Eleonora Mærsk* and continued with Captain J.D. 'Dusty' Miller on *British Consul* and Major March-Phillipps.[456]

It is a distinctive and recurring theme in many descriptions of encounters with Lassen that he was agitated and tense, like a 'tightly coiled spring'. Those who served alongside him in spring and early summer 1944 described Lassen as impatient, unable to relax and unbalanced. This is perhaps not surprising considering what he had been through since boarding the M/T *British Consul* in October 1940. On the other hand, Lassen could also be

> the friendliest, most delightful fellow, very shy and kind and rather quiet. But he always had a smile and a joke, and all of us, men and officers, loved to be with him.[457]

Lassen was on leave from 29 May until 4 June 1944. However, instead of taking some well-earned rest, he went on raids with the Greek Sacred Squadron under the command of Colonel Tsigantes, who later wrote about him: 'His legendary courage, his extraordinary dynamism and his brilliant comradeship was the main reason for fabulous successes on several occasions.' On 5 June, Lassen was back on duty, training new reinforcements.[458]

Lassen undoubtedly needed some form of rest after more than four months on board *Tewfik* or on raids, and no one would have expected him to do anything but take all of the leave to which he was entitled. Nonetheless, he chose instead to spend part of it with Tsigantes' men in the Aegean Sea. Perhaps his hatred of the Germans and his determination to fight for Denmark's freedom and honour made him feel that relaxing while others were fighting was a waste of time. Or maybe he simply missed the war, where he was an important person with great responsibility and freedom of action, where he was doing something that he enjoyed and was good at, and for which he received recognition. Maybe, like so many other soldiers, he had become addicted to the excitement and adrenaline. Maybe, at the age of 23, he had felt the proximity of death and tried to live in the present, to achieve what he had set out to do before his time was brought to an end.

Porter Jarrell said of Lassen:

> It was as if a fever were burning inside him. He defied death and exposed himself to the greatest dangers. He was like a restless dynamo, charged with energy. He had to do something to translate his thoughts into action. Also when he was on leave, it was as if he knew that he had

courted disaster too often and had to fill these short hours with the life that was running away from him.[459]

The many testimonies to Lassen's mood swings, restlessness and enormous energy and stamina in the field, as well as his corresponding periods of depression during leave, make it reasonable to think that maybe he was one of the hundreds of thousands of soldiers who developed a short-lived or prolonged amphetamine habit.

Amphetamine products, which were originally marketed as antidepressants, were used extensively by the British, American, German and Japanese armed forces during the war. RAF fighter pilots were particularly heavy users. However, the British gradually cut down on their use, partly because the RAF found that the amount of amphetamines needed to prevent trembling hands and a lack of coordination could have an adverse effect on judgement. The US military continued to use Benzedrine throughout the war. The SOE and special forces like the SBS also included Benzedrine tablets as part of the standard kit when agents and raiders were sent into action.

As well as the desired effects – increased energy, alertness and concentration – Benzedrine enhanced sociability, self-confidence and sexual desire. It also led to side effects such as euphoria, anxiety, irritability, aggression, pyschomotor agitation and sense of power and superiority. Users developed a tolerance quite quickly and needed to up the dose and frequency to achieve the desired effects and avoid a comedown. Chronic users who stop taking amphetamines may suffer withdrawal symptoms – depression, anxiety, exhaustion, irascibility, suicidal thoughts and psychosis involving paranoia, hallucinations and delusions.

There is nothing to suggest that Lassen was psychotic or suicidal, but he did exhibit most of the other symptoms. One of Lassen's men noted that the members of his patrol 'never got any Benzedrine tablets because Lassen kept them all for himself.'[460]*

Chapter Thirty-Three

The Adriatic, July–August 1944

For some minutes Guy stood in the dark hall. This building [the HQ of LFA] was a pre-fascist structure designed in traditional style round a sunless cortile. A broad flight of shallow stone steps led up into the darkness, for the glass roof had been shattered and replaced by tarred paper. 'The light ought to come on any time now,' said the sentry. 'But you can't rely on it.'
(Evelyn Waugh, *Unconditional Surrender*)

Land Forces Adriatic

When the Allies landed in Normandy on 6 June 1944, it effectively rendered conjuring up the illusion of a major offensive through Greece irrelevant. The intensity of the SBS campaign in the Aegean tapered off. Raiding was left to the Greek Sacred Squadron. In August the SBS relocated to southern Italy to operate in Yugoslavia and on the Adriatic islands.

In Italy the SBS came under the command of the new Land Forces Adriatic, which had its HQ in a former police station in the centre of Bari. As well as the SBS and LRDG, LFA included commandos from the Army and Royal Marines, field artillery and various support units.[461]

Ian Lapraik was one of the few SBS men to remain in the Aegean with Turnbull's greatly reduced Raiding Force – but this left M Squadron without a commander. George Jellicoe entrusted Lassen with the role.[462]

* * *

The SBS's new quarters were a camp in an olive grove outside Monopoli, 25 miles south of Bari, where the SOE also had a base; and in a school building in Monte Sant'Angelo, 60 miles north of the city. The medieval town of Monte Sant'Angelo is on the Gargano Peninsula, the forested mountains of which made an ideal training ground. The LRDG was already in the area and had been active in Yugoslavia for some time. Old acquaintances were renewed and the new arrivals benefited from the advice and experience of those with greater experience.

* * *

On 23 August, King Michael of Romania deposed the pro-German dictator Marshal Antonescu and asked General Sănătescu to form a government. Sănătescu broke with Germany and gave their troops a deadline to leave the country. On 25 August Romania declared war on Germany. On 31 August the Russians entered the capital, Bucharest. Bulgaria underwent a similar process – on 24 August the Prime Minister demanded that the German military mission and all their troops leave the country. On 26 August he declared the country neutral. On 5 September Soviet forces advanced into Bulgaria, and on 9 September the Communists seized power in a coup and installed a pro-Soviet government. These dramatic events in the two Balkan countries heightened the strategic focus on Yugoslavia – both as a transit country for German forces moving from Greece to Austria and Germany, and as an area in which Britain attempted to exert influence and compete with the USSR and its Communist allies.

Operation Health Able, Yugoslavia, August–September 1944[463]

At 23:59 on Sunday 27 August 1944, an RAF high speed launch set Lassen, Lieutenant J.C. Henshaw (a new member of the SBS) and sixteen men from S Squadron's O and K patrols ashore on the Croatian coast. They were met on the beach by Lieutenant Skipworth from the LRDG and 20 Yugoslav partisans. By 02:30 the raiders' equipment and several hundred pounds of plastic explosives had also been landed. These were hidden in a nearby thicket right away, after which Skipworth and the partisans led Lassen and his men to a hideout roughly a mile inland.

The operation, called Health Able, was part of a major, week-long campaign to impede the German withdrawal from Greece that had begun in late summer. Lassen's task was to blow up a railway bridge over a gorge at Karasovici, 15 to 20 miles south of Dubrovnik. After that he was to attack any targets he found on the railway or roads down towards the Albanian border. For the raiders this was business as usual – exactly what they had been doing on the Aegean islands, only now it was on the mainland. The SBS was responsible for the attacks and sabotage, while the LRDG men led them through countryside that they had carefully reconnoitred and observed for days before the raiders arrived.

For the first two days, the raiders remained in hiding during daylight hours. They marched at night, with the LRDG men as guides and the partisans carrying the explosives. On 30 August at 03:30, as dawn was breaking along the mountain tops, they at last reached Plocice, approx. two miles south of the target. The raiders remained in hiding all day, enjoying food and wine provided by locals. At 20:00 the SBS men set out for the bridge with their explosives. It took them an hour to get there. The partisans covered the access routes while the explosives team placed charges in holes that the partisans had drilled in the pillars. The explosives were in place by 21:15.

> We set it up electrically. A couple of us did the wiring while a Royal Engineers corporal made a junction box with a primer cord to each charge. The wiring from the plunger to the detonator was less than 150 feet, shorter than we would have liked for 500 lb of ethyl-ammonal.
>
> The rest retreated while Lassen and I stayed behind. We pressed the plunger but nothing happened. Lassen told me to clean the plunger so I unscrewed the terminals, polished and replaced the wires, we pressed once more. Again nothing. In the meantime, the RE corporal had lit the safety fuse. We sat there for a couple of minutes and still nothing happened. Lassen said: 'We'll have to do something.' I said that perhaps the safety fuse hadn't yet burned through. He wouldn't listen, he said: 'It must have burned by now.' Finally, I talked him into waiting just a little longer but he was restless and stood up … as he did so, the bridge exploded and a piece of masonry fully five-foot square whistled past his head.[464]

After the explosion, the SBS patrols met with the LRDG men and the partisans at a predetermined location further along the railway track. From there they marched to the partisans' headquarters at Duboki. At 07:30 they reached their destination – ten miles further inland and around 4,000 feet higher up in the mountains. The raiders stopped to rest for two days, but at 02:30 on 2 September the alarm sounded. Three patrols of *Ustaše* (fascist militia) were heading towards the camp, led by German officers using whistles as signals.

After consulting with the leader of the partisans, Lassen decided to stay and fight despite the enemy's superior numbers, instead of trying to escape into the darkness. He sent Lieutenant Henshaw and five men out to occupy a ridge on the camp's right flank. When the battle began at dawn, his patrol succeeded in killing or wounding three enemies. Henshaw tried to manoeuvre his way behind the Ustaše and attack them from the rear, but had to give up because there were too many of them.[465*] At 10:00, Henshaw withdrew his patrol and went into hiding until darkness fell.

The main force under Lassen also engaged the enemy. Again he and Holmes disagreed about what to do:

> We grabbed our rucksacks but were told by Andy to leave them where they were then he led us to a spot where we were to make our stand.

The spot was a hollow, overlooked for a good part of its circumference, a feature that would enable our adversaries to approach unseen and drop grenades among us, a fact that seemed to have escaped Lassen's notice. … We gathered in the hollow waiting for the enemy to arrive, knowing that we were not likely to survive the skirmish due to Lassen's choice of a battleground. Being cowardly by nature and reluctant to forfeit my life for a ridiculous, forlorn cause, I stationed myself on the rim, keeping a watchful eye on our Yugoslav allies. As the Ustashi split into two groups, intent on encircling our little force, I spotted several partisans leaving the scene, heading north. In no time at all they would all be gone leaving us on our own. When I told Andy what was happening he did not believe me but rushed to the ridge just in time to see the last of our friends disappearing round a bend in the path. Wasting no time we followed their example, sans packs which contained food, water, warm clothing and the like. For three days we roamed the mountains existing on rain water collected in the depressions in rocks and patches of wild potatoes. When the partisans found us we were near the end of our tether and we were delighted when the launch picked us up several days later, happy to escape with our lives. With so many excellent defensive positions to choose from I found it hard to comprehend Lassen's choice.[466]

Anders Lassen (right) in the Aegean. Before the raid on Santorini.

Lassen wrote in his report: 'Later a withdrawal was ordered and carried out successfully except for RE who was taken prisoner along with two LRDG personnel after a 3hr fight.'[467]

Holmes was not the only SBS man with reservations about Lassen's tactical abilities. Sergeant Nicholson, who was awarded the Military Medal for his gallantry in Crete in July 1943 and the Distinguished Conduct Medal for his endeavours on Santorini and Paros, considered him reckless. He thought that Lassen placed his men's lives in danger unnecessarily.

Sergeant Les Stephenson admired Lassen greatly, but found him 'immature' and thought he must really irritate soldiers accustomed to more traditional officers.

> He wouldn't suffer fools gladly, he would say what he thought. Some people didn't like that. I could understand people not getting on with him because he could put salt in the wound. There would be no 'ifs' and 'buts'. This was part of his leadership. He didn't want you standing there arguing or hesitating. A very positive man who didn't have trouble making his mind up.[468]

All in all, one dead and two captured must be considered relatively modest losses after a three-hour clash with a numerically superior enemy force and three days of flight through the mountains.

* * *

On the night of 5/6 September, Lassen's two patrols and the two remaining LRDG men made it to the pick-up site where Henshaw and his five men had been waiting in hiding since the night before. The men gathered in small clusters on the beach and sent the predetermined coded message out to sea – but the signal faded as the batteries in the lanterns drained. Two men stood guard while Lassen stood perched on a cliff, peering into the darkness through his binoculars.

After a long and nerve-wracking wait, artillery fire was heard a little further up the coast. A German coastal battery had caught sight of the British motor torpedo boats that were to pick up the raiders. The Germans had tried to signal to the torpedo boats to lure them closer to shore but did not know the code. When that gambit failed, they opened fire, albeit at too great a distance to do any harm.

At 01:45 the torpedo boats finally reached the rendezvous point. One sailed close to the beach, the other waited further out to sea. The raiders could only see the closest boat, but they were expecting two. Lassen ordered his men to take cover behind nearby rocks, ready to fight in case it was a German patrol boat putting troops ashore. Before the situation could escalate, Lord Jellicoe, who had made the trip to pick up his men, made his presence known loudly. His shout was answered from the beach. A dinghy and a few inflatables were launched and the SBS men and their two comrades from LRDG were taken on board. The patrol boats docked in Bari at 06:00 that morning.

* * *

The raiders had brought with them large quantities of lire, captured from a German transport column that they had attacked on the road to the coast: 'It was a terrible slaughter – mules, men and horses stomping around in blood and baggage.' The column was transporting a fortune in German Reichsmark and Italian lire. Since Lassen and his men were unable to lug all of the money with them, they decided to burn the German notes and keep the Italian ones – on the grounds that the Reichsmark was likely to be worthless when Germany collapsed, whereas the lira would retain its value. It was the wrong call. The Reichsmark remained in circulation until 1948, while the Italian lira was replaced by the occupation currency 'the AM-lira'.[469]

Leave in Bari, September 1944

In Bari the men had time to relax. Lassen went into town with the Danish-born Lieutenant P.B. Jensen (RNVR) and the American Howard Reed. Lassen and Jensen had become acquainted in March 1944 when the latter was serving on a patrol boat in the Aegean. Jensen had never met anyone who harboured such hatred for the Germans or had such a reputation for absolute composure in action. He noted that a member of Lassen's patrol described him as 'our tame killer'. Lassen had met Reed, a fellow raider, on Leros in October 1943. They had fought together in the Aegean, where Reed had admired Lassen's calmness and willingness always to lead from the front in dangerous situations. They had also spent time on leave together in Palestine and Egypt, where he had found Lassen quiet, friendly and shy, but always with a joke at the ready. Now they met again in Bari. Reed was preparing to depart for Alexandria to join the new Force 140 which was mainly made up of III Corps. Under the newly appointed Commander Land Forces, Greece, Lieutenant General Ronald Scobie, its role was to make sure that the British and the Greek government-in-exile controlled Greece. Lassen was heading straight back to Greece with the SBS.[470*]

Chapter Thirty-Four

Back to Greece, September–October 1944

The 'Tommy Gun' has a short barrel and fires blunt-nosed pistol ammunition. It is therefore a short range weapon & by reason of the heavy calibre of the bullets and the high rate of fire it is a valuable weapon for any type of close combat fighting, such as Street and House Fighting, etc.

(SOE Syllabus)

Operations Manna and Noah's Ark

As mentioned previously, Lassen's raid in Croatia was part of a larger operation, which started in September 1944 – the Greek part of which, Operation Noah's Ark,[471*] sought to tie down as many Germans as possible in Greece. The idea was to ensure that any units that managed to escape were so damaged and worn down that it would take time to reinforce and re-equip them before they would be ready for action in Western Europe. At the same time, a strong British naval force (Force 120, organized around seven escort aircraft carriers) was preventing the Germans from evacuating islands in the Aegean or concentrating their troops on the 'fortress islands': Crete, Rhodes, Leros, Kos, and Samos. Both of these operations were part of the preparations for talks soon to be held in Moscow on the future of the Balkans.

Churchill met with Stalin at the Moscow conference, 9–19 October 1944, and the two leaders agreed to share influence in the Balkans: the USSR was to have 90% influence in Romania, Britain and the other Allies 10%; Yugoslavia would be split equally; Hungary and Bulgaria was to be divided up 80/20 in favour of the Soviets. Greece, on the other hand, would be divided 90/10 in favour of Britain.

Winston Churchill was determined that it would be the royal government-in-exile, led by the Liberal Georgios Papandreou, and not the Communist resistance organization EAM and its armed wing ELAS, that took power in Greece once the Germans withdrew. It was envisaged that Lieutenant General Scobie's Force 140 would play a dual role: fighting the Germans and working with anti-communist partisans to harass them as they withdrew, and then taking control of the country before EAM/ELAS did. Papandreou

The Western Aegean and the Greek mainland.

and the EAM leadership may have agreed at Caserta that Scobie should command all resistance forces in Greece, but there was no guarantee that local ELAS leaders would work with the British.

Scobie's work to secure control of Greece for the British and Papandreou started even while the horse-trading was going on in Moscow. The operation was codenamed Manna. The British Cabinet had determined its purpose as 'a. to install the Greek government. b. to accept the German surrender. c. to pave the way for the introduction of relief.'[472*] This was a top-secret operation, at the very highest political and strategic level, and it is extremely doubtful whether George Jellicoe (for example), who would play a central role in it, knew the full scale of the plans. Without doubt, the officers at Anders Lassen's level knew little more than that they were to inconvenience the Germans as far as possible, that they were to establish a British military presence in liberated Greece, and that relations with the Communist partisans in ELAS were often particularly strained.

Kythera and Antikythera, September–October 1944[473]

On 14 September 1944, Anders Lassen's M Squadron embarked from Taranto, bound for the island of Kythera, about six miles south of the Peloponnese. M Squadron was now part of Foxforce, under the command of Lieutenant Colonel Ronnie J.F. Tod, who led the very first commando raid on the north coast of France in June 1940. Foxforce also included the Scottish 9 Commando, a patrol from the LRDG and some units of the Raiding Support Regiment, complete with 75 mm guns and mortars. The Greek Sacred Squadron was incorporated into the force later on.

On 9 September an SBS patrol parachuted into Kythera to destroy a German radar station that was thought to pose a danger to the planned landing on the Greek mainland.[474] The patrol reported that the Germans had evacuated the island. The Royal Navy decided to use Kythera as a forward base for its operations along the Greek coast. Foxforce was initially charged with protecting this new naval base, and landed on Kythera on the evening of 15 September.

A small Royal Navy force consisting of, at least, a destroyer and, probably, an LCT arrived at Kythera at 8 a.m. of Wednesday 20 September with orders to secure the ports on the islands and support the Royal Hellenic Navy. ELAS controlled Kythera and there were 300–400 'British Greeks' on shore. The port was bombed by German planes as soon as the British landed. After the attack, a RN LCT sailed round to Nicoto Bay to pick uo 350 men of 9th Commando and 'Andy Lassen and his S.B.S thugs'.[475*]

From Kythera, the SBS and LRDG sent reconnaissance patrols up to the islands in Saronikos Bay to prepare to take the capital. Lassen and his men clashed with German patrols and garrisons on several of these expeditions – but other dangers lurked on these islands too. In many areas, enmity between royalist and leftist guerrillas had broken out into pitched battles. Lassen's colleague Lieutenant Robert Bury was killed when a group of right-wing partisans on Spetses mistook his patrol for ELAS men.[476*]

M Squadron did not just operate on its own. Lassen and his men were also used as scouts and guides when a commando force was sent to occupy the island of Antikythera, approx. twenty-four miles south-east of Kythera.

The landing was a rush job and poorly planned – unlike the SBS men, the commandos were unaware that there were no Germans on the island. This led to an episode that illustrates the men's sometimes difficult relationship to more traditional military authorities, as well as Lassen's loyalty to his own men and his fearless contempt for anything he considered *bullshit*. The landing was to be made in the dark. Dick Holmes and Roger Wright were to row into the harbour in a folboat and show the landing craft the way:

> When we reached the entrance to the harbour I suggested to the officer that he should drop us off but he decided that it was not necessary. Another ALC sped past us and disappeared into the gloom. There was a tremendous crash which we later learned was caused by one of the ALCs colliding with the mast of a sunken ship. Our craft breasted the surf and came to an abrupt halt. The ramp thudded down and the young officer, walking stick in one hand, pistol in the other, motioned to his men to follow him and rushed down the ramp – into several feet of water!! Roger and I pissed ourselves as some of his platoon followed his lead, but the rest stayed in their seats. The bosun of the landing craft reversed his charge and chose another section of the beach to discharge his cargo. At the second attempt the rest of the platoon reached the beach comparatively dry. Roger and I carried our folboat ashore without getting our feet wet. As we plodded higher up the sandy strip we passed the young officer who had just waded ashore, soaked to the skin.
>
> 'Get out of those wet clothes. You'll get your death of cold!' Roger advised him.
>
> We turned our boat upside down, slid out of our ruck-sacks and sat down on it, while all around us the commando 'chappies' were feverishly digging in the sand.
>
> 'Jesus Christ! What are they doing that for?' Roger muttered loud enough for everyone to hear.

At that point the gung-ho officer, soaked to the skin, probably incensed by my companion's earlier remark, headed in our direction.

'Why aren't you men digging in?' he growled.

'We don't do that sort of thing,' I replied, 'especially when there are no enemy in the vicinity.'

He went away. As soon as he was out of sight we picked up the folboat, lifted it over the drystone wall at the top of the beach and climbed over after it. Roger lit his cigarette while I brewed up. We finished the tea, removed our boots, slid into our sleeping bags and went to sleep. Several hours later we woke to find our commando friends busily digging slit trenches on this side of the wall. We ignored them and prepared our breakfast. No sooner had we finished eating than the officer who had been on our ALC appeared, still soaked to the skin.

'Why aren't you men digging in?' he demanded.

'We don't do that sort of thing,' I replied.

'Anyway, we've nothing to dig with,' added Roger.

The officer crossed to one of his section, picked up a small entrenching tool and brought it over to us with the remark, 'You have now.'

I stood up, accepted the implement, removed a shovel full of earth then handed it to Roger.

'Your turn,' I smiled.

He did the same then handed the tool back to the officer.

'Why are we digging in? There are no fucking Germans on the island!' he protested.

We sat back on our boat and began to clean our weapons. Our tormentor looked at us for several seconds, unsure just how to handle this situation, one he had never faced before, I felt sure, then turned on his heels and strode towards a group of commando officers that included the CO of the commando. He began talking excitedly, glancing over his shoulder in our direction as he did so, then he and his CO detached themselves from the group and walked towards us. We got to our feet and stood at a casual attention.

'Don't you salute officers?' the CO barked.

'Not often, sir,' I replied.

'Never on active service, sir,' Roger added.

'Why is that?' demanded the CO.

'Might provide enemy snipers with a target, sir,' Roger answered.

'You said there were no Germans on the island,' the lieutenant protested.

'We've been wrong before,' Roger answered with a shrug.

The CO looked us up and down, an expression approaching disgust on his face.

'Who are you?' he asked brusquely.

'Sergeant Holmes.'

'Sergeant Wright.'

'Do you always dress like this?' the CO's face began to redden.

'Only on active service, sir,' Roger replied.

I was wearing khaki shorts, calf-length boots, a windproof jacket that displayed the detritus of several other raids, which included gun oil, food stains, mud and the odd spot of blood (not my own). A web belt about my waist supported a water bottle, a fighting knife, a web holster with the top cut away held a .45 Colt and a homemade canvas pouch contained three spare mags for my Tommy gun. I suppose I did look scruffy compared to these commando jokers. Roger was similarly attired.

'Mr Watson! Put these men under close arrest!!' the CO barked.

The lieutenant waved two men over and they stood in front of us.

'Disarm them!!' he ordered.

'I don't think so,' I said quietly but firmly.

'I suggest you find our officer, Captain Lassen,' Roger informed him.

The CO nodded agreement and a soldier was despatched to find Andy. We sat down on our boat.

One of our guards looked at us. 'Are you two in the army?'

'More of it than in it,' Roger replied, leaving the guard to figure that out.

Within minutes our fearless leader appeared, an angry expression on his face. He too was wearing a windproof jacket in much the same condition as our own, an old denim beret on his hand and sewn over the left breast of his jacket were two rows of medal ribbons, in pride of place his MC with two silvery shapes, crudely cut from the inner lid of a Players cigarette tin.

'What's going on here?' he barked and we could see the two commando officers taken aback by his appearance. We wandered over to listen in on the exchange.

'Your men refused an order to dig in!' the CO replied eyeing Andy's medal ribbons.

'We don't believe in that shit!!' scoffed Andy.

Then the CO opened his mouth and really put his foot in it.

'But look how they're dressed!!' the CO complained.

Andy looked him up and down before replying.

'My men don't have to be well dressed to be good soldiers. That's sergeant Holmes,' he said pointing in my direction.' He won the MM for single-handedly destroying a fuel dump in Crete in 1943. He was with me last year when we destroyed a bridge in Yugoslavia as well as many other successful raids. The other man is Sergeant Wright, also an MM. He helped us blow up the bridge in Yugoslavia.' He paused for breath before continuing. 'Both of these men have been in the army since the outbreak of war and have probably killed more Germans than you have ever seen.'

Neither of the two officers could think of a suitable reply so Andy resumed.

'Now, if you've finished with my men I'll take them with me. We've got more important things to do than dig fucking holes!' He turned on his heels and strode away; we picked up our boat and followed him. As we plodded along behind him I gave vent on my feelings.

'Sometimes I love that man!'[477]

Jellicoe – with Bucketforce from Araxos to Athens, September–October 1944

While Ronnie Tod's Foxforce felt their way forward along the eastern side of the Peloponnese, George Jellicoe was put in charge of *Bucketforce*, which was to land on the opposite side of the peninsula. Bucketforce consisted of approx. 450 men from the SBS L Squadron, two companies of the Highland Light Infantry, 2908 Squadron RAF Regiment, a patrol from the LRDG, half a platoon from 40 (Royal Marine) Commando, and various support and maintenance units. Between 23 and 25 September, Bucketforce occupied the airfield at Araxos on the west side of the Peloponnese. They met no resistance. From there they proceeded rapidly to Patras, which was captured before the Germans managed to render the important harbour unusable, and then further east along the coastal road to the Corinth isthmus, between the Peloponnese and the rest of the Greek mainland. On 7 October, L Squadron crossed the Corinth Canal on a makeshift ferry. Lieutenant Bimrose led three patrols north towards Thebes. Along the way they engaged the German rearguard and one of the men was killed. Meanwhile the commander of L Squadron, Ian Patterson, sent a caique out to reconnoitre Athens Bay, east of the Corinth isthmus. The skipper, Lieutenant Balsillie, decided to go ashore in the Athens port of Piraeus – the first uniformed British soldier to set foot there as part of Operation Manna.

The rest of Bucketforce (except for the RAF Regiment, which was busy taking care of the Greek security battalions who had collaborated with the Germans and were now surrendering in large numbers on condition that the

British protected them from their countrymen) advanced on Piraeus and Athens along the coast road on the northern shore of the Bay of Athens.

Jellicoe spent a couple of days negotiating a *modus vivendi* between the ELAS partisans and the British forces, to maintain the peace, law and order in the liberated areas and avoid revenge killings and summary executions. He was then ordered to Athens to establish a military and political presence post-haste as the Germans withdrew from the city. The British presence needed to be at a certain level if it was to give the impression that a major force was heading for Athens. On 9 October, Jellicoe had been promoted to 'local acting colonel'.[478*] However, this was deemed insufficiently senior, so the colourful Brigadier Joseph Patrick O'Brien-Twohig, commander of 183 Infantry Brigade (Adriatic Brigade), promoted Jellicoe on the spot to acting brigadier and gave him the red collar patch from his own uniform so that he could act with the requisite authority. Milner-Barry was promoted to colonel in the same manner.[479]

The Germans were still blocking the coast road to Athens and were thought to have mined the city's airfield. As a result, on the night of 11 October, 11 of Jellicoe's men, under the command of the SOE-man Major Frank Macaskie (known as 'Greece's Scarlet Pimpernel'), sailed to the port of Skaramagas, west of Athens. They marched the rest of the way and were the first British troops to reach the Greek capital, on the morning of Thursday, 12 October.[480]

At 05:00 on 13 October, Jellicoe and Milner-Barry boarded a caique along with the Greek-speaking correspondent of the *New York Times*, A.C. 'Shan' Sedgwick, who acted as an interpreter, Bill Reid (not identified in any more detail) and their military escort Corporal Newton. This small party sailed along the north side of Salamis to Eleusis on the western outskirts of Athens. Here they met Ian Patterson, who had arrived by road. Jellicoe and Patterson mounted bikes and headed for the city. The rest of the party followed by car later.

According to Milner-Barry, the reception in Athens was 'overwhelming; tears, shouts, kisses, handshakes, blows on the back, dragged into houses and nearly suffocated.'

In Athens, Jellicoe, Milner-Barry and Macaskie sought out the local ELAS leaders and the royal Greek government's military governor of Athens – the fiercely anti-Communist General Panagiotis Spiliotopoulos, whom ELAS considered a German collaborator. Early on the morning of Saturday, 14 October, Jellicoe and Macaskie appeared on the balcony of the elegant Hotel Grande Bretagne on Constitution Square, where a mass demonstration was taking place. For the rest of the day, Jellicoe, Milner-Barry and Patterson were repeatedly called back out onto the balcony to wave to the crowd and make impromptu speeches in a mixture of English and Greek.

Athenians celebrating the liberation of their city.

Rumours of how the British had prevented a bloodbath in Patras after the Germans left had preceded them. The sight of Jellicoe and his compatriots on the hotel balcony, as well as the arrival in the city of the SBS, helped to curb unrest during this critical period following the German withdrawal.[481*]

'Verk before vimmin' – on the way to Athens – Poros, October 1944

During one of his reconnaissance patrols, Lassen ascertained that the Germans had abandoned Poros, off the east coast of the Peloponnese in the southern part of the Bay of Athens. Due to the strategic importance of its harbour, Foxforce boarded a handful of minesweepers on 30 September and sailed from Kythera to Poros. This was to serve as the base for the combined naval and land forces' final leg to Athens. First they had to neutralise enemy coastal batteries on the neighbouring island of Aegina, eight miles north of Poros, which controlled the entrance to the Bay of Athens and therefore to Piraeus. The small island of Fleves, at the eastern end of the bay, also had to be overrun before the attack on Piraeus and Athens.

In preparation, M Squadron, under the command of Lassen, carried out another series of covert reconnaissance patrols – this time far up into the Bay.

After one such mission, Lassen (who had been promoted to acting major on 9 October, a few weeks after his 24th birthday[482*]) reported to Brigadier Ronnie Tod that the Germans were preparing to evacuate Aegina, and that they would leave behind a battalion of somewhat rebellious – and therefore incarcerated – Arab volunteers under the command of an Italian NCO. Men from the Arab Free Corps had raped several Greek women, and Lassen thought that the locals would annihilate every last member of the battalion as soon as the Germans left. Tod took Lassen's advice and decided to evacuate the Arabs. Operation Freikorps Rescue was launched for humanitarian reasons, but also because Lassen knew that there were ELAS people on the island. He suspected that a massacre of the Arabs might serve as cover for revenge attacks on ELAS's political opponents. Poros was receiving a steady stream of refugees from the Peloponnese, where ELAS was forcing men into service, confiscating food from villages and killing its political opponents. Tod and his staff were fully aware of what might happen on Aegina if the situation were to spiral out of control.

According to Ronnie Tod's deputy, Colonel Donald Hamilton-Hill, while he and Tod discussed the details of Operation Freikorps Rescue with Lassen,

> Tod noted … that the three other ranks of the SBS whom Andy had brought with him were lolling about outside our window, cigarettes dangling out of the corners of their mouths; they did not either get up for or salute the many officers moving in and out of the building. Andy Lassen himself was somewhat irregularly dressed, in a filthy pair of shorts and shirt and was almost – but not quite – ill-mannered in his approach to his Force Commander – which was Ronnie – and as he left the office he omitted to salute.
>
> Ronnie spoke to me: 'Donald, you know these odd bods better than I do – sort out their discipline.'

Colonel Hamilton-Hill followed Lassen and invited him into his office 'for a chat'.

> Softening my rocket to him, I started out by saying that we thought he and his section were doing an excellent job with their night infiltration, but there had been complaints that their ration drawings had been three or four times the amount required for the numbers involved. Andy was quite open about it all. 'We use our golden sovereigns that you gave us for payment for information in our nightly poker game and we buy our information with 'C' rations.'

This was apparently quite normal practice in all their previous operations during the preceding years, and he seemed to think that I was being quite unreasonable in asking for a regular account of such money. I had to disillusion him somewhat abruptly and further insist that he and his men must in future conform to the Force discipline – which in the case of 9 Commando was as strict as any in the British Army, including the Guards and the Highland Brigade! He only managed a half-hearted salute as he went out, but I could sense that he would conform in due course.

The next morning, Hamilton-Hill saw one of Lassen's sergeants on the way to the clearing station with his mouth and face wrapped in bandages. He sent for Lassen and asked him if any of his men had been injured.

In his funny sing-song Danish accent he said – this time with a decent salute: 'I thought I would have good discipline as you said, sir, and last night when I got back to our forward base on Megathon [the neighbouring northward isthmus] I found my men sitting round in a circle playing poker for sovereigns as usual. I said to the Sergeant 'Don't you ever get up when your CO comes into the room?' The Sergeant did not stop smoking and said 'No' – so I kicked him hard three times in goolies. As he lay on the ground I then kicked his teeth out. We are now disciplined, sir.'

'Good heavens, Andy, one complaint from him and I would have to set up a Court of Enquiry and you might well come off second best.'

'Don't worry, sir, there will be no complaint – furthermore, I've told all the men, in future, *verk before vimmin.*'

Andy was quite right; there was no complaint, either then or later, though when I made a private enquiry from our doctor at the CCS – Casualty Clearing Station – he told me that the sergeant had lost several teeth and was in considerable pain and discomfort. I breathed a sigh of relief. Whatever his faults, Andy was an engaging character and an incredible gatherer of information.[483]

It says something about Lassen's status among his superiors – 'an engaging character and an incredible gatherer of information' – that Hamilton-Hill let him off with such gross misconduct. It also says something about Hamilton-Hill, and perhaps about the British army in general, that the Colonel evidently considered Lassen's lack of respect for his superiors and for the army's equipment and money to be a bigger problem than the fact that he kicked a subordinate's teeth in. It is less clear what the sergeant's silence says about his personal relationship with Lassen, or about Lassen's status among his men. He may have kept quiet because he was too fond of the Dane to complain about him, or he may have been too scared of him. Maybe involving outsiders in an internal matter would have been against the macho ethos of the SBS men and their sense of belonging. In any case, it was not the only time Lassen used his fists to put a subordinate in his place.[484]

When Lassen demolished the two officers on the beach on Antikythera, this was him in his element. He was in action and free to do what he wanted, he was self-assured and full of an authority that largely rested on the accomplishments of himself and his men and on the recognition they had brought him. He also had a loyal audience with whom he shared values, while his opponents were outside that circle. On the other hand, when he sat across from Hamilton-Hill in the latter's office, he was alone, confronted with an authority stronger than his own, which he could not challenge without serious consequences. He had to accept a reprimand, which sat badly with his pride, rebellious temperament, urge to assert himself and need for recognition.

When Lassen left Hamilton-Hill's office with 'a half-hearted salute', he was presumably boiling over with humiliation and anger. Nevertheless, his reaction to a man who had, after all, only done what he himself encouraged his men to do was unusually brutal – even by his own and the SBS's standards – and completely out of proportion to the offence. His propensity towards violence may have been down to his amphetamine use, but must also, to some extent, be seen as a consequence of the heavy mental strain of years of service as a raider. Or as Lassen himself is supposed to have put it: 'You can do some of it, part of the time, for quite a while. But you can't do all of it, all the time, for very long.'[485]

Poros, Aegina, Piraeus and Athens, October 1944

On Poros, planning continued for the attack on Aegina and the advance on Piræus and Athens. Despite persistent requests to LFA in Bari, there was little in the way of aerial reconnaissance, but Lassen's patrols continued to gather intelligence. PoWs and Greek caique skippers were questioned, and, from the heights on Poros, British observation posts kept an eye on German troop movements on Aegina, approx. eight miles to the north.

On 11 October plans were drawn up for the attacks on the coastal batteries at Perdika and Tourlos on Aegina. On 12 October raids would be launched to 'soften up' the German defences. The following day, the actual attack would commence. However, on 11 October, word came that the Germans had evacuated the Perdika battery, and on the afternoon of the 12th, patrols reported that the Germans had left Aegina completely. The rest of the day was spent on an intense exchange of signals between Poros, LFA HQ in Bari which controlled the air support, and the Middle East Command HQ in Alexandria which coordinated the naval effort. It was decided that Aegina was no longer a problem. On the evening of 12 October, Foxforce received orders to call off the attack, secure the port of Piraeus and the Kalamaki airbase near Athens, and prevent any sabotage attempts by the Germans. The operation was scheduled for 14 October, but on the night of the 13th observation posts reported hearing blasts in Piraeus. The same day, a patrol also confirmed that the Germans had abandoned Fleves. The sea route to Piraeus lay open. At 21:00, Foxforce embarked from Poros to Piraeus on board two landing craft, accompanied by 70–100 caiques.

The Germans had mined the waters between Aegina and Piraeus, but the improvised transport fleet managed to pass through, losing only three boats. At dawn on 14 October, the landing vessels were within sight of the port of Piraeus. The rumour that the British were coming by sea had spread. The harbour was packed with people and an armada of small boats and caiques sailed out to welcome Foxforce. The Germans had left Piraeus the day before. They had sabotaged the main harbour but the smaller one was undamaged. The British went ashore there after clearing a beachhead into the enthusiastic crowd which filled the whole quay. Jellicoe wanted Foxforce to move into Athens as soon as possible to give his mission greater substance. Immediately after the landings, the troops changed from combat fatigues to parade uniform, after which they were driven in local buses to the outskirts of Athens. Here they met a reduced company of 4 Independent Parachute Battalion which had landed at Megara. The two small contingents marched through jubilant crowds into Constitution Square, where they were inspected by the military governor, General Spiliotopoulos. They then continued to the tomb of the Unknown Soldier, where Brigadier Tod laid a wreath.

On 18 October, Prime Minister Georgios Papandreou and his government (including seven ministers from the Communist-dominated National Liberation Front (EAM), of which ELAS was the military wing) arrived in Athens.

* * *

It is not entirely clear where Anders Lassen was during all of this. Maybe he went ashore in Piræus and was transported from there to Athens along with the rest of Foxforce. However, it is possible that he (along with Lieutenant

Anders Lassen behind the wheel.

James Henshaw and a small patrol) had landed in the elegant suburb of Faliron, a few miles south of Piraeus, where 'a sweet, young Greek girl' provided him with civilian clothes so he could go into Athens on a secret errand, presumably to reconnoitre in advance of the parade.[486]

Like a number of other British officers, Lassen moved into the Hotel Grande Bretagne, where he spent some days sharing a room with a comrade from the evacuation of Samos, the tennis star Colonel Max Bally. The liberation celebrations were extensive, with demonstrations, torchlight processions, music and dancing in the streets. Through it all, the happy – and thoroughly inebriated – British soldiers were the centre of attention. Every morning, Lassen's unofficial batman, a Greek called Dimitri whom he had picked up while reconnoitring the island of Hydra, went through his sleeping employer's pockets and scoured the floor in search of any money left over from the night's excesses.[487]

Chapter Thirty-Five

Thessaloniki, October–November 1944

These are basic guerrilla tactics: surprise and subterfuge. Surprise, to take the enemy unawares; subterfuge, to trick him by various ruses into doing the wrong thing, miscalculating your strength or position.

('Yank' Levy: *Guerilla Warfare*)

Pompforce moves north

After the triumph in Athens, Jellicoe continued north, now commanding the improvised Pompforce, made up of the 4th Independent Parachute Battalion, the SBS, airborne engineers, a contingent from the RAF Regiment and a battery of 75 mm guns, totalling approximately 950 men. Pompforce was part of Operation Noah's Ark, which sought to impede and delay the German withdrawal from Greece by enabling guerrillas, SOE agents and small, fast-moving regular units to attack their rearguards and block their way. An order from AFHQ in Caserta to the Balkan Air Force stated: 'Our main objects are to prevent enemy from withdrawing and to kill maximum number of Germans.'[488] In reality, lack of resources to implement Operation Noah's Ark at anything like full strength meant that Pompforce was one of its few tangible outcomes.

On 24 October, Jellicoe attacked Kozani, about 200 miles north of Athens. Despite valiant efforts, especially by the paratroopers, he was unable to take the town. The Germans evacuated Kozani the following morning and continued a series of forced marches, mostly on foot, north-west to Florina on the border with Yugoslavia.[489*] During the autumn, the Yugoslav Communist leader Josip Broz Tito had moved closer to the USSR, and his partisans had linked up with the Red Army. Tito had expressed displeasure with the Western Allies operating in his territory, and Jellicoe received orders not to cross the border into Yugoslavia. Nevertheless, he succeeded in launching another attack against the rear of the last German column to leave Florina on the evening of 1 November. As Pompforce was unable to pursue the Germans into Yugoslavia, Jellicoe instead sent an SBS patrol led by Milner-Barry into Albania. It made contact with David Sutherland and his S Detachment, which had set up its HQ in Korçë, about twenty miles west of the border.⁴⁹⁰

* * *

Scrumforce – on the road to Thessaloniki

While Pompforce advanced towards Yugoslavia and Albania, Lassen and M Squadron pushed up the east coast of Greece through the Sporades archipelago, bound for Thessaloniki – the second biggest city in the country, with a population of 320–350,000, significant industry, a major railway hub, an important port and two airfields near the border with Bulgaria and Yugoslavia.⁴⁹¹*

On 23 October, after a pleasant stay in a villa in Faliron⁴⁹² – perhaps the home of the young lady whom Lassen may have visited on his way to Athens – M Squadron sailed from Piraeus aboard the gunboat ML458.⁴⁹³ In addition to their usual weapons and equipment, the men of the newly dubbed Scrumforce had two PIATs (anti-tank weapons similar to the

Thessaloniki about a week after the arrival of Scrumforce. The famous White Tower is seen in the background.

American bazooka) and were accompanied by Royal Engineers and Royal Navy personnel.[494]

M Squadron was the core of Scrumforce – a reconnaissance outfit under Lassen's command. Its main aim was to prepare for the occupation of Thessaloniki, which the Germans were getting ready to evacuate. On 25 October, the day after Scrumforce set sail, the German admiral in command of the Aegean moved his headquarters from Thessaloniki to Vienna. All air traffic to and from the city stopped the same day. On 26 October, Army Group E HQ, which had already moved out, received word from Thessaloniki that thirty fully loaded trains were ready to leave, and that the deadline for the evacuation, which had been set for 28 October, could only be met if they left very soon.[495] The British may not have been aware of all of the German preparations for withdrawal, but they had SOE and OSS spies on duty and intercepted German radio traffic.[496] One particular message on 22 October revealed that the German forces in the city were not to leave until 24 hours after the hospital ship *Gradisca*, due to dock on 26 October, had departed again.[497] Lassen and Scrumforce had orders to secure the Megalo Mikra airfield, 7.5 miles south-east of the big port, and set up a command post. The engineers were to repair the airfield after German attempts to sabotage it. Scrumforce was not to operate inside Thessaloniki itself, except for patrols and small reconnaissance groups just ahead of the first wave of the occupying force Kelforce (2nd Independent Parachute Brigade Group, under the command of Brigadier C.H.V. Pritchard).[498]

On the morning of 24 October, M Squadron reached Skopelos, which the Germans had vacated. That night they continued to the neighbouring island of Skiathos. The plan was that Scrumforce would reach the island on D-Day -5 – in other words, five days before Kelforce arrived in Thessaloniki.[499] The Germans had also abandoned Skiathos, but Lassen encountered resistance from an unexpected source. Just as he was about to go ashore, he was flagged down by a patrol boat carrying a landing force from Turnbull's Raiding Forces. They thought that Skiathos was 'their' island and that the SBS had no business there. After a short debate, it was decided that Turnbull's men would go ashore a few minutes before Lassen and his team. The double landing took place before dawn and caused some concern among the islanders until they realised that the incomers were British, rather than returning Germans. The guests were served wine and brandy before breakfast and then invited to a church service at the cathedral to celebrate the liberation of the island.

On Skiathos, Scrumforce was reinforced by an LRDG patrol, meaning that Lassen now had 8 officers and 68 NCOs and men (SBS: 6/55 and LRDG: 2/13).[500] It also had a jeep with a trailer, which may have cheered

Lassen, who was otherwise somewhat dissatisfied with once again being sent to sea while his colleagues Sutherland and Patterson, who led S and L squadrons, were to fight on land. Lassen had complained to Jellicoe, but his otherwise accommodating boss threatened to demote him unless he did as he was told.[501]

The British did not know if the Germans had evacuated the northern Sporades or whether Scrumforce risked running into hostile forces. As a result, the fast and well-armed but highly conspicuous ML458 was replaced with two more discreet caiques from the Levant Schooner Flotilla under the command of Lieutenant Alec McLeod of the Royal Navy Commandos. Unloading a jeep and trailer from a caique would be no easy task, but Lassen ensured Kelforce HQ that it could be done, and the vehicle was loaded on board.[502]

Scrumforce continued heading north at a sedate pace, in bright, warm sunshine. On the morning of Wednesday 25 October, the caiques laid to beside a British navy vessel that Lassen's Greek interpreter Jason Mavrikis described as 'a huge battleship'. Whatever kind of ship this 'monster of the seas' was, it made the men in the caiques feel 'like mice'. Lassen climbed on board to speak with the captain while the British sailors bombarded the caiques with chocolate, biscuits and whatever other food they had at hand – a welcome supplement to the usual 'compo' rations. Early on 26 October, the two caiques docked in the small port of Nea Potidaea, about thirty-four miles south of Thessaloniki. They managed, albeit with some difficulty, to manoeuvre the jeep onto land. A local dignitary offered the guests shelter in his home near the harbour, where Lassen set up his command post.

That afternoon, Lassen, Mavrikis, and two of their comrades drove north in the jeep on a reconnaissance mission. As was the norm when Lassen was behind the wheel, they travelled at breakneck speed. At 21:00 they stopped in a forest to relieve themselves and heard German voices in the dark. They crept closer, saw 3 or 4 men chatting around an armoured car and overpowered them without firing a shot. After destroying the engine of the armoured car, the four scouts squeezed two of the prisoners on board the now packed jeep and drove to Nea Potidaea with them.

At 05:00 on Friday 27 October, Scrumforce was joined by Major D.S.L. Dodson of the SOE. Along with his interpreter, Maniatopoulos, and his radio operator, Sergeant Parker, he had been sent to assist Kelforce. They were supposed to land on Epanomi, on the southern outskirts of Thessaloniki, but the weather was too poor to land their heavy and fragile radio equipment safely, so their patrol boat continued to Nea Poteidaia. After discussing the situation, Lassen and Dodson decided that the latter should try to get as close to Thessaloniki as possible – preferably all the way into the city. Lassen gave Dodson an escort of six LRDG men, under the command of a Lieutenant Barker. At 15:00, Dodson and his group left Nea Poteidaia in a commandeered bus. After taking a winding route, they arrived in the village of Mantzarides, on the south-eastern outskirts of Thessaloniki, at 21:00. Mantzarides was an ELAS outpost, and the partisans were preparing to attack the military airfield at Sedes, around four miles south of the village. Lieutenant Barker was keen to join the battle the following day, so Dodson left him and his men behind with the partisans. Dodson himself, along with the interpreter and the radio operator, continued to the village of Panorama, just under four miles north-east of Thessaloniki. The hilltop village lived up to its name, providing an excellent view over the whole of the city and its environs. After some wrangling with the local ELAS people, a house was made available, where Dodson billeted his men before darkness fell. He then went to meet the local ELAS divisional commanders for a progress report, which the radio operator, Sergeant Parker, then sent to SOE HQ in Cairo. Dodson knew that the Communist partisans, with some justification, considered the Allied liaison officers to be their enemies in the struggle for power in Greece. With this in mind he said nothing about the SOE and claimed to be the head of a British vanguard company that was in Nea Poteidaia and that he had gone ahead to reconnoitre.[503]

While Major Dodson was in Panorama, Lassen also made contact with ELAS. Scrumforce was not just carrying out reconnaissance ahead of Kelforce's landing at Thessaloniki; Lassen and his men were also charged with gathering intelligence on the ELAS forces in the area, and playing a role in another one of 'A' Force's decoy operations.

Following the morning meeting with Dodson, Lassen had made contact with some local ELAS people. His interpreter Jason Mavrikis quizzed them about their organization, strength, weapons, etc. After a quick lunch, Lassen, Mavrikis, McLeod and Lassen's driver Sam Trafford drove thirty miles north to the ELAS HQ in the district capital, Polygyros. Arriving at 16:00, they met with a large group of officers who were clearly surprised to see British soldiers so far north. The partisans plied their guests with water and – in Mavrikis' opinion – 'doubtful' coffee, after which Lassen and McLeod, with the help of the interpreter, began to question their hosts about German minefields in the area, both at sea and on land, asking that they be marked on McLeod's map. Lassen and McLeod asked about minefields not just on the road to Thessaloniki but also along the coast at Kavala – a town about 80 miles east of Thessaloniki and about 30 miles south of the border with Bulgaria. During a break in the three-hour conversation about minefields, some of the ELAS people asked Mavrikis why the British were so interested in the waters and beaches at Kavala. Mavrikis 'unwittingly let the information pass that a very large Allied convoy with a strong armada with at least 3 Army divisions with armour, artillery, and all necessary paraphernalia was awaiting our signal to start an invasion in that particular area.'

Mavrikis' 'gaffe' was, like Lassen and McLeod's demonstrative interest in the situation in the Greek-Bulgarian border region, part of 'A' Force's Operation Second Undercut. The aim was to expand the small British force in Greece by massively reinforcing the existing III Corps – also known as 'Headquarters Land Forces, Greece' – with the fictitious British 34th and 57th Infantry divisions and 5th Airborne Division. In contrast to 'A' Force's past performances, which had been mainly staged for the benefit of the Germans, the audience for Second Undercut was ELAS, and through them the Soviet leadership. The British did not trust Stalin to adhere to the Moscow Agreement under which control of Greece would be left to the British. Reinforcing III Corps was designed to deter the Russians from supporting an attempted takeover by ELAS or moving Red Army troops from Bulgaria into Greece. It is not known whether the message about British interest in Kavala actually reached Red Army Command in Bulgaria, but the Soviets did remain north of the border.[504*]

When night fell, Lassen and his companions drove back to Nea Poteidaia. The next morning, 28 October, Scrumforce started to advance towards Thessaloniki. That evening the raiders came across German troops near the American agricultural college on the outskirts of the city. During the fighting the two PIATs, which were designed to fire grenades in a straight trajectory at armoured vehicles or buildings, were instead used as mortars. Further skirmishes ensued on the outskirts of the city. There were also verbal clashes with some ELAS partisans who did not share Lassen's interest in attacking the Germans but preferred to let them withdraw without a fight – presumably with a view to filling the power vacuum that they would leave in their wake.

Lassen set up his command post in an American school close to the agricultural college and spent the evening on reconnaissance. Lassen's second-in-command in M Squadron, Captain Henshaw, and Lieutenant Commander Martin Solomon, RNVR, who had commanded a small naval force tasked with securing ports on the islands and along the coast of mainland Greece, and who now acted as Lassen's liaison officer to the Royal Navy, set out to find a coastal battery that, according to the locals, the Germans were about to evacuate. Along the way, they managed to surprise and destroy a supply truck that was heading out to the battery. This success encouraged them to try to bluff the Germans into surrendering. Henshaw, who spoke German, sent a letter to the German commander, stating that he was surrounded by a large British force and that immediate surrender was the wisest course of action. While Henshaw and Solomon waited for their interpreter to return with a response, they were unexpectedly joined by two Germans on their way back from the pub. In the darkness they mistook the British for their own side and were taken prisoner. The German battery commander was not fooled by Henshaw's ruse and had apparently raised the alarm. The sound of engine noise pierced the darkness. Suddenly Henshaw and Solomon were all but surrounded by a larger German force in trucks, accompanied by tanks and self-propelled artillery. The two officers beat a swift retreat, taking their prisoners with them, but leaving behind Lassen's jeep. Once they were out of immediate danger, the full gravity of their self-inflicted predicament dawned on them. The thought of returning to Lassen without his beloved jeep was too horrible to contemplate. Henshaw and Solomon spent a restless night in the woods with their prisoners. Shortly before dawn, Henshaw sneaked back to the spot where they had left the jeep. Luckily it was still there. When the Germans began blowing up their gun emplacements, Henshaw drove off, using the noise as cover. When they arrived back at the command post they told Lassen what had happened. 'You have done well,' he said, 'but had you not brought *ze jeep* back, I would have slit your throats.'[505] 'I really think that he would have done it,' Solomon wrote later. Whether or not Solomon really believed this of Lassen, it is certainly significant that his story about the episode – like Hancock's story about the fiasco on Paros – was as much about the fear of Lassen's fiery temperament and brutality as it was about the encounter with the enemy.

In Thessaloniki

On Saturday 28 October, Dodson and his companions saw columns of smoke rising above the city from the mountains between Panorama and Thessaloniki. While he could not see what was going on, he did not doubt that the Germans would withdraw very soon.[506] Massive destruction preceded the departure – German engineers spent days rendering the port useless. Forty-four scuppered ships blocked the approach, the shipyard had been razed to the ground, holes had been blown in the outer pier, and the Germans were preparing to blow up other plant and installations.[507]

The next morning, Dodson secured his interpreter a pass from the local ELAS people and sent him down into Thessaloniki to find a house where the major could wait for the Germans to leave the city. However, around noon

ELAS started to descend Hortiatis mountain, heading into Thessaloniki. When Dodson asked the local ELAS commander to accompany him into the city that evening, it proved more difficult to obtain a pass this time. The ELAS man referred Dodson to divisional HQ for the pass. Later that evening the major met a Greek who worked for the International Red Cross and was due to enter Thessaloniki the following morning. He agreed to accompany Dodson into the city. They set off early on Monday 30 October, before the local ELAS commander could stop them. He reached Thessaloniki about 08:00. He stopped a car and persuaded the reluctant driver to take him to Queen Olga Avenue in the city centre. Dodson noted that there were still German patrols around and that ELAS did not seem minded to take them on.[508]

After seizing control of Thessaloniki on 29 October, ELAS now aggressively patrolled the streets in search of people that the Communists regarded as enemies of the new order: collaborators, anti-Communist resistance fighters, and so on. All around the city, official and more or less spontaneous demonstrations, processions and festivities were held in honour of ELAS.

While in Thessaloniki, Dodson heard that Lassen and his men were on their way towards the city and had engaged a German unit that was cut off to the south of it. He hurried back to Panorama and sent a message to Lassen that the road was clear further north.[509]

Lassen was indeed on his way to Thessaloniki with Scrumforce. ELAS had told him that only a few Germans remained in the city, so he decided to move in.[510] His motives are unclear. Perhaps he presumed Kelforce's arrival was imminent (in fact they were delayed by sea mines and would not arrive until 8 November) and that it would be in line with his orders to march into the city now. Or perhaps he had decided that to prevent the Germans from destroying more of the city's infrastructure, or to establish a British military presence before ELAS took control, he had to act immediately – Kelforce or no Kelforce. Or maybe he just could not resist the prospect of marching into the liberated city at the head of his men.

Early on Monday, 30 October, Lassen led Scrumforce into Thessaloniki. It started out as a part triumphal procession, part circus parade: Lassen's driver Sam Trafford was at the front, on a horse that had been chewing grass by the roadside when the raiders arrived. Then came Lassen's jeep and four fire trucks with ringing bells that Lassen's men had picked up along the way. Bringing up the rear was a contingent of ELAS partisans with bandoliers across their chests. The strange procession attracted a growing number of jubilant Greeks who threw flowers and pelted the British with gifts of food and wine while the prettiest local girls were invited to climb aboard the fire engines.

John O. Iatrides, who lived with his parents in a side street off Queen Olga Avenue, (perhaps) saw Lassen's entry:

> The parade I saw marched on Queen Olga Avenue (eastern end of the city) heading west, toward the center. The avenue, its side-walks and side-streets were crowded and noisy as the marchers made their way through the excited spectators. We were standing on the second-floor balcony of the house we occupied, on Kriezotou Street, looking left toward Queen Olga Avenue, about 60–80 ft away. (The building across from us had been evacuated by a German unit the day before). We could see the parade (formations of marching ELAS, [the communist youth organization] EPON, other groups of civilians) on Queen Olga Avenue, in the space between the buildings astride Kriezotou clearly but only for a few moments as the marchers came into view and quickly went by to our left. We did not see the start (head) of the parade but later heard there were ELAS men on horseback. For a few moments we watched a single jeep go by, carrying four or five (?) men in khaki British field uniforms, officers' caps (two?) and round khaki berets. It was surrounded by cheering pedestrians and we could not see the occupants' faces clearly. Could that have been Lassen's jeep? Impossible to say! (We later heard stories that British troops had landed from a submarine somewhere along the Chalkidiki coast and I remember wondering how they got the jeep off the submarine …).

Regarding the British journalist Henry Maule's[511] account of people in Thessaloniki hanging Union Jacks from their windows in the days following the liberation, Iatrides recalls:

> My family had to take down its homemade British flag when threatened with violence by the local EAM.[512]

The triumphal procession moved into the centre of town and passed a square where some local Communist resistance leaders were waiting to receive the British and the ELAS partisans – or perhaps just holding one of probably several public meetings that day. Lassen ignored whatever was going on in the square and continued towards the harbour.

Again, his motives are unclear. Did he not understand what was going on and that it would have been polite and diplomatically opportune to stop and greet the local dignitaries? Did he miss an opportunity to portray the British as liberators and steal some of the limelight from ELAS? Or did he want to show that it was not ELAS but the Greek Royal Government and its British allies who were masters of Thessaloniki and that the Communist partisans did not have the status to bid Scrumforce welcome?

As the procession approached the docks, the celebrating crowds started to disperse quietly. Suddenly German snipers opened fire on the raiders. They missed, but the raiders and partisans found themselves in a prolonged firefight with a group of Germans who were preparing to blow up a fuel depot. The raiders, who had split into two attack groups under Lassen and Henshaw, took what little cover there was and returned fire until they began to run out of ammunition. Some of the Germans managed to escape but a number were killed. One raider took a bullet to the shoulder. The fuel depot was saved.[513]*

The next day, Tuesday 31 October, the last Germans left Thessaloniki. Lassen telegraphed Cairo: 'I have the honour to report that I am in Salonika.' Jellicoe replied, 'Give your estimated time of arrival Athens.'[514]

Almost two weeks would pass before Lassen could comply with Jellicoe's request to return to the capital. Kelforce did not arrive until 8 November, and its reinforcement and replacement, Glisforce (7th Indian Infantry Brigade), would not be ready to take over until 11 November.[515] Until then, and until transport back to Athens could be procured, Scrumforce would have to stay in Thessaloniki.

Like Dodson, Lassen received all sorts of practical help from the Greek major George Diamantopoulos, who was head of SOE's mission 'Jeanne', which had been operating since the summer of 1944 in northern Greece and since September in Thessaloniki. In September, Diamantopoulos held negotiations with a representative of the Germans in Thessaloniki. They had expressed their willingness to surrender if conditions could be agreed, but negotiations eventually broke down, as they did in several other parts of the country. The enterprising Diamantopoulos was now acting as a procurer of transport and accommodation, as well as an interpreter and liaison to ELAS, for Lassen, Dodson and later for the first of the British officers who arrived with Kelforce.[516]

Widespread violence had broken out across Thessaloniki in the final weeks before liberation, and continued for the first few days afterwards, especially in the outlying districts. EAM/ELAS quickly rounded up its most prominent opponents and began monitoring all political activity and the press. The city was also running out of food, a situation exacerbated by EAM's arbitrary confiscations.[517] In Athens, from 5 December to early January, the British forces waged open warfare on ELAS, using every means at their disposal (including Spitfires, Sherman tanks and naval artillery). Thessaloniki, however, was essentially controlled by EAM, with the British and Indian occupation forces remaining in the background. Even though EAM/ELAS were in control of Thessaloniki and Greek Macedonia they refrained from declaring a separate regime, from attacking the outnumbered British forces, and from trying to expel them, before the armistice was signed in Athens on 1 January 1945. On 17 January 1945 representatives of the government in Athens assumed control of it.[518*]

Martin Solomon described his and Lassen's role in the first week as a sort of self-appointed military governors:

> I shall never again have as much power or enjoy anything so much. Dictators for a week … Andy and I prevent riots and murder, we pass laws, we pardon and pass sentences. If we had not come, much blood would have been spilt.[519]

Given the size of Thessaloniki, the complexity of the situation in the city, and, in particular, the fact that ELAS had a firm and very aggressive grip on power by the time Lassen and Solomon and their force of approximately seventy-five men arrived in the city, it is hard to imagine that the two young officers really made the huge difference that Solomon described. However, by keeping on the move constantly and maintaining an active presence they might have been able to give the impression of a much larger and more powerful force – although ELAS was probably relatively well informed about the real numbers. Scrumforce may have been able to exert some control over a single neighbourhood, perhaps on the outskirts of town towards the Megalo Mikra airbase, which they and Diamantopoulos's 'Jeanne' mission were responsible for securing. To pave the way for the rest of Kelforce and Glisforce, Lassen and Solomon organized civilian work battalions from the areas around the port and the airbase to clear rubble and repair sabotage damage to runways.

Occasionally local people approached the two British officers in the hope that they could solve various everyday problems. Among them were black marketeers who more or less openly asked for help in smuggling their ill-gotten fortunes out of town, probably fearing confiscation by ELAS. Lassen took their money and pretended to arrange for it to be sent securely to Athens – but in fact he doled it out among his own men. By the time the black-marketeers found out, Lassen and Solomon were long gone, and the victims of their scam had nowhere to turn to complain.[520]

M Squadron did not fly to Athens on leave until 10 November, when space started to be available again on flights.[521]

Interlude in Athens

Athens was the scene of a couple of weeks of parties, booze, women and the kind of piratical approach to the miltary's resources and money that was typical of Lassen and many of his comrades in the SBS. Lassen was usually to be found in Eddie's Bar, which acted as an unofficial HQ for the SBS, and in the sumptuous Hotel Grande Bretagne. It was in the hotel that he blocked a lift when he tried to take an American jeep he had stolen – to replace his own, which had been stolen shortly before – up to his floor to stop it being stolen again. It was also here that, after swapping rooms with his fellow officer Charlie Clynes, he avoided an encounter with a very angry Greek husband armed with a pistol.

None of the accounts confirm whether the change of rooms, which earned Clynes a bullet in the leg, was down to chance or yet another example of Lassen's legendary ability to obtain intelligence.

On Thursday, 30 November, the commander of the SBS's HQ Squadron, Walter Milner-Barry, noted in his diary:

> Breakfast with Andy Lassen at a black market restaurant for about 15/. Andy tells me he [is] able to keep himself nearly by selling Diesel fuel!! Amoral but a modern Robin Hood.
>
> He solemnly offered to give me a part of the proceeds, and was quite surprised when I declined![522]

There were also quieter, more contemplative moments. While Lassen was in Athens he was a regular guest of the Danish diplomat Sven Peter Duurlo and his wife Ebba, who offered him a peaceful Danish refuge from the war and from his English-speaking surroundings. Ebba, who plied Lassen with traditional Danish pork and all the trimmings (the pork was supplied deep-frozen from Canada by a Swedish ship's captain), later described him as relaxed, smiling and funny, and full of ideas about agriculture, which he – at least on that occasion – imagined would be his career when he returned to Denmark after the war.[523]

Chapter Thirty-Six

Senforce, Crete, December 1944–February 1945[524]*

Things are always confusing and mysterious in war.
(Ernie Pyle, *Catnap and Fire*, 7 July 1944)

Back to Crete

On 29 September 1944, Hitler issued an order that as many combat-ready troops as possible were to be flown from Crete and Rhodes to Athens, and move north via Thessaloniki and Belgrade to other fronts. They were to leave their vehicles behind but take any weapons and equipment that might be needed if they ran into enemies along the way. The Kriegsmarine was to transport as much heavy weaponry as it could. In the first weeks, the Luftwaffe made 40 to 80 sorties a day, but the airlifts were soon interrupted as planes were diverted to evacuate Belgrade and (according to a British liaison officer on the island[525]) to operations in Finland and Estonia. On 25 October, Army Group E ordered that the 'fortresses' (Crete, Rhodes and Leros), as well as Kos and Milos, should be 'defended to the last bullet' to tie up as many enemy troops as possible in the Aegean. The German forces on the five islands consisted of 11,700 men on Crete, 6,000 on Rhodes, 3,500 on Leros, 1,000 on Kos and 200 on Milos. The Kriegsmarine also had 4,115 men who could not be shipped off the islands. In all some 26,515 German soldiers and sailors were left behind in the Aegean, more or less cut off from any other Axis forces by the Royal Navy.[526]*

When the airlift and sea evacuation came to a halt on 20 October, the commander of Fortress Division Crete, Major General Hans-Georg Benthack,[527]* decided that his German/Italian occupation force did not have the resources to hold the entire 3,000-square-mile island. He vacated the capital, Heraklion, and concentrated his troops on the plains he had fortified along the north coast, between Georgioupolis in the east, the airfield at Maleme in the west, and the mountain range of Lefka Ori (the White Mountains) in the south. As they withdrew to their last redoubt, the Germans blew up every bridge leading into the area.[528]

On 23 October the SOE agent Lieutenant Colonel L.T. Dunbabin wrote (alluding to the start of Caesar's *Commentaries on the Gallic War*) that 'Crete now falls into two parts – the three eastern departments which are completely free of Germans, and the CANEA department, most of the north east of which is still held by the enemy.' He also wrote that the situation in the free part of the island was 'very satisfactory', without serious clashes between the two sides in the civil war, and that the acts of violence that had occurred were motivated by private feuds rather than ideology. Several of Dunbabin's colleagues had a bleaker view. Major E.H. Watson and Patrick Leigh Fermor thought that EAM/ELAS might attempt to seize power in a coup – despite their relative weakness on Crete – leading to a potentially bloody conflict with the nationalist/anti-communist resistance organization EOK which had very much been created by SOE. Watson pointed out that Force 133 (the SOE headquarters in Bari, which was in charge of activities in the Balkans and northern Italy) had repeatedly asked for at least a symbolic British military presence on the island. The plea fell on deaf ears, presumably due to a lack of resources.[529]

The British military leadership in Cairo did indeed have difficulty complying with the SOE's call to station regular troops on Crete at the time. It was difficult enough sparing men to counter ELAS/EAM expansion on the mainland because fresh troops were needed in Italy to replace the units transferred to Montgomery's Army Group in north-west Europe. In late November, when the decision was taken to send a force to Crete, the only troops available were from the SBS – who should have been heading back to Bari and Monte Sant'Angelo to fight in Italy or on the islands along the Dalmatian coast – and men from the LRDG.

Lassen was put in command of this improvised force, called Senforce after the last syllable of his surname. It comprised four jeep-borne platoons made up of men from M Squadron – minus Lassen's old Irish Patrol, the members of which had been used to bolster other units – as well as a large number of new faces, many of them unfamiliar to Lassen. As a first for the SBS, the force also had a field-artillery platoon. According to the instructions from III Corps, the military HQ to which Senforce was directly subordinated, Senforce's job was to keep an eye on German and Italian forces and alert the RAF and Royal Navy detachments in Heraklion, as well as the new headquarters for 6 District, if the enemy moved out of their enclave and acted in a manner deemed sufficiently threatening that the British liaison officers would need to seek safety in the interior of the island.[530]

(6 District was a department of Allied Military Liaison which coordinated the work of the British SOE and the American OSS with the partisans

behind enemy lines in Greece, the Balkans and Italy. After the German retreat on Crete, 6 District, i.e. the SOE on Crete, had assumed responsibility for running 'Free Crete' in collaboration with representatives of the Royal Greek Government. The new advance headquarters would be responsible for supplying food and other relief via Heraklion.)

On Friday, 1 December, Milner-Barry and Lassen lunched together in Athens and then drove out to Piraeus so that Milner-Barry could help with the practical arrangements in connection with Senforce's departure to Crete the following day. Milner-Barry, who was not the type to be easily rattled, wrote in his diary that the journey was: 'A terrifying drive during which I reached, I suppose, the extremity of human terror, because I had the feeling that Andy simply didn't care if he did knock somebody down and killed him.'[531*]

Senforce sailed to Crete aboard a destroyer and landed in Heraklion on 3 December.

Nothing in Lassen's career so far could have prepared him for all of the many political and diplomatic challenges associated with his new position – despite the fact that the instructions from III Corps suggested a relatively limited role. Nonetheless, he considered it an honourable job, which promised to be 'very interesting and very responsible and very independent' (as Lassen had once said of the time he spent training guerrilla fighters in Nigeria).

Lassen (left) and Captain Walter Milner-Barry, probably in August 1943, on their way to a dance held by the Jewish Hospitality Committee of Tel Aviv in honour of David Sutherland's Squadron of the SBS.

While the men were settling into their temporary quarters in Heraklion, Lassen met Captain Percival from the SOE, who explained that ELAS and EOK were taking up positions around Heraklion and the second important port on the north of the island, Rethymnon, around forty miles to the west. The Germans had entered into a non-aggression pact with the partisans and were delighted to see their enemies at each others' throats.

Although the Communists were a minority on Crete, and

ELAS was weaker than EOK, the overwhelming majority of Cretans were Republicans, opposed to the restoration of the monarchy, and indignant at British support for King George II. Moreover, as noted by Dunbabin, local groups were often less ideological, being defined primarily by kinship, clan ties, local alliances, and personal friendships and enmities. The large numbers of weapons in circulation and the partial anarchy that reigned in the wake of the German withdrawal into their last stronghold meant that violence frequently erupted. It is uncertain to what extent Lassen and his colleagues in Senforce understood all of these complications.

After setting up his command post in Heraklion, Lassen and some of his men spent the evening in one of the local brothels.[532]

The day after the landing, Senforce blocked the three roads that the Germans might use to break out of their new position and launch an attack. A platoon manned each roadblock while the fourth platoon remained in reserve in Heraklion. Off the harbour lay the Hunt-class destroyer HMS *Catterick*, ready to support the SBS if required. Over the next few weeks, Lassen and *Catterick*'s commander, Lieutenant C.J.M. Rickards, saw quite a lot of each other. Rickards thought Lassen was

> a real soldier and born adventurer. I really cannot ever see him settling down to the ordinary routine of civilian life. He appeared to me to be at his best at that kind of irregular guerrilla warfare and really to enjoy it. He sometimes used to say that after the war he would travel from one

Giannis Bandouva.

Georgios Petrakoyeorgis.

country to another and look for a wife – but I think he was half joking – he would I think have gone on travelling about, but I cannot imagine him settling down.[533]

Lassen's attack on the airfield at Kastelli Pediadas in July 1943 was the stuff of local folklore, and word of his return to Crete soon spread. On 4 December a large and enthusiastic crowd gathered in the main square to welcome him.

Later that day, Lassen met with the main local resistance leaders, Georgios Petrakis (known as Petrakogiorgis) and Manolis Bandouvas, as well as the ELAS chief (*kapetanios*), Giannis Podias. Lassen knew Manolis Bandouvas, and especially his brother Giannis,[534*] from the attack on Kastelli in July 1943, but all he knew of the others was that he should be wary of them. The SOE head had warned him about Podias in particular. ELAS may well have had fewer men than the other resistance groups, but it was better organized, and Podias was hostile to the British.

Some hours after the meeting with the resistance leaders, Lassen was surprised to receive a phone call from the adjutant of the German garrison in Maleme. It turned out that the ordinary civilian telephone system was still working and now served the British as well as the Germans and various resistance groups – despite the risk of calls being tapped. The German officer bid Lassen welcome, wished him luck in his new post and explained that the Germans intended to remain passive. Their only contact with the world outside Crete consisted of occasional flights between Maleme and Athens (until 9 October) and Thessaloniki (from 10 October until the base at Thessaloniki closed on 24 October).[535] They bought their food locally, mostly from resistance groups.

Over the months that followed, Lassen and his German counterpart met regularly to discuss prisoner exchanges, relations with the civilian population and other issues of common interest.

* * *

In December, rumours flourished that the Germans were planning to leave their enclave to attack the partisans. Lassen sent two patrols, under captains Henshaw and Bimrose, to the area around Episkopi, some ten miles south-east of Heraklion. They were to meet 100 partisans, probably from the anti-Communist EOK groups, whom the captains, based on an agreement with the EOK leader general Papadakis, would 'train and discipline in the art of war', not least in fighting German armoured vehicles. They brought with them a 3-inch mortar, two Bren Guns, a German MG 34 machine gun and a PIAT, along with ammunition: 500 rounds for each of the machine guns, 18 bombs for the PIAT, 12 high-explosive shells and 18 smoke shells for the mortar. In his instructions to Henshaw and Bimrose, Lassen stressed:

The port of Heraklion.

> The role of Special Boat Service patrols is to provide heavy support to any attack or defensive actions which may take place in the near future. In addition it is believed that the presence of regular, disciplined troops in their ranks will have a heartening effect on the Partisans. It is of vital importance that all ranks realise that the success of this experiment depends on their setting a high standard of discipline and bearing as an example to the Partisans. It is also considered important that serious exercises and training of the partisans be carried out. This training should commence at once [noon on 14 December] and every endeavour made to complete it by 18 DEC.[536]

Unfortunately the sources do not report on the outcome of the training programme. However, it is clear from the instructions that Lassen – and, one must assume, the SOE men – believed that there was a need to make the partisans more disciplined and military.[537*]

* * *

Lassen would have liked to do more than just teach the partisans how to defend themselves against the Germans. Major Oxland, who served on the staff of Force 133, noted in a report:

> An SBS (Special Boat Service) Squadron had recently arrived in IRAKLION. Its task was to establish a warning link with their short

ranged W/T sets between IRAKLION and the GERMAN perimeter. This Unit was commanded by Maj LASSEN, M.C., who throughout his stay consistently put up schemes for attacking the enemy upon which we equally consistently had to throw 'cold water' because of the reprisals they would have caused.[538]

Sutherland takes over

While, with some difficulty, Lassen was settling into his new role, George Jellicoe made an unexpected and unwelcome announcement to his colleagues at the top of the SBS: he had decided to accept an offer to take the staff course at the Middle East Staff College in Haifa from January 1945. On Wednesday 6 December, the head of S Squadron, David Sutherland, and the head of HQ Squadron, Walter Milner-Barry, had breakfast with Jellicoe after having dined, the evening before, 'most alcoholically and amusingly' at the Allied Officers Club in Bari, from which Sutherland drove home at top speed. Seizing the opportunity, they confronted their superior and demanded an assurance that he would return to the SBS after the course and lead the unit to the Far East to fight the Japanese. Jellicoe agreed. The trio continued their discussion over lunch in the Officers' Club 'when many candid opinions were expressed'.[539]* The 26-year-old Jellicoe was replaced as head of the SBS by David Sutherland, who had just come back to Bari after a trip to Albania, and now 'at the ripe old age of 24 … became a Lieutenant-Colonel and the proud commander of an exceptional unit.' To celebrate his appointment, Sutherland flew to Heraklion to spend Christmas with Lassen.

> He and his men had taken over the largest and best hotel in Heraklion for Christmas. Immediately he sent for the town band with all its brass instruments. There were so many tubas, cornets, saxophones and trumpets that they occupied three floors of the hotel and began playing at random. The noise was deafening. The whisky, beer and cigarettes went around. Anders rose, swaying a bit, and ordered: 'Play the Danish National Anthem.' No one knew it. He hummed merrily, puffing on a cigarette. The band reciprocated, and the whole hotel and street outside shook. The noise which went on for twenty minutes, was ear-shattering. Everyone in the town came into the hotel. Anders, standing on the stairs, cigarette in mouth, conducted with a napkin. Then the band changed to the Greek National Anthem, and later to 'God Save the King'. And all the time Anders' terrible dog Pipo was peeing on everybody's trousers, mine included. What a night![540]

* * *

294   Special Forces Hero

On New Year's Day 1945, Lassen took part in a more solemn celebration. As commander of the only regular British ground force on the island, he attended a public thanksgiving service in the cathedral in Heraklion. The congregation was somewhat taken aback to see the top British officer arrive in an ordinary army greatcoat with no badges of rank or unit and wearing heavy-duty commando boots. A few days later, when Lassen and Captain Bimrose met with Major General Benthack in Georgioupolis, the German officer too expressed surprise at his counterpart's attire. Lassen explained that he kept a low profile to avoid assassination attempts by Podias's partisans. Benthack and his colleagues understood. During a meeting with Captain Henshaw a German police officer had quipped: 'It's a pity you are so few. Otherwise we might have considered surrendering to you. As it is, with these wild men … these Andartes [Greek resistance fighters] … all about us, to give up our arms would be suicide.' Considering the hundreds of Cretans the Germans had murdered during their three-and-a-half-year occupation of the island, the German was probably correct in his assessment of the local population's attitude to him and his comrades.[541]

Uneasy diplomacy

Although Lassen would have preferred to be allowed to attack the Germans, he was still able to relax and show a humorous attitude in their company. The SOE officer Major D.J. Ciclitira[542]* described a diplomatic meeting with the purpose of arranging an exchange of prisoners in which he participated together with a 'very tall SBS officer', who in all probability was Lassen:

> I wrote several letters to the GERMANS through the BISHOP, who was still acting as GOVERNOR GENERAL of the occupied area. In the end they agreed to send a senior GERMAN officer and an interpreter in the company of the BISHOP to meet me at DRAMIA, the first few houses in the liberated areas.
>
> On the given morning early in Jan I proceeded, together with a very tall SBS officer, his Jeep and a suit I had borrowed from one of his corporals. We had taken the precaution of equipping ourselves with tea, milk, biscuits, candies, good Virginian cigarettes and a bottle of whisky. By the time the GERMANS arrived we had a very good spread ready for them. They arrived looking most serious and gave the NAZI salute every two minutes. The senior officer turned out to be a rather shabby Major called BERNARD and the interpreter a 2/LT GROMAN, who could only interpret GREEK and was one of the leading lights of the GFP. The Major produced a paper written in GERMAN and very bad ENGLISH stating that he had authority to

discuss this exchange with Maj DYONISIOS (my pseudonym); this paper he would not let me keep. The meeting as a whole was certainly a victory for us – the chief reason being that I had the facts, etc. in my head while the poor old GERMAN had his written on a sheet of paper, which I could easily read over his shoulder. It saved me mentioning names, for seeing the ones he had written down I knew that he would mention them all in due course. After the business had been concluded – it consisted of agreeing to an exchange at the rate already mentioned for seven agents, one of which was Cpl G. COHEN whom they had written down as Lt. G. COLLIN; that I should ask my HQ for permission for an exchange of a further three agents; and would also find out if we were interested to exchange three BRITISH officers and nineteen ORs held PW in RHODES – we had a little social chat. The GERMANS showed no signs of being in any hurry to depart, though it was obvious that GROMAN was the man to say when to leave and when not to. The SBS officer, who could not speak either GREEK or GERMAN, had sat listening without understanding what it was all about. When we were sipping tea and passing the time of day he suddenly asked me to suggest challenging them to a game of football as a means of making them a little more human and less the stiff NAZI officials.[543*] At first the interpreter declined to translate this joke to the Major, but when pressed did do so. The Major seemed to take it in good spirit, and when the BISHOP offered to act as referee the party became quite hilarious. By this time the GERMANS had become quite normal beings, and what is more showed no signs of departing. I could not refrain from informing them of the escape of Capt BARKHAM, that he was now safe in CAIRO and how unfortunate it was that they had not tried to evacuate all our prisoners, as it would have saved so much trouble. The interpreter denied any knowledge of BARKHAM, but I later learnt that GROMAN was one of the officers present at his interrogations. The Major laughed when the conversation was translated to him and shrugged his shoulders, as much as to say – 'We are surrounded; what do you expect?' The meeting broke up just before lunch – they to proceed to CANEA, I to go and meet Col DUNBABIN and arrange for a double list of GERMAN names to be produced in order that the GERMANS could select half. The list I am afraid had not turned up some six weeks later and the GERMANS were using this fact as good propaganda against us, stating that it was the BRITISH's fault that our agents were still in prison. I would certainly have liked to give the staff officers responsible for this hold up a taste of a GERMAN prison and also the mental torture of being informed that they were to be shot every morning.[544]

* * *

A few days into January, Senforce gained a valuable new member. Staff Sergeant Les Stephenson was an atypical addition to a unit already made up mainly of atypical men. When Crete had been evacuated in 1941, Stephenson, a private and acting unpaid sergeant major in the Royal Engineers at that time, was one of the 5–7,000 British and ANZAC troops left behind. He was taken prisoner by the Germans but escaped and spent almost two years in the mountains, where he taught himself Greek, worked with the local resistance and the SOE – and met the woman who would later become his wife. In June 1943 he arrived in Cairo, where he helped interrogate refugees from Greece and the Balkans. Jellicoe brought Stephenson into the SBS as an intelligence officer because of his language skills and extensive knowledge of the situation in the Balkans and Greece. He 'wasn't so much a fire power number as an intelligence gatherer.' Stephenson felt that there was a special bond between him and Lassen. This may have stemmed from an episode in the Aegean when he, Lassen and the Greek helmsman were the only people on a caique not below deck suffering seasickness; or maybe it was due to Lassen's respect for Stephenson's achievement in surviving for two years in the Cretan mountains. 'Lassen was hooked on success,' Stephenson thought, 'and he had this knack of recognising success in other people.' In Senforce, Stephenson acted as an interpreter and intelligence officer, as well as Lassen's advisor on local issues. 'He was always asking me about Crete. He was interested in the local people and made friends with them and any resistance people we happened to meet.'[545]

* * *

Despite Lassen's ability to make friends with both civilians and the resistance, relations between the SBS and ELAS deteriorated badly during January 1945. The partisans tried time and again to prevent the British from going about their duties. Civilians in Communist-dominated areas began shouting abuse at British patrols, and the ELAS men camped on hilltops and slopes above British control posts and barracks. Lassen warned the ELAS leader Podias that if necessary he would fight fire with fire. Lassen had sympathy for the Cretans and admired the courage and fighting spirit they had displayed when he fought alongside them in July 1943, but the increasingly hostile atmosphere and relentless pressure began to sour his mood.

Lassen and his men lacked training and experience in civil administration. Otherwise they might have ignored the constant disobedience and disrespect or countered intrigue with intrigue. As things stood, their forte was action, not diplomacy and politics. Lassen would have liked to put down ELAS once and for all,[546] but had neither the mandate nor the military might to do so – nor did he have permission to use the conservative forces on Crete against the Communists. Instead Lassen followed his orders, which forbade him from taking sides in local conflicts.

In the first half of January, clashes between ELAS and EOK in Heraklion became commonplace. In Rethymnon, ELAS ramped up the pressure on the town, which was otherwise dominated by EOK. ELAS also set up checkpoints between Free Crete and the German-occupied part of the island and used them to monopolise trade with the Germans. Lassen sent a patrol to the area to stop the flow of food across the divide, and ELAS soon removed their posts. They found other ways of maintaining their lucrative trade with the Germans though. Lassen's agents reported a significant increase in caique traffic between ports in Free Crete and the German ports of Georgioupolis and Suda. Lassen asked the Royal Navy commander on Crete to patrol the coast with motor gunboats and torpedo boats. This reduced the traffic to a certain extent, but there were too many small bays and coves under German control along the 80-mile-long coastline to stop it altogether.

The presence of the Royal Navy and the Royal Greek Navy in Heraklion were occasional bright spots in an otherwise dark period. HMS *Catterick* did not remain in Heraklion throughout Lassen's stay on Crete, but called occasionally during her patrol and convoy duties in the Mediterranean, Aegean and Adriatic. Lieutenant Rickards (RNVR) and his colleagues were always gracious hosts and good company, and the officers' mess was a welcome diversion from the political intrigue on land. HMS *Catterick* left Heraklion on 6 December to be relieved by the Greek destroyer *Kanaris*. A naval officer who remained on Crete noted in his diary, 'They have been grand to us throwing everything open to us. Much stores are taken off … Firing at night. Andy disgruntled.'[547]

Increasing tension

In general however, the mood in and around the SBS grew worse and worse. ELAS ratcheted up the pressure, and civilians (both men and women) obstructed British patrols when they appeared in the towns and villages. Communist supporters held noisy parades late into the night outside the British quarters. 'British go home' was daubed all over the place.

On 13 January a brawl in a brothel in Heraklion resulted in one dead and five wounded, and led to bans on off-duty partisans carrying weapons in town and 'firing of arms casually in the street'. A curfew was introduced and all restaurants were forced to close at 20:00.[548] Lassen moved two SBS patrols into Heraklion to maintain law and order – and, as far as possible, kick ELAS out of town.

In mid-January, ELAS stepped up its presence in Rethymnon, where the clashes between ELAS and EOK had become even more regular and violent – some politically motivated, some for other reasons. On 17 January the bloody strife culminated in the killing of the nephew of EOK officer Pavlos Gyparis.[549] The same night saw clashes between German forces and ELAS near Rethymnon. Fourteen ELAS men were killed, twenty wounded and sixty taken prisoner. German casualties were four dead and seven wounded.[550] Lassen feared that the situation would get out of hand, and sent three patrols to Rethymnon to chase ELAS out.

The raiders knew that the approx. 45-mile-long winding coast road between Heraklion and Rethymnon was dotted with obvious spots to stage ambushes. They travelled at high speed, with automatic weapons at the ready, but not a shot was fired at them. As the jeeps approached, two gunboats cast anchor in Rethymnon's small Venetian harbour and made a show of pointing their guns at the town.

When Bimrose's jeeps came roaring into the narrow streets, they were greeted by a jeering crowd pushed forward by ELAS soldiers. Bimrose ordered his men to fire warning shots over the mob. The shocking noise of their automatic weapons echoed back and forth between the walls of the houses. The demonstration quickly dissolved. Bimrose imposed a curfew throughout the town, which helped to restore order but hardly endeared the British to the locals.

The following day, snipers on the roof of a factory at the harbour fired on a jeep patrol. No one was hit, but the SBS men shot out every window in the three-storey building.

The next day, when Lassen arrived in Rethymnon, all was quiet. Many of the ELAS men had sneaked out of town during the night because they expected that the British would search every inch of it at dawn. Lassen was on his way to a German checkpoint a few miles west of the town to negotiate the release of two prisoners. One was the Australian war correspondent Keith Hooper, who had strayed into German territory. The other turned out to be a German who had disguised himself as a British major to escape the siege on Crete. Lassen took him back to Heraklion too.

On 23 January, fighting again broke out outside Rethymnon, and Lassen sent patrols into the town to stave off a new attempt by the Communists to seize control of it.

Armed clashes between the two Greek factions, with casualties on both sides, were now a daily occurrence throughout Free Crete. On 27 January the fighting in Heraklion cost three guerrillas their lives, and many more were wounded. Lassen informed his superiors in Athens that the situation was becoming highly dangerous. Later that day, two nationalist leaders were abducted and four EOK men killed in an ambush near Rethymnon. It looked as if the much bloodier unrest that had ravaged the rest of Greece since December was on its way to Crete.

On 29 January, Lassen was ordered to Athens to discuss firmer action to stem the violence. A few hours after his plane took off, fighting again broke out between ELAS and EOK in Heraklion – this time, triggered by an incident the previous day at a local brothel where ELAS had shot two EOK men (one of whom died) and abducted two others. Once the fighting had started, none of the leaders on either side was able to stop it.

Captains Charles Bimrose and Charles Maurice Clynes MC immediately set off in the direction of the airfield to safeguard Heraklion's link to the outside world. Clynes was sitting in the passenger seat of the jeep, with Bimrose atop the backrest. About half a mile from the airfield, the jeep and their motorcycle outrider, Private Cornthwaite, were hit by fire from an 18-year-old ELAS sympathiser. A bullet passed through both of Bimrose's legs and continued through Clynes' head. Both the car and the motorcycle hurtled off the road and hit a stone wall. Bimrose's life was saved by 'a big Greek woman' who came running out of her house, picked up the nearly 6′ 2″ Bimrose 'as if I was an infant', carried him into her house and bound his wounds. The three wounded men were taken to a hospital, where Cornthwaite died the same day. The incident shocked the warring parties so much that the EOK leader Bandouvas, along with Heraklion's Greek military governor Lieutenant Colonel Andreas Nathenas and one of his staff officers, managed to bring the fighting to an end.[551]

Early in the morning of 30 January, Lassen and Brigadier Karl Vere Barker-Benfield, commander of Force 133, landed at Heraklion airfield in a Wellington bomber.

Based on his observations during a previous visit to Crete, Barker-Benfield had suggested to Allied Middle East Command, AFHQ, that the various British and Greek forces, authorities etc, in Crete be brought

Brigadier Karl Vere Barker Benfield inspecting Senforce. Behind him, on the left, Anders Lassen.

under a single structure headed by a 'Senior Military Officer Crete', who should lead and coordinate military efforts and maintain contact with the Greek civil authorities, the Greek gendarmerie, the Red Cross and District 6. Barker-Benfield's proposal said:

1. ….
2. At present operations against the enemy are not properly co-ordinated, i.e. the Andartes, Senforce, R.A.F. and R.N. are all engaged in various activities, but often quite independent of each other.
3. Reports, which are sometimes conflicting, are being sent out by various H.Qs. Demands for equipment, stores and relief are being made to on ATHENS, CAIRO and BARI.
4. It would be an advantage if the CRETAN civil authority had a local British authority to deal with the problems of policy and co-ordination.[552]

Farewell to Crete

Barker-Benfield now returned to the island as Senior Military Officer Crete, seeking to create order in what was now called Creteforce, and take over direct military command on the island, heading up a bigger force once Senforce had left.[553]* The 8th Army had requested that Senforce be transferred to Italy. An amphibious force was needed in the northern Adriatic, and since no commandos were available, they sent for the SBS. Senforce consisted of men from two different squadrons, and it was expected that it would take a month to incorporate them back into their original units. As such there was no time to waste getting Lassen and his men to Italy. Following repeated requests, relief and sea transport from Crete to Italy were finally arranged, raising the prospect that they would soon be leaving.[554]

Shortly after landing back in Heraklion, Lassen drove his jeep slowly and provocatively through the village where ELAS HQ was based. During the afternoon he conducted an investigation into the shooting. The ELAS leadership denied any involvement by their people, but eyewitnesses contradicted them.

The episode caused Lassen and Barker-Benfield to make a drastic decision: all resistance groups in Free Crete were to lay down their weapons immediately. The edict was announced to the Greeks on 1 February. Three days later, Lassen held a parade for SBS and the partisans at which he explained the reasons for laying down arms. On 5 February, Barker-Benfield inspected the SBS force at another parade in Heraklion. This was both a prelude to SBS's upcoming departure from Crete and a show of strength to the locals and the partisans. Once the parade was over:

Andy and his men pelted into a line of armed jeeps, drawn up in the background, and with a roar and a cloud of dust they were away, a very gallant motorcade. The jeeps were Force 133 property, and there was some concern that Andy should smuggle them away with him to his next destination.[555]

At 02:00 on 6 February, Captain Clynes died of his wounds. At 09:00 the next morning the SBS men lined up at their barracks, all uncharacteristically well groomed and wearing clean and correct uniforms. They were transported to the hospital in Heraklion, from where they marched through the streets in formation. Three officers and three sergeants from the SBS formed the honour guard. Three Greek priests led the way, followed by a gun carriage that bore Clyne's body in a 'luxurious coffin' wrapped in the Greek and British flags, and behind it the SBS, a detachment of the Greek army, Brigadier Barker-Benfield and his staff, the acting Metropolitan of Crete, the Greek government's representative on the island, the Greek military commander for Crete and Heraklion, and a whole host of other Greek officers, clerics and officials. The parade moved slowly through Heraklion and ended at the cemetery, where Squadron Leader Church of the RAF and the representative

The funeral of Captain Charlie Clynes, Heraklion, 7 February 1945. Anders Lassen is in the far right of the picture.

of the Greek government made speeches. Leading partisans and most of the other local dignitaries were in attendance.[556*] Later that day, the first contingent of the force that would replace Senforce on Crete arrived. The SBS patrols gladly handed over their posts to the new men and boarded the destroyers that would take them to Bari the next day.

The deaths of Clynes and Cornthwaite had affected their comrades badly, especially Lassen and Bimrose, who had worked closely with Clynes. The timing of their deaths made them even more difficult to bear. Lassen and his colleagues accepted the risk of being killed or wounded in regular fighting against a real enemy, but being shot in an ambush by people who were supposed to be their allies in the fight against the Germans seemed meaningless – especially as it was clear to everyone that the war was drawing to a close.

* * *

By no means all of the partisans on Crete complied with the order to lay down their weapons, but Senforce's efforts (not to mention the arrival of a more substantial British force) ensured that the situation on Crete was relatively quiet at a time of widespread political violence elsewhere in Greece.

Major General Benthack surrendered to the British on 9 May 1945. His men were disarmed on 23 May.

The civil war between Greek government forces (supported by first Britain and then the United States) and Communist rebels (backed by Yugoslavia, Bulgaria and Albania), which broke out in the spring of 1946 and ended with victory for the government forces in the summer of 1949, also reached Crete, where, although its extent was more limited, was just as cruel as in the rest of the country. The civil war on Crete effectively ended in 1948 when government troops dispersed the remaining few hundred ELAS soldiers who had taken refuge in the Samaria Gorge in the south-west of the island.[557]

Chapter Thirty-Seven

Italy

The Hand Grenade is a very deadly close weapon under certain circumstances. It should be taught as such and every endeavour should be made to make Live Throwing practices as practical as possible.

(SOE Syllabus)

'The big war'

When Lassen arrived in Italy in early February 1945, the front had remained stationary for months along the approx. 210-mile Gothic Line, which stretched from the Reno River on the Adriatic coast, north of Ravenna and south of Bologna, to Massa Carrara and La Spezia on the west coast. The Gothic Line consisted of countless well-built fortifications that took advantage of natural conditions, especially the mountains in the middle of the peninsula and the Po Delta's mighty wetlands along the Adriatic coast.

Although the line was well-defended, the commander of the German forces in Italy, Colonel General von Vietinghoff, knew that his troops risked being wiped out if they were caught between the superior advancing Allied ground forces and the Po, where the Allied air forces were busily destroying ferries and bridges. If he acted quickly to pull his divisions back behind the great river, he would be able to fight a rearguard action for a little longer. Hitler, however, forbade any such withdrawal.

In early January 1945, the American Lieutenant General Mark W. Clark,[558] commander of Army Group XV and head of Allied ground forces in Italy, had issued the master plan for the imminent attack. The British 8th Army, under Lieutenant General Richard McCreery, was to initiate the attack at the eastern end of the front. This would draw German reserves away from Major General Lucian K. Truscott's US 5th Army, which was ready to attack further west. McCreery was to advance along a line that ran through the small towns of Massa Lombarda and Budrio, west of an approximately 10 x 10-mile area that the Germans had flooded by blowing up the dikes and disabling the pumping system that kept the low-lying plains south of Ferrara dry. The Massa Lombarda–Budrio line would lead the 8th Army over open terrain,

giving McCreery an opportunity to deploy his armoured forces and attack the road and railway hub of Bologna from the rear. According to Clark's plan, this manoeuvre would provide the 5th Army with the opportunity to advance rapidly past Bologna and continue north to Verona and the Brenner Pass. As the Americans advanced north, the 8th Army was to crush the German forces trapped south of the Po.

McCreery was unhappy with a supporting role for the Americans. He would have preferred to attack via the Argenta gap, a strip of land about five miles wide, east of the flooded area and west of Lake Comacchio. Here, Highway 16 led from Ravenna directly up to Ferrara, where McCreery wanted to cross the Po and continue north towards Trieste and Gorizia.

McCreery's plan was more complicated than Clark's. It involved a number of preparatory operations aimed at securing the southern shore of Lake Comacchio. From there commando forces would cross the south-west part of the flooded area in amphibious vehicles, the so-called 'Fantails'. They would then continue east and north of Argenta to pave the way for the main attack from the south on Highway 16, via Bastia and Argenta to Ferrara. Along with the commando attack east of Argenta and the advance along Highway 16, various diversionary manoeuvres would take place along the east and north shores of Lake Comacchio.

* * *

The American tracked amphibious vehicle LVT-4, also known as Fantail, Buffalo or Water Buffalo, was 26 feet long, 10 feet wide and weighed 13.7 tons. It had a crew of three and could take 30 passengers or 2.9 tons of cargo. For the sake of buoyancy, it was only lightly armoured. Its top speed was 20 mph on land and 8 mph in water. The US Marine Corps had used Fantails in the Pacific, but this would be the first time they were deployed in Europe.

McCreery had asked for 600 Fantails for the offensive, but received only 190, of which 81 had American crews. The British 9th Armoured Brigade was responsible for organizing, training and leading the new amphibious force, which comprised personnel from the Royal Army Service Corps (RASC) so was dubbed the RASC Regiment. The RASC men came from more than thirty different units. None had worked with tracked vehicles or under combat conditions before. They were put through a wide-ranging training programme to transform them into a coherent unit and teach them how to drive and maintain tracked vehicles, read maps, use signals, and several other disciplines. They were also trained in the very difficult art of sailing Fantails and manoeuvring these clumsy vehicles up and down shores. To keep the new secret weapon hidden from the Germans for as long as possible, the training took place on Lake Trasimeno in Umbria, where conditions are similar to Lake Comacchio. There the brigade was joined by the US 755th Armored Battalion, supplemented with men from the British 27th Lancers, along with another 200 Fantails. Responsibility for the enormous task of hiding the existence of almost 400 Fantails fell on the 9th Armoured Division's intelligence officer, the Dane serving in the British Army, Captain Henrik O. Karsten – whose sister, Ellen, had written such rapt letters about her encounters with Lassen in London three years earlier. As well as sending up smokescreens during the exercises on the lake, Karsten posted guards and patrols along the lake, strictly censored all post and evacuated some of the local civilians.

Captain Karsten was responsible for security and camouflage when the 9th Armoured Brigade moved to the area north of Ravenna in early April. The big, mosquito-infested pine forests there provided effective cover and prevented the Germans from spotting the brigade from the air.

He was also responsible for collecting, processing and disseminating technical information and intelligence on enemy dispositions, on the terrain around the lake, and on sailing conditions. It was a huge and difficult task, not least because the 9th Armoured Brigade's units were spread along the entire 8th Army front. As if all this were not enough, Karsten was busy studying aerial photographs and reconnaissance reports of lakes Trasimene and Comacchio to identify places where amphibious vehicles would be able to cross the great rivers Po and Adige.[559]

* * *

On 24 March, Clark issued instructions for the upcoming offensive, which represented a compromise between his original plan and McCreery's. The 8th Army would cross the Senio and Santerno rivers and then advance along two axes: Bastia–Argenta (to the east, as McCreery wanted) and Massa Lombardo–Budrio (west of the flooded area, as per Clark's original plan). The attacks were to be supported by amphibious operations and paratroopers. Depending on how the attacks went, Clark and McCreery would then jointly decide whether the 8th Army would continue to Ferrara or Budrio and Bologna. McCreery, however, had decided in advance on Ferrara and the straight road to Po.

The attack by the 8th Army was codenamed Buckland, that of the 5th Army, Craftsman. Operation Buckland would start the day the 8th Army attacked across the Senio. Two days later the 5th Army would move into action. Truscott's main job was to break through to the Po Plain. He was also to either occupy or circumvent Bologna. Five days before the offensive was due to commence, US forces would attack Massa at the Italian west coast, and from there advance on La Spezia.

During the first days of the offensive, Allied air forces were to prioritise support for the 8th Army, partly in the form of massive raids on Argenta and the surrounding small towns and villages which were to be attacked by heavy bombers. When the 5th Army began its attack, the air support would move to its part of the front.[560]

On 11 February, Lassen and M Squadron arrived at SBS HQ in Modugno on the western outskirts of Bari. Preparations for Operation Buckland were in full swing. The 8th Army, which had its HQ in Ravenna, was to use light amphibious forces for reconnaissance on and around Lake Comacchio. The idea was that they would lead the way for the commandos when the offensive began, and carry out diversionary operations to distract attention from the real attack.

On 15 February, S Squadron sailed to Zadar, on the Adriatic coast of Croatia, to operate on the islands along the Dalmatian coast. L Squadron was to join it a few weeks later. In the meantime, Lassen's M Squadron was deployed around Comacchio. They were to be part of 'the big war' now, but once again as a decoy on the fringes of the main action.

Reorganization and leave

On 16 February, Lassen travelled from Modugno up to the SBS camp at Monte Sant'Angelo, where M Squadron was to be reorganized and trained before further action. Two days later he returned to Modugno. On 21 February he travelled to Rome on leave in a group which included Captain Bimrose, Sergeant Les Stephenson and the Italian-speaking Private Fred Green.

Stephenson, who spoke Greek, would have preferred to be somewhere else. He did not speak Italian and knew nothing about the country or its people. But Lassen was adamant that he should stay – and Stephenson:

> would have followed him anywhere. Here was someone you could rely on. He wouldn't say, 'Oh, you go off and I'll give you covering fire.' He'd say,: Come on, you come with me.' ... We'd got good officers, but there was no doubt about it that here was a man who was a hundred per cent going to lead and after the operation wouldn't forget all about you ... He sort of had an affection for people. Once he'd sorted you out, you were his man, in his eyes anyway, sorting the sheep from the goats.[561]

In Rome, Lassen stayed at the classy Hotel Excelsior on Via Veneto. The week-long leave gave him a chance to resume his acquaintance with an English WAAF girl he had met the year before. In the morning they went shopping, and Lassen looked for antique porcelain figurines of the kind his mother collected. In the evening – if Lassen was not throwing another party for his men – they went to restaurants and danced to his favourite song *Lili Marlene*.

Lassen's generosity towards his men reflected not only his personality but the SBS's close-knit community (albeit a community that was gradually being somewhat diluted by successive reorganizations and personnel changes). 'When you went out socially, it was not your money, my money, his money but only our money. All for one, one for all.'[562] Lassen also talked about the prize money that was still to come his way from the hijacking of *Duchessa d'Aosta*, *Likomba* and *Bibundi*. As the number of men in for a cut decreased, so Lassen's portion increased. He promised his comrades in the SBS that he would share his good fortune with them. Stephenson often heard Lassen say to his men that they should not worry about what they would do after the war – he would see to it that they had enough money. On other occasions, Lassen talked about a beach he had seen in Africa, where diamonds were just lying around waiting for him and his companions to return and pick them up after the war.[563]

After his leave in Rome, Lassen took part in SBS recruitment work. Among other things this involved an officer and a sergeant visiting British military camps in Italy and the Middle East and talking with potential raiders. On one such trip, Lassen met the Danish sailor Svend Ove Bent Knudsen, who in January 1941 had been among those who signed the oath of allegiance to Christian X in Børge Francks' Bible, and had been with Lassen at No. 1 Special Training School. Knudsen, now 23, was a marksman, probably in the Buffs, but Lassen persuaded him to apply for the SBS.[564]

Anders Lassen talking to a war correspondent on Crete or in Italy.

When Lassen was not on the lookout for new recruits to the SBS, he spent his time training M Squadron, which had a lot of new men. During February and March he was reunited with a whole patrol and a number of other men who had been transferred to other service while Lassen was in Crete with Senforce. M Squadron was to be a functioning unit again, once the new men attained the same level of skill and stamina as the old ones. When asked about his plans for the men's training, Lassen's answer was simple: 'Zey will march.' And after that: 'Zey will march again.'[565] No doubt fresh in his mind was the poor marching condition of so many of the new troops in Santorini.

Pipo in front of Anders Lassen's tent.

The training took place first at Monte Sant'Angelo and then in a camp near Ravenna, to which M Squadron relocated in the second half of March to be closer to its new theatre of operations. On moving to Ravenna, Lassen left Pipo and his newly acquired canine companion Dog Tom in the care of the entourage he had gathered over time – his Greek batman Dimitri, the Italian barber Zeppi, a couple of Greek cooks and a shoeshine boy. When Lassen left, a sergeant called Rally saw his chance to shoot Dog Tom. Pipo, however, despite having earned many enemies among the raiders, went unscathed.[566]

Comacchio[567]*

Had it not been for the billions of mosquitoes that swarmed over Lake Comacchio and the surrounding area day and night, Anders would surely have loved to have taken his bow and arrow and gone duck hunting and fishing in this vast wetland on the southern outskirts of the Po Delta. But this was no playground. It was a battleground – one like no other Lassen had seen.

It is somewhat misleading to use the term 'lake' about *Le Valli di Comacchio*. This is an area of lagoon and swamp with an average water depth of 1 to 5 feet, divided into a number of large sections called *valli* by natural ridges and low dikes, and full of more or less hidden sandbanks. In 1945 the 'lake' covered approx. 32,000 hectares. In the 1920s and '30s, the northern *valli* –

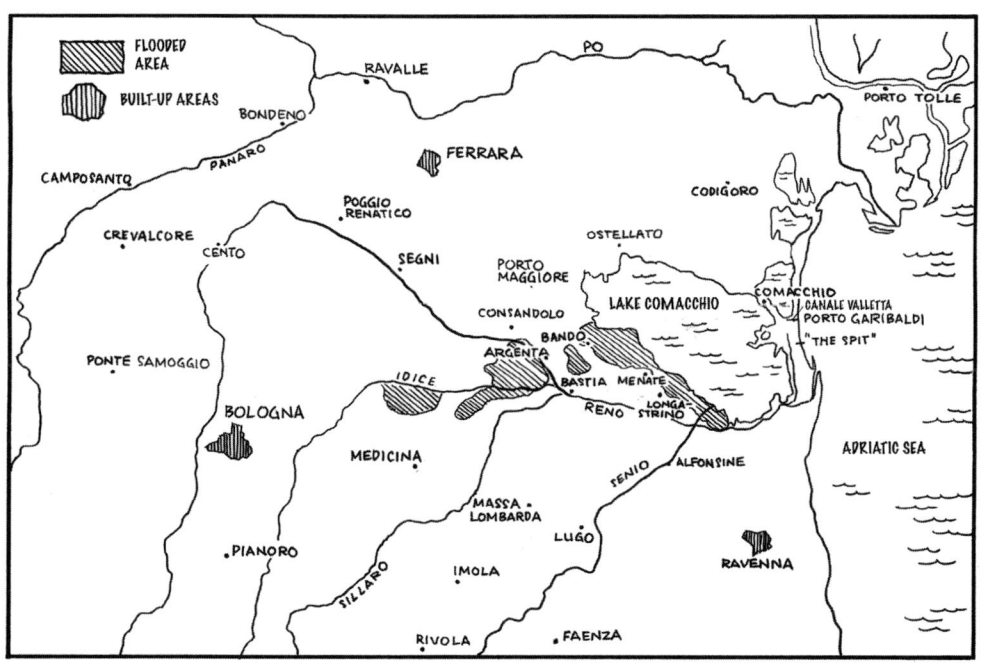

Trebba, Ponti and Isola – had been drained and cultivated. But here too, like the area to the west of Argenta, the Germans had blasted holes in the dikes and stopped the pumping plants. The 5,207 hectares were flooded, and Lake Comacchio more or less merged with Valle Bertuzzi, north of Comacchio.[568*] The Germans had also blown up dikes in the south-west corner of Lake Comacchio, the flooding from which stopped just 2.5 miles short of Argenta.

Lake Comacchio was separated from the Adriatic by a 1 to 2 mile-wide isthmus that the British called *the Spit*. This consisted of two parallel strips of land: the one to the east was relatively narrow, covered by dunes with low trees and scrub; the western strip was broader, with fields, gardens and scattered settlements. Between the two lay a swampy area, which had been flooded before the war to attract ducks and wild geese. It now formed part of the German defence system. There were several bodies of water on the Spit. It was criss-crossed by rivers and ditches, as well as two canals that were partially navigable and used to regulate the salinity of the lake and guarantee the best possible conditions for the eels and mullet that sustained the local population. From the south bank of *le valli*, a 3 to 4-mile peninsula, Boscoforte, cut into the water. At the end were a handful of small, flat islands, some of which had simple stone buildings used by fishermen or the officials charged with preventing poaching. These guardhouses often had towers that afforded a good view of the lake.

After the northern *valli* had been flooded again, the small town of Comacchio was surrounded by water on all sides. It was only connected to land by Via Romea, which ran along the Adriatic coast and stretched down over the western part of the Spit, south of the town, and a road that led north-westwards to Ferrara, about thirty miles inland. Immediately south of Comacchio was the small fishing village of Porto Garibaldi, where Canale Valletta connected the lake to the Adriatic. A railway line ran north from Porto Garibaldi, through Comacchio and on to Ferrara. Everything that moved on the lake and far out into the surrounding flat landscape was visible from the church tower in Comacchio.

The defence of *le valli* had been left to the 162nd (Turkestan) Infantry Division. Set up in May 1943 by volunteers from Turkestan, Azerbaijan and Georgia, the division had arrived in northern Italy in October the same year and distinguished itself in fierce fighting on various sections of the frontline. On 27 February 1945 it had relieved the 114th Jäger Division at Lake Comacchio and along the Adriatic coast. Its three regiments now stretched from Ostellato, twelve miles west of Comacchio, along the north side of the lake, through Comacchio and down along the Spit to the Reno River, just south of the lake. In addition to the three infantry regiments, the division also had at its disposal two reconnaissance battalions, a machine-gun battalion, howitzers and strong armoured and air defence units, equipped with artillery and heavy machine guns. Six sets of manned searchlights were set up along the north shore of the lake, heading west from Porto Garibaldi, to light up the banks in the event of a night-time attack. It was a substantial defence force, made up of solid veterans familiar with their positions and fortifications. The key points in the German defences were around Porto Garibaldi and the southern end of the Spit.[569*]

Operation Roast, 1–5 April 1945[570]

On Wednesday 18 March, Lassen's M Squadron was placed under command of 2nd Commando Brigade and Brigadier Ronnie Tod (whose dissatisfaction with Lassen's way of running his squadron had cost a sergeant his teeth on Poros). Tod's 2nd Commando Brigade was to prepare and support the 8th Army's advance through the Argenta gap – by first securing the Spit and then attacking west along the south and west coasts of the lake.

The taking of the Spit, codenamed Operation Roast, was to start on the night of 1/2 April. The operation involved four commandos: 2 Commando, 9 Commando, 40 and 43 (Royal Marines) Commandos. The isthmus was to be attacked both by land and from the water. However, neither the available maps nor aerial photographs sufficiently clearly showed which areas were lake and which were flooded farmland, nor where the water was deep enough for

Commandos and raiders on the shore of Lake Comacchio. Anders Lassen is 2nd from right in the foreground, with a white canteen on his hip.

the commandos' boats and amphibious vehicles. This information had to be acquired by other means. The British were working with the local partisans of the 28th ('M. Gordini') and 35th ('M. Babini') Garibaldi Brigades, which had waged guerrilla war on the Germans on the lake and south of Reno all winter. The 28th had taken part in the liberation of Ravenna on 4 December 1944. On 12 January it had been accorded the status of a regular unit in the British 8th Army, and its 600 members had been kitted out in British uniforms. Many of the partisans were fishermen and hunters. They were used to crossing the lake in their traditional long, flat-bottomed punting boats, known as *batane* and had in-depth knowledge of the navigable channels and the many hidden obstacles that lurked among the reeds and in the murky water. The Germans had forbidden the local population from sailing on the lake, but since they had nothing else to live on, there was still extensive illegal traffic of fishermen and partisans pretending to be fishermen. Their information was supplemented by intelligence gathered by the SBS, who paddled out at night in their folboats to measure water depths, look for minefields and try to draw up a picture of German positions on the banks. This information, along with that gleaned by the canoe-borne Combined Operations Pilotage Parties (COPP), would lead the attacking forces to the shore. When the attack started, Wagner's *Ride of the Valkyries* and *Lohengrin Preludes* blasted out over the lake from large speakers that the British had used for days to mask the noise of their movements.[571]

Despite all these preparations, Operation Roast got off to a very bad start. The twenty Fantails, which should have set 2 and 9 Commandos ashore on the Spit from the sea, ran aground – as predicted by the local partisans – in the muddy lake bed, just yards from their starting point off the southern shore. The commandos transferred into the *Storm* and *Assault* boats that had been brought along as spares, but the drought of recent weeks meant the water level was six inches lower than anticipated, and they ran aground too. The commandos had to push and pull the boats, laden with their equipment, through mud, darkness and increasing confusion. Only after struggling on like this for 1,400 yards were they able to climb aboard and start the outboard engines on the big Storm boats, each of which pulled four of the smaller Assault boats. Despite the unfortunate start, they pushed ahead with the attack, and in the face of fierce German resistance and heavy artillery fire, 2 Commando was in position along the Caldirolo channel, roughly in the middle of the isthmus, by 11:00. During the day, 40 and 43 RM Commando advanced overland to conquer the whole of the southern part of the isthmus. In the afternoon, 43 RM Commando also reached the Caldirolo canal. The following day, 3 April, 2 Commando and 43 RM Commando advanced further north towards Canale Valletta, supported by artillery and tanks. In the afternoon the commandos clashed with the German forces defending the settlement of Scagliocca, 300 feet south of the canal. The British took Scagliocca, but beyond this point there was nothing but flat and open terrain all the way to the canal. The Germans had demolished every structure to give themselves a free view and field of fire. Some Germans, caught between the advancing British and the canal, were taken prisoner but when the commandos tried to approach the river, both they and their prisoners came under heavy fire from machine guns in a row of houses on the north side of the canal. Corporal Tom Hunter of 43 RM Commando climbed onto a pile of rubble and returned fire with his Bren gun, covering his comrades long enough for them to get out of the line of fire. He continued firing until he was killed by machine-gun fire.

For the rest of the afternoon, Porto Garibaldi came under fire from British artillery and was attacked by South African fighter-bombers, but the British attack failed to regain momentum. Every move immediately drew fire from the German positions. During the night of 3/4 April, the commandos were ordered to maintain their positions, around 400 yards south of the canal, until they could be replaced by the 24th Guards Brigade. They were relieved the following night, and withdrew to Ravenna to take part in the impending attack on the south and west sides of the lake. The Germans were surprised that the British did not exploit their enormous material superiority and continue on to Canale Valletta and into Porto Garibaldi. The Germans were not impressed by the 24th Guards Brigade either, and noted that their reconnaissance activity around Canale Valletta ceased as soon as the first patrol had been captured by the 303rd Infantry Regiment.[572]

Operation Fry, 4–11 April

Parts of M Squadron were involved in the preparations for Operation Roast and in piloting the attacking forces to the shore. They also formed part of 2nd Commando Brigade's reserves during the attack itself. Even the SBS folboats would have had difficulty crossing the shallow lake. Stephenson, sailing with Lassen, had to keep jumping into the water to disentangle the boat from plants or push it clear of mud flats. All the while Lassen loudly cursed and swore about the delays. Lassen tried to navigate using a ship's compass, but eventually conceded that it was misleading. He threw it overboard and navigated by the stars instead.[573]*

Lassen was also busy elsewhere on the lake. A little before 19.30 on 14 March he was met near the southern bank by the 20-year-old partisan Giuseppe Folegatti, a member of the 28th Garibaldi Brigade. His brigade

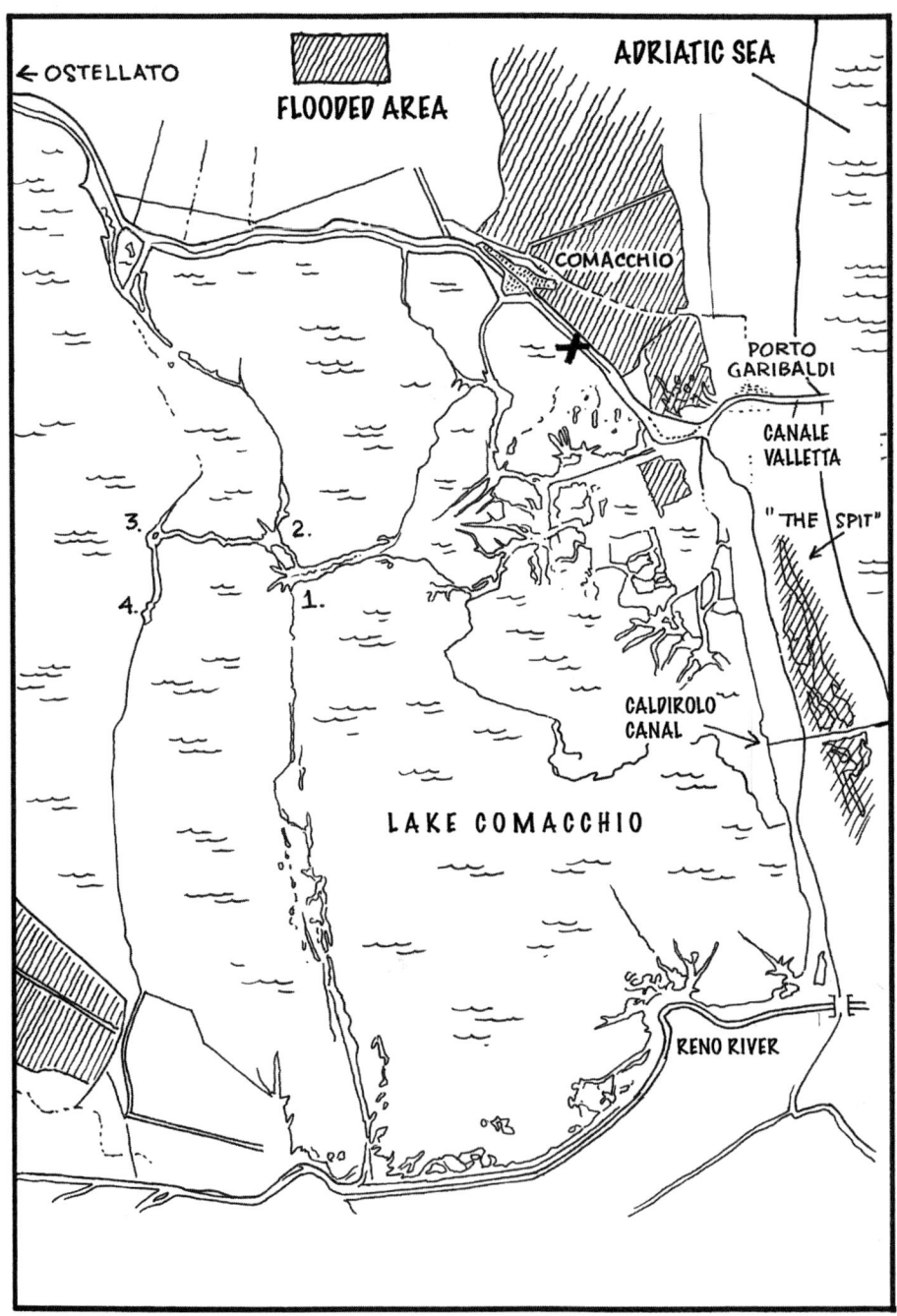

Lake Comacchio. 1 and 2 are the two islands occupied by the SBS, while 3 and 4 were occupied by Italian partisans. The cross shows where Lassen's patrol landed during the night between 8 and 9 April 1945.

commander, the famous partisan Arrigo 'Bülow' Boldrini, had ordered Folegatti to sail an English major close to the German positions.

> I took up position with the boat close to a tamarisk bush. After some time, I saw a shadow. I pointed to it with my machine gun and asked for the password. 'Roma,' he said. I gave the agreed response: 'Remo'. It was the Allied officer I was waiting for. I took him on board and then we sailed eastwards, out towards the sea, in the direction of Caldirolo. The major gave me a small bag of food, concentrated coffee, cigarettes and chewing gum. I started chewing the gum. We sailed a long trip around the lake, and from time to time the major … slipped into the water and dived. I wondered what he was up to. Whether it was due to the stress – we were right beside the German positions – or the gum, I developed a very stiff jaw.[574]

Caldirolo was one of four small islands just north of the Boscoforte peninsula. The 2nd Commando Brigade was to occupy it to ensure that the forces due to advance against the Argenta gap were protected from attacks from the east. The islands were also to be used as a base for raids against the north and north-east shores of Lake Comacchio, designed to tie up as many of the enemy as possible in the Porto Garibaldi–Comacchio–Ostellato area. The total defence force was believed to consist of about sixty German soldiers.

Comacchio, April 1945, sketch by the artist Eric Manning who served with 8th Army. The 'Spit' at the centre of the picture divides the Adriatic Sea on the right from Lake Comacchio on the left.

The attack was to begin three days after Operation Roast, i.e. the night of 4/5 April.

Two attack forces were assigned to the four islands, which lie in pairs close to each other. Force 1, which consisted of M Squadron (about 60 men), 3 to 4 men from 42nd Field Company Royal Engineers (mine sweepers, etc) and a small platoon of the 28th Garibaldi Brigade, was to occupy the easternmost islands, Agosta and Caldirolo. Force 2, which consisted of around sixty partisans from the 28th Garibaldi Brigade, was to attack the two more westerly islands. The operation was to take place at night – and if possible, silently – but first the targets were softened up by air strikes on the evening of 4 April. The operation was codenamed Fry. Lieutenant Colonel R.P. Menday MC of 2nd Commando Brigade was put in command of the newly dubbed Fryforce.

On the night of 3/4 April, Force 1 took up position on the Boscoforte peninsula, where it remained throughout the following day. The wooded peninsula offered some cover against observation from the church tower in Comacchio and from the German-occupied islands. It was not the worst place on the lake to wait to go into action, but the mosquitoes and the need to remain hidden at all times ratcheted up the tension. At 19:00, fighter-bombers attacked the few buildings and sheds on the islands, and each target was hit several times. At least eight Germans were killed. Thirty, including four wounded, left the islands in 7 or 8 boats and sailed to Comacchio.

Later in the evening, Force 2 (the Italian partisans) made their way to the east side of the peninsula, where the two forces were to meet before the attack. The operation was due to start at 00:30, but some of the men from M Squadron were still on piloting duties for Operation Roast and did not arrive on time. The attack was postponed for two hours. Around 23:00, the whole of Fryforce was finally able to embark – the British in folboats and other rowing boats, the partisans in the Comacchio fishermen's *batane*. Force 1 rowed straight north to the islands of Agosta and Caldirolo, while Force 2 sailed over to their two islands. The partisans went ashore at 02:30 and ascertained that while the Germans had indeed left, both islands were strewn with mines. Clearance started right away, and the two islands were reported clear at 02:55.

Force 1, which had been delayed by radio problems that severed the link to Force 2 and to the Brigade HQ, landed an hour later. Stud Stellin's folboat turned upside down during the landing, but all of the SBS men made it ashore in one piece and soon established that the Germans had abandoned the two islands.

While the British were landing on their islands, a group of partisans who had sailed west from the islands to prevent the Germans from escaping in that direction announced that a boat was approaching. It was allowed to pass, but as soon as the occupants disembarked, they were taken prisoner by the SBS. The PoWs turned out to be a German and a Turkoman NCO, four Turkmen soldiers and two Italian boatmen who had been sent out from Comacchio to examine the results of the shelling.

The two Italians were the 32-year-old Ettore Tomasi and his companion Mario Foschini Cavalieri, who were local fishermen – and, in Tomasi's case, a fishery officer – whom the Germans had forcibly conscripted into service on Lake Comacchio. Tomasi and Cavalieri were offered a choice between prison camp and helping the British. The two men, who had wives and children in Comacchio, chose to help the British liberate their hometown. In the days to follow, they acted as pilots and boatmen during the raiders' reconnaissance sorties on the lake.

On 5 April, Lieutenant Colonel Menday returned to 2nd Commando Brigade HQ. Lassen took the reins of Fryforce, establishing his command post in the ruins of a house on Caldirolo. In the course of the day, the raiders were reinforced by a platoon of Troop 4 of 9 Commando, who were to secure the two eastern islands and facilitate SBS raids on the north and north-east shores. The idea was to fool the Germans into thinking that the 8th Army was going to cross the lake and continue its offensive northwards up the Spit. This would entice the Germans to redeploy troops to this part of the front – or at least not move them away – and divert their attention from the imminent attack on the southern shore (Operation Lever).

The raiders and commandos spent the following day hiding on the flat, almost completely barren islands. The following night, 5/6 April, the Germans sent a second patrol to the islands, this time in three boats. The first boat was allowed to sail past Caldirolo, where Lassen's men were hiding, and right up to Agosta, which was occupied by Stellin's patrol. The second boat was allowed to sail close in before the British opened fire. The third and most distant boat slipped away in the darkness. The firefight resulted in one dead German and five prisoners. The prisoners belonged to 129th Panzer Reconnaissance Battalion, from the 29th Panzergrenadier Division. They told their captors that their division was actually heading back to Germany, but that their unit, the last to cross the Po, had been called back in haste to the Comacchio area to counter an impending attack. For the British, this news was an encouraging sign that Operation Roast had served its purpose of drawing German forces to Comacchio.

On 6 April, the German guns around Comacchio opened fire on Caldirolo and Agosta. A couple of men were wounded by shrapnel. The SBS men and commandos had been sheltering in what was left of the buildings on the two islands, but it was now obvious that these were the Germans' target. Once again, they had to do what SBS men otherwise 'did not do', but had done so many times during the recent reconnaissance missions in Lake Comacchio: dig themselves in. Lassen and his men dug into the stinking mud and covered themselves with either the camouflage nets they had brought with them or whatever branches and twigs they could find. Neither option offered any protection from mosquitoes. This was how they spent the daylight hours. It was hard to get anything to eat and drink, and they had to relieve themselves where they lay.

They had no way to return the Germans' fire, because all available artillery had been moved south of the lake to support Operation Lever, which began the same day.

* * *

Operation Lever was carried out by the British 167th Infantry Brigade (56th (London) Division). From the area around the small town of Sant'Alberto, due south of the Boscoforte peninsula, the troops crossed the Reno River on two ferries, a Bailey bridge, and Storm and Assault boats. Here the British received valuable assistance from the partisans of the 28th Garibaldi Brigade, who had occupied part of the terrain north of the river and knew the area well. When Operation Lever ended on 8 April, the British had conquered the whole of the partially flooded wedge-shaped area (*the Wedge*) between the southern shore and the river Reno. The wedge was to serve as a basis for the subsequent amphibious assault, Operation Impact, at the eastern end of the Argenta gap.

'Forward, you bastards!' – Operation Fry, 6–11 April[575]

Even after Operation Lever had started, the British tried to maintain the illusion of an impending attack on the north coast. On the night of 6/7 April, two SBS patrols, each consisting of nine men and an officer, sailed to the north shore and attempted to land. They came across a dike and a deep channel that ran parallel to the shore, behind which was another dike. The moon was about to come out and the raiders could hear German patrols on the coast road. They abandoned the plan to go ashore but blew holes in the dam with plastic explosives to let the enemy know they had been there.

On the night of 7/8 April, Lassen sent three folboats to Comacchio to reconnoitre the coast between Comacchio and Porto Garibaldi, where he planned to go ashore with a force the following night. In one of the boats was Greece expert Sergeant Les Stephenson, who still felt rather out of place in these strange surroundings, and Trooper Freddie Crouch, a former policeman from London who had recently been plagued by nocturnal out-of-body experiences – which he interpreted as an omen of his own death. The three patrols were rowing into a fierce headwind and made very slow progress. It was shortly before dawn when they finally approached their goal. This meant that they had to return without achieving their objectives, to avoid being caught in the middle of the lake when the sun came up, which would have given away the fact that the raiders were interested in this part of the coast.

Lassen was concerned about the lack of reconnaissance, but 2nd Commando Brigade maintained that the operation should go ahead.[576]

On 8 April the men on Agosta and Caldirolo again had to spend a whole day hiding in mud holes. But that night they were to carry out the biggest attack of Operation Fry. Lassen divided his men into four groups and sent them into action at various locations along the northern shores – some to fight and draw attention to themselves, others to reconnoitre without being detected. The Royal Engineers detachment was sent up to the dike that demarcated the lake to the west, to investigate whether patrols could be sent ashore east of Argenta. A small patrol from M Squadron landed at the salt works in the north-east corner of the lake, where they conducted a thorough reconnaissance and questioned local people – a sure-fire way of ensuring that the Germans would get wind of British interest in this area.

One of Lassen's two combat groups, under the command of Captain Stud Stellin, made another attempt to climb the high dike and cross the deep channel along the northern shores west of Comacchio, but had to retreat when they were spotted by German sentries.

Lassen himself led the last of the four groups – seventeen men divided into two patrols – which would disembark on the shores of Comacchio and Porto Garibaldi and from there head north-west along the coast to Comacchio. Their job was to kill as many Germans as possible, take prisoners for interrogation and cause maximum confusion. This would presumably give the Germans the impression that a much larger force had landed in advance of a major attack on this part of the front. Lassen led E Patrol, which consisted of ten men besides himself. Lieutenant Turnbull, a newcomer to the SBS, had six men under him in Y Patrol.[577]*

The sun went down over Lake Comacchio at 20:00 and the attacking force sailed from Caldirolo shortly after. The waning moon had not risen yet. Some of the raiders sailed in folboats, others in larger craft. Lassen, Stephenson and Sergeant Waite sailed with Ettore Tomasi and Mario Foschini Cavalieri in their *batana*. From Caldirolo they sailed towards Valle Fattibello, crossed the Cona and Fosecchie dams, sailed on through the Pallotta Canal and into the dam along the shore by the village of Raibosola, just south of Comacchio.[578*]

As they lay off the dam, Lassen produced a bottle, took a swig, and passed it to Tomasi and Cavalieri. The drink was strong and Tomasi had not tasted it before. Lassen asked where they should go ashore. Tomasi pointed out the German positions and left the rest up to Lassen.

As Lassen led his men ashore, they first had to cross a canal that ran parallel to the shore, before moving up to the road between Comacchio and Porto Garibaldi. The road, which was around fifteen feet wide, ran parallel to the railway track on a low dam, with the canal to the west and a flooded area of six-foot-deep mud to the east. Lassen sent two scouts up the road, followed by the rest of E Patrol, with Y Patrol about 100 yards further back. He himself was in the rear of E Patrol from where he could maintain contact with Y as well.

After about 500 yards, the raiders were challenged by a guard shouting from a dug-in machine-gun post.[579*] Lassen did not entirely trust the two fishermen, so he had left them at the boats. The force's only Italian-speaking member, Private Freddie Green, was sent up to join the scouts. He told the guards that he and his comrades were fishermen from Sant'Alberto on their way to Comacchio. Out of sight, the raiders had taken up positions in the darkness behind Green, ready to intervene if something went wrong. Green had no experience in bluffing, especially not enemy machine-gunners. Nonetheless, he succeeded in delivering his message and repeating it three or four times. At first, the Turkmen sentry seemed to be convinced by Green's Italian. But just as the raiders were about to advance on the position and silently despatch the men occupying it, two machine guns in the post opened fire.[580*] The opening salvo wounded the two scouts and Freddie Crouch, and alerted the two machine-gun positions further up the road. The three posts had been positioned so that the ones at the back could fire over the top of those in the front. The raiders returned fire, but in the darkness and confusion some of the men had advanced too far and risked being hit by friendly fire. It was a hugely difficult situation – but Lassen acted decisively to save his men. Lassen had been just behind Green when he tried to fool the sentries. When the machine guns opened fire he had thrown himself to the ground. Now he ran towards the machine-gun position and threw two hand grenades in quick succession before storming it, followed by his men. Lassen was known for his ability to throw far and accurately, and the grenades did their job. Four Turkmenian soldiers were killed, either by the grenades or by bullets.

The two machine-gun positions further up the road then opened fire, as did a fourth position slightly to the left of the road, about 300 yards further away. Five or six machine guns were now firing down a road that was just fifteen feet wide. Lassen braved the hail of bullets to run towards the next position, to the left of the road. This allowed his men who had taken up positions on either side of the first machine-gun nest to shoot freely without risking hitting him. From here, Lassen threw three hand grenades towards the second German position. This shocked the crew so much that they ceased fire momentarily. Lassen seized the opportunity to lead another assault. He fired a green flare and stormed forward, alternately blowing his whistle and yelling at his men: 'Come on! Forward, you bastards!' This position too was manned by four soldiers with two machine guns. Two of the defenders were killed in the attack, the other two were taken prisoner and sent back for interrogation.[581*]

In the meantime, the third machine-gun position in the row, as well as the fourth, further back in the dark, had sent up flares. They now concentrated their fire on the position that the raiders had just stormed. The heavy fire killed Fusilier Stanley Raymond Hughes and Corporal Edward Roberts. Sergeant Waite was hit in the leg and was unable to move, but continued shooting from a prone position. Sean O'Reilly was also wounded, his shoulder shattered by a machine-gun bullet. The total force was now down to ten men armed with handguns, a Bren gun and hand grenades.

Disarray and confusion reigned among the raiders. Trying to get away from the road and the railway line, they took cover in the water and mud on both sides of the dam. Lassen gathered his men and ordered them to concentrate their fire on the third and nearest machine-gun position. He had already used all of his grenades but took more from Stephenson – who in return received a lecture because he had not pulled out the pin.

> The thing is you don't pull that till the last minute, you don't run around with a loose pin. But that went over my head, I knew that was Lassen, it didn't bother me, those remarks, one would expect that, it was almost a compliment.[582]

From inside the machine-gun position they now heard the cry 'Kamerad', the standard call meaning that the crew wanted to surrender. Lassen stood up, but ordered his men to remain under cover. He stepped onto the road and ran towards the machine-gun position. He stopped around three yards away and shouted in German to the defenders that they should come out. At that, a machine gun opened fire from the left side of the post.[583*] Maybe it was a trick by the defenders, or maybe they were unsettled to see Lassen running towards them holding weapons while unseen enemies were still firing on them. Lassen's men could barely see the machine-gun position. They had seen Lassen run up to it and then fall or throw himself to the ground and disappear from sight. They did not know if he had been hit or sought cover. When the shots were fired, Lassen threw a hand grenade into the post and wounded some of the defenders. One of the machine guns continued to fire, but the raiders responded in kind – and it fell silent.

After 'a few seconds but it seemed like twenty minutes' the raiders heard Lassen shouting: 'SBS! Major Lassen wounded!' Stephenson was the first to react. 'I heard him shout again so I then went across to the pill box, you've got to make your mind up.' Stephenson found Lassen lying on his back, apparently unconscious, to the right of the entrance to the post. He had been hit by gunfire in the side of the abdomen or groin. Stephenson put his arm under Lassen and supported him against his knee, trying to lift him up. Lassen started to talk. He said that he was dying and that Stephenson should leave him, because trying to evacuate him would just put the other raiders' lives at risk. Stephenson was to tell Lieutenant Turnbull to take command and continue the attack.[584*] Stephenson reached into his back pocket and fished out the morphine tablets that raiders always carried with them on operations. He placed one on Lassen's tongue. He again tried to lift the wounded man up to carry him back to the others. But Stephenson was not a big man, and had difficulty lifting the wounded Lassen, who weighed around 12½ stone. His backpack then got tangled in a phone line that had been downed by one of the explosions. He tried again to carry or drag Lassen away and yelled at his comrades. At last another raider joined them. Stephenson wanted him to help carry Lassen, but the man said, 'Oh, he's dead, there's no point.' Leaving Lassen behind, Stephenson and his companion headed back through the darkness and the shooting to find Turnbull.[585] According to the report that Turnbull wrote a month after the event, he shouted 'Andy, Andy!' and heard the reply 'Carry on, carry on!'

Regardless of which order Turnbull received from Lassen, and when and how he received it, he decided to abort the operation. By now the raiders had almost exhausted their ammunition – and without Lassen to spur them on it was pointless trying to continue. Turnbull fired a red flare as a signal to retreat. As well as Lassen, who was either dead or dying, the force left behind two dead and five missing, of whom at least two were wounded. Some of the boats had been hit by gunfire and were useless. Tomasi and Foschini used mud to patch holes in their *batana*, and took eight men on board instead of the three on the outward journey. O'Reilly, his shoulder smashed and bleeding heavily, tried to soothe the pain with cigarettes.[586] When the raiders sailed out onto the lake, they left one of their boats on the shore in the hope that the missing men would find it and escape.

It was around 03:00 when Tomasi and Cavalieri punted their boat out on the lake. To get out of range of the German weaponry as fast as possible, they steered first south-west and then west. This was not the course set by the British. '[They] were angry with me because I did not follow the routes that they had stipulated. But afterwards they understood it.'

When the remains of the force made it back to Caldirolo, O'Reilly's wound was treated, but it proved impossible to remove the bullet with the limited medical resources on the island. The next morning, he was sailed down to the south coast and taken by jeep to Ravenna, from where he was flown to a hospital. The other wounded were transported to Sant'Alberto, just south of the lake, and treated there.[587]

Of the five missing raiders, Alfred John Crouch was killed, but the two unharmed men managed to help their wounded comrades on board the abandoned boat and row to a nearby island, where they remained hidden until they were extracted safely the following night.[588]

* * *

At dawn on 9 April, the Germans and Turkmen brought their dead to Comacchio but left their enemies where they had fallen. The people of Comacchio did not dare venture out of town after the gunfire during the

The graves of Lassen, Hughes and Roberts in the old cemetery inside Comacchio. The site is now the playground of a local nursery.

night. Nor did they dare show sympathy for the Germans' enemies, so the corpses were left there until the town priest, Don Francesco Mariani, did something about it. He had repeatedly risked his life to help escaped Allied prisoners of war with shelter and money. Now, with the aid of some of the townswomen, he collected the bodies of Lassen, Hughes and Roberts (Crouch was not found until later and was buried where he fell). The bodies were brought into Comacchio, after which Don Francesco and the women prepared them for burial and laid them to rest in the town's old cemetery. It had been demolished during Napoleon's reign but was brought back into use after the flooding perpetrated by the Germans had made the newer cemetery southeast of Comacchio inaccessible.[589*]

The news of M Squadron's losses reached the other SBS units during 10–12 April.[590] Private Ken Smith, who knew Lassen from the Aegean, responded with a shrug when he heard that 'Lassen's 'ad it' and that Roberts, Hughes and Crouch had also lost their lives. Neither Smith, nor the other raiders who responded similarly, were particularly unfeeling. It was just that

> after five years of war, human life was just not as precious as it is in peacetime. We had lost a lot of friends, and we all knew that we could be killed at any time. So, when we heard that Lassen and the others had died, we shrugged, said 'Oh well' and drank another mug of coffee.[591]

Those closer to Lassen responded more strongly of course. Freddie Green, who himself had almost been killed during the battle on the Spit, 'cried incessantly for two days'. Others reacted with sorrow, shock and disbelief.

David Sutherland was in the Yugoslav mountains when he received word:

> I went as white as a sheet, we all did, we simply couldn't believe it. We thought that this man was totally indestructible. He'd been through so much and this was the last thing that he'd get killed doing. We were very upset about that and morale went down, absolutely rock-bottom.[592]

Operation Buckland and the end of the war

The 8th Army offensive, Operation Buckland, started the day Lassen and his comrades died. At 13:45 a large force of Allied aircraft – first heavy bombers, and then fighter-bombers and fighters flying at low altitude – started a bombardment of the area west of the River Senio and south of Lake Comacchio, where British forces were to attack that evening. Other parts of the German defences were also subjected to air strikes and artillery bombardments. At 19:20 the 8th Army's V Corps advanced across the Senio.

The next day, the big amphibious operation Impact Plain began, with around 100 Fantails attacking Longastrino and Menate, 5 to 6 miles east of Argenta, from the lake.

On the night of 10/11 April, the rest of M Squadron, who had already learned of their losses, carried out their last raid under Operation Fry. Using a smokescreen as cover, patrols opened fire with machine guns on the north shore of Lake Comacchio. The Germans responded with machine guns and mortars, but the raiders withdrew without casualties. The next day, M Squadron was relieved on the islands by the 28th Garibaldi Brigade and the raiders returned to base at Ravenna.

Impact Plain ended on 12 April. During the operation, the 15th and then the 71st Panzergrenadier Regiment of the 29th Panzergrenadier Division arrived at the Argenta gap. This division, one of the best in the German army, had been on its way to Germany when von Vietinghoff decided to send its reconnaissance battalion to Comacchio to defend the Spit. Despite the Allies' diversionary tactics, von Vietinghoff was in no doubt that the main attack would come via Argenta – and it was there that he sent his reserves.

On 13 April, the next major amphibious operation in the Impact series started. Impact Royal was an attempt to attack Argenta from the north-east with 102 Fantails. It was a disaster. The amphibious vehicles were unable to climb the steep banks at Fiorana and came under heavy fire from German artillery. The British losses were between 160 and 200 dead and wounded. The follow-up, Operation Impact Slam, which was supposed to lead to the capture of Portomaggiore, north-west of Argenta, was cancelled.

When the 8th Army finally took Argenta on 17 April 1945, 75% of the town's buildings had been destroyed by gunfire and bombs. (Sketch by Eric Manning, April 1945).

It would be 17 April before the British 56th Infantry Division finally crossed the channel and reached Bando, four miles north-east of Argenta. The night before, the 78th Infantry Division's 38th (Irish) Infantry Brigade crossed the river Reno at Bastia, four miles south of Argenta, and was now advancing on the town. In Argenta and its slightly more northerly neighbour Sant'Antonio, the remains of the 29th Panzergrenadier and 42nd Jäger Division, equipped with just a handful of tanks and twelve cannons, held out against forces from the 78th Infantry Division, 2 Commando and 43 RM Commando, which were pressing the Germans from all sides. On the evening of the 17th, following an artillery bombardment, the British infantry, supported by flamethrower tanks, heavy Churchill tanks and fighter-bombers, attacked. By the time darkness fell, the British had full control of Argenta. Three-quarters of all buildings in the town had been destroyed. On the night of 18 April, the British beat back a German counterattack with tanks. That same day they captured Consandolo and Portomaggiore, just north of Argenta. The last German resistance around Sant'Antonio was quelled in the early hours of 19 April. The battle for the Argenta gap was over. The 8th Army could now continue to Po and the north of Italy.

On the evening of 20 April, von Vietinghoff ordered the German forces in Italy to retreat north of the Po. The next day, the 28th Garibaldi Brigade, along with local partisans, entered Porto Garibaldi. At 15:00 they marched into Comacchio.

The Argenta Gap War Cemetery was inaugurated on shortly after the end of the fighting. The crosses were later replaced by the standard headstones used in British War Cemeteries all over the world.

While fighting continued in the Argenta gap, an Italian battle group and the Polish II Corps, both part of the 8th Army, advanced towards Bologna on Via Emilia, south of Argenta. Here too the Germans put up stiff resistance – but on 21 April the Poles entered Bologna.

The US 5th Army's offensive, Operation Craftsman, began on 14 April, two days late due to bad weather. The Americans circumvented Bologna and reached Verona on 25 April. On the same day, the National Liberation Committee for Northern Italy (CLNAI) issued an order for an uprising against the Germans and the remnants of Mussolini's regime in the north of the country. On 28 April the British reached Venice. Italian partisans captured Mussolini as he tried to flee across the border to Switzerland at Lake Como. The dictator was executed and his corpse put on public display and desecrated by a mob in Milan. On 1 May the 8th Army reached Udine, close to the Yugoslav border. The following day, the British reached Trieste. The Americans reached Turin and Milan on 2 May. On the morning of 4 May, the small South Tyrolean town of Colle Isarco/Gossensass was the scene of the first meeting between the 5th Army's vanguard, which was advancing from the south, and the front units of the US 7th Army, which had just crossed the Brenner Pass from Austria. On the same day, the BBC's Danish news service announced the surrender of German forces in the Netherlands, north-west Germany and Denmark.

Five days after the liberation of their country, the Lassen family in Nyhavn learned of Anders' death.

'Unit disbanded and all personnel now gone'

In the final weeks of April, S and L Squadron completed their operations in Dalmatia and returned to Italy, where the SBS headquarters and camps were slowly beginning to wind down their activities. M Squadron left the front on 4 May and arrived at the camp in Monopoli the next day. Some officers and crew began taking leave, others transferred to units in the Middle East or Britain. The adjutant's war diary entries[593] increasingly said only 'NTR' – 'Nothing To Report'. On Tuesday 8 May, the day the war officially ended in Europe, he wrote, laconically, 'V.E. DAY. Schooner arrived MONOPOLI from ANCONA.' Milner-Barry described the festivities in more detail:

> The war's over, and tomorrow we celebrate officially. But began today, and after dinner I found myself lured into the men's canteen and made to sing a song; my usual 'Oh, Mabel, Darling Mabel'. Avoided the Sergeants Mess afterwards so wasn't too badly off.

VE-Day on Tuesday was a riot of gaiety. We organized a funfair for the troops with unsuitable Officers dressed up as ballet girls, a wine bar, Fox telling fortunes, Stud showing them how to flog kit, Paterson giving advice on sex questions, etc. We had filled a tank cart with wine, so everybody got drunk by about 6.00 and started firing para flares. The situation appeared to be getting out of hand, and finally I was deputed by David [Sutherland] to address the troops to stop shooting, as it was becoming a possible danger to our neighbours. In order to make myself heard I mounted on a pedestal wearing a top hat, which I had somehow acquired, and managed to make myself heard by shouting at the top of my voice, and succeeded in quelling the near riot.[594]

In the following days, there was nothing to report. On Monday 14 May, the whole force was sent on two weeks' leave. One hundred and one men went to Rome, thirteen stayed in Bari, thirteen went on a 'cruise round the coast of Italy (in Dories)', and the remaining eighteen visited everywhere from Brenner to Rhodes. All of them reported for duty again on Monday, 28 May.

On 25 May, fifty men under the command of Captain John Lodwick[595*] had their leave shortened when they were sent to the military prison camp in Bari to stand guard over a group of disgruntled Lebanese port workers who had mutinied.

On 30 May, M Squadron was relocated to San Menaio, a pretty little town with magnificent beaches on the north side of the Gargano Peninsula. S Squadron moved to Sorrento. The first two weeks of June were largely uneventful. A few officers left to rejoin their old units or to transfer to another service. David Sutherland returned following visits to England and to Allied HQ in Italy, in the colossal royal palace at Caserta. The purpose of the visit was presumably to discuss the future of the SBS – but there was something else on Sutherland's mind too.

* * *

Immediately after Sutherland returned to Monopoli from Dalmatia, he had spoken to the men who had accompanied Lassen on his final raid. Their reports had convinced him to nominate Lassen for a posthumous Victoria Cross. Sutherland discussed the matter with Captain Bimrose, who then wrote a recommendation based on Lieutenant Turnbull's report. The recommendation was accompanied by two almost identical eyewitness accounts of Lassen's actions, written by Company Sergeant Major Workman and Bombardier Crotty.

Armed with this material, Sutherland went to Brigadier Tod, whose 2nd Commando Brigade had authority over the SBS in Italy. Tod was reluctant to recommend Lassen because he had already recommended Tom Hunter from his own brigade for a posthumous Victoria Cross for his deeds at Canale Valletta. It was unlikely that such a rare honour would be given to two soldiers who had participated in the same relatively small diversionary manoeuvre on the Italian front. On 16 June, however, Sutherland persuaded Tod to approve his recommendation. On 7 July the commander of V Army Corps, Major General H. Murray, also signed. Sutherland clambered into his jeep and drove up to 8th Army Command, near Klagenfurt. Here Sutherland met with an old friend from Eton, Tony Crankshaw, who was assistant to the army commander, Lieutenant General McCreery. Crankshaw made sure that the case was presented to McCreery in an appropriate manner. On 19 July, McCreery also signed the recommendation – but the matter was not settled yet. There were still people in the military system who did not like the special forces, and for whom it was a problem that Lassen was not a Commonwealth citizen.[596]

* * *

The end of the war made it easy for those in the military establishment who disapproved of 'private armies' to argue that the SBS had had its day. On Thursday 21 June the adjutant wrote: 'Signal from AFHQ stating unit to be disbanded.' Two weeks later all three squadrons were again gathered in the camp, where they were told that the dissolution of the SBS had been postponed. Over the following weeks, the SBS gradually shrank as the officers were assigned other duties. Sutherland again visited AFHQ, but the decision to close down the SBS was not to be overturned. The SBS suffered its final casualty of the war on 28 July when one of the newer officers, Captain Case, broke his neck during a swimming accident and was hospitalised. The next day 6 officers and 108 privates and NCOs who had volunteered for service in the SAS and the Far East travelled to Naples. From there they continued on to England.

Once the volunteers had left, work began on closing down the Monopoli camp. Most of the vehicles, signals equipment and REME stores were returned to the respective corps. The armoury and some tents were sent to Returned Stores Depot (RSD) in Naples.

> 'M', 'L' and 'S' Sqns cease to exist and the remainder of the personnel are concentrated as one unit in the Boathouse under command of Major STELLIN with Capt. BIMROSE 2 i/c.[597]

On 31 July the men continued to pack away the tents to send them elsewhere. Some of the boats were sent by truck to Naples and Venice. Captain Case died of his injuries at 11:30 on 31 July. The following afternoon he was buried with full military honours at the British military cemetery in Bari.

By 2–3 August the camp in Monopoli had been almost completely cleared. All that remained were the field kitchen, which was still in use, and the Boat House, which served as quarters for the remaining men and the office of the adjutant and his staff. On 4 August the SBS relinquished all of its vehicles and boats – except eight dories, ten kayaks, two rigid boats and twelve dinghies, which were put on board a landing craft to transport them to Malta on the orders of the Royal Navy Commander-in-Chief Mediterranean.

On 8 August, David Sutherland left the camp in Monopoli to travel to Naples. From there he flew to England, where, after four years with the SBS, he would be assigned to another service. The following four days were uneventful, except for final notifications of new postings and travel orders.

On Wednesday 15 August the adjutant wrote: 'Unit disbanded and all personnel now gone.'

Anders Lassen's decorations, from left to right: King Christian X's Commemorative Medal for participation in the War 1940–45 (Danish); Victoria Cross; Military Cross with two Bars; Greek War Cross in bronze; 1939–45 Star; Africa Star; Italy Star; Defence Medal; War Medal 1939–1945. Except for the three MCs all the decorations were awarded posthumously.

Chapter Thirty-Eight

Legacy

Thanks to, among others, Jellicoe and Sutherland's old friend Bob Laycock, who was Chief of Combined Operations, Anders Lassen's Victoria Cross was approved. On 7 September 1945, the War Office officially announced that it had awarded Lassen the rare distinction. Shortly afterwards, Suzanne Lassen placed ads in *The Times* and *Daily Express*, 'seeking details to complete a book of her son's legendary exploits in the Commandos'. She wanted to hear from anyone who knew anything about his whereabouts from 1939 until his death. Over the following year, Suzanne corresponded with several of her son's comrades-in-arms and other people who had met him more or less fleetingly or knew someone who had known him. She met some of them in England, others came to Denmark. The War Office and Combined Operations were also very helpful – at least up to a point. It was forbidden to divulge any 'operational technique', *Maid Honor* was not to be mentioned, and Suzanne was asked to submit her book for approval.[598]

Suzanne Lassen in Greece in the summer of 1947.

On 21 April 1947, Suzanne, Emil and Bente travelled by train from Copenhagen Central Station down through war-ravaged Germany to Italy to follow in Anders' footsteps. Over the following three months, they visited Comacchio, where they spoke with Ettore Tomasi among others. They also went to Greece, where, as guests of the British military authorities and the Greek government, they sailed by caique around the Aegean, visiting most of the islands on which Anders had operated. Stud Stellin, who had found it hard to settle down back home in New Zealand, accompanied them for most of the trip. Suzanne also met other British military personnel who had been in Greece, as well as Greek eyewitnesses to Anders' work – from Colonel Tsigantes to caique skippers and islanders who had met her son during the war. Emil had to return to Denmark before they visited Crete, but Suzanne and Bente met partisans from both sides of the civil war. They travelled with two sets of passports: one to show ELAS members and one to show their pro-government enemies. It was rarely possible to tell just by looking at them to which side the big, bearded men with cartridge belts across their chests belonged – but even when Suzanne took out the wrong passport, she was still lifted into the air and kissed as soon as the partisans realised that she was the mother of the man who had helped them in their struggle for freedom.

Throughout the journey, Suzanne diligently took notes in English or Danish, whichever seemed most natural in the moment. She returned home on board the Swedish freighter SS *Vikingland*, which sailed from Alexandria to Copenhagen via Oslo. Her efforts to trace Anders' steps were an important part of the material for her book about his life. Other important sources were her own family and friends' memories of him before he went to sea – not least, his many letters home from *Fionia* and *Eleonora Mærsk*, which she had carefully saved. She also had copies of military reports that Anders either wrote himself or in which he was mentioned, his hunting journals – particularly the last in the series, which had also served as a diary and scrapbook – and the collection of travel documents, membership cards, and private and official letters that Anders had collected and saved during the war. This material and more formed the basis for the book *Anders Lassen, Sømand og Soldat – Beretninger samlet af hans Moder*, ('Anders Lassen, Sailor and Soldier: Reports collected by his mother'), which was published in 1949 and widely read for many years. The book was published in an English translation in 1965 under the title *Anders Lassen VC*. The Danish version was last reprinted in 2000.

In May 1950, Anders received another posthumous reward when Suzanne was paid £44 12/- shillings by the Admiralty – her son's share of the prize money for *Duchessa d'Aosta*.

* * *

Suzanne's book may have cemented Lassen's status as national hero in Denmark, but Jørgen Halck, who fought in the South African Army, had started the process in 1946 with his poetry collection *Sange paa Rejsen* (*Songs along the Way*), which included this poem:

MAJOR ANDERS LASSEN V.C., M.C. & 2 BARS
Killed in battle on 9 April 1945 on the Italian Front

IN MEMORIAM

You knew war, the cold demands of battle, its hot hatred;
the sour-sweet stench where young men bled to death;
the painful harmony of pent in longing
and comradeship born of a thousand dangers shared.

The proudest German feared the glint of your steel
in the desert mist and in the moonlight of Crete.
Your name shall live forever in a saga full of deeds,
as long as Denmark's youth honours Denmark's heroes.

We know that the chalice of life, which you so often drained to the bottom,
frothed at its most fiery when your rush of youth was spilt,
and that you greeted death as your greatest adventure
and leapt expectantly into the great nothing.

Therefore, just a greeting without sorrow to your proud memory.

In 1947, Halck broadcast a radio lecture about Lassen, which was subsequently published in the newspaper *Information*. The same year, he published a short book *En dansk soldat, Major Anders Lassen, V.C., M.C.* (*A Danish Soldier, Major Anders Lassen, V.C., M.C.*). John Lodwick's book on the SBS, *Filibusters*, was published in Danish in 1948. *Unge Anders Lassen* (*Young Anders Lassen*) by the Norwegian author Frithjof Sælen was published in 1950. It was based mainly on Suzanne Lassen's book, as he pointed out in the foreword, but underpinned by his own studies and wartime notes. In the foreword, Sælen also thanks Suzanne Lassen for reading his manuscript.

In the 1960s the British adventure comic *The Victor* featured at least two stories starring Anders Lassen: 'Dangerous Decoys' on the Kastelli attack, and 'V.C. for a Dane' on Lassen's last battle (no 254, 1 January 1966 and no. 273, 14 May 1966). Anders Lassen also appears in the album *Koinsky racconta…due o tre cose che so di loro* (1993) by the Italian comic book artist Hugo Pratt, and Emil and Suzanne Lassen make an odd cameo appearance in Pratt's album *Corto Maltese. Mu, The Lost Continent* (IDW Publishing, 2020).

Shortly after the war, the British authorities established the Argenta Gap War Cemetery just north of Argenta, close to the site of the final battles in the area on 19 April 1945. The bodies of 625 Commonwealth soldiers who fell during the fighting were laid to rest there. Lassen and his companions Hughes, Roberts and Crouch were moved there from their original graves in the old cemetery inside Comacchio and on the battlefield. The second Victoria Cross recipient from the fighting at Comacchio, Private Tom Hunter, RM, was also laid to rest there.

In Denmark, busts of Anders Lassen have been placed in front of the Museum of Danish Resistance in Copenhagen, Jaeger Corps HQ at Airbase Aalborg, the Frogman Corps HQ at the naval station Kongsøre, at Lassengården at Herlufsholm, and in the park at the Lassen family's estate Holmegård. Roads have been named after Anders Lassen in Fakse Ladeplads and at the Danish Resistance Memorial Cemetery in Copenhagen. A memorial in his honour can be seen at Saint Peter's Chapel in Sjolte, close to Bækkeskov.

A memorial grove in Israel also commemorates his exploits. In England, Lassen is remembered with a bust in front of 22 Special Air Service Regiment HQ in Hereford and at the SBS HQ in Poole. In Scotland, D Squadron of the 23rd Special Air Service is based in Lassen House in Invergowrie, and a bench at the Glenfinnan Monument in the north-west Highlands has been dedicated to his memory. Photographs of Anders Lassen hang in the Special Forces Club, the SAS Regimental Association and the Imperial War Museum. In Kastelli on Crete, and in other towns on the Greek islands, Lassen is remembered with portraits in local libraries, etc. At the time of writing, locals in Kastelli were working to have a monument to Lassen erected.

Shortly after the liberation of Denmark, *Hjælpefondet for danske Frivillige i de allierede Styrker og deres Efterladte stiftet i 1946 til Minde om Major Anders Lassen, V.C., M.C. and two Bars (Foundation for Danish Volunteers in the Allied Forces and their Survivors, founded in 1946 in memory of Major Anders Lassen, VC, MC and two Bars)* was set up to provide financial assistance to former resistance fighters. It only lasted for a few years. In 1996 the current *Anders Lassen Foundation* was set up with HRH Crown Prince Frederik as

patron. The foundation has several aims: to provide financial support and encouragement to members or former members of the Danish army's and navy's Special Operations Forces or their survivors; to support injured Danish military personnel; to support individuals or their survivors for special humanitarian efforts; and to raise the profile of Anders Lassen as a source of inspiration for the two modern-day Danish special corps.

On the occasion of the hundredth anniversary of Lassen's birth – 22 September 2020 – the Anders Lassen Foundation introduced a new medal for acts of exceptional valour, the Major Anders Lassen Medal. The medal's patron is HRH Crown Prince Frederik (a former member of the Danish Navy's Frogman Corps). The medal's design incorporates references to Lassen's service in the SOE and SBS and to the Victoria Cross, as well as the motto "Strength, Will, Courage", words used about Lassen by Lord Jellicoe in a letter to Suzanne Lassen.

Major Anders Lassen VC, MC and two bars, SBS, 20 September 1920 to 9 April 1945.

On 9 April 2002, Comacchio Council inaugurated a memorial on the site where Lassen, Crouch, Hughes and Roberts were killed – or at least as close to this location as the changeable lagoon landscape allows. The inscription commemorates and expresses gratitude to the men who 'at this location, far from their homeland, laid down their lives for the freedom of the peoples'. The local council, civil and military authorities and local veterans' associations lay a wreath at the monument every year on 25 April, which is Liberation Day in Italy. The British Commando Veterans Association visited the monument in 2005 and 2006. On 9 April 2015, a detachment from the Home Guard from Haslev near Bækkeskov held a memorial service at Lassen's grave in Argenta complete with colour party and band. The British military attaché in Rome, the Mayor of Comacchio and representatives of many Italian military and civil bodies, veterans' organizations, etc. also attended. In 2016 and 2017, delegations from the British Army Land Warfare Centre also visited the monument to Lassen and his comrades in arms. On 6 November 2017 Greek organizations in Melbourne (the world's third largest 'Greek city' after Athens and Thessaloniki) cooperated with the Danish Consulate General in organizing an event to commemorate Anders Lassen's role in the liberation of Thessaloniki. On 22 September 2020, the centenary of Anders Lassen's birth was commemorated in the Memorial Cemetery in Copenhagen, where Denmark remembers its fallen Resistance heroes as well as the Danes who sacrificed their lives in the service of their nation and of the Allies during the Second World War.

Anders Lassen's Service in the British Army

20 May 1942 – Appointed as an emergency commission as 2nd Lieutenant, General List (specially employed without pay and allowances from Army Funds)

20 November 1942 – War Substantive Lieutenant

1 March 1943 – Posted to SAS Regiment

10 September 1943 – Posted to Special Boat Squadron

13 September 1943 – Appointed Acting Captain

13 December 1943 – Appointed Temporary Captain

9 October 1944 – Appointed Acting Major

9 January 1945 – War Substantive Captain, Temporary Major

This list is based on Anders Lassen's Army Form B199A (P/234907).

Acknowledgments

This book could not have been written without the help of numerous individuals and institutions. I hope I have lived up to their faith in me.

For reasons of space, I can only name a few of the many to whom I owe gratitude. They, of course, are not liable for any mistakes or omissions. Responsibility for those lies solely with the author.

Andy's War is based on the 2018 edition of *Anders Lassens krig*, which was originally published in Danish in 2010 and has since appeared in several new editions and reprints. Every time the book was slightly improved thanks to corrections and new information offered by kind readers or, in many cases, by people who had particular knowledge of the events described, often because their fathers or grandfathers had participated in them. I am very grateful for all these contributions. Keep them coming!

However, the 2018 edition is the result of a more systematic and extensive revision, focussing particularly on the Greek chapters of Lassen's story. I am much indebted to the historian Lars Bærentzen and his colleagues John O. Iatrides and Ioannis D. Stefanidis who, with overwhelming generosity, shared their great knowledge and insight with me (John Iatridis even provided an eyewitness account of (perhaps) Lassen's entry into Thessaloniki). I am also hugely grateful to Nina Stähle, MA, MSc, who – under the motto 'I try to treat every project I work on as if it were my own' – searched British, German, and Greek archives for me and contributed an endless stream of helpful advice and ideas.

Nikos Nikoloudis shared with me his detailed knowledge of the Greek Sacred Squadron and guerrilla warfare in the Aegean. The former Danish cultural attaché in Athens, the distinguishd translator Panagiota Goula, found Greek sources and translated them for me. Patricia McGoldrick gave me access to interesting finds from her own archival research, Mariann Fines Evison and Philippa Field helped improve the chapter on *Maid Honor* and Operation Postmaster, as did Graham Robinson with the chapter on Sark, and the journalist and author Michael Smith helped me understand the fate of Graham Hayes. Helen Tzortzopoulos provided material on events on

Kithera. Thank you also to Nicholas Jellicoe for interesting conversations on his father, to Gavin Mortimer, author of *The SBS in World War II* for discussing the fate of the Alimina patrol with me, and to Fiona Lapraik for allowing me to use her father's private papers. Thank you to Børge Franck's son and granddaughter, Julian and Esther Franck, for additional information and for permission to use Franck's letter to Krøyer Kielberg. Georgios Papadoiannis, who lived on Crete as a boy during the war, has been a constant encouragement with his year-long kind interest in my work. Thank you also to Helen Forbes for genealogical assistance, to Søren Dalsgaard for investigations in the field in our hunt for Esther Molloy, and to the historians Susanne Brand and Sebastian Remus for their help at, respectively, The National Archives, Kew, and BAMA, Freiburg.

Thank you to Henry G. Wilson for believing in the project, to Barnaby Blacker (whose grandfather, Colonel Latham Valentine Stewart Blacker OBE, invented the Blacker Bombard and the PIAT) and Matt Jones for their meticulous editing, and to the entire team at Pen & Sword Books for their efficiency and enthusiasm. And a special thank you to my translator colleague Tam McTurk for his brilliant work.

* * *

For their help with the original version of this book I must thank Anders Lassen's sister, Bente Bernstorff-Gyldensteen, and his niece, Suzanne B.D. Lassen; Poul Lyngsøe, former President of the Danish Anders Lassen Foundation, the late Erik Heimann Olsen of the Danish Association of Resistance Veterans, Grenville Bint of the SAS Regimental Association; the historian Jakob Sørensen; Henrik Lundbak, Chief Curator of the Danish Resistance Museum; J. Kunze Christensen and his colleagues at the Danish Defence Library; Kaj Andersen, Næstved; Ejnar Christiansen; Jenny Bimrose and Alan Brown; Valerie Bond; Bob Perkins; Anders Sandberg, Iain Farmer, Claus De La Porte; Louise C. Larsen; Simon Bang; the Italian historians Silvio Tasselli and Rino Moretti; Andrea Casciotta; George Poulimenos; Niels Henrik Sliben; Jens Post; Poul Erik Branebjerg; Peter Edelberg; Morten Nielsen; Rolf Hesse; Lena Hoff; Aage Sækmose, former teacher at the Academy of Physical Education, Ollerup; Sarah K. Minney; David List and Bob O'Hara.

A special thank you to Lieutenant General Kjeld G. Hillingsø, who gave me advice and practical help during my work and read the finished manuscript, and to my old friend Christopher Munthe Morgenstierne (whose family owned Bækkeskov 1741–1795), who read the manuscript as I wrote it and gave me valuable comments and advice based, not least, on his apparently inexhaustible knowledge of everything that has ever sailed on the sea.

And last but first, I must thank my wife, the author and translator Lene Ewald Hesel, without whose patience, support and help neither this book nor most of whatever else I do would be possible – and without whom it wouldn't feel very meaningful.

All this goodwill would probably have brought me nowhere, had it not been for financial support from the following sources: Kunstrådet, A.P. Møller og Hustru Christine McKinney Møllers Fond til almene Formaal, Danske Banks Fond, Dronning Margrethes og Prins Henriks Fond, Harboefonden, Kong Christian den Tiendes Fond, Konsul George Jorck og Hustru Emma Jorck's Fond, NTI Fonden, Overretssagfører L. Zeuthens mindelegat, Prins Joachim og Prinsesse Alexandras Fond.

* * *

In April 2002 I visited Comacchio to participate in the inauguration of the town's monument to Lassen and his three comrades. Among the organizers of the beautiful event was Massimo Cavalieri, who worked in the municipal Culture and Tourism Admnistration, and his wife, the historian Sandra Carli Ballola. Massimo's and Sandra's engagement in their hometown's culture and history and their warm and generous hospitality – both on that occasion and when my family and I retured to Comacchio during the summer – made a strong impression on me and stimulated my desire to learn more about what happened around Comacchio and Argenta in the spring of 1945. Massimo was killed in a hunting accident on Lake Comacchio on 10 October 2002. I often thought about him while working on this book.

* * *

To the best of my knowledge, all quotes from texts in copyright are within the limits of 'fair dealing' as described in The Society of Authors' *Guidance on Copyright and Permission*. Every effort has been made to identify and track down any copyright holders for the illustrations and gain permission for use. If any mistakes have been made, I apologise unreservedly.

Acknowledgments

Sources of maps and illustrations
All maps drawn by Simon Bang (www.simonbang.art/).
The majority of the illustrations have been made available by the Lassen/Bernstorff family. This collection includes photos from family albums, material from Anders Lassen's Hunting Journal, photos taken by Suzanne Lassen and/or her travel companions in 1945–47 as well as photos acquired by her from a variety of unknown sources – presumably her son's friends and comrades – during the same years.

ix, 225: Hoffmann family collection, courtesy of Anders Fogh.
1, 2, 4, 5, 7, 9, 11, 26, 30, 37, 78, 89, 105 (bottom), 107, 146, 164, 170, 189, 192, 204, 211, 215, 219, 251, 258, 274, 276, 289, 292, 299, 301, 308, 311, 323, 326, 331, 336: Collection of the Lassen/Bernstorff family, courtesy of Bente Bernstorff-Gyldensteen.
3: Illustration by Suzanne Lassen in *Bentes Fuglebog*, 1932, courtesy of Bente Bernstorff-Gyldensteen.
48, 49, 50, 58, 146, 249: Danish National Museum.
13, 51, 62, 65, 67, 108, 110, 117, 129, 183, 187, 269, 330: public domain.
66: Madrid Police.
75, 76, 95, 96, 136, 143, 183, 187: TNA.
93, 94: Courtesy of Peter Quartermaine.
87, 91: Courtesy of Mariann Fines Evison.
100: Courtesy of Philippa Field.
105 (top): Courtesy of Nina Stähle.
147: Courtesy of Nicholas Jellicoe.
156, 158, 290: Courtesy of Georgios Kalogerakis.
141, 154, 218, 222: David Sutherland's scrap book/courtesy of SAS Regimental Association.
315, 325: *The Italian Campaign, 3 Sep 1943–2 May 1945*, RAC.
335: the author's collection.

Glossary

AB	Able Seaman
AFHQ	Allied Forces HQ (HQ of the allied forces in the Mediterranean)
ANZAC	Australian and New Zealand Army Corps
COHQ	Combined Operations HQ
COPP	Combined Operations Pilotage Parties
CoS	Chiefs of Staff Committee (a subcommittee of the War Cabinet consisting of the professional heads of the three services meeting regularly under the chairmanship of the CIGS, General Alan Brooke)
CIGS	Chief of the Imperial General Staff, the professional head of the British Army; the post was held by General Alan Brooke 25 December 1941–25 June 1946.
CSDIC	Combined Services Detailed Interrogation Centre (CSDIC ran prisons where PoWs, espionage suspects etc. were interrogated)
DMWD	Royal Navy Department of Miscellaneous Weapons Development, also known as Directorate of Miscellaneous Weapons Department, Admiralty department responsible for the development of unconventional weapons.
DSO	Distinguished Service Order (decoration for meritorious or distinguished service during wartime, typically in combat; until 1993 only officers were eligible)
EAM	Greek: National Liberation Front, resistance organization established in September 1941 as a coalition of six left wing parties; eventually dominated by the Communists
EDES	Greek: National Republican Greek League, the largest of the non-communist resistance groups, its military wing, the National Groups of Greek Guerrillas (EOEA) was mainly active in Epirus.
ELAS	Greek: National Liberation Army; guerrilla organization created by the Communists in December 1941; the first armed groups were formed during the summer of 1942
EOK	Greek: National Organization of Crete (informal alliance of non-Communist Cretan resistance groups, from centre-left

	to the republican right) EOK was the dominant resistance organization on Crete
GFP	Geheime Feldpolizei; German secret military police.
ISLD	Inter Services Liaison Department (codename for SIS in the Middle and Far East)
ISRB	Inter-Services Research Bureau (cover name for SOE)
LFA	Land Forces Adriatic
LRDG	Long Range Desert Group
LS	Levant Schooner (the caiques of the LSF; named 'LS' followed by a number, e.g. 'LS1')
LSF	Levant Schooner Flotilla
MC	Military Cross (award for gallantry given to captains and officers of lower rank)
MI5	the UK domestic intelligence service
MI6	the UK foreign intelligence service (SIS)
MI9	Secret organization established to set up escape networks for PoWs, downed airmen etc.
MI(R)	Military Intelligence (Research)
ML	motor launch (various types of British patrol vessels, with a length of app. 20–35 m and a tonnage of 21.5–57 grt; built for anti-submarine warfare, harbour defence, rescue operations etc.; typically armed with 20 mm (0.787 in) and 7.7 mm (.303 in) machine guns and depth charges etc.)
MM	Military Medal (award for gallantry given to NCOs and privates)
MTB	motor torpedo boat
MVSN	Milizia Volontaria per la Sicurezza Nazionale (paramilitary organization of the Italian Fascist Party; the Blackshirts)
Neucols	Neutral colonies (the section of SOE's West African organization in charge of the colonies of neutral countries)
OCTU	Officer Cadets Training Unit
OKW	*Oberkommando der Wehrmacht* (high command of the German armed forces)
OSS	Office of Strategic Services (US intelligence service; the precursor of CIA)
PERO	Political and Economic Research Organization (cover name for SOE's organization in West Africa)
PIAT	Projector Infantry Anti-Tank (British anti-tank weapon)
RAF	Royal Air Force
RAMC	Royal Army Medical Corps
REME	Royal Electrical and Mechanical Engineers

RFHQ	Raiding Forces Headquarters
RM	Royal Marines
RN	Royal Navy
RNVR	Royal Navy Voluntary Reserve (Civilian voluntary reserve officers of the RN)
RSI	Repubblica Sociale Italiana (fascist state under Mussolini's leadership, established in Northern Italy on 23 September 1943)
RTU	Returned to Unit
SAAF	South African Air Force
SAS	Special Air Service
SBS	Special Boat Section 1941–43; 1943–44: Special Boat Squadron; 1945: Special Boat Service
SIS	Secret Intelligence Service, aka MI6
SOE	Special Operations Executive.
SSRF	Small Scale Raiding Force.
STC	Special Training Centre
VE Day	Victory in Europe Day (8 May 1945, the day the Allies accepted Germany's unconditional surrender)
WAAF	Women's Auxiliary Air Force

Notes

Chapter 1: Childhood and Family
1. Unless otherwise indicated, this chapter is based on Suzanne Lassen: *Sømand og Soldat* (1949/1965) as well as on the author's interviews with Anders Lassen's sister, Bente Bernstorff-Gyldensteen.
2. Jessien: Interview by Anders Sandberg, 2008.
3. Jessien: Interview by Anders Sandberg, 2008.
4. *London Gazette, no. 30975, 26 October 1918*. The Victoria Cross is Britain's greatest honour for bravery. The VC is awarded 'for most conspicuous bravery or some daring or pre-eminent act of valour or self-sacrifice, or extreme devotion to duty in the presence of the enemy'.
5. AL's report cards, etc. in the Lassen family archive.
6. AL's report cards etc., in the Lassen family archive.
7. EL: Letter to headmaster Krarup, 20.06.33, Krarup, J.: Letter to EL, 24.06.33 and EL: Letter to headmaster Friis-Hansen, 24.06.35.
8. About Herlufsholm: Prince George, quoted in Langley 1988/2016, p.31. About Lundby Lower Secondary: Christiansen, Einar: 'Lundby High School', unpublished manuscripts, e-mail, 26.08.09; Jessien: Interview by Anders Sandberg, 2008.
9. Christiansen, Ejnar: 'Lundby High School' and 'The Funen Bike Trip', unpublished manuscripts, e-mail 26.08.09.
10. Christiansen, Einar: 'The Funen Bike Trip', unpublished manuscripts, e-mail 26.08.09.
11. Jessien: Interview by Anders Sandberg, 2008.
12. 'General Preparation Exam Certificate', Lundby Lower Secondary, 06.25.38, Lassen family private archive; Christiansen, Einar: 'Lundby High School', unpublished manuscripts, e-mail 26.08.09.

Chapter 2: M/S *Fionia*, January–May 1939
13. AL: Letters 1 and 2, n.d., from *Fionia*.
14. Prince Georg, quoted in Langley 1988/2016, p.26.
15. AL: Letter 9, n.d., Port Said/Suez; AL: Letter 7, n.d., Dunkirk; AL: Letter 12B, 02.28.39, Colombo.
16. AL: Letter 10, 10.02.39, Port Said/Suez.
17. AL: Letter 12B, 03.19.39, Colombo.
18. AL: Letter unnumbered, 01.04.39, Bay of Bengal.

Chapter 3: Bækkeskov, May–June 1939
19. Lassen, p.27; Langley 1988/2016, pp.39–40; AL, holiday card, Copenhagen, 24 May 1939.
20. Muus 1994.
21. AL: Trainee ship's mate contract, Copenhagen, 1 June 1939
22. The exchange is reproduced from Langley 1988/2016, p.40. As a first lieutenant in the celebrated Infantry Regiment 9 Potsdam, Axel von dem Bussche watched a group of SS and SD men shoot more than 3,000 Jews on an airfield near Dubno in Ukraine in October 1942. After this he saw it as his duty to save Germany from Hitler. He became part of the resistance circle around Claus von Stauffenberg, and in 1943 he volunteered to assassinate Hitler. A tall, impressive figure, he was chosen to model a new uniform for the Führer.

The idea was that he would physically grab hold of Hitler and detonate a bomb hidden on his person. Bussche's 'patriotic suicide', as he called it, was foiled by an Allied air raid on Berlin that destroyed the goods wagon shipping the new uniforms to Rastenburg. It was impossible to reschedule the modelling assignment before February 1944. In the meantime he returned to his unit on the Eastern Front. On 30 January 1944 he was so badly injured by a Soviet grenade that one of his legs had to be amputated. He spent several months in an SS field hospital, which saved him from the wave of arrests and executions that followed in the wake of the failed attempt on Hitler's life on 20 July 1944. Axel von dem Bussche died on 26 January 1993 (Von Medem 1994; Dönhoff 1994).

Chapter 4: The Art of Guerrilla Warfare 1 – MI(R)
23. Gubbins: *The Art of Guerrilla Warfare.* Quoted from Mackenzie (2000/2002), p.40.

Chapter 5: M/T *Eleonora Mærsk*, 1939–40
24. AL: Letter, 12 December 1939.
25. AL: Letter 03, 29 June 1939, Falmouth.
26. AL: Letter, n.d., but July 1939, 'Dear Mother'; Christiansen: *Beretning.*
27. AL: Telegram, 5 August 1939, *Eleonora Mærsk.*
28. Lassen, S. 1949/1965, pp.14.
29. AL: Letter, n.d., but the end of September/start of October 1939, 'Dear Mother…'; AL: Letter, 'Atlantic Ocean five days south-west of Calais in France'; AL: Letter, 16 August 1939: 'Dear Dida…'.
30. AL: Letter, 30 September 1939, Willemstad, *Eleonora Mærsk.*
31. AL: Letter, 19 September 1939, *Eleonora Mærsk*, Weymouth.
32. Christiansen: *Beretning*; Bennike, 1945; Chapter 1; AL: Letter, 19 September 1939, Weymouth.
33. AL: Letter, 19 September 1939, *Eleonora Mærsk*, Weymouth.
34. AL: Letter, n.d., but early October 1939, 'Dear Dad…'.
35. AL: Letter (19 September 1939), *Eleonora Mærsk*, Weymouth.
36. AL: Letter, n.d., but early October 1939, 'Dear Dad…'.
37. AL: Two letters (n.d., but late September/early October 1939). 'Dear Mother…' and 'Dear Dad…', *Eleonora Mærsk*, Antwerp.
38. AL: Letter (n.d., but late September/early October 1939), 'Dear Mother…'; Letter (n.d., but early October 1939), 'Dear Dad…'; Letter (October 4, 1939) *Eleonora Mærsk*, Antwerp.
39. AL: Letter, n.d., but early October 1939, 'Dear Dad…'.
40. AL: Letter (26 September 1939) *Eleonora Mærsk*, 'North of Davns End'.
41. AL: Letter, n.d., but early October 1939, 'Dear Dad…'.
42. Christiansen: *Beretning.*
43. AL: Letter, n.d. but 1940, *Eleonora Mærsk*, Rangoon.
44. AL: Letter, n.d., but 11 December 1939; on Lassen's racism: Langley 1988/2016, pp. 71–2..
45. AL: Letter, n.d. but 1940, *Eleonora Mærsk*, Rangoon.
46. AL: Letter, n.d., but 11 December 1939.
47. AL: Telegram, 24 December 1939.
48. SL: Letter to AL, 1 November 1939.

Chapter 6: The Art of Guerrilla Warfare 2 – The Snowballers, November 1939–March 1940
49. This chapter is based mainly on Allan 2007, p. 28–32 and Windmill 2005, p.10.

Chapter 7: 'Good luck – aim between the eyes' – February–March 1940
50. AL: Letter, n.d., 'Dear Mum, Docked in Abberdan…'.
51. SL: Letter to AL, 28 January 1940.
52. AL: Telegram no. 22 14, n.d., *Eleonora Mærsk.*

Chapter 8: M/T *Eleonora Mærsk*, 1 January–9 April 1940
53. AL: Letter to E. and S. Lassen and Kristine Carlsen ('DIDA'), n.d., but 1940, *Eleonora Mærsk.*
54. Lassen 1949/1965, p.19.

55. Christiansen: *Beretning*.
56. AL: Letter, 14 March 1940.
57. AL: Letter, 20 March 1940, 'Dear Dad…'.

Chapter 9: M/T *Eleonora Mærsk*, 9 April 1940–October 1940
58. The descriptions of events on board *Eleonora Mærsk* between April and October 1940 in this and the following chapters are largely based on S.N. Christiansen's *Beretning*, second mate C.A. Lang's *Dagbog*, radio operator Arne Bennike's *'Gnisten' paa Eventyr*, 1945), AL's *Jagtjournal 1938–1942* and Tortzen 1981, 1, pp.499–521.
59. SL: Letter to 'Fritz', n.d., but shortly before Christmas 1941.

Chapter 10: The Art of Guerrilla Warfare 3 – Independent Companies and Operation Knife
60. This chapter is based mainly on Allan 2007, particularly the chapter 'The Big House'.
61. Allan: 2007, p.37.
62. Smith, I.C.D.: *Private Papers*, IWM.

Chapter 11: M/T *Eleonora Mærsk* in British Service, 4 May 1940–October 1940
63. Christiansen: *Beretning*.
64. According to Suzanne Lassen (Lassen 1949), Anders and the ship's radio operator tried to join the Royal Air Force in Colombo but were rejected on the grounds that the RAF did not enlist foreigners (which it did in large numbers, including Danes). Suzanne Lassen does not mention her source. Anders did not refer to the incident in his diary nor in any other preserved document, and *Eleonora Mærsk*'s radio operator, Arne Bennike, says nothing about it in his memoir *Gnisten paa Eventyr* (Sparky's Adventures, 1945), in which he otherwise talks extensively about their time in Colombo.
65. Lang: *Dagbog*.
66. Tottenham: Letter, 5 April 1948.

Chapter 12: The Art of Guerrilla Warfare 4 – Commandos
67. Ladd: 1978, p.17.
68. Cited from Allan 2007, p.84.
69. Cited from Ramsey 1981, p.129.
70. The actual Commandos had not yet been set up, so men from MI(R)'s ten independent companies were forged into a new unit called 11 Commando/Independent Company (Ladd: 1978, p.17).

Chapter 13: M/T *British Consul*, October–December 1940
71. Lassen: 1949/1965, p.20.
72. Langley 1988/2016, pp.27–30; wikipedia.org/wiki/SS_British_Consul, acc. 4 April 2018.

Chapter 14: Britain, December 1940–January 1941
73. Jespersen 1998 I, pp.155–6.
74. In this and the following chapters, the account of Iversen and his relationship with SOE, etc, is based mainly on Sørensen (2009 and 2011), Hollingworth (1947) and Jespersen (1998).
75. HS 2/106; ADM 1/18250.
76. Hollingworth 1947.

Chapter 15: The Art of Guerrilla Warfare 5 – SOE – Set Europe Ablaze
77. Brown 1975, p.563.
78. Hollingworth 1947; Jespersen 1998, I, p.80.

Chapter 16: In the SOE
79. Hollingworth 1947.
80. Sørensen 2011, pp.173–9; ADM 1/18250.

81. Hollingworth 1947.
82. *Orders for Wednesday 15th January, 1941, No. 1 Special School*, Danish National Archives, Captain W.M. Iversen's Archive, 1939–47 folder 29.
83. Rigden 2001; Cunningham 1998.

Chapter 17: The Art of Guerrilla Warfare 6 – The SOE Schools

Chapter 18: 'Good with an out-and-out independent nature'
84. Rigden 2001, p.4.
85. Sørensen 2011, p.233.
86. Quoted from Cook Ridge 1966, p.560; information about Bruhn otherwise mainly from Jespersen 1998, pp.153–4.
87. Sørensen 2011.

Chapter 19: The Art of Guerrilla Warfare 7 – Commandos
88. Ramsey 1981, p.90.
89. DEFE 2/842.
90. Lodwick 1947/1990, p.16.
91. Waugh 1941, p.493; Windmill 2005, p.12.
92. Lodwick 1947/1990, p.20.
93. Lodwick 1947/1990, p.19.
94. The description of the early days of the SAS is mainly based on Warner 1971, ch. II.
95. Holt 2004, p.23.

Chapter 20: Special Training School 21, Arisaig House
96. Allan 2007, p.169; Lassen 1949/1965, p.26.
97. SOE Syllabus, p.255.
98. SOE Syllabus, p.256.
99. SOE Syllabus, pp.276–9.
100. SOE Syllabus, pp.361–2.
101. SOE Syllabus, p.362.
102. SOE Syllabus, pp.368–9.
103. SOE Syllabus, pp.369, 372.
104. SOE Syllabus, p.382.
105. Grossmann 1995/2009; but see also Bourke 1999.
106. Lassen 1949/1965, p.26.

Chapter 21: Gumley Hall
107. SOE HQ Files 242: History of the Training Section of the SOE 1940–45, HS 8/435; Hollingworth 1947.
108. Rigden 2001 [introduction to SOE Syllabus]; Allan 2007; Cunningham 1998; Crowdy 2008.
109. HS7/215, War Diary, Vol. 4, Survey of Global Activities, April 1941.
110. Sørensen 2011.
111. Anonymous member of the Danish contingent ('seaman by profession'), Suzanne Lassen, cited by Lassen 1949/1965, pp.28–9.
112. HS 9/888/2; Lassen 1949/1965, p.29.
113. Captain Iversen, archive; Hansson, 2007.
114. Lassen 1949/1965, p.27.
115. Lassen 1949/1965, p.30.
116. Hancock, interviews with Mike Langley.

Chapter 22: The Art of Guerrilla Warfare 8 – *Maid Honor*
117. Jespersen 1998, I, p.58.
118. Howe: Interview, with Mike Langley, 1985.
119. Appleyard 1947, chapters 1 and 2; Lean 1998; Fournier & Heinz 2006, chapter 1; Langley 1988/2016, chapter 4; HS 9/1183/2.

120. Appleyard 1947, chapters 1 and 2; Lean 1998; Fournier & Heinz 2006, chapter 1; Langley 1988/2016, chapter 4; HS 9/48/11.
121. Appleyard, 1947, p.53.
122. Nasmyth: Interview, with Mike Langley.
123. Appleyard, 1947, p.57.
124. Mackenzie (2000/2002), p.248.
125. BT 119–1253
126. Nasmyth: Interview by Mike Langley.
127. HS/9/680/5.
128. Appleyard, 1947, pp.105–6.
129. Prout: 'Major A.F.E.V.S. Lassen V.C. M.C.' in HS 9/888/2.
130. Appleyard 1947, p.106.
131. Appleyard, 1947, p.106; Ogden-Smith, interview by Mike Langley; Perkins: e-mail: 25 and 26 February 2010.
132. Appleyard, 1947, pp.67–8; Fournier & Henitz 2006, p.22.
133. Langley 1988/2016, p.55.
134. The fourth participant, the Nazi Jørgen Børresen, was imprisoned by the British and handed over to the Danish authorities for prosecution in 1945. Lauridsen (ed.), pp.199–202; HS 9/538/1; about Jørgensen: HS 9/812/5; HS 9/1494/6 Tvermose. Letter from Børge Franck to the President of the Danish Council in Great Britain, F.M. Krøyer Kielberg, written in Brixton Prison, London, 14 October 1940 (copy of English translation by Mikkel Plannthin in the author's archive).
135. Nasmyth: Interview by Mike Langley. Jørgensen and Franck were identified based on a letter of 7 August 1942, from Alfred Jørgensen in 'Niggerland' to Anders Lassen, in which Jørgensen refers to a mutual acquaintance, 'Bugger Frank', who appears to have been at Anderson Manor and in West Africa with them.
136. Nasmyth: Interview by Mike Langley.
137. Lassen: *Jagtjournalen* (Lassen's Hunting Journal); tottenham.name/index, retrieved 26 February 2010.
138. Tottenham: Letter to Suzanne Lassen, 20 September 1946.
139. Special Operations Executive Operation Postmaster Preparations, Major C.V. Clarke Collection, IWM, Cat. no. MGH 432; ADM 223/480; Langley 1988/2016, p.54; Appleyard, 1947, p.71.
140. Richards 2004, p.92.
141. HS 33/93 S.O.E. West Africa no. 23.
142. Langley 1988/2016, p.56; Nasmyth: Interview by Mike Langley; ADM 223/480.
143. AL: Note to the War Office: Bow and Arrow Used in Modern Warfare, n.d., but presumably summer 1941.
144. Appleyard, 1947, p.119.

Chapter 23: Operation Postmaster
145. The National Archives in Kew contain very extensive material on Operation *Postmaster*. Here the reference is to HS 3/86-93.
146. HS 3/92.
147. The account of the *Maid Honor*'s travels is based mainly on Langley 1988/2016, pp.59–67, which in turn is based on the ship's logbook.
148. The date is based on Langley 1988/2016, which in turn is based on *Maid Honor*'s logbook. However Appleyard (1947) gives the date as Thursday 14 August. The Perkins Collection, IWM, contains some pages of the *Maid Honor's* logbook (September 1941–February 1942).
149. Nasmyth: Interview by Mike Langley.
150. Lett, chapter 'The Voyage to West Africa'; Langley, chapter 5. I am indebted to Ernest Fines Evison's daughter, Mariann Fines Evison, who drew my attention to inaccuracies in my previous attempts to track the *Maid Honor* Force's movements.
151. Nasmyth: Interview by Mike Langley.
152. Appleyard, 1947, p.84.

153. Mackenzie, (2000/2002) pp.325–6; Pearce 1983, p.426; HS 9/538/2.
154. *War Diary 6, Vol. 2, Survey of Global Activities, August 1941*, HS 7/219.
155. HS 3/88
156. *SOE West Africa No. 23*, HS 33/93.
157. Appleyard, 1947, p.86.
158. Appleyard, 1947, p.85; Langley 1988/2016, pp.69–70.
159. Appleyard, 1947, p.89.
160. *SOE West Africa No. 18*, HS 3/89.
161. HS 9/635/2.
162. Coded telegram from *Neucols*, no. 185, 28 12:41, HS 3/86.
163. CO 537/4286
164. Penultimate Report on Tour No. 3, by W25 (Richard Lippett), HS 3/89.
165. After the war, *Maid Honor* was sold as a fishing boat in Freetown (Howe: Interview by Mike Langley).
166. Appleyard, 1947, p.108.
167. Jørgensen: Letter dated 7 August 1942; Langley 1988/2016, p.74.
168. Report by W10, HS 3/92.
169. *Ibid*.
170. Report by W10, HS 3/92.
171. Report by W10, HS 3/92.
172. CO 537/4286.
173. Vice-Consul C.W. Michie had left Fernando Po in early December 1941 to go on a prolonged leave. Towards the end of the month he was replaced by the SOE agent B. Godden (W51) who was reinforced, on 6 January, by Peter Ivan Lake (W53). (Lett 2012/2013, p. 86; HS 9/877/5.) Correspondence between the British consulate the Spanish Governor General; Report by W.51; Private Memorandum from C.G. Duala, and other documents, HS 3/92. Lett, 2012, contains a great deal of interesting details on Operation Postmaster. This author, however, does not agree with Lett in assuming that the Maid Honor Force was sent to West Africa with the explicit purpose of participating in Operation Postmaster.
174. 26 January 1942, HS 3/89. 'Caesar' was a South African arms dealer, Julius Hanau, who had worked for the SOE in the Balkans. According to one colleague, he knew more about the Balkans than any living Englishman – and therefore, with typically British military reasoning, in the summer of 1941 he was placed in charge of the SOE's activities in Africa (Harrison 1999); HS 9/652.
175. PREM 3/405/3.
176. HS 3/89
177. HS 3/89.
178. Tottenham: Letter to Suzanne Lassen, 4 April 1946; Langley 1988/2016, p.79–80; HS 9/1183/2; HS 9/4811; Pearce 1983, p.430.
179. Dismore: *Dragon he be Strong Ju-Ju! (Some Reminiscences of a Private Army)*, no date; HS 9/434/5.

Chapter 24: Small Scale Raiding Force
180. Parker 2000, p.62.
181. Ramsey 1981, p.141.
182. Brown 1975, chapter I, 4.
183. Appleyard, 1947, p.119.
184. Kemp 1958/1960, p.50.
185. Foot 1966, p.185; Kemp 1958/1960, p.52.
186. 'Anderson Manor, Near Blandford, Dorset, Report upon visit 13th April 1942' refers to an arrticle in *Country Life*, 3 April 1915; Arthur Oswald: *Country Houses of Dorset*, and Garner & Stratton: *Domestic Architecture*. (Private Papers of Major L.E. Prout, IWM).
187. Lassen 1949/1965, pp.46–7.
188. Lassen 1949/1965, pp.38–9.
189. SL: Letter to 'Fritz', April 1942.

190. SL: Letter to Fritz, 10.05.42.
191. The description of Anderson Manor is based primarily on Langley 1988/2016, chapter 7 and Appleyard, 1947, chapter 5.
192. Appleyard, 1947, p.120.
193. Lady Marling (Marjorie March-Phillipps): Interview by Mike Langley.
194. Ellen Branth (née Karsten), interview by the author, 2011; Ellen and Henrik Karsten's diaries and letters are quoted extensively in Harder & Hesel 2018.
195. Messenger 1985, p.153; Kemp 1958/1960, p.54.
196. DEFE 2/1093 'Notes on Landing from Dories and Rubber Dinghies', App. C.
197. According to German reports, the attackers threw five hand grenades, only four of which exploded.
198. RH 26-320/3.
199. RH 26-320/3.
200. Combined Operations Headquarters, report on Operation Barricade, DEFE 2/109.
201. Grossman 1995/2009; Bourke 2009; for some background: Bateman 2007; Engen 2011.
202. Charles Mann, SBS, interview by Anders Sandberg.
203. Brown, 1975, p.81.
204. Brown 1975, pp.80–91.
205. Kemp 1958/1960, p.54.
206. Ramsey 1981/2005, pp.146–7; SOE HS 6/304.
207. SOE HS 6/304.
208. Lassen 1949/1965, pp.65; Langley 1988/2016, p.97.
209. The description of Operation Aquatint and Hayes' fate is based on HS 9/680/5 and on Fournier & Heinz 2006, pp.95–214. This is an extremely thorough and detailed account based on a great deal of British, German and French material.
210. Hayes first went into hiding in a peasant's cottage in a small village near the Normandy coast. From there he made it to the Paris suburb Garches where he stayed with a man named Hortet, alias Aymand, who was probably an SIS agent. Hortet put Hayes in touch with a British woman living in Garches whose South African husband was interned. She helped Hayes send a Red Cross letter to his fiancée in South Africa. The letter was intercepted by the Censorship Department. In early October Hortet accompanied Hayes to the Spanish border. En route they stopped at Limoges to gather information for Hayes to take away. Hortet brought Hayes and other refugees to a frontier village where they passed into Spain through the house of a priest which was located exactly on the frontier.

    Hortet was killed in 1943, probably in connection with a black-market business which he ran in parallel with his work for the SIS.

    Shortly after arriving in Spain, Hayes was arrested by the Spanish police and, presumably, handed over to the Vichy-French authorities who transported him to the Gare d'Austerlitz in Paris where he was arrested by the Germans on 28 October 1942. He was sentenced to death on 22 February 1943 and executed on 13 July of the same year, probably not based on the Commando Order, but rather for carrying out espionage activities. (Important parts of Hayes' story emerge from HS/680/5, but I'm grateful to Michael Smith for access to his very extensive and extremely thorough studies of other British, German, and French sources.)

    Hall and Burton spent the rest of the war in a German PoW camp for officers. Winter was first placed in Stalag VIIIB in Lamsdorf (now Łambinowice) in Poland, but towards the end of the war, as Soviet forces approached, Winter and many fellow prisoners were moved to Stalag XIB in Fallingbostel, Germany. The British forces reached the camp on 16 April 1945, shortly after Winter had escaped and made it to the British lines. Orr died in German captivity on 12 April 1945. Hellings, the Dutchman, was also sent to Stalag XIB, where he met Winter, but his fate is unknown. The Frenchman Desgrange escaped from a camp for officers, made it back to England and rejoined the war effort. Francis was admitted to a hospital for PoWs in Germany and was returned to Britain via Sweden for health reasons in 1943. Fournier & Heintz 2006, pp.153–219 and 223–33.
211. Fournier & Heintz 2006, p.118.

212. Ramsey 1981/2005, pp.148–157; Langley 1988/2016, pp.108–112; HS 6/304 SOE Channel Islands No. 1, Report on Operation 'BASALT', signed Appleyard, 6 October 1942; DEFE 2 109. On Redborn: Lassen 1949/1965, p.51–4. Doubts about the existence of Redborn and a meticulous study of the available sources referring to the participants in Operation Basalt: Robinson 2015 and 2016. See also Lee 2016.
213. Foot 1966, p.187; Kemp 1958/60, p.63.
214. According to some versions of the story of Operation Basalt, the purpose was to bring back a Polish SOE agent who was hiding on the island. (Fournier & Heintz 2006, pp. 234–5 and Messenger 1985, p.158.) This version is based on an eyewitness account from a certain Leslie 'Red' Wright, who served in the Royal Marines from 17 June 1942 to 16 January 1946, but neither in the Commandos nor the SSRF. At no time did Wright leave Britain during his military service, but he managed nonetheless to fool journalists, writers and many others with his carefully prepared tall tales. Excerpts of his service records, etc, are in the SAS Regimental Archive.
215. Parker 2000, p.111.
216. RW 49/662; Ramsey 1981/2005, p.156; Langley 1988/2016, pp.109–12.
217. The full text is available at: documentarchiv.de/ns.html (retrieved 6 December 2017). RH 49/662. There was apparently some uncertainty about how the order should be executed – or perhaps some officers just did not like the order to shoot enemy prisoners. In June and November 1944, the head of Sipo SD/IV A2a Amt M, Colonel Hansen, impressed upon OKW several times that when the Wehrmacht took enemy commandos prisoner, the unit concerned was responsible for carrying out the order. The prisoners were not, as was the standard practice for other enemy combatants, to be handed over to Sipo, but immediately 'killed in combat' or 'while escaping'. If it was considered appropriate to interrogate the prisoners, the Sipo should be brought in, but afterwards the unit was still responsible for shooting the commando (RW 5/244; RW 5/502).
218. RW 49/97 letter from Abwehrleitstelle Frankreich to OKW, 22 December 1942.
219. Ramsey 1981/2005, p.150; Messenger 1985, p.160.
220. Scorries House, Redruth, Cornwall; Lupton House, Dartmouth; Wraxall Manor, Dorchester; Inchmery, Exbury, Hampshire. Messenger 1985, p.160.
221. Stirling had taken part in the SOE's Yak Mission – an attempt to plant agents in groups of Italian prisoners of war and find out what their fellow PoWs had failed to divulge under interrogation. It is not entirely clear what Stirling did after he left the SOE in March 1942. It is known that he worked for the British Chiefs of Staff and may have been seconded to the Ministry of Supply. In October 1942, he was transferred to the SOE from the Middle East Command. HS 1418/6 Bill Stirling; Messenger 1985, p.161.
222. DEFE 2/109.
223. Brown 1975, p.367.
224. Kemp 1958/1960, p.72.
225. DEFE 2/109.
226. DEFE 2/1093.
227. Langley 1988/2016, pp.119–24.
228. Kemp 1958/1960, p.51.
229. Kemp 1958/1960, pp.73–4.
230. Reventlow: Letters to the AL, 26 and 27 August 1942 and 9 September 1942.

Chapter 25: SAS/SBS – Jellicoe
231. Gilbert 2014, pp. 102-113; Sutherland 1999, pp. 63–9; Windmill 2005.

Chapter 26: The SSRF – The End
232. Anders Lassen was named 'War Substantive Lieutenant', i.e. the rank applied as long as the war lasted.
233. Messenger 1985, p.236.
234. Messen 1985, p.236.
235. Kemp was posted to Cairo where he joined SOE's Albanian section and subsequently spent ten months underground in Albania before returning to Cairo by way of

Montenegro and Yugoslavia. Towards the end of 1944 Captain Harold. B. Perkins (an uncle of the *Maid Honor*'s engineer, Buzz Perkins), who headed SOE's Polish Section, sent Kemp to southern Poland where, when the Russians entered Poland, he was arrested by the Soviet security service NKVD. Kemp returned to Britain via Moscow and in the summer of 1945 he parachuted into Siam from where he smuggled weapons to the French in Laos, who were fighting both the Japanese and the Viet Minh partisans. During the revolt in Hungary in 1956, where Kemp acted as correspondent for the catholic journal *Tablet*, he helped Hungarian students escape to Austria. He was in the Belgian Congo during the unrest that in 1971 led the country to independence under the name Zaïre (now the Democratic Repulic of Congo), and he took part in the Vietnam war. Kemp reported from revolts and revolutions in Central and South America and visited Albania, where he predicted ethnic conflicts between Albanians and Serbs. When Kemp was not travelling, fighting, or reporting he sold life insurance and wrote the books *Mine Were of Trouble* (1957) about his experiences in the Spanish Civil War, *No Colours or Crest* (1958) about his time in MIR and SOE, and the autobiography *The Forms of Memory* (1990). Peter Mant MacIntyre Kemp died in 1993, at the age of 78. Foot (1993).

236. Frants Lassen joined the Danish section of the SOE in May 1943 and completed the full training programme. His various teachers gave him excellent reports. In February 1944 he parachuted into Jutland and met his old friend Varinka Wichfeld. Now active in the resistance movement, she accompanied him to Copenhagen and put him in touch with the SOE agent Fleming Muus (whom she later married). Frants spent six months working underground, organizing arms drops, training resistance fighters and securing radio links with Britain. In late summer 1944, Muus ordered Frants and the other members of the resistance group Holger Danske to prepare for a sabotage operation on ships in the port of Copenhagen. On 1 September, Frants was arrested by the Gestapo, interrogated and tortured. He revealed several addresses, including meeting places that he was convinced were no longer in use. Unfortunately a big meeting had just been moved to one of these old locations. The resistance operative storing the explosives for the planned sabotage was also arrested. Frants was then transferred to a prison where he was interrogated for another three weeks before being moved to the Dreibergen-Bützow prison, twenty miles south of Rostock in northern Germany. He spent six months there until he was liberated by the Swedish Red Cross on 14 April 1945.

    Among resistance veterans, opinions on Frants were divided. Some thought that he had betrayed them by giving information to the Gestapo – or at least by not waiting longer before he did so. Others found it unfair to condemn a man for succumbing to torture. Frants Lassen died in 1997, aged 75. HS 9/888/3.
237. Brown 1975, p.247.
238. The LRDG were specialists in using customised jeeps and trucks to penetrate deep behind enemy lines, and often acted as a 'taxi service' for the SAS. PPA, officially known as No. 1 Demolition Squadron, was founded by and under the command of the half-Belarusian, half-Belgian Major Vladimir 'Popski'. The unit carried out many successful attacks on German/Italian airfields etc deep in the desert hinterland.
239. DEFE 2/1093; Sutherland: Aide memoire in scrapbook, SAS Regimetal Association.
240. 'Application by a Traveller for the Examination of Prohibited Documentary, Printed or Pictorial Matter Intended to be Conveyed out of Great Britain'; Personal Paper/Army Form B199A P/234907. In 1944, Esther Molloy married the Belgian SOE agent Count Philippe E.R.A. de Liedekerke (HS 9/922/7).
241. Ellen Branth (née Karsten): Interview by Anders Sandberg, 2008. Ellen Karsten (Branth), diary.
242. Branth (née Karsten), interview by author; Lassen 1949/1965, p.61.
243. Private Papers of Major L E Prout (IWM).
244. DEFE 2/957.

Chapter 27: Special Boat Squadron
245. Pitt 1983, p.61.
246. WO 218/97 SAS Regt. January–April 1943.

247. Morris 1989, p.163.
248. Sutherland 1999, p.99.
249. Verney 1966, p.17.
250. Verney 1966, p.18.
251. Jellicoe: Interview, with Mike Langley.
252. Verney 1966, p.26.
253. Sutherland 1999, p.99.
254. Maclean 1949.
255. Holmes: 'The Saga of Captain "G"'.
256. Lodwick 1947/1990, pp.128–9; about the raid and plundering, Holmes, *Ibid*.
257. Hastings, 1994, p.79.
258. Sutherland, 1999, p.101.
259. Brown 1975, p.275; Churchill quoted from Macintyre p.34.
260. The 90th Panzergrenadier division replaced the 90th Light Division, part of Rommel's Afrika Korps that had been wiped out in North Africa.
261. Brown 1975, pp.287–8; Melis 2006; RM 35-III/58.
262. *Le operazioni delle unità italiane nel settembre-ottobre 1943*, chapter XV.

Chapter 28: Operation Albumen, Crete, 23 June–11 July
263. The description of Operation Albumen is based mainly on Sutherland 1999, chapter 10, the participants' official reports in WO 201/136, and Greek eyewitness accounts in Kalogerakis 2009. The SOE's contributon to the operation is described in Woodhouse 2–5, 'Joint Operations and Assistance Given to Other Organizations'.
264. Milner-Barry MS, 17 June 1943.
265. Langley 1988/2016, pp.136–7
266. *Morgenmeldung vom 7.7.43*, RM 35-III-57.
267. Leigh Fermor was born in 1915. At the age of 18 he walked from Hoek van Holland to Constantinople. The journey took him a little over a year and along the way he studied local languages, dialects and landscapes. When the war broke out Leigh Fermor, who at the time was living with a Romanian princess in Moldavia, returned to Britain and joined the Irish Guards, but because of his language skills he was posted to Albania as liaison officer and subsequently took part in the fighting in Greece and on Crete. During the German and Italian occupation he did tours of duty on Crete where, under the cover names Michalis and Filedem, he lived in the mountains, leading one of the SOE missions that cooperated with, and tried to coordinate and control, the local resistance movement. After the war, Leigh Fermor settled in Kardamyli, in southeastern Peloponnese. He died in 2011, aged 96, leaving behind a large body of literary work that had made him one of the great stars of English memoir and travel literature. (PLF's personnel file: HS 9/507/4; PLF's biography: Cooper 2012; The political role of SOE on Crete: Damer & Fraser 2018).
268. *Veste Kreta* (German military newspaper), 4 July 1943, Historical Archive of Crete, German Occupation Archive.
269. Poulies and Nipiditos according to Zografakis; Handruk and Niploclitos according to Lassen's operation report.
270. 'Giannis Androulakis' account' (έκθεση του Ιωάννου Ανδρουλάκη) in Kalogerakis 2009.
271. 'Kimon Zografakis commemorates Lassen' (Major Anders Lassen – Ταγματάρχης Άντερς Λάσσεν) in Kalogerakis 2009.
272. 'Giannis Aslanis' account (son of Nikolaos Aslanis) from Kato Poulies' (Κάτω Πουλιές) in Kalogerakis 2009.
273. 'Andonis Alexakis' account by Nipiditos (Νιπιδιτό)' in Kalogerakis 2009.
274. *Erdverteidigung*, RL 7-602; Morgenmeldung vom 7.7.43, RM 35-III-57, Bundesarchiv.
275. Kimon Zografakis.
276. 'Michalis Petrougakis' account of the sabotage action' (Ο Μιχάλης Πετρουγάκης αφηγείται για το σαμποτάζ) in Kalogerakis 2009.
277. DEFE 2-970.
278. Vick 1995, p.59.

279. In her book, Suzanne Lassen cites one Nereanos Georgios, who told her that he led Lassen and Jones up to the barbed wire fence, but waited outside 'in front of the building' when the two raiders sneaked into the airfield. Georgios told Suzanne that her son was attacked by an Italian sentry and Lassen killed him with his commando knife. Giorgos Kalogerakis does not mention Nereanos Georgios in his otherwise very thorough collection of eyewitness accounts about Operation Albumen, but explicitly mentions two other locals who showed Lassen and Jones the way to the fence. It is also difficult to imagine how Georgios could see what was going on inside the airfield when it was shrouded in darkness. Further, it is worth noting Lassen's report makes no mention of a knife. None of this, of course, excludes the possibility that among the Greek guides there was *also* a Nereanos Georgios and that he actually did see Lassen stab an Italian to death. However, it seems more plausible that among the many people from the area surrounding the airfield who directly or indirectly came into contact with the raiders, there was a Nereanos Georgios who told Suzanne a story that he had heard from a friend of a friend of a friend. It is worth remembering that Lassen and his British companions could only speak directly with the few locals who spoke a little English, and that their attempts to explain what had happened on the airfield were probably heavily laden with gestures.
280. 'Michalis Petrougakis' account of the sabotage action' in Kalogerakis 2009.
281. Lassen later described his attack on the western side of the airfield as a diversion to draw the guards away from the east side and facilitate Nicholson and Greaves's work. This was probably post-rationalisation. Zografakis describes very clearly Lassen's determination to blow up the planes in this side of the airfield. Nicholson also contradicts Lassen's version of the story: 'That was no diversion, it was a bungle, Lassen and Jones were meant to be as silent as me and Greaves.' (Langley 1988/2016, p.140).
282. 'What became of Lassen after the action?' (Τι απέγινε ο Λάσσεν μετά το σαμποτάζ) in Kalogerakis 2009.
283. *Morgenmeldung vom 7.7.43*, RM 35-III-57; *Morgenmeldung vom 16.7.43; Morgenmeldung vom 20.7.43*, RM 35-III/58.
284. *Morgenmeldung vom 7.7.43*, RM 35-III/57, *Morgenmeldung vom RH 26-22/79*, 5. Juli 1943.
285. RH 26-22/79.
286. Report on Patrol C Western attack on KASTELLI PEDIADA aerodrome on the night 4th July 1943. (WO 201/136).
287. Sutherland, 1999, p.68.
288. Order issued by General Hellmuth Felmy, 17.09.43, RH 24-68/16, Bl. 9 f, reproduced in Jureit (ed.) 2002, p.532; Mazower 1993, chapters15 and 17.
289. The saboteurs' barbed wire cutters: Spyridon Karyotakis' account (το ψαλίδι των σαμποτέρ - η μαρτυρία του Σπυρίδωνα Καρυωτάκη) in Kalogerakis 2009.
290. WO1 201/136.
291. WO1 201/136.
292. The execution order was signed by the CO of 22nd Infantry Division, Major General Friedrich-Wilhelm Müller ('The unknown executions of 20 Greeks, 5 July 1943' (Η άγνωστη εκτέλεση των είκοσι πατριωτών στις 5 Ιουλίου 1943)) in Kalogerakis 2009; *Morgenmeldung vom 07.07.43* RM 35-III-57. In 1946, a Greek court condemned Müller to death for war crimes. He was executed by firing squad on 20 May 1947, the anniversary of the German attack on Crete.
293. 'Letter from Patrick Leigh Fermor to Cretan freedom fighters and residents' (Επιστολή Πάτρικ Λη Φέρμορ (προς τους αντιστασιακούς και τους κατοίκους της νήσου Κρήτης)) in Kalogerakis 2009. An SOE man tasked with attaching limpet mines to ships docked in Heraklion to divert attention away from the attacks on the airbases wrote: 'I sincerely hope that these raids were essential because in this area it has caused much havoc to morale, and caused much anti-British feeling. Nevertheless, it will probably all vanish if things go well in SICILY.' (WO 106/5431: Extract from Progress Report for Period Ending 15th July 1943). According to Artemis Cooper, the SOE man was Patrick Leigh Fermor (conversation with author, Copenhagen, 26 January 2018).

294. Holmes: 'Anders Lassen …'
295. The plan to kill the prisoners and leave the civilians to their fate is not mentioned in Sutherland's report, but in 'Kimon Zografakis' account' (Διήγηση Κίμωνα Ζωγραφάκη) in Kalogerakis 2009.
296. WO 201/136 – doc 110; Sutherland 1999, pp.110–12.
297. Sutherland 1999, pp.110–12.
298. Sutherland, 1999, p.111.
299. Sutherland, 1999, p.110.
300. Jellicoe was supposed to lead Operation Hawthorn but handed over command to Verney because malaria had cut the number of SBS men involved; Tasselli 1993 & 2001. The National Museum of the Royal Navy has a file Operation Hawthorn containing inter alia various reports by George Jellicoe. I am grateful to Nicholas Jellicoe for making me aware of it.
301. Tasselli 1993, 2000 & 2002. The SOE had already landed agents in January 1943 to contact Lussu's people on the island. They were arrested by the Italian authorities (Brigaglia 2004; Giacobbe 2000; Patucchi 2007).
302. Comando della Piazza di Rodi, Diramazione No 5, No 1/5787/S di prot. P.M. 550 li, 2 Agosto 1943 = *OGGETTO: Notizie sullo Special Boat Service Britannico*.

Chapter 29: The Battle for the Aegean Sea – 1
303. Quoted from Gooderson 2002.
304. Maltoni 2002.
305. Koburger 1999, pp.84–7.
306. Maltoni 2002.
307. The letter was stamped by Field Post Office 6 at the New Zealand Forces Club in Cairo. (Brown 1960, p. 87).
308. Grossman 1995/2009, pp.149–55.
309. Quoted from Langley 1988/2016, p.189–90.
310. Lassen 1949/1965, pp.81–2; Jellicoe 2002.
311. This account is based on four pages from a longer report written by Lord Jellicoe (Jellicoe 1943, copy in David Sutherland's scrapbook, SAS Regimental Archive); Major Dolbey's *A Report on RODELL* (HS 5/715), on Dolbey's account (Dobrski 13) at LHCHA, King's College; Maltoni 2002; Lamb 1993, chapter 8; Gooderson 2002; and the official Italian war history *Le operazioni delle unità italiane nel settembre-ottobre 1943*, chapter XV. Campioni's surrender is described from the German point of view in Hauptmann Dr. Bayer: *Erlebnisbericht über die Kampftage vom 8.-11. September 1943* (RH 26-2007/5); on Dolbey/Dobrski: HS 9/437/4.
312. Dobrski 13, p.25; Jellicoe's report, p.3, Sutherland's scrapbook, SAS Regimental Archive.
313. At 05:25 on 11 September, a German listening station informed Kleemann that at 23:20 a signal from Rhodes to Rome had been intercepted. It stated: 'The English have just arrived. We are in possession of our weapons. Request immediate decision' (RH 26 2007/5). The chronology would have been easier to understand if the message had been sent on the evening of 9 September, when Jellicoe & co actually arrived, and not a day or so later. Regardless of when the message was sent to Rome, the Germans had also learned from a spy that Campioni was meeting with three Englishmen, one of whom was Lord Jellicoe.
314. It is unclear whether Jellicoe & co travelled directly from Rhodes to Kastellorizo, or via Symi. An Italian eyewitness on Symi told of a motor torpedo boat and a seaplane that brought three British officers, one of whom was a major and one was wounded, to the island (Cavallari, 1943).
315. Sturm-Division Rhodos,17.09.43, *Verlustmeldung der Kampftage vom 9.-13. Sept 1943*.

Chapter 30: The Battle for the Aegean Sea – 2
316. Koburger (1999) describes the war at sea in the Aegean. Gartzonikas (2003) provides a strategic/operational analysis of the Allied deployments in the Aegean, 1943–5.
317. Lodwick 1947/1990, p.84; *Le operazioni delle unità italiane nel settembre-ottobre 1943*, p.572.

318. Gooderson, p.10.
319. *Le operazioni delle unità italiane nel settembre-ottobre 1943*, chapter IV, gives the number of British soldiers as 22; Italian eyewitness Maria Luisa Caporali Cavallari mentions 55 Australians and New Zealanders led by a Scottish major, probably Lapraik; Langley writes about 'some forty men' without specifying his source.
320. Unfortunately Lapraik's notes contain no information on the source of the signal that made M Detachment land on Symi, nor on the identity of the unknown BORDER who, according to Lapraik, was the intended recipient of the signal. (Col J.N. Lapraik 1/5, IWM).
321. Hancock: Interview by Mike Langley.
322. Langley 1988/2016, p.161.
323. Col J.N. Lapraik 1/5, IWM.
324. Cavallari 1943.
325. On *Guardia di Finanza*, Cecini, Giovanni (2014): *La Guardia di Finanza nelle isole italiane dell'Egeo 1912–1945*. Gangemi. Rome
326. WO 201/1663.
327. *Le operazioni delle unità italiane nel settembre-ottobre 1943*, chapt. IV.
328. rhodesianafricanrifles.co.uk/alan-gardiner-redfern-mbe-%C2%B7-november-11-1943/ and unithistories.com/officers/Army_officers_R01.html (both acc. 16 December 2018).
329. Lassen 1949/1965, p.85; HS 5/716; *Report on Erratic* Operation *conducted from Cyprus Base between 22 Sept 1943–8 Oct*.
330. *Long Range Desert Group, Operation Report No. 99*, in Private Papers of Major General D.L. Lloyd Owen CB DSO OBE MC at the IWM.
  According to Suzanne Lassen's account, 'After a few days had elapsed, Anders contacted the Abbot and managed without the knowledge of the Italians, to get a radio operator installed on the mountain behind the monastery... The Greek who was to operate the set was introduced to the monks as the Abbot's nephew.' (Lassen 1949/1965, p.85). Suzanne Lassen does not mention the source of her information. It seems unlikely that both the SBS and the LRDG (which by now was specialised in this form of work) would have an observation post in the same place, or, if in fact they did, or if Lassen had helped the LRDG party set up its observation post, that Redfern would not mention it in his report.
331. Cavallari 1943; Lodwick 1947/1990, p.83.
332. In a German radio message intercepted by the British, the two men were described as 'Turkish agents from the police in Marmaris, Andreas and Leonidas' (Sofia to Istanbul September 24, 1943, HW 19/141); WO 201/1663 Aegean Lapraik Broxton.
333. MacKenzie (2000/2002) chapter VII; Foot & Langley 1979/80, pp.87–93; Rees 2004.
334. Ferris: Report.
335. Hancock: Interview by Mike Langley.
336. *To: 292 From: Broxton, Date: 26 Sep 43*, WO 201/1663.
337. *Long Range Desert Group, Operation Report No. 99*, in Private Papers of Major General D.L. Lloyd Owen CB DSO OBE MC at the IWM; *Unternehmen 'Esperia', Angaben und Aussagen des Bürgermeisters über die Insel Calchis*, (RH 26-1007).
338. In Lassen 1949 it says on p.99 'he put every man through *assault course*'. It cannot be ruled out that the SBS men really did build – or at least had the Italians build – a makeshift assault course. However, it seems more likely that the story is based on a misunderstanding, or that Lassen and his comrades perhaps amused themselves by forcing the Italian *carabinieri* to run, jump and do push-ups.
339. *Gefechtsbericht über das Unternehmen gegen die Insel Calchi vom 16. bis 18.10.1943* (RH 26-1007).
340. Lassen 1949/1965, pp.87–9; *Long Range Desert Group, Operation Report No. 99*, in Private Papers of Major General D.L. Lloyd Owen CB DSO OBE MC at the IWM.
341. Lodwick 1947/1990, p.83; Lassen 1949/1965, pp.88–9
342. http://durhamlightinfantry.webs.com/1stdlikos.htmLamb 1989, p.145; Gooderson 2002, pp.11–16; Lodwick 1947/1990, p.85–6; Foot & Langley 1979/1980, pp.198–9; *Le operazioni delle unità italiane nel settembre-ottobre 1943*, chapt. III; Gilbert 2017, pp.89–99.

343. Ferris: Report.
344. *Betr.: Unternehmen 'Trianda', Sturmdivision Rhodos, 6.10.43* (RH 26-1007/6); operation reports RH 26-1007/10).
345. Cavallari 1943.
346. The various German accounts (RH 26-1007/10) do not fully concur on this point, nor on the geography, but taken together they suggest that the Germans felt that the antenna was on or in the immediate vicinity of the citadel where Lassen had positioned his patrol and his 20 mm cannon.
347. Cavallari 1943.
348. Langley 1988/2016, pp.160–1.
349. Hancock: Interview by Mike Langley; Langley 1988/2016, p.177. Here Langley also quotes Porter Jarrell and Dick Holmes, who again cite an unnamed eyewitness.
350. Lassen 1949/1965, p.90.
351. RM 35-III/63; RH 26-1007/2.
352. The German casualty figures are taken from Fresemann's *Gefechtsbericht über das Landungsunternehmen Simi*, 1 November 1943 (RH 26-2007/10). These figures are significantly lower than those in Lodwick and Suzanne Lassen and Lapraik's account, cited in *Le operazioni delle unità italiane nel settembre-ottobre 1943*, Ch. III, from which the Italian casualty figures are taken.
353. *Long Range Desert Group, Operation Report No. 99*, in Private Papers of Major General D.L. Lloyd Owen CB DSO OBE MC at the IWM.
354. Col J.N. Lapraik 1/5, IWM; *Le operazioni delle unità italiane nel settembre-ottobre 1943*, chapt. III; Cavalari 1943.
355. *Gefechtsbericht über das Unternehmen gegen die Insel Simi vom 1. bis 3.11.1943* (RH 26-1007/7).
356. *Long Range Desert Group, Operation Report No. 99*, in Private Papers of Major General D.L. Lloyd Owen CB DSO OBE MC, IWM. In his war memoirs, *Providence Their Guide*, Lloyd Owen is very critical of the planning behind the the Aegean campaign and the defence of Leros. Lieutenant (T/Captain) Alan Gardiner Redfern was killed in action on Leros on 12 November 1943. He is buried in the Leros War Cemetery – unithistories.com/officers/Army_officers_R01.html (acc. 16 December 2018).
357. Langley 1988, p.181.
358. *Gefechtsbericht über das Unternehmen gegen die Insel Simi* vom 1. bis 3.11.1943 (RH 26-1007/7); Abendmeldung 2.-3. november 1943 (RM 35-III/65).
359. Unless otherwise stated, the account of the events on Leros is based on Gooderson 2002; Lodwick 1947/1990; *Le operazioni delle unità italiane nel settembre-ottobre 1943*, Ch. V, Schenk 1995.
360. Gooderson 2002, pp.17–23.
361. *Le operazioni delle unità italiane nel settembre-ottobre 1943*, chapter V.
362. Gooderson 2002, pp.17–23.
363. Kay 2008.
364. Lassen 1949/1965, p.99.
365. Sutherland 1999, p.129.
366. Sutherland, 1999, pp.129–30.
367. Lassen, *Operational Report, Boat: HMS LS7*. The report does not mention exactly when the rescue operation took place. The date field is left blank except for »Oct', which has been added by hand. The report was probably written some time after the operation, when Lassen had forgotten the exact date. (Sutherland's scrapbook.)
368. Benyon-Tinker 1947, p.101.
369. Waugh 1949, pp.111–12; Windmill 2005, pp.52–3.
370. Lassen 1949/1965, pp.99–101.
371. Sutherland, 1999, p.130; Langley 1988/2016, p.183. Half a century after the events, Jellicoe told his biographer (Windmill 2005, p.86) that on 11 November he ordered Sutherland to 'join Lassen and the others on Samos'. However, this is not consistent with Sutherland's own recollections.
372. Langley 1988/2016, p.183.

Notes   359

373. Now Pythagoreio.
374. Hamson had been awarded the MC for his role in the sabotage of the railway bridge at Gorgopotamos on the Greek mainland in November 1942. On 9 June 1944 he was parachuted into France to organize the resistance movement in the Lozere and Cevennes region where in August 1944 he was in charge of about 4,500 French partisans. (WO 373/46; WO 373/78/389; WO 373/98/713.)
375. RM 35-III/66.
376. Foot & Langley 1979, pp.89–91; Lassen 1949/1965, pp.113–14.
377. *Dodecanese December 1942 to the Loss of Leros 1943 – Report by M.O.1 (Records)*, WO 32-11430.
378. Lassen 1949/1965, pp.113–14.
379. *Dodecanese December 1942 to the Loss of Leros 1943 – Report by M.O.1 (Records)*, WO 32-11430. The same report also states: '19 November SAMOS All British and important Greek personnel evacuated' and '20 November 1,000 Greeks, 400 Italians and patrol of Special Boat Squadron evacuated by caique. Further 3,000 Greeks and Italians evacuated to KUSADASI in Turkey.' On the night of 21 November, General Soldarelli came to Kusadasi with his division staff and the entire 8th Infantry and 27th Artillery Regiment (PM 167 of 5 December 1943 from the Italian military attaché in Ankara to the Italian Chief of Staff, reproduced in *Le operazioni delle unità italiane nel settembre-ottobre 1943*, pp.586–7).
380. Lassen 1949/1965, pp.113–14.
381. Holmes, letter to Iain Farmer, February/March 2008 and 'Anders Lassen, VC, MC: The Man and the Myth'. According to Holmes, the lifeline was Lassen's idea, but Suzanne Lassen believes that he was opposed to it (Lassen 1949/1965, pp.113–16.)
382. According to Suzanne Lassen, the number of evacuees was about 10,000 (Lassen, 1949/1965, p.116); about the German prisoners: RM 35-III/66.
383. Lassen 1949/1965, p.116–17.
384. Holmes: 'Anders Lassen, VC, MC: The Man and the Myth'.
385. The Italian soldiers who had made the trip from Samos via Turkey and Aleppo to Palestine were sent on to Egypt, where they joined various engineering units and work squads. According to the official Italian war history, they were also 'subjected to various humiliations' *(Le operazioni delle unità italiane nel settembre-ottobre 1943*, p.572).
386. Holmes: Letter to Iain Farmer, n.d.

Chapter 31: Raiders in the Aegean, 1944
387. MO 3/3376, quoted from Tasselli 2002 C; WO 218–108
388. Koburger 1999, pp.64–5; Seligman 1996, p.3.
389. WO 218/108.
390. *GHQ Middle East Force Directive No. 200, 12 Mar. 44*, copy in David Sutherland's papers, SAS Regimental Archive; Sutherland 1999, pp.132–3.
391. GHQ Middle East Force Directive No. 200, 12 Mar 44, copy among David Sutherland's papers at the SAS Regimental Archive; Sutherland 1999, pp.132–3. Among the papers of J.N. Lapraik at the IWM is a large collection of documents on the planning and execution of Operation Fireeater. (Colonel J N Lapraik 1/5, IWM).
392. Seligman, 1996, pp.12–17.
393. Rigopoulos, 'A Testimony from the Alimnia Mission', http://www.athensnews.gr/articles/13071/18/06/2004/15231 retrieved 24 July 2010.
394. Army Form B199A P/234907; Langley 1988/2016, pp.188–9.
395. Quoted from Langley 1988/2016, p.189.
396. By this time, the Special Boat Squadron had been renamed the Special Boat Service, and the former Detachments were now called squadrons.
397. Benyon-Tinker, 1947, p.136.
398. Benyon-Tinker, 1947, pp.140–2.
399. Koburger 1999, p.64.
400. Milner-Barry TS, p.278; RM 35-III/76, 6 April 1944; RH 19-XI/11, 16 and 18 April 1944.

401. Langley 1988/2016, pp. 198–9.
402. *'S' Detachment Operational Report*, 17 June 1944, (WO 218–112).
403. Milner-Barry, MS, 26 March 1944
404. Sutherland, 1999, pp. 133–4.
405. This and the following quotes are from Lodwick 1947/1990, p.110. The War Diary of Sturm-Division Rhodos gives the date of Lassen's landing as 1 February (RH 26-1007/12, entry for 11 February 1944).
406. Lodwick 1947/1990, pp. 110, 138.
407. Milner-Barry, TS, p.270; MS, 12 February 1944
408. Halck 1948, pp.9–11. Halck had a reputation for embellishing the truth, but the fact that he mentions a real Danish family and we know Lassen visited them suggests that we should perhaps give this particular story the benefit of the doubt. It should, however, be noted that the German officer whom Halck mentioned in a 1947 radio lecture had, in the 1948 retelling, changed his name from 'Kurt Wöllner' to 'von Steinertz' and that the reward had shrunk from RM 30,000 to RM 20,000. It seems strange that the reward was offered in German marks, not Italian lire (the legal tender on Italian islands in the Aegean Sea). In his memoirs *I streng fortrolighed* ("In strict confidence", Thanning & Appel, Copenhagen, 1958), Halck said:

> 'At that time the Dane Major Anders Lassen was the great heroic role model for every soldier in the Near East. His name and deeds were on everybody's lips, and his reputation was legendary. As I too was a sort of Dane, Colonel Fennimore Powys and the entire G.U.F.F.A.W. expected quite a lot from me. But even though I can have the occasional fit of temper, I've never been known for any notable gallantry, and thus I'm afraid I let down their expectations. I took only two German prisoners, and they were both quite small.'

409. hsozkult.geschichte.hu-berlin.de/forum, retrieved 22 July 2010.
410. Holmes, letter to Iain Farmer, n.d., 'Just a few lines …'.
411. Lodwick 1947/1990, pp. 100–101.
412. Reed: Letter to SL, 24.07.46.
413. Langley 1988/2016, pp. 147–50, 168; Lassen 1949/1965, p.132–3
414. NN, *Diary*, 6, 22, 23 March 1944.
415. NN, *Diary*, 6, 22, 23 March 1944; Windmill 205, pp. 89–91; Lassen 1949/1965, pp.131–2; Langley 1988/2016, p.148.
416. RM 45-V/155; HS 5/716; Lassen 1949/1965, p.93–4.
417. Lodwick 1947/1990, s. 128–34; Sutherland 1999, s. 136; RH 26-1007/12; RM 45-V/155.
418. Raiding Forces Intelligence Report No. 7, WO 218–108; *'S' Detachment Operational Report*, 17 June 1944, WO 218–112.
419. HW 19-168. According to the War Diary of Sturm-Division Rhodos the raiders left the island on 25 March and brought 45 Italians with them. (RH 26-1007/12, entry for 25 March 1944).
420. WO 218/989.
421. *LS24*'s usual commander, Lieutenant Rigas Rigopoulos, had undergone the Greek Sacred Squadron's raider training and was parachuted onto Samos in October 1943. He spent considerable time training his men in the use of weapons, but they were far from fully trained when *LS24* was sent to Alimnia and Halki. Shortly before 5 April, Rigopoulos was sent to Kastellorizo – so it was not him but Tuckey who commanded the vessel on its last voyage (Rigopoulos 2004).
422. German sources refer to the vessels as 'U-Jäger'. These were presumably patrol boats kitted out with depth charges, but could, in principle, have been any type of vessel equipped to attack U-boats.
423. RH 26-1007/12.
424. RH 19-XI-11
425. Mortimer 2013, Chapter 11 Waldhheim Collection 646, Wiener Library.

426. An entry in the War Diary of Sturm-Division Rhodos for 13 April reads: 'The Wehrmacht Communiqué for 11.4 published on 12.4 reports inter alia: "A British Commando unit which had landed on the western coast of Rhodes was destroyed in combat to the last man." This report does not correspond to the facts as all Cdo. members were taken prisoner and not killed! All prisoners were flown to the mainland and put at the disposal of Army Group E. Subsequent whereabouts unknown.' (RH 26-1007/12). As the German historian Harald Gilbert has noted, it would appear that somebody on the staff of Sturm-Division Rhodos found it important to distance the division from the murdering of PoWs. (Gilbert 2017, 233)
427. Accounts of the incident on 6 April 1944, interrogation of the German participants, etc: RH 26-1007/15, RH 19-XI/11 and Waldheim Documents, 646, Wiener Library, London. One of the documents concerning the execution of the prisoners (as per Hitler's Commando Order of October 1942) was signed by Captain Kurt Waldheim – a staff officer in Army Group E who later became President of Austria and UN Secretary General. Other sources for the Alimnia Patrol: 'S' *Detachment Operational Report*, 17 June 1944 (WO 218/112); Sutherland 1999, p.136 and pp.149–52; Lodwick 1947/1990, pp.134–5; Rigopoulos 2004. The killing of the presumed spy is mentioned by Lodwick (p. 134) and Langley (p. 205). Langley is alone in naming Lassen and the members of the Irish Patrol as the executioners. The discussion between Sutherland, Lassen and Thanos is mentioned by Sutherland in his memoirs (published in 1999). Sutherland also mentions Walter Milner-Barry among the participants, but this must be due to a memory slip as Milner-Barry's diary (which is kept at the IWM) shows that he left the SBS on 31 March to travel to England on leave and did not see Sutherland again until they met in Cairo on 27 June.
428. The War Diary of Sturm-Division Rhodos notes that if the Wehrmacht Communiqué had not mentioned the capture of *LS24* the British would not have known that the codebooks etc were in German hands (*LS24* might have been sunk or lost at sea and the codebooks might have gone down with it), and so would presumably have continued to use the codes, signals etc laid down in them until 15 April when they were due to be replaced by a new set of codes etc. This would have given the Germans access to a great deal of valuable operational information, but this opportunity was lost because of the communiqué. (RH 26-1007/12, entry for 13 April 1944).
429. 'S' *Detachment, Special Boat Squadron – Operation Instruction No. 13 – Thira*, signed by Sutherland 'FIELD 19/4/44'.
430. There were 20 shillings (/-) to a pound (£). A gold sovereign had a nominal value of £1, but its real value was £5. The 15 sovereigns Lassen's men brought with them on the voyage to Santorini was the approved bribe for a caique of 30 tons. A newly enlisted infantry private in the British Army was paid 2 shillings a day. The hyperinflation, huge price swings, and the equally huge differences in conditions in different parts of Greece during the war years make it impossible to be precise about the purchasing power of their 400,000 drachma. The war correspondent Richard Capell noted in October 1944: 'For a pound sterling you can get 2,000 million drachma, six times as much for a gold sovereign. A cigarette costs 7½ million, an egg 40 million' (Capell 1946, p.28).
431. Langley 1988/2016, p.217.
432. Stephenson: Interview by Mike Langley.
433. Hancock: Interview by Mike Langley; Holmes: Interview by Anders Sandberg, 2009.
434. Kirk 1997, p.105. The account of the maritime part of the Santorini operation is based on Kirk 1997, chapter 7. This in turn is based on an account by Lieutenant Geoffrey Kirk, who was on board *LS11* and wrote his account shortly after the operation. The account of the events on land are based on Sutherland's 'S *Detachment, Special Boat Squadron, Operation Instruction No. 13, Thira*; Anders Lassen's 'S *Detachment, Special Boat Squadron, Operation report No. 13, Thira*; Lodwick 1947/1990, pp.138–42; Langley 1988/2016, chapter 17; and, first and foremost, Sergeant Nicholson's long account in Lassen 1949/1965, pp.135–46.
435. Lassen 1949/1965, p.141.
436. Reeves and Nicholson are quoted in Langley 1988, pp.215–16.

437. Kirk 1997, p.122. Kirk's version of his encounter with Lassen contains both minor inaccuracies and a serious implausibility. Apart from the fact that Sergeant Nicholson doesn't seem to have mentioned anything about Lassen wanting him to wake up the sleeping Germans when he talked to Mike Langley in 1987, it is hard to imagine that very many of the Germans and Italians slept for long after the shooting began. It is also improbable that Lassen thought he could cut the throats of that many sleeping men without waking their roommates, or that he really would have preferred the awkward and difficult work with the blade rather than the quick and relatively easy shooting for which he had been trained at the SOE school and elsewhere. On the other hand, it is not hard to imagine that Lassen, in his state of stress and exhaustion, and perhaps shock at the unexpected adversity, not to mention his anger and sorrow over Kasoulis's death, said something about wanting to cut the throats of the Germans. Nor is it inconceivable that in his fury he might really have tried to attack an enemy with his knife instead of with the machine gun, but was held back by Nicholson.
438. *Detachment Operational Report*, signed by Sutherland, 17 June 1944 (WO 218–112).
439. RM 35-III/77; RM 35-III/171. Kurowski 1997 gives a brief, uncritical, but nevertheless interesting account of the activities of Division Brandenburg's Küstenjäger units. A broader and academically solid description of German warfare in the Aegean is to be found in Gilbert 2017.
440. Brown 1975, p.275, 601–3; on the D-Day deception campaign in general (and in a great deal of fascinating detail): Hesketh 1999.
441. Cooper p.180.
442. Disagreement within SOE about whether the plan should be carried out or not: Clogg, pp. 12–13; Sweet-Escott p.198. The plan's inception and development can be traced through HS 5/723 Dunbabin's 1. Report, 16 April–16 May 1942; Dunbabin's 3. Report, April 1942–February 1943; HS 5/724, various reports by Dunbabin; HS 5/728, PLF's 3. Report, May–June 1943; PLF's Report, 30 March 1944; PLF's Report on the capture of Kreipe, 16 May 1944; HS 5/726, Fielding's letter of 28 July 1943; Fielding's Report, January 1944.
443. Private papers of Mrs A.M. Street, IWM.
444. WO 208/4208. Kreipe was initially interned in a PoW camp in Canada, but was subsequently transferred to Island Farm Camp in Wales, from which he was released for health reasons in 1947. Kreipe died in 1976. (Personnel file and German documents on the abduction: PERS 6/300062 and PERS 6/252023; health: WO 309/1722). The abduction of Kreipe has generated a large number of books in English, German, and Greek. The first was the SOE officer W. Stanley Moss's partly autobiographical *Ill Met by Moonlight: The Abduction of General Kreipe*, which was first heavily censored by SOE and much edited by the original publishers (HS 9/507/4), and then held back by the War Office until it was finally allowed to appear in 1950; it has been in print ever since, and in 1957 it was made into a film by Michael Powell and Emeric Pressburger. Among the most recent books on the 'hussar stunt' is Patrick Leigh Fermor's posthumous (ed. Peter & Chris White, 2014) *Abducting a General*, John Murray, London. The latter book's homepage provides a useful overview of some of the documents that tell the story of the plan's inception: abductingageneral.info/publication-history
445. The Historical Archive of Crete at Chania (German Occupation Archives, 13). The archive has a large collection of proclamations and other German documents from Bräuer's time as the island's commandant which show the range of reprisals from mass executions and the burning of villages to hostage taking and forced labour to collective fines paid in kind – e.g. poultry, cattle, olive oil etc – and various forms of curfew. Müller and Bräuer were sentenced to death by a Greek court and executed in 1947.
446. Gilbert 2014, p.152; Report on Crete by Lt Col T.J. Dunbabin (4th Report, 3rd series) 20–30 Aug 44, HS 5/724. I am grateful to Lars Bærentzen, John Iatrides and Nina Stähle (the latter also helped me get an overview of the sources and searched the Historical Archive of Crete in Chania on my behalf) for helpful discussions and email exchanges about this famous but under-researched episode.
447. Brown 1975, p.275. 601–3.

448. The description of events on Paros is based *'S' Detachment Operational Report*, signed by Sutherland, 17 June 1944 (WO 218/112); Sergeant Nicholson's account in Lassen 1949/1965, pp.146–50; Langley 1988/2016, pp.218–22; Manolis Mpardanis: 'To Germaniko aerodromio ton Marmaron tis Parou Erevna kai epimeleia' ('Έρευνα-Επιμέλεια': Μανώλης Μπαρδάνης, naxosdiving.com (acc. 13 December 2017)). The parts referring to Nikolas Stellas, von Merenberg, and certain other details are based on Savidis 2001, Cotts & Massaliotis 2010 and Clark 2010. The chronology cannot be pinned down definitively. For example, the website of the Hellenic National Defence General Staff, www.geetha.mil.gr/en/component/k2/4425-14-5.html (acc. 1 February 2018), states that the attack on the airfield took place on 14 May. It also says that the attack was carried out by 'Greek guerrilla elements of the Sacred Band of Paros', and completely fails to mention the SBS; on the four Beaufighters: Air 27/2080.
449. Sutherland, 1999, p.143.
450. *'S' Detachment Operational Report*, signed Sutherland, 17 June 1944 (WO 218/112). A report signed by Turnbull – *Raiding Forces and Coastal Forces Combined Results for Operations in Eastern Aegean From 1 Feb to 30 Apr 1944* (which therefore also includes SBS activities) – shows that during this period 25 islands were visited a total of 49 times, and a total of 38 ships, with a total tonnage of 1,938 grt, were hijacked, destroyed or purchased. LSF and Coastal Forces lost one motor torpedo boat, one patrol boat (HDML), one caique and one 'LS craft' due to enemy fire or severe weather, while one patrol boat (HDML) suffered slight damage. German and Italian losses totalled 161 dead, wounded and captured. Losses among the British and the Greek Sacred Squadron amounted to 6 dead, 13 wounded and 12 missing. Three telegraph lines, eight phone lines, two radio stations and one cable station were destroyed. Seven major deliveries of food supplies were made to Nisyros (on two occasions, three and seven tons), Sesklio, Lipsi (twelve tons) and Ios, among many others that were not reported to headquarters. According to the war correspondent Richard Capell, who was close to Turnbull in autumn 1944, over a 22-month period, Raiding Forces carried out 381 landing operations in the Aegean, killing 288 enemies, wounding 119 and taking 3,724 prisoners. The raiders' losses amounted to 93 (19 dead, 35 wounded and 39 captured), of whom 58 were Greeks and 35 were British (Capell 1946, p.19).

Chapter 32: Fatigue and Addiction
451. Hancock 2008, interview by Iain Farmer.
452. Holmes, interview by Anders Sandberg, 2009.
453. Bourke 199, pp.66–7.
454. Benyon-Tinker 1947, pp.104 and 181.
455. Langley 1988/2016, p.221; Holmes: 'Anders Lassen…'; Stephenson: Interview by Mike Langley.
456. Hancock, interview by Iain Farmer 2008.
457. Reed: Letter to SL, 24.07.46.
458. About Greek Sacred Squadron: Nikoloudis Tsigantes: letter to the Danish ambassador in Athens, 17 August 1945. Unfortunately, beyond Tsigantes' praise, there are no records of Lassen's work with the Greek Sacred Squadron. Lassen's whereabouts in June 1944: WO 218/112; Greek Sacred Squadron: Nikoloudis, 'The Sacred Squadron …'.
459. Lassen 1949/1965, p.208.
460. Hancock, interviews with Iain Farmer (Hancock's observation is contradicted by the fact that Lassen, at least on Santorini, handed out Benzedrine to his men); on amphetamines in wartime: Rasmussen, Nicolas (2008): *On Speed: The Many Lives of Amphetamine*, New York University Press, New York.

Chapter 33: The Adriatic, July–August 1944
461. Roberts 1987, p.229.
462. Windmill 2005, p.93; Lodwick 1947/1990, p.172.
463. The main sources for this section are: *Special Boat Service 'S' Squadron – Operation Instructions No. 26* in WO 140/4012; *'S' Squadron Special Boat Service – Operation Report No. 26* by Lt. J.C. Henshaw; *'S' Squadron Special Boat Service – Operation Report No. 26*

by Capt. A.F.E.V.S. Lassen MC (copies of both reports in Sutherland's scrapbook, SAS Regimental Archive); Lassen 1949/1965, p.155; Holmes: 'Anders Lassen, VC, MC: The Man and the Myth'.
464. Holmes, quoted in Langley 1988/2016, p.221.
465. In his report, Henshaw estimated the number of enemies to be around 200, while Lassen thought there were twice as many. Forty years later, Holmes stated that he felt that there had been 'about 100'.
466. Holmes: 'Anders Lassen, VC, MC: The Man and the Myth'.
467. 'S' *Squadron, Special Boat Service. Operation Report No. 26* by Capt. A.F.E.V.S. Lassen, MC. O.C. 'S' Squadron, 6 Sept 1944.
468. Stephenson: Interview by Mike Langley, before 1988.
469. Hancock, interview by Iain Farmer.
470. Jensen: Letter to Suzanne Lassen, 8 October 1945; Reed: Letter to Suzanne Lassen, 24 July 1946. Force 140 consisted of HQ III Corps, 23 Armoured Brigade, 2 Parachute Brigade, 139 Infantry Brigade (46 Infantry Division) and a brigade of 4 Indian Infantry Division, as well as Commandos, SBS, LRDG, etc. On Scobie and the British campaign in Greece 1944–45: Maule.

Chapter 34: Back to Greece, September–October 1944
471. The code name 'Noah's Ark' appears as early as in the minutes of a meeting of the Middle East Command's Joint Operational Staff held on 2 January 1944. (IWM: Lapraik 1/5).
472. CAB 80/86, COS [44] 768 [O]25.8.1944. In summer 1944 feelers were put out via various channels and at different levels, and negotiations were conducted between German and British military commanders and officials about a German capitulation in Greece. The negotiations stalled however, due to the two sides' conflicting demands: the Germans wanted to leave Greece unimpeded, the British wanted the German troops to remain in place (thus preventing ELAS from seizing power) and surrender to British troops as they advanced up through the country (Bærentzen 1980 and 2011).
473. WO 204/8505 Naval Instructions for the Conduct of Kithera Raiding Operations, Short Title: CONKROM; WO 204/8506 Operations against Kithera; WO 204/8461.
474. On the German radar station on Kythera, sketches of 'Freya' and 'Würzburg' and how to destroy them: WO 204/844.
475. NN, *Diary*, 20 September 1944. It is not clear what NN meant by 'British Greeks': whether they were members of ELAS or other, pro-British, Greek resistance fighters.
476. Signal from Lassen, 30 September 1944: 'Regret BURY killed. MACPHERSON and HUNTER wounded off Spetsai whilst enroute from KITHERA to me at ERMIONI. Shot by EDES patriots of Colonel Zervas in mistake for EAM' (WO 204/8506); Lassen 1949/1965, p.163. In April 1944, Bob Bury had participated in the abduction of General Kreipe on Crete.
477. Holmes 2008.
478. Jellicoe wore the insignia of a colonel and drew a colonel's pay, but the promotion did not count towards his seniority.
479. Milner-Barry, MS, 13 October 1944
480. Capell 1946, pp.43–5.
481. The account of Bucketforce's operations and Jellicoe and Milner-Barry's actions is based primarily on Pitt 1983, pp.166–75; Milner Barry MS and TS, and on Windmill 2005, pp.95–107. It is unclear who had organized the demonstration on 14 October. According to Windmill (p. 105) it was organized by General Spiliotopoulos, but this appears unlikely. EAM organized demonstrations on 13 and 15 October, and anti-EAM/Nationalist groups organized their own demonstrations on 15 October. (Thanks to Professor Ioannis D. Stefanidis for these observations.)
482. Lassen now had the rank of temporary captain and acting major. On 9 January 1945 he was promoted to 'war Substantive Captain', i.e. captain for as long as the war lasted, and from acting major to temporary major.
483. Hamilton-Hill, 1973, pp.143–5.
484. Lassen 1949/165, p.164; Sutherland, interviews with Mike Langley.

485. Pitt 1983, p.147.
486. Lassen 1949/1965, pp.164–6.
487. *History of 9 Commando – Overseas, 11 Sep 43–8 May 45*; Lassen 1949/165, p.170.

Chapter 35: Thessaloniki, October–November 1944
488. WO 201/1598 (quoted from Bærentzen 1987, p.258).
489. WO 204/8512, *LRDG Operation Report No 155B*; Woodhouse: Report on Final Phase of Allied Military Mission in Greece. Geoffrey Chandler, an SOE officer in western Macedonia, described Jellicoe's arrival at Kozani, the fighting, and the political situation before and after the German withdrawal and the British passing through the town in *The Divided Land – An Anglo-Greek Tragedy* (1959). In this (beautifully written) book, Chandler, who went on to have a career as a director of Shell oil, director-general of the National Economic Development Office, and a pioneering campaigner for ethical business practices, was highly critical of the British failure to support more moderate Greek elements and help avert the bloody civil war which followed the German defeat. telegraph.co.uk/news/obituaries/finance-obituaries/8478562/Sir-Geoffrey-Chandler.html (acc. 20 August 2018).
490. Woodhouse: Report on Final Phase of Allied Military Mission in Greece; Milner-Barry, MS, 2 November 1944; Sutherland 1999, pp.157–62.
491. The population figures are from WO 204/9102 Progress Reports 3 District, reports of 21–25 and 26 November 1944. They recorded a population of 350,000 (of whom 130,000 were refugees from the Bulgarian-occupied parts of Greece) within a 9.5-mile radius of the city and 320,000 (of whom 108,000 were refugees) in the city itself. Thessaloniki's 50,000 Jews had been deported during the German occupation.
492. Mavrikis 2000.
493. WO 204/8828, Naval Message from CS 15.
494. Lodwick 1947/1990, p.188.
495. RH 19-7/27; RM 35-III/96.
496. HW 1/3294. Helias Doundoulakis, who after the war had a distinguished career in aerospace engineering, described his work as an OSS agent in Thessaloniki in the very entertaining memoirs *I was trained to be a Spy* I-II (Xlibris Corporation, 2008 and 2012/14).
497. HW 1/3294.
498. WO 204/8828, orders from III Corps to Kelforce, 31 October 1944; orders from Kelforce to Scrumforce/Sea Patrol; WO 204/8830.
499. WO 204/8828, Outline Plan for Operation '*Kelso*', 27 October 1944.
500. WO 204/8830, 'Occupation of Salonika', sign. Brig. Pritchard, 22 October 1944.
501. Lodwick 1947/1990, p.188.
502. WO 204/8828, signal from Kelforce to Skiathos Sea Patrol.
503. HS 5/785: Final Report on Third Visit to Greece by Major D.S.L. Dodson.
504. Mavrikis 2000; Holt 2004, pp.622, 625 and Appendix III. In autumn 1944, Allied newspapers (e.g. *The Times* on 11 and 29 September 1944 and the *Sydney Morning Herald* on 18 September 1944) and the German news agency (quoted in *The Times* on 14 September 1944) carried reports that Soviet troops had crossed the Bulgarian/Greek border. There were, however, neither Soviet troops nor Soviet officers with the Bulgarian units which remained on Greek soil until 25 October. The newspaper articles may have been misinformation circulated by the British or by the Germans – or by both, each for their own purposes.

The German military authorities and the German Foreign Ministry also announced several times during September and October that the Soviet military had entered northern Greece (RM 35-III/92; RM 35-III/95, KTB, 2 October 1944).

It is well documented that a Soviet military mission arrived in Greece in July 1944 and held meetings with the EAM/ELAS leadership. The mission advised the Greek Communists not to attempt a takeover and advised them to cooperate with the British (Moscow did not want to imperil the beginnings of an understanding with Britain that would give the USSR control of the rest of the Balkans).

The above is a highly simplified representation of the complicated relationship between the KKE and the USSR, and the role of the Soviet military mission. Interested readers should refer to Bærentzen (1986 and 2011) and Macrakis (1988).
British speculation about the point of the Russian mission: WO 202/175.
505. Capell 1945, p.72.
506. HS 5/785: Final Report on Third Visit to Greece by Major D.S.L. Dodson.
507. Capell 1945, pp.70–1.
508. HS 5/785: Final Report on Third Visit to Greece by Major D.S.L. Dodson.
509. HS 5/785: Final Report on Third Visit to Greece by Major D.S.L. Dodson; thanks to John O. Iatrides for the description of conditions in Thessaloniki.
510. Langley 1988/2016, pp.225–9; Mavrikis 2000; HS 5/785: Final Report on Third Visit to Greece by Major D.S.L. Dodson.
511. In the book *Scobie, Hero of Greece: The British Campaign, 1944–45*. Arthur Barker, 1975.
512. Iatrides, e-mail of 10 October 2017.
513. Langley 1988/2016, pp.225–9; Lodwick 193; Capell 72–3. The information about German casualties varies considerably. Suzanne Lassen says both 22 and 60 were killed, and mentions that Henshaw personally killed 12 and Lassen 8 (Lassen 179). Lodwick says 60 dead Germans, of whom Henshaw was responsible for 11 and Lassen for 8 (Lodwick, p.193). Prof. Iatrides confirms that the Greek sources also mentioned the incident, but present it as a clash between ELAS and the Germans without British involvement. Iatrides, e-mail of 10 October 2017.
514. Lodwick, p.194.
515. WO 204/9102, HG 3 District, M.L. (Greece), Progress Report No. 1: (Covering period up to 25 Nov '44); WO 204/8692.
516. HS 5/785, Report by Major Diamantopoulos (Arty), Leader of 'Jeanne' mission at Thessaloniki. About the German/British negotiations in general, see Bærentzen 2011.
517. Thanks to Professor Ioannis D. Stefanidis for this summary of the situation in Thessaloniki, Stefanidis, e-mail, 11 October 2017.
518. Another possible explanation for why ELAS did not seize control of Thessaloniki is that once the fighting in the Athens area had started in earnest (following demonstration of Dec 3) the communist party (KKE) leadership ordered the main ELAS units in northern Greece to attack the anti-communist Colonel Napoleon Zervas's weaker EDES forces in Epirus which had to be rescued by British troops and ships that transferred them to Corfu. Some weeks later ELAS's commander in the Thessaloniki area was ordered by the KKE to take Thessaloniki but he refused, claiming that his forces were now inadequate for the task. (Thanks to Professor Iatrides for this observation.) On the British perception of EAM/ELAS's rule in Thessaloniki: Alexander 1980.
519. Quoted from Langley 1988/2016, p.229.
520. Lassen 1949/1965, p.181.
521. WO 204/8828: Signal from Kelforce to III Corps, 10 November 1944.
522. Milner-Barry, MS 30 and TS p.328.
523. Lassen 1949/165, pp.187–91; Langley 1988/2016, pp.222–3.

Chapter 36: Senforce, Crete, December 1944–February 1945
524. Unless otherwise stated, this chapter is based on Lind 1994, chapter 19, Lassen 1949/165, pp.190–209, WO 204/9235 CRETEFORCE SITREPS and WO 204/9240 SENFORCE SITREPS. Suzanne Lassen's account is based in part on an 'official diary', presumably a Senforce war diary. Despite an extensive search of the National Archives, Liddell Hart Centre for Military Archives, the SAS Regimental Archive archive and the Lassen/Bernstorff-Gyldensteen family archive, this source has not been traced. Suzanne may have read the war diary during her visit to the War Office in London – or perhaps it was shown to her by some Senforce veteran who, breaching all regulations, had kept it as a souvenir. What has since become of it is not known.
525. WO 204/4483, Daily Sitrep 2 Oct-44; Sirotti.
526. About the evacuation order, the number left behind and the order to defend: RM 7/1417 1 SKL; RM 35-III/91 4 KTB, September: RM 7/1418; RM 35-III/96, KTB 23 October 1944.

527. The German troops consisted of remnants of various units brought together around the staff of Fortress Division 133. When the commander of the division, Lieutenant General Ernst Klepp, fell ill, the artillery commander, Colonel Benthack, was promoted to major general and appointed his successor. As well as the Germans, there were about 5,000 troops from the armed forces of the fascist Italian Republic (RSI), including 'blackshirts' from the elite units of the MVSN (party militia) and a few hundred Russian Wehrmacht volunteers (Russians, blackshirts and other Italians: RH 34/418; Sirotti).
528. On the withdrawal to the Chania-district: Gilbert 2014, pp.203–11.
529. About the withdrawal area: Report on Crete by Major T.J. Dunbabin, Fifth Report, Third Series, 3–18 Sep 44; 'Crete now in two parts': Report on Crete by Major T.J. Dunbabin, Sixth Report, Third Series, 18 Sep-12 Oct 44; Seventh Report, Third Series, 11–23 Oct 44 in HS 5/724. Major Baton's reports: HS 204/8813; on SOE's political role on Crete: Damer & Frazer 2018.
530. 3 Corps Sig Instr, 29 Nov 44 in WO 204/9422.
531. Milner-Barry, MS, 1 December 1944. It is interesting, perhaps, that where Stephen Hastings saw Lassen's dangerous driving as a sign of fearlessness, Milner-Barry thought of it as recklessness .
532. Langley 1988/2016, pp.230–1.
533. Lieut. C.J.M. Rickards, RNVR: Letter to Suzanne Lassen, 21 June 1945.
534. The three Bandouvas brothers, Giannis, Manolis and Nikos, were leading figures of the Cretan Resistance.
535. Flights to and from Thessaloniki discontinued on 24 October: RM 35-III/96.
536. *Special Boat Service 'M' Squadron Operation Instruction No. 5 Senforce*, 13 December 1944, WO 170/7529; HS 5/730: Maj S. Oxland: Report part III 'Period 5 Dec-21 Dec 44, my first visit to Crete as Staff Officer to Brig Benfield' by Maj S. Oxland.
537. Around New Year 1943, the British officer Lieutenant Colonel J.M. Stevens wrote a report on the situation in central Greece, where he had just spent three months with the partisans. He wrote about ELAS, among other things: 'As bandits they are first class, as guerrillas good, as soldiers mediocre' (*Report of Lt.-Col. J.M. Stevens on Present Conditions in Central Greece*, reproduced in Bærentzen 1982).
538. HS 5/730: Maj S. Oxland: Report part III 'Period 5 Dec-21 Dec 44, my first visit to Crete as Staff Officer to Brig Benfield' by Maj S. Oxland.
539. Milner-Barry, MS, 5–6 December 1944. According to Jellicoe's biographer, Lorna Almonds-Windmill, Jellicoe went to Haifa because David Stirling, who was a prisoner at Colditz Castle, had indicated to Winston Churchill, 'via various clandestine means', that he wanted Jellicoe as his staff officer in a special forces contingent which he expected to command in operations against the Communists in China after the war. Windmill quotes Sutherland (p. 172) as her source, but even though Sutherland does mention the anti-Communist project he says nothing about Jellicoe being part of Stirling's scheme. George Jellicoe's son, Nicholas Jellicoe, can't remember his father ever mentioning Stirling's Chinese plans as his reason for going to Staff College. (Nicholas Jellicoe, conversation with the author, Copenhagen, 26 June 2017.)
540. Sutherland, 1999, p.164.
541. Lodwick 1947/1990, p.199.
542. Dennis John Ciclitira (1918–2000) was born in Patras but brought up in Westcliff-on-Sea, Essex, where his father Demosthenes, also a native of Patras, had set up a dried fruit import business. After completing his education at Wycliffe College in 1936, he went to Greece to learn the family business. Back in England he joined the Territorial Army in March and was commissioned in April 1940. His fluency in Greek made him a natural choice for operations in the Eastern Mediterranean and after a couple of years with the South Staffordshire Regiment he joined the SOE in Cairo, looking after Greek affairs. (Obituary, *The Times*, 23 June 2000).
543. In a typed memoir, presumably written quite some time after the war, Ciclitira says that the unnamed SBS officer proposed the football match, to be played between Germans and 'his unit which were in the mountains' as a means of settling the discussion, 'winner take all'. Ciclitira, TS in Private Papers of Major D J Ciclitira, IWM.

544. HS 5/722, Final Report by Maj D.J. Ciclitira.
545. Stephenson, interview by Mike Langley, before 1988.
546. Burn, letter to Milner-Barry, 19 April 1948.
547. NN, *Diary*, 6 December 1944. Mason 2004.
548. WO 204/9255, Weekly Report no. 7.
549. HS 5/731, Third Report (New Series) by Major J. Smith-Hughes.
550. WO 170/7575, WD 6 District, 17 January.
551. HS 5/731, Third Report (New Series) by Major J. Smith-Hughes; e-mail from Professor Jenny Bimrose, 16 August 2010.
552. WO 204/9305, Proposal for Appointment of a Senior Military Officer, CRETE, 27 December 1944.
553. Barker-Benfield was replaced as head of Creteforce and Senior Military Officer Crete by Colonel Macalester on 23 February 1945 (WO 204/9255).
554. WO 204/8393.
555. Burn 1947, pp.184–185.
556. WO 204/9107, App. 'A' to HQ 6 Dist Progress Report No. 10, 'Extract from NIKE Newspaper of 8 February 45'; Squadron Leader Church's speech and other details are based on the long entry in the 'War Diary' quoted by Suzanne Lassen (Lassen 1949/1962, p.207. Unfortunately, it has not been possible to identify Squadron Leader Church. It would seem reasonable to assume that he was a chaplain, but the RAF List seems to contain no chaplain by that name.
557. Rickards, letter to Suzanne Lassen, 21 June 1945; Beevor 1991, chapter 28; on the partisans' treatment of captured Germans and traitors within their own ranks: Gilbert 2014, pp.133–5.

Chapter 37: Italy
558. Clark was promoted to General on 10 March 1945.
559. Harder & Hesel 2018, pp.234–5, 241.
560. Moretti 2005, pp.28–9 and 209–11.
561. Stephenson, interview by Mike Langley.
562. Green, quoted from Langley 1988/2016, p.236.
563. Stephenson, interview by Mike Langley.
564. Lassen 1949/165, p.215.
565. Lodwick 1947/1990, p.208.
566. Langley: Letter to Anders Sandberg, 21 December 1990; Lassen 1949/165, p.215.
567. The description of Operation Buckland, the operations on and around Lake Comacchio and the fighting in the Argenta gap are based primarily on Moretti 2005 & 2008, and Pieraccini 2000; Renata Vigano's novel *L'Agnese va a morire* (1949) is a masterly literary depiction of the war as experienced by the partisans and civilians.
568. The draining continued after the war, and *Le Valli di Comacchio* now covers approx. 11,000 hectares.
569. *162. (Turk.) Infanterie-Division. (Einsatz in Rahmen der 10. Armee)*, RH 26-162/64; Vuerich 2009. Of the three infantry regiments, 303 was Turkmen, while 314 and 329 were Azerbaijani. In July 1944 the ratio of Germans to foreign volunteers had been 1:1 in the division as a whole, and 1:3 in the combat units. However, during winter, the division sent so many German officers and soldiers to other units that the ratio was now about 1:10.
570. The description of Operation Roast is based primarily on Pieraccini 2000.
571. Pitt 1983, p. 189; Sutherland, 1999, p.169; Snelling; McConville 1992/2013, p. 105.
572. *162. (Turk.) Infanterie-Division. (Einsatz in Rahmen der 10. Armee)*, RH 26-162/64; Vuerich 2009.
573. A week later, Lassen again sailed with Folegatti. He brought along a radio, which he used to draw down such a fierce artillery bombardment of the German lines 'that you would've thought it was broad daylight'. Stephenson: Interview by Mike Langley, before 1988.
574. *'Il racconto di Giuseppe Folegatti – Ho condotto la batana col danese vicino ai tedeschi'*, article in La Nuova Ferrara, early 1990, author's collection.

575. The description of the events of 6–11 April 1945 is based mainly on Pieraccini 2000; 2nd Commando Brigade's orders, reports, etc, in WO 218/76; as well as on Lieutenant Turnbull's, Company Sergeant Major Workman's, and Bombardier Crotty's eyewitness accounts in WO 373/47.
576. Lassen 1949.
577. As well as Lassen, E Patrol consisted of Company Sergeant Major Workman, Corporal O'Reilly, Bombardier Crotty, Trooper Crouch and privates Shaw, Thompson, Barbour, Medcalfe, Green and Stephenson. Y Patrol consisted of First Lieutenant Turnbull, Sergeant Waite, corporals Roberts and Watkins, Fusilier Hughes and privates Williams and Hunter. The men had not volunteered for the operation but had been handpicked by Lassen.

    Ken Smith of the SBS described a violent row between Lassen and another officer. According to Smith, Lassen wanted to lead the whole of his force towards Comacchio and preferably into the town, perhaps to carry out a raid like the ones he was used to in the Aegean Sea. The other officer insisted that he should divide the force into multiple groups to create as much commotion as possible – which is what was ultimately done. Smith called the other officer 'Turnbull', but it seems unlikely that Lieutenant Turnbull would have seen fit to give his superior orders. It is not entirely clear when this alleged altercation took place. On the other hand, given Lassen's temperament and attitude to authority, it is highly likely that while in Italy he had one or more violent clashes with a superior. It is known, for example, that during a long and apparently boring briefing at the 8th Army HQ in Ravenna, he simply got up and walked out (Langley, 237–8).
578. The countryside around Comacchio has changed much since 1945. The land that the Germans had flooded was drained again after the war. Since then, several other new areas have also been drained. Part of the route that Lassen's force sailed would today cross the dry land north of the lake.
579. In British sources, these machine-gun positions are often referred to as 'pill boxes', which suggests a small concrete structure aboveground. In fact they were foxholes, which were presumably covered with turf-lined boards. The German infantry's foxholes for light machine guns were generally intended for a single weapon operated by a gunner and an assistant. However, the positions on the Spit were apparently wider, with room for two machine guns operated by a total of four men (Langley 1988/2016, p.234; in general on German field fortifications: Rottmann 2004).
580. According to Tomasi, he asked Lassen, as they parted on the lakeshore, if he knew the password. Lassen said that he did, but that very night the Germans had changed the password, and so the sentries opened fire on Green and his comrades. None of the British witnesses mention any password.
581. The prisoners belonged to 6th Company, 2nd Battalion, 303rd Infantry Regiment, 162 (Turk.) Infantry Division (*2 Cdo Bde Report on Op 'FRY'*, WO 218/76). About the green flare: Sergeant Waite, quoted in Lassen 1949, p.226.
582. Stephenson: Interview by Mike Langley.
583. According to *2 Cdo Bde Report on Op 'FRY'* (WO 218/76) of 17 April 1945, the men in the machine-gun post came out with their hands up. Another position to the northwest then opened fire. This description of events is inconsistent with that of Stephenson, Lieutenant Turnbull, Company Sergeant Major Workman and Bombardier Crotty. It is difficult to imagine who might have been able to see the Turkmen leave their position. The brigade report also fails to mention one of the German machine-gun posts. According to this report, the raiders defeated the first post without losses, but then Lassen was killed in front of the second in the row – and not, as in the other reports, the third.
584. Shortly after the war, Stephenson sent Suzanne Lassen a written account of the night's events. He told her that Lassen had said that he should give Turnbull the order to withdraw (Stephenson: interview by Mike Langley). However, according to Turnbull's own report of 8 May 1945, Lassen had given the order to press home the attack. In principle, the two versions are not mutually exclusive. Lassen may well have given the order to continue the attack but impressed on Turnbull that he should get his men out safely.
585. Stephenson: interview by Mike Langley.

586. Tomasi: interview by M. Paiola.
587. Tomasi interview by M. Paiola.
588. *2 Cdo Bde Report on Op 'FRY'* (WO 218/76).
589. Nazareno Bellini: Interview by author, Comacchio, 9 April 2002. Don Francesco Mariani helped 1,034 Italian and Allied soldiers cross the Gustav Line into Allied territory during the war. For this effort, and for providing pastoral care and practical assistance to the victims of the Allied air attacks in 1945, Comacchio council honoured him with a gold medal in 1955.
590. Milner-Barry TS, pp. 341–2.
591. Kenneth Herbert Smith: Interview by author, Comacchio, 9 April 2002.
592. Sutherland, 1999, p.143. Interview by Mike Langley.
593. WO 170/7529.
594. Milner-Barry, TS, p.345
595. John Lodwick's adventurous life and interesting writing is described in Geoffrey Elliott's fine biography *A Forgotten Man – The Life and Death of John Lodwick* (I.B. Tauris, 2017).
596. The recommendation: WO 374/47; Brown & Bimrose, e-mail to author 16.08.10.
597. WO 170/7529.

Chapter 38: Legacy
598. HS 9/888/2; Lassen Family Archive; Private Papers of Major L E Prout at IWM.

Bibliography and Sources

Books and articles etc on Anders Lassen

de la Billière, Sir Peter (2004/2007): 'Major Anders Lassen' in *Supreme Courage, Heroic Stories from 150 Years of the Victoria Cross*, Abacus, London

Halck, Jørgen (1948): *En dansk Soldat, Major Anders Lassen, V.C., M.C.*, Thaning & Appels Forlag, Copenhagen.

Holmes, Dick (n.d.): 'Anders Lassen, VC., MC., – The Man and the Myth' in *Mars & Minerva*.

Kofod-Hansen, Mogens (1987): *'Andy' – et portræt af danskeren, major Anders Lassen som – efter at være faldet i anden verdenskrig – blev tildelt Victoriakorset*, Frihedsmuseets Venners Forlags Fond, Copenhagen.

Langley, Mike (1988/2016): *Anders Lassen, VC, MC of the SAS*, New English Library. Republished with a foreword by William Langley by Pen & Sword Military, Barnsley, 2016.

Lassen, Suzanne (1949): *Sømand og Soldat*, Gyldendal, Copenhagen. All references are to the English version: *Anders Lassen VC*, translated by Inge Halck. Frederick Muller. London, 1965.

Sælen, Frithjof (1950): *Unge Anders Lassen*, John Griegs Forlag, Bergen.

Other published sources

Alanbrooke (1957/2001/2003), *War Diaries 1939–1945*, ed. Alex Danchev & Daniel Todman, Weidenfeld & Nicholson, London.

Alexander, George M. (1980) 'British Perceptions of EAM/ELAS Rule in Thessaloniki' in *Balkan Studies* 21.2, pp.203–16.

Allan, Stuart (2007): *Commando Country*, National Museums Scotland, Edinburgh.

Appleyard, J.E. (1947): *Apple. Being the Story of "Apple" of the Commandos and Special Air Service Regiment*, Blandford Press, London.

Bacci, Marcello; Gandini, Giorgio; Modonesi, Carlo (1997): *La stretta di Argenta*, Guaraldi, Rimini.

Bateman, Robert L. (2007): *The long-dead hand of S.L.A. Marshall misleads historians, Military History*, February 2007, www.historynet.com/long-dead-hand-s-l-marshall-misleads-historians.htm. (downloaded on 26 July 2020).

Bærentzen, Lars: (1980): 'Anglo-German Negotiations during the German Retreat from Greece in 1944', *Scandinavian Studies in Modern Greek*, nr. 4, 1980, s. 23–62.

Bærentzen, Lars (ed.) (1982): *British Reports on Greece 1943–44* by J.M. Stevens, C.M. Woodhouse & D.J. Wallace, Museum Tusculanum Press, Copenhagen.

Bærentzen, Lars: (1986): 'The Arrival of the Soviet Military Mission in July 1944 and KKE Policy: A Study of Chronology' in *Journal of the Hellenic Diaspora*, årg. 13., nr. 3–4, New York.

Bærentzen, Lars: (1987): 'The German Withdrawal from Greece in 1944 and British Naval "Inactivity"' in *Journal of Modern Greek Studies*, Vol. 5, Number 2. October 1987, pp.237–65.

Bærentzen, Lars: (2011): 'A letter from the Peloponnese dated September 17, 1944' in Pirjevčev zbornik – Poti zgodovine med sevenrnim Jadranom, srednjo in vzhodno Evropo: ob 70. obletnici akad. prof. dr. Jožeta Pirjevca, ed.: Gorazd Bajc & Borut Klabjan, Universitena Založba Annales, Koper.

Ballola, Sandra Carli (1997): *Il paesaggio delle valli di Comacchio come luogo di guerra e di Resistenza (1944–45)*, Comune di Comacchio, Assessorato alle Istituzioni culturali, Comacchio.

Beevor, Anthony (1991/2005): *Crete, The Battle and the Resistance*, John Murray, London.

Bennike, Arne (1945): *"Gnisten" paa Eventyr*, Carl Allers Bogforlag, Copenhagen.

Benyon-Tinker, W.E. (1947): *Dust Upon the Sea*, Hodder & Stoughton, London.
Bourke, Joanna (1999/2000): *An Intimate History of Killing, Face-to-Face Killing in Twentieth-Cenury Warfare*, Granta Books, London.
Brigaglia, Manlio (2004): 'Salvatore Mannironi e lo sbarco alleato sulle coste della Sardegna' in *Il Messaggero sardo*, September 2004.
Brown, Anthony Cave (1975): *Bodyguard of Lies*, Quill/William Morrow, New York.
Brown, A.J. (1960): *Forces Postal History Society*, Newsletter No. 41, JANUARY/FEBRUARY 1960.
Burn, Lambton (1947): *"Down Ramps!", Saga of the Eighth Armada, A Story of the Men who Fought and Sweated and Cursed in the long struggle from Tobruk, 1941, to Kiel, 1945*, Carroll & Nicholson, London.
Capell, Richard (u.å., men 1946): *Simiomata, A Greek Note Book 1944–1945*, Macdonald, London.
Cavalli, Giuseppe (1954/1995): *Il calvario di due ammiragli, Ricordi di un compagno di carcere*, APC, Parma.
Cecini, Giovanni (2014): *La Guardia di Finanza nelle isole italiane dell'Egeo 1912–1945*. Gangemi. Rom
Chandler, Geoffrey (1959): *The Divided Land – An Anglo-Greek Tragedy*, Macmillan, London.
Clark, Katherine (2010): *Closing the Circle*, paroslife.parosweb.com/story.html?story=2773, acc. 27 July 2010.
Clayton, Anthony (2006): *The British Officer, Leading the Army from 1660 to the Present*, Pearson, Harlow.
Clogg, Richard (2018): *Greek to Me – A Memoir of Academic Life*, I.B. Tauris. London, New York
Cookridge, E.H. (1966): *Inside S.O.E., The Story of Special Operations in Western Europe 1940–45*, Arthur Barker Limited, London.
Cooper, Artmis (2012): *Patrick Leigh Fermor: An Adventure*. John Murray, London.
Cotts, Cynthia & Massaliotis (2010): Nikolas Stellas, a Paros boy who redefined bravery, paroslife.parosweb.com/story.html?story=2703&issue=136, acc. 27 July 2010.
Crang, Jeremy A. (2000), *The British Army and the People's War*, Manchester University Press, 2000, s. 55, note 8.
Crowdy, Terry (2008): *SOE Agent, Churchill's Secret Warriors*, Osprey, Oxford.
Cunningham, Cyril (1998): *Beaulieu: The Finishing School for Secret Agents*, Leo Cooper, London.
Damer, Sean & Frazer, Ian (2018): 'SOE in Wartime Crete: An Instrument of Control,' in *Journal of Modern Greek Studies* 36 (2018).
Deakin, F.W. (1962): *The Brutal Friendship, Mussolini, Hitler and the Fall of Italian Fascism*, Weidenfeld and Nicholson, London.
Dinter, Elmar (1982): *Held oder Fegling, Die korperlichen und seelischen Belastungen des Soldaten im Krieg*, Mittler, Herford.
Dönhoff, Marion (1994): *"Um der Ehre willen". Erinnerungen an die Freunde vom 20. Juli*, Berlin.
Doundoulakis, Helias (2008 & 2011/(rev.) 2014), *I was Trained to be a Spy I-II*, Exlibris
Dourlein, Pieter (1953) *Inside North Pole: a secret agent's story*, London.
Elliott, Geoffrey (2017) *A Forgotten Man – The Life and Death of John Lodwick*. I.B. Tauris, London, New York.
Ellis, John (1980/2009): *The Sharp End, The Fighting Man in World War II*, foreword by Max Hastings, Aurum Press, London.
Engen, Robert: (2011): »S.L.A. Marshall and the Ratio of Fire: History, Interpretation, and the Canadian Experience«, *Canadian Military History* 20, nr. 4 (autumn 2011), www.canadianmilitaryhistory.ca/wp-content/uploads/2012/03/4-Engen-Marshall-under-fire.pdf. (downloaded on 26. July 2020).
Fermor, Patrick Leigh (ed. Peter & Chris White, 2014): *Abducting a General*, John Murray, London.
Field, Philippa (née Jeffers), e-mail corr., 2013–2020

Fleck, Dieter & Bothe, Michael (1999): *The handbook of humanitarian law in armed conflicts*, Oxford University Press, Oxford.
Folegatti, Vincenzino, e-mail, 16. July 2020.
Foot, M.R.D. (1966): *SOE in France, An Account of the Work of the British Special Operations Executive in France 1940–1944*, HMSO, London.
Foot, M.R.D. (1993): 'Obituary: Peter Kemp' in *Independent*, 4 November 1993.
Foot, M.R.D. & Langley, J.M. (1979): *MI9, Escape and Evasion 1939–1945*, The Bodley Head, London.
Fournier, Gérard & Heintz, André (2006): *'If I Must Die …'. From 'Postmaster' to 'Aquatint', The Audacious Raids of a British Commando 1941–1943*, Eng. transl. Heather Costil, Orep Editions, Cully.
Gartzonikas, Panagiotis (2003): *Amphibious and Special Operations in the Aegean Sea 1943–1945. Operational Effectiveness and Strategic Implications*, Naval Postgraduate School, Monterey, California.
Giacobbe, Simonetta 'L'insurrezione mancata' in Rojch 2000.
Gilbert, Harald (2014) *Das besetzte Kreta 1941–45* (PELEUS/Studien zur Archäologie und Geschichte Griechenlands und Zyperns, Bd. 63), Harrassowitz, Wiesbaden
Gilbert, Harald (2017) *Der Krieg in der Ägäis 1943–1944* (PELEUS/Studien zur Archäologie und Geschichte Griechenlands und Zyperns, Bd. 78), Harrassowitz, Wiesbaden.
Gooderson, Ian (2002): 'Shoestring strategy: the British campaign in the Aegean, 1943', *Journal of Strategic Studies*, 25: 3, 1.
Grossman, Dave (1995/2009): *On Killing, The Psychological Cost of Learning to Kill in War and Society*, Back Bay Books/Little, Brown and Company, New York.
Grossman, Dave (2004/2008) (with Loren W. Christiansen: *On Combat, The Psychology and Physiology of Deadly Conflict in War and Peace*, Warrior Science Publications.
Gubbins, Colin: *The Art of Guerilla Warfare* & *The Partisan Leader's Handbook* available on the internet in a number of different editions. Gubbins is not credited as the author and the year of publication is not mentioned.
Hæstrup, Jørgen (1974): *Christmas Mollers Londonbreve, Christmas Mollers korrespondance med hjemlandet 1942–1945*, Gyldendal, Copenhagen.
Halck, Jørgen (1946): *Sange fra rejsen*, Thanning & Appel, Copenhagen.
Halck, Jørgen (1958) *I streng fortrolighed*, Thanning & Appel, Copenhagen.
Hamilton-Hill, Donald (1973): *SOE Assignment*, William Kimber, London.
Harder, Thomas & Hesel, Lene Ewald (2018): *Kareste Kek – Et dansk soskendepar i britisk tjeneste*, People's Press, Copenhagen.
Harokopos, G. ((2002): *Die Entführung von General Kreipe* (German translation by Elisa Zoccolan; the title of the Greek original is not mentioned), V. Kouvidis-V. Manouras, Heraklion.
Harrison, E.D.R. (1999): 'British Subversion in French East Africa, 1941–42: SOE's Todd Mission' in *The English Historical Review*, Vol. 114, No. 456 (April 1999), pp. 339–69.
Hastings, Stephen (1994): *The Drums of Memory – An Autobiography*, Leo Cooper, London.
Heiberg, Morten & Pelt, Mogens (2003) *Emperadores del Mediterraneo. Franco, Mussolini y la guerra civil espanola*, Critica Contrastes, Barcelona.
Hesketh, Roger (2000): *Fortitude – The D-Day Deception Canpaign*. St. Ermin's, London.
History of 9 Commando – Overseas 11 Sep 43 – 8 May 45, commandoveterans.org, acc. 9 August 2010.
Holt, Thaddeus (2004/5): *The Deceivers, Allied Military Deception in the Second World War*, Phoenix, London.
Jensen, Ole Helmer (1968): *Anden Verdenskrig Hvornar-Skete-Det*, Politikens Forlag, Copenhagen.
Jespersen, Knud J.V. (1998): *Med hjalp fra England*, Odense Universitetsforlag.
Jespersen, Knud J.V. (2000): 'Mogens Hammer og hans rolle i modstandskampen 1941–43' in *Krigshistorisk Tidsskrift*, 36:3.
Jureit, Ulrike (red.) 2002: *Verbrechen der Wehrmacht, Dimensionen des Vernichtingskrieges 1941–1944*, Hamburger Institut für Sozialforschung, Hamburg.

Kalogerakis, Giorgos (2009): *To aspradi tou avgou, epihirisi ALBUMEN (το ασπράδι του αυγού, Επιχείρηση ΑΛΜΠΟΥΜΕΝ)*, Heraklion.
Kay, R.L. (2008): *Long Range Desert Group in the Mediterranean*, nzetc.org/tm/scholarly/tei-WH2-1Epi-c4-WH2-1Epi-l-0.html, acc. 17 June 2010.
Kemp, Peter (1958/1960): *No Colours or Crest*, Cassell, London.
Kirk, Geoffrey (1997): *Towards the Aegean Sea, A Wartime Memoir*, Square One Publications, Upton upon Severn.
Koburger, Charles W. Jr. (1999): *Wine-Dark, Blood Red Sea, Naval Warfare in the Aegean, 1941–1946*, foreword by G.W. Searle, Praeger, Westport, Conn., London.
Kurowski, Franz (1997): *The Brandenburgers – Global Mission*, translated by David Johnston, no mention of German original title, Fedorowicz, Winnipeg.
Ladd, James (1978). *Commandos and rangers of World War II*, Macdonald and Jane's.
Lamb, Richard (1993): *War in Italy 1943–1945, A Brutal Story*, Penguin, London.
Lauridsen, John T. (red.) (2007): *Over stregen – under besættelsen*, Gyldendal, Copenhagen.
Le operazioni delle unita italiane nel settembre-ottobre 1943, Ministero della Difesa, Stato Maggiore dell'Esercito, Ufficio Storico, Rom, (1975).
Lean, Mary: 'Obituary: Ian Appleyard' in *The Independent*, 16 june 1998, independent.co.uk/artsentertainment/obituaryian-appleyard-1165285.html, acc. 23 February 2010.
Lee, Eric (2016): Operation Basalt, The History Press, Brimscombe Port
Lett, Brian (2012): *Ian Fleming and SOE's Operation Postmaster: The Top Secret Story Behind 007*, Pen & Sword Books, Barnsley.
Lind, Lew J. (1994): *The Battle of the Wine Dark Sea*, Kangaroo Press, Kenthurst.
Lloyd Owen, David (1980/2003): *Providence their Guide – The Long Range Desert Group 1940–1945*, Leo Cooper, Barnsley.
Lodwick, John (1947/1990): *Raiders from the Sea, The Story of the Special Boat Service in WWII*, with a foreword by Lord Jellicoe, Naval Institute Press, Annapolis.
Macintyre, Ben (2010): Operation *Mincemeat, The True Spy Story that Changed the Course of World War II*, Bloomsbury, London.
Mackenzie, William (2000/2002): *The Secret History of S.O.E.: Special Operations Executive 1940–1945*, with a foreword and notes by M.R.D. Foot, St. Ermin's, London.
Maclean, Fitzroy (1949/1956): *Eastern Approaches*, Pan Books, London.
Macrakis, Michael S. (1988): 'Russian Mission on the Mountains of Greece, Summer 1944 (A View from the Ranks)' in *Journal of Contemporary History* (SAGE, London, Newbury Park, Beverly Hills og New Delhi), vol. 23 (1988), 387–408
Maltoni, Luciano Alberghini (2002): 'Rodi 1943' in *Storia Militare* nr. 105.
Mariager, Rasmus (red.) (2009): Danskere i krig 1936–48, Gyldendal, Copenhagen.
Mason, Geoffrey B. (2004): »Service Histories of Royal Navy Warships World War 2, HMS CATTERICK (L 81) - Type III, Hunt-class Escort Destroyer including Convoy Escort Movements«, http://www.naval-history.net/xGM-Chrono-10DE-Catterick.htm (downloaded on 26 June 2020).
Maule, Henry (1975): *Scobie, Hero of Greece – The British Campaign 1944–45* (Arthur Barker, London).
Mavrikis, Jason (2000): 'The Big Bluff', in *Mars & Minerva*.
Mazower, Mark (1993): *Inside Hitler's Greece, The Experience of Occupation, 1941–44*, Yale University Press, New Haven & London.
McConville, Michael (1992/2013): *Nothing Much to Lose - The Story of 2nd Battalion Royal Marines, 1940–1943 and 43 Commando Royal Marines, 1943–1945*, Naval & Military Press, Uckfield.
von Medem, Gevinon (1994): *Axel von dem Bussche*, with an introduction by Richard von Weizsäcker, Mainz 1994.
Melis (2006): 'Il mio faccia a faccia con le spie inglesi' in *L'Unione Sarda*, 30.01.2006.
Messenger, Charles (1985): *The Commandos 1940–1946*, foreword by Brigadier Peter Young, DSO MC MA FSA, William Kimber, London.
Montagu, Ewen (1953/2001): *The Man Who Never Was, World War II's Boldest Counterintelligence Operation*, Naval Institute Press, Annapolis.

Moretti, Rino (2005): *Argenta Gap, L'ultima battaglia della campagna d'Italia aprile 1945*, Mursia, Milano.
Moretti, Rino (2008): *La battaglia dell'Argenta Gap, Guida storico-turistica*, Edisai, Ferrara.
Morris, Eric (1989): *Guerillas in Uniform, Churchill's Private Armies in the Middle East and the War Against Japan, 1940–45* Hutchinson, London.
Mortimer, Gavin (2004/2005): *Stirling's Men, The Inside history of the SAS in World War II*, Cassell, London.
Moss, W. Stanley (1950): *Ill Met by Moonlight: The Abduction of General Kreipe*, George C. Harrap, London.
Nikoloudis, Nikos: 'The Sacred Squadron – The struggles of an elite military unit from the deserts of Africa to the islands of the Aegean during WW2', academia.edu/26856342/The_Sacred_Squadron_-_The_struggles_of_an_elite_military_unit_from_the_deserts_of_Africa_to_the_islands_of_the_Aegean_during_WW2 (retrieved, 24 October 2019).
O'Carroll, Brendan (2020): The Long Range Desert Group in the Aegean, Pen & Sword Books, Yorkshire – Philadelphia
Owen, David Lloyd (1980/2003): *Providence their Guide – The Long Range Desert Group 1940–1945* (foreword by John Keegan), Pen & Sword Books, Barnsley.
Parker, John (2000/2005): *Commandos, The Inside Story of Britain's Most Elite Fighting Force*, Bounty Books, London.
Patucchi, Marco (2007): 'I segreti di John Armstrong la spia venuta dal nulla' in *Repubblica*, 19.07.2007, repubblica.it/2007/05/sezioni/spettacoli_e_cultura/lettere-spia/lettere-spia/lettere-spia.html, acc. 21 May 2010.
Pearce, Robert: 'Espionage in Africa: The Case of the Duchess', *The Historical Journal*, 26, 2.
Pieraccini, Giuseppe (2001): *Finale – VIII Armata – Offensiva finale – Dal fiume Reno al Panaro e Po 13–28 aprile* 1945, Società Editrice »Il Ponte Vecchio«, Cesena.
Pitt, Barrie (1983): Special Boat Squadron, The Story of the SBS in the Mediterranean, Century, London.
Ramsey, Winston G. (1981/2005): *The War in the Channel Islands Then and Now*, After the Battle, Old Harlow.
Rasmussen, Nicolas (2008): *On Speed: The Many Lives of Amphetamine*, New York University Press, New York.
Rees, Tom (2004): Levantine Heritage, levantineheritage.com/testi46.htm, acc. 13 June 2010.
Richards, Brooks (2004): *Secret Flotillas: Clandestine Sea Operations in the Mediterranean, North Africa and the Adriatic, 1940–44* Vol 2 (Government official histories), Frank Cass, London.
Rigden, Denis (2001): 'Introduction' in *SOE Syllabus, Lessons in ungentlemanly warfare World War II*, Public Records Office, Richmond.
Rigopoulos, Rigas (2004): 'A Testimony from the Alimnia Mission' in *Athens News*, 13071, athensnews.gr/articles, acc. 24 July 2010.
Roberts, Walter. R. (1987) *Tito, Mihailović, and the allies, 1941–1945*, Duke University Press, New Brunswick.
Robinson, Graham (2015): 'Sergeant Joseph Henry 'Tim' Robinson and the men from E Troop 12 Commando', operationbasalt.apps-1and1.net/page/4/ (acc. 3 April 2018).
Robinson, Graham (2016): 'Remarks by Graham Robinson on Sark, 21 May 2016', operationbasalt.apps-1and1.net/remarks-by-graham-robinson-on-sark-21-may-2016/ (acc. 3 April 2018).
Rogers, Anthony (2003): *Churchill's Folly. Leros and the Aegean.* Cassell.
Rojch, Antonio (2000): *Storie di un capo tribu, Lussu oltre la leggenda*, Grafica Mediterranea, Bolotana.
Rottmann, Gordon L. (2004): *German Field Fortifications 1939–45*, Osprey, Oxford.
Schenk, Peter (1995): 'The Battle for Leros' in *After the Battle*, nr. 90, London.
Schreiber, Gerhard (1990): *Die italienischen Militärinternierten im deutschen Machtbereich 1943–1945 – Verraten – Verachtet – Vergessen*, R. Oldenbourg Verlag, München.
Searle, Geoffrey (1994/2005): *At Sea Level*, foreword by The Rt Hon The Earl Jellicoe, The Book Guild Ltd. Lewes.
Seligman, Adrian (1947): *No Stars to Guide*, Hodder & Stoughton, London.

Seligman, Adrian (1996/1997): *War in the Islands, Undercover Operations in the Aegean 1942–4, Recalled by Men of the Levant Schooner Flotilla, The Greek Sacred Company and Aegean Raiding Forces*, Sutton, Phoenix Mill.

Sevaldsen, Jørgen (ed.) (2003): *Britain and Denmark: political, economic and cultural relations in the 19th and 20th Centuries*, Museum Tusculanums Forlag, Copenhagen.

Sirotti, Luigi: 'Le isole italiane dell'Egeo – 1945–1947 – Amministrazione Britannica', ilpostalista.it/sirotti/sirotti11.htm (acc. 20 November 2017).

Snelling, Steve: *Commando Valour at Lake Comacchio – Tom Hunter VC*, www.britainatwar.com/2018/08/17/commando-valour-at-lake-comacchio-tom-hunter-vc/ (downloaded on July 2020).

SOE Syllabus, Lessons in Ungentlemanly Warfare, World War II, introduction by Denis Rigden, Public Records Office, London, 2001.

Stafford, David (2001): *Secret Agent, The True Story of the Covert War Against Hitler*, Overlook Press, Woodstock & New York.

Sutherland, David (1999): *He Who Dares, Recollections of Service in the SAS, SBS and MI5*, foreword by Lord Jellicoe, Naval Institute Press, Annapolis.

Sørensen, Jakob (2009): 'Werner Michael Iversen: Hvervningen af danske statsborgere til britisk militærtjeneste 1940–45' in Mariager (ed.) (2009).

Sørensen, Jakob (2011): *For Danmarks ære, Danskere i allieret krigstjeneste 1939–45*, Informations Forlag, Copenhagen

Tasselli, Silvio (1993): 'L'insidia sottile', *Almanacco di Cagliari, 1994*, Cagliari.

Tasselli, Silvio (2000): 'Le spie venute dal mare', *Almanacco di Cagliari, 2001*, Cagliari.

Tasselli, Silvio (2001); 'Le operazioni 'Marigold' e 'Hawthorn'', *Storia Militare*, n. 96, anno IX, september 2001, Albertelli Edizioni Speciali, Parma.

Tasselli, Silvio (2002A): 'Operazione ›Bathtub‹ in Sardegna', *Storia Militare*, n. 111, anno X, december 2002, Albertelli Edizioni Speciali, Parma.

Tasselli, Silvio (2002B): 'Paracadutisti nel cielo di Siliqua', *Almanacco di Cagliari, 2003*, Cagliari.

Tasselli, Silvio (2002C): 'Il Capitano Terence Bruce Mitford nei Corpi Speciali Inglesi' in *Storia & Battaglie*, nr. 20.

Verney, John (1955): *Going to the Wars, A Journey in Various Directions*, Collins & The Book Society, London.

Verney, John (1966): *A Dinner of Herbs*, Collins, London.

Vick, Alan (1995): *Snakes in the Eagle's Nest, A History of Ground Attacks on Air Bases*, Rand, Santa Monica.

Viganò, Renata (1949): *L'Agnese va a morire*, Einaudi, Torino.

Vuerich, Cosimo (2009): 'La Turkistan Division' in Cavalloni, Centenari, Conti, Gropello (ed.) and Vuerich: *Deutsche Truppen in Italien, La Repubblica Sociale Italiana – R.S.I. e la "Turkestan Division"*, II, (Museo per la fotografia e la comunicazione visiva di Piacenza)

Waldheim Report, The, Submitted February 8, 1988 to Federal Chancellor Dr. Franz Vranitzky by the International Commission of Historians, Museum Tusculanum Press, Copenhagen, 1993.

Warner, Philip (1971/1980): *The Special Air Service*, William Kimber, London.

Waugh, Evelyn (1941): 'Memorandum on LAYFORCE; July 1940–July 1941', in Waugh 1976.

Waugh, Evelyn (1965) *The Sword of Honour Trilogy* (*Men at Arms*, 1952, *Officers and Gentlemen*, 1955 & *Unconditional Surrender*, 1961). Quoted from the Everyman's Library edition, London, 1994, with an introduction by Frank Kermode.

Waugh, Evelyn (1976), *The Diaries of Evelyn Waugh*, ed. Michael Davie, Little, Brown and Company, Boston & Toronto.

Windmill, Lorna Almonds (2005): *A British Achilles, The Story of George, 2nd Earl Jellicoe KBE, DSO, MC FRS*, foreword by Sir Patrick Leigh Fermor DSO CB, Pen & Sword Military, Barnsley.

Woodhouse: *Report on Final Phase of Allied Military Mission in Greece, Sept '44 – Jan '45 by Col. The Hon. C.M. Woodhouse, S.S.O., O.B.E.* in Bærentzen (ed.) 1982.

Bibliography and Sources

Archive material etc.
Where nothing else is stated, the letters, telegrams etc to and from Anders Lassen and Anders Lassen's personal documents etc are kept in the private archive of the Lassen family.

Rigsarkivet, Copenhagen
Kaptajn W.M. Iversens Arkiv, 1939–47.

The National Archives, Kew
ADM 1/18250 Resolution forwarded by the Danish Seamen's Organization requesting permission to serve on Brisih warships
ADM 223/480 MAID HONOR Transference to Freetown
AIR 27/2080 Operations Record Book, No. 603 Squadron R.A.F., M.E.
CAB 80/86, COS [44] 768 [O]25.8.1944.
DEFE 2/109 "Branford""Dryad""Musketoon""Fahrenheit""Barricade""Aquatint""Facsimile" "Basalt" and "Batman" Vol 1A.
DEFE 2/338 JUBILEE, Part 7
DEFE 2/842 Canoes MK II
DEFE 2/957 Small scale raiding force: procedures, responsibility etc
DEFE 2/970 Special Boat Unit (SBU) Operations, Operation ANGLO
DEFE 2/1093 Small scale raiding force: policy, formation, responsibility etc
HS 2/106 SOE Denmark 77 – Danish Seamen in Newcastle
HS 3/86/92 SOE West Africa No. 17–23
HS 3/89 SOE West Africa No. 18.
HS 3/92 POSTMASTER report by head of West Africa Mission
HS 3/93 S.O.E. West Africa No. 23.
HS 5/715 SOE – Dodecanese Islands – Rhodes – voyage, landing and operational reports
HS 5/716 SOE – Dodecanese Islands – Scarpanto, Symi – voyage, landing and operational reports
HS 5/722 SOE/Greece 862, Reports Various – Individual Reports, Crete; Personnel B-D
HS 5/723 Crete; Lt Colonel T J Dunbabin; part 1
HS 5/724 SOE Greece – Reports Various Individual Reports, Crete: Lt.Col. T.J. Dunbabin (Part 2)
HS 5/726 Crete; Major A W Fielding; part 2
HS 5/728 Crete; Major P M Leigh-Fermor
HS 5/730 Crete; personnel O – R
HS 5/730 SOE/Greece 862, Reports Various – Individual Reports, Crete; Personnel O-R
HS 5/731 SOE Greece – Crete, Situation Reports from Major J. Smith-Hughes
HS 5-785 Greece – Reports Various Individual Reports: Jeanne: Maj Diamantopoulos
HS 6/304 Support of military and naval operations: PETRIFY, BRANFORD, DRYAD, BASALT, HUCKABACK
HS 7/215 War Diary, Vol. 4, Survey of Global Activities, April 1941
HS 7/219 SOE – survey of global activities, August 1941
HS 8/435 SOE training section 1940–1945
HS 9/48/1 John Geoffrey Appleyard
HS 9/437/4 Julian Anthony Dobrski
HS 9/538/2 Louis Franck
HS 9/539/1 Børge Franck
HS 9/635/2 Guise
HS 9/644 Jørgen Halck
HS 9/652/2 Hanau
HS/9/680/5 Graham Hayes
HS 9/812/5 Alfred Jorgensen
HS 9/877/5 Peter Ivan Lake
HS 9/888/2 AFEVS Lassen
HS 9/888/3 Lassen FA
HS 9/922/7 Liedekerke

HS 9/1183/2 Gustavus Henry March-Phillipps
HS 9/1418/6 Bill Stirling
HS 9/1494/6 Tvermose
HS 204/8813 Sitreps 6 District
HW 19/141 Italian resistance to Germans on Greek islands
HW 19/168 Government Code and Cypher School: ISOS Section and ISK Section: Decrypts of German Secret Service (Abwehr and Sicherheitsdienst) Messages
HW 1/3294 Signals intercept by Government Code and Cyphers School
MO 3/3376 LRDG Future Policy
PERS 6/1519 Kreipe
RH 19-VII/27 Oberkommando der Heeresgruppe E (Oberbefehlshaber Südost)
RH 26-1007/23 Sturmdivision Rhodos, Abteilung 1c, Anlagen zum KTB
WO 32/11430 OVERSEAS (MIDDLE EAST): (Code 0(A/O)): Dodecanese – planning and operations – Dec. 1942 to loss of Leros 1943. OPERATIONS (NARRATIVES OF): General (Code 46(A)): Dodecanese – planning and operations – December 1942 to the loss of Leros 1943
WO 106/5431 Crete: miscellaneous and general
WO 140/4012 Special Boat Service – Land Forces Adriatic
WO 170/7529 SBS Jan-July 1945
WO 170/7575 WD 6 HQ Crete District Mil.
WO 201/136 Crete: Operation ALBUMEN and FACULTY
WO 201/1598 Operations: Force 133 and 266
WO 201/1663 Miscellaneous situation reports by Majors Lapraik and Broxton
WO 202/175 Russian Mission to Greece July–August 1944
WO 204/4483 Sitreps Force 133
WO 204/8393 Moves Special Units
WO 204/8401 WE Special Boat Service (Sept 44–May 45)
WO 204/844 Operations against Greek Islands – Independence – April–August 44
WO 204/8461 Summary 9 Commando/Foxforce activities in Aegean September 1944
WO 204/8505 Operation against Island of Kithera – Aplomb
WO 204/8506 Operations against Kithera
WO 204/8512 Orders and reports – Operations against Greek coast 9/44–4/45
WO 204/8692 Sitreps Greece 3 Corps
WO 204/8828 KELSO
WO 204/8830 GLISSADE
WO 204/9102 Progress reports – 3 District
WO 204/9107 District Reports – 6 District
WO 204/9235 CRETEFORCE sitreps
WO 204/9240 SENFORCE sitreps
WO 204/9255 AIS Reports, Crete District, Nov 44–July 45
WO 204/9305 Reorganization of Units – Crete, Dec 44–Jan 45
WO 204/9422 Relief of Crete
WO 208/4208 Ger/PoW Interrogations Kreipe
WO 218–76 2 Commando, 1945 Jan.- Apr., July – Sept.
WO 218/97 1 Special Air Service (1 S.A.S. Regt) including 1 Special Boat Section. Raiding Forces…
WO 218/108 HQ Raiding Forces
WO 218/112 SBS
WO 309-1722 Kreipe Heinrich
WO 373/46 – Special Operations and Escapes: 24 Feb 1942–4 Jan 1945 Mediterranean: 5 Oct 1944–4 Oct 1945. Combined Operations (St Nazaire): 5 July 1945.
WO 373/78/389 Recommendation for Award for Hamson, Dennis Harry Rank: Captain
WO 373/98/713 Recommendation for Award for Hamson, Dennis Harry Otho Rank: Temporary Major
WO 374/47 Recommendarion for VC, Anders Lassen

SAS Regimental Archive, London
Sutherland, David: Scrapbook.
Mike Langley's Archive
Dismore, Leonard H.: *Dragon he be Strong Ju-Ju! (Some Reminiscences of a Private Army)*, undated.
Jellicoe, George: Report on Rodell.
Dr. Ferris: Report.

Liddel Hart Centre for Military Archives, King's College, London
Dobrski 13
Woodhouse 2–5

Imperial War Museum, London
Private Papers of Major D J Ciclitira
Special Operations Executive Operation Postmaster Preparations, Major C V Clarke Collection, IWM, kat. nr. MGH 4321.
Private Papers of Colonel J N Lapraik DSO OBE MC, Documents.16249
Private Papers of Major General D L Lloyd-Owen CB DSO OBE MC at the IWM
Milner-Barry Manuscript (MS): Diary
Milner-Barry Typescript (TS): The Unrepentant Hedonist
Private Papers of F C Perkins
Private Papers of Major L E Prout, Box 09/40/1, Documents 17255
Smith, I.C.D.: Private Papers.
Private papers of Mrs A M Street, Box 95/34/1, Documents 6433.

National Museum of the Royal Navy, Portsmouth
Operation Hawthorn, various documents concerning Operation Hawthorn, including Reports etc by George Jellicoe.

Wiener Library, London
Waldheim Collection, 646

Bundesarchiv, Militärarchiv, Freiburg
PERS 6/252023 Kreipe
PERS 6-300062 Kreipe
RH 19-VII/27 Oberkommando der Heeresgruppe E (Oberbefehlshaber Südost)
RH 19-XI/11 Oberbefehlshaber Heeresgruppe F
RH 24-68/16 Sonderstab F, Anlagen zu KTB Juli-Dezember 1943
RH 26-22-79 22. Infanteriedivision, Abteilung Ic
RH 26-22-80 22. Infanteriedivision, Abteilung Ic
RH 26-320/3 320. Infanteriedivision, KTB, 1.12.1942–31.12.1942.
RH 26-162/64 162. Infanterie Division
RH 26-1007/2 Sturmdivision Rhodos, Abteilung 1a, KTB Nr. 2, 1. Juli – 31. Dezember 1943
RH 26-1007/5 Sturmdivision Rhodos, Abteilung 1a, Anlagen zum KTB, 30. August–30. September 1943
RH 26-1007/6 Sturmdivision Rhodos, Abteilung 1a, Anlagen zum KTB, Oktober 1943
RH 26-1007/7 Sturmdivision Rhodos, Abteilung 1c, Anlagen zum KTB, 1. November–15. November 1943
RH 26-1007/12 Sturmdivision Rhodos, KTB Nr. 3 (Rekonstruktion durch den früheren Kriegstagebuch-Führer, Lt. Müller (Karl August) nach Unterlagen aus den Beständen des Militärarchivs), ohne Anlagen 1. Jan. – 30. Juni 1944
RH 26-1007/15 Sturmdivision Rhodos, Abteilung 1c, Anlagen zum KTB, Juli-August 1944
RH 26-1007/25 Kommandant Ost-Ägäis, Abteilung 1c, Tätigkeitsberichte, 1. Juli-15. September 1944
RH 49/662 Materialsammlung zur Geschichte der „Brandenburger"
RL 7-602 Luftwaffenkommando Südost, Richtlinien für Bau und Führung von Flugplätzen

RM 7/1417 1 SKL Räumung Ägäis – Operationsgruppen – Ägäis
RM 7/1418 1 SKL Räumung Ägäis, Aug 44–Jan 45
RH 34/318 Tagebuch der Ortskommandantur I/921
RM 35-III/57 Marinegruppenkommando Süd, KTB, 1.-15. Juli 1943
RM 35-III-58 Marinegruppenkommando Süd, KTB, 16.-31. Juli 1944
RM 35-III/63 Marinegruppenkommando Süd, KTB, 1.-15. Oktober 1944
RM 35-III/65 Marinegruppenkommando Süd, KTB, 1.-15. November 1944
RM 35-III/66 Marinegruppenkommando Süd, KTB, 16.-28. November 1943
RM 35-III/75 Marinegruppenkommando Süd, KTB, 16.-31. März 1944
RM 35-III/76 Marinegruppenkommando Süd, KTB, 1.-15. April 1944
RM 35-III/77 Marinegruppenkommando Süd, KTB, 16.-30. April 1944
RM 35-III/91 Marinegruppenkommando Süd, KTB, 1.-15. September 1944
RM 35-III/92 Marinegruppenkommando Süd, KTB, 16.-30. September 1944
RM 35-III/95 Marinegruppenkommando Süd, KTB, 1.-15. Oktober 1944
RM 35-III/96 Marinegruppenkommando Süd, KTB, 16.-31. Oktober 1944
RM 35-III/171 Marinegruppenkommando Süd, Eigene Kommandounternehmen und Erkundungen
RM 35-IV/75
RM 45-V/155 Kommandant der Seeverteidigung Dodekanes, KTB, Januar-Juni 1944
RW 5/244 Chef der Sicherheitspolizei und des SD/IV A2a an Amt M (Oberst Hansen): Kommandounternehmen (Führerbefehl vom 18. Oktober 1942)
RW 5/502 Angelegenheiten der Sicherheitspolizei – Behandlung Angehöriger von Kommandounternehmen Juni und November 1944
RW 49/97 Amt Ausland/Abwehr Kanalinseln 1942–44
RW 49/662 Div. Brandenburg

Historical Archive of Crete, Chania
German Occupation Archive

Italian Sources
Cavallari, Maria Luisa Caporali: *Relazione sugli avvenimenti a Simi…*, 10.11.1943.
Comando della Piazza di Rodi, Diramazione No 5, No 1/5787/S di prot. P.M. 550 li, 2 Agosto 1943 = OGGETTO: Notizie sullo Special Boat Service Britannico, kopi hos forf.

Unpublished sources
Andersen, K.A.E.: *Fra min tid på Bækkeskov*, unpubl. memoirs, 2010.
Christiansen, Ejnar: 'Lundby High School', unpubl. manuskripter, e-mail, 26.08.09.
Christiansen, N.S. (Cabin boy of *Eleonora Mærsk*): *Beretning*.
Hansson, Nicolai (2007): *Danskere i allieret krigstjeneste under Anden Verdenskrig*. MA thesis, Historisk Institut. Aarhus Universitet, February 2007. (Copy at Museet for Danmarks Frihedskamp, Copenhagen).
Hollingworth, R.C. (1947): *Beretning afgivet af Commander R.C. Hollingworth, Chef for den danske Sektion af 'S.O.E.' 1940–45*, dictated to the Danish historian Jørgen Hæstrup, revised, expanded and annotated by Hollingworth. (Danish Resistance Museum).
Holmes, Richard 'Dick' (n.d.): The Saga of Captain 'G'
Lang, C.A. (second mate of *Eleonora Mærsk*): *Dagbog* (Diary).
Conversations, interviews, correspondence etc.
Bellini, Nazareno: interview by author, Comacchio, 9 April 2002.
Bernstorff-Gyldensteen, Bente: conversations with author.
Branth, Ellen: conversation with Anders Sandberg, 2008.
Evison, Mariann Fines: e-mail correspondence with author, June 2015.
Field, Philippa (née Jeffers), e-mail corr., 2013–2020.
Folegatti, Vincenzino, e-mail, 16 July 2020.
Hancock, Hank: interview by Mike Langley
Holmes, Richard 'Dick': interview by Anders Sandberg, 2009.
Holmes, Richard 'Dick': letter to Iain Farmer, February/March 2008.

Howe, Stanley: interview by Mike Langley 1985.
Jellicoe, Nicholas: conversation with author, 26 June 2017.
Jessien: interview by Anders Sandberg, 2008.
Nasmit, Jan: interview by Mike Langley.
Ogden-Smith: interview by Mike Langley.
Perkins, Bob: E-mail to author: 25 and 26 February 2010.
Savidis, Mary (2001): letter to Bente Bernstorff-Gyldensteen.
Smith, Ken: interview by author, Comacchio, 9 April 2002.
Tomasi, Ettore: interview by M. Paiola, 2002.

Mike Langley used much of the material from his interviews in his book on Anders Lassen. Langley quoted his sources very faithfully, but nevertheless I have, as far as possible, used the original transcripts of his interviews which, together with Langley's other research material concerning Lassen is preserved on tape and paper in the Mike Langley Archive at the SAS Regimental Archive.

Index

Names, places, etc.
Aalborg, 334
Abadan, 23, 25–6, 38
Abbots Langley, 59
Achnacarry, 138
Aden, 7, 19, 23
Adriatic coast and sea, 217, 255, 288, 297, 300, 303, 306, 310, 315, 327–8
Aegean Sea and Islands, 63–4, 175, 177–9, 181–7, 189–91, 193–5, 197, 199, 201, 203, 205, 207–209, 211, 213, 215–23, 225, 227, 229–33, 235, 237, 239, 241, 243–4, 247, 249, 252–3, 255–6, 258, 260–2, 277, 287, 296–7, 324, 332, 338
Aegina, 269–70, 272–3
Agios Giannis, 161
Agios Nektarios, 162
Agios Savvas, 156
Agosta, 316–19
Agrelia, 194
Ahlefeldt-Laurvig-Bille, Gregers, 4
Alanbrooke *see* Brooke, Alan
Albania, 44, 153, 275–6, 293, 302, notes 235, 267
Alderney, 123–4
Aleca, 226
Aleppo, 214, note 385
Alexakis, Andonis, 159
Alexakis, Manolis, 158–9
Alexander II, 248
Alexandria, 63–5, 140, 142, 148, 154, 178, 220, 223–4, 226, 260, 273, 332
Algeria, 173
Algiers, 145
Alimnia, 191, 194–5, 227–30, 240, 249, notes 421, 427
Alinda Bay, 207–208
Amiens, 3
Amorgos, 227, 241
Ancona, 327
Anders Lassen Foundation, 334
Anders Lassen VC., 332
Anders Lassen, Sømand og Soldat – Beretninger samlet af hans Moder, 332
Anderson, Desmond, 188

Anderson Manor, 110–12, 114, 136, 139, note 135
Andreas, note 332
Androulakis, Giannis, 155–7
Ankara, 211, 221–2, note 379
Anson, Peter, 93, 94
Antelope Hotel, 78, 85, 114
Antikythera, 264, 272
Antimachia, 187, 196
Antonescu, Ion, 256
Antwerp, 7, 17–18
Anydros, 232–3, 239
Apayina, 157
A.P. Møller, 12, 15, 25–7, 29, 38
Apoini, 156–7, 161, 163–4
Appleyard, Ian, 76
Appleyard, John Ernest, 76
Appleyard, John Geoffrey, 61, 76–9, 84–5, 87–9, 92–4, 97–8, 105, 109, 110–11, 114, 123–33, 136, 139, 143, 145
Appleyard, Joyce, 76
Araxos, 267
Arctic, 177
Argenta, 304, 306, 310–11, 315, 318–19, 325–7, 334, 336, 340
Argenta Gap War Cemetery, 334
Arisaig House, 59–60, 67, 69–71, 83, 131, 162
Arkoi, 228
Armenians, 216
Arne peninsula, 78
Art of Guerrilla Warfare, The, 14
Arvand, 23
Aslanis, Giannis, 157–8
Aslanis, Nikolaos, 157
Aspronisi, 233
Astypalaia, 179, 217, 227
Athens, 64, 229–30, 233–4, 247, 264, 267–9, 272–6, 284–7, 289, 291, 298–300, 336, 338, note 458, 518
Athens bay, 267–9
Atlantic Wall, 109, 121
Atlit, x, 148–51, 153–4, 169, 213–15, 250
Auchinleck, Claude, 64–5
Australia, 19, 23, 78

Austria, 152, 256, 327, notes 236, 427
Axel, Prince, 6, 9, 11
Aymand, note 210
Azerbaijan, 310
Azores, 88
Azzib, 148, 182, 215–16, 220, 223

Badoglio, Pietro, 175, 182
Bækkeskov, 1, 3–6, 11, 15, 86, 112, 334, 340
Bahrain, 19, 20, 25–9
Bairaman or Bairamian, interpreter, 196, 203
Baird, Brigadier, 211
Baker Street, 51
Baker, Arthur 'Pop', 78, 85
Baleine Bay, 129
Balisu Bay, 230–2
Balkans, 63, 153, 177, 183, 217, 230, 261, 288–9, 296, notes 174, 504
Bally, Max, 274
Balsillie, Keith, 230, 234, 236–7, 267
Bando, 326
Bandouvas, 299, note 534
Bandouvas, Giannis, 159–60, 291
Bandouvas, Manolis, 291, 299
Bangkok, 7
Barbaiannis, 232
Barbour, Private, note 577
Bardia, 63, 155–6
Barfleur, 116–17, 125, 127
Bari, 182, 243, 255, 260, 272–3, 288, 293, 300, 302, 306, 328, 330
Barker, Lieutenant, LRDG, 279
Barker-Benfield, Karl Vere, 299–301, note 553
Barkham, Captain, 295
Bastia, 304, 306, 326
Bathurst, 93
Bayeux, 125
Beagley, Sergeant, 168
Beaulieu, 55
Behl, Johannes, 148
Beirut, 152, 178, 182, 220, 226–7
Belgian Congo, 105, note 235
Belgrade, 287
Bennike, Arne, 17, 25, 35
Benthack, Hans-Georg, 287, 294, 302, note 527
Benyon-Tinker, W.E, 220
Bere Regis, 114
Bernard, Major, 294
Bimrose, Charles, 201, 267, 291, 294, 298–9, 302, 307, 328–9
Biscay, 18
Black Sea, 177, 218
Blacker bombard, 82, 339
Blagdon, Major, 203

Blandford Forum, 110
Bleyer, August, 133
Blixen, Karen, 3
Blyth, Bill, 148, 228–9, 230, 240
Bodrum, 222
Boer War, 33, 40
Boldrini, Arrigo 'Büow', 315
Bologna, 303–304, 306, 327
Borneo, 23
Boscoforte, 310, 315–16, 318
Boulogne, Boulogne-sur-Mer, 39, 41
Bourdillon, Bernard Henry, 90, 95, 102
Bourne, Allan, 40, 42
Bourne, Frederick 'Freddie' William Parnall, 116–17, 123, 125–7, 131–2
Bournemouth, 80, 114–15, 125
Bramley, 76
Branth, Ellen *see* Karsten, Ellen
Bräuer, Bruno, 243–4, note 445
Brazil, xii, 24
Brenner, 152, 304, 327–8
Brindisi, 181
Brittany, 75, 137–8
Brixham, 75, 77
Brockhall, 54, 57, 59
Brooke, Alan, 144, 175, 187
Bruhn, Carl Johan, 58–60
Bruneval, 108
Bucharest, 14, 256
Budrio, 303–306
Bulgaria, 64, 197, 242, 256, 261, 276, 279–80, 302, notes 491, 504
Burhou, 124
Burton, John, 125, 127, note 210
Bury Street, 115
Bury, Robert, 264, note 476
Bussche-Streithorst, Axel von dem, 3, 11–12, 113, note 22
Bussche-Streithorst, Cuno von dem, 3, 11–12, 113

Caesar, 103, note 174
Caesar, Gaius Julius, 288
Cairo, 65, 140, 142, 145, 148, 153, 159, 163, 166, 168, 171, 182, 184, 201, 203, 211, 215, 218, 224–5, 236, 243, 279, 284, 288, 295–6, 300, notes 235, 307, 427, 542
Cala Gonone, 173
Calais, 109
Caldirolo, 312, 315–19, 323
Cambridge, 21, 76, 100, 140
Cameroon, 92
Campioni, Inigo, 182–5, note 313
Campo Imperatore, 175
Canada, 121
Canale Valletta, 310, 312–13, 329

Canea *see* Chania
Cap Barfleur, 116–17, 125, 127
Cape St. Vincent, 88
Cape Town, 23, 24, 38, 43–4, 105
Cape Verde, 82, 88, 90
Carl, Swedish Prince, 74
Carlsen, Kristine, 29
Carmel, Mount, 148–9
Carmichael, Hoagy, 92
Casablanca, 144
Case, Captain, 329–30
Caserta, 263, 275, 328
Castelrosso, 179, 187, 202
  see also Kastellorizo
Casulli 223, *probably* Kasoulis
Cator, H.J., 148
Caucasus, 152
Cavalieri, Mario Foschini, 317, 320, 323
Cavalieri, Massimo, 340
Cavallari, Maria Luisa Caporali, 189
Cedars, 152, 220
Cephalonia, 64
Çeşme, 194
Ceylon, 29
Chalkias, K., 245
Chalkidiki, 283
Chamberlain, Neville, 35
Chamonix, 21
Chania, 288, 195, note 445
Channel (English), Channel Coast, Channel Islands, 16–18, 39, 41, 87, 92, 109, 116, 119, 121–3, 127, 132, 154, 217
Chapman, Freddy Spencer, 20
Cherbourg Peninsula, 117, 137, 144
Chevalier, Harold Gordon, 209
Chico, 92
China, 13, note 539
Chios, 193–4
Chnarakis, Grigoris, 163
Chostos, 158
Christ College, 100
Christian X, 6, 58, 74, 308
Christiana Islands, 234, 238
Christiansen, S.N., 27, 35
Chrysos, Stylianos, 245
Church, Squadron Leader, 301, note 556
Churchill, Randolph, 21, 62, 140
Churchill, Winston S., 35, 39, 40–2, 51, 103, 108, 122, 137, 140, 144, 153, 177–8, 187, 205, 261, note 539
Ciclitira, D.J., 294, note 542–3
Clark, Mark, 303, 306, note 558
Clarke, 203–204
Clarke, Captain, 249
Clarke, C.V., 81

Clarke, Dudley Wrangel, 39–41, 65–6, 153, 173
Clynes, Charles Maurice, 286, 299, 301–302
Coats, J.S., 20–1, 32
Cohen, G., 295
Colditz, note 539
Cole, Lieutenant, 224
Colle Isarco, 327
Collin, G, *see* Cohen, G.
Colombo, 7, 25, 29, 35–7, note 64
Comacchio, Lake and town, xi, 304–306, 309–11, 314–20, 323–6, 332, 334, 336, 340, notes 568, 577–8
Comce, 221
Commando Order, 135, 229, notes 210, 217, 427
Como, Lake, 327
Cona dam, 320
Conby, 223
Connan, Anne, 58
Consandolo, 326
Constantinople, note 267
Constitution Square, 268
Cooper, Artemis, 243
Copenhagen, 7, 11, 74, 113, 327, 332, 334, 353
Corfu, 64, note 518
Corinth, 267
Cornthwaite, Private, 299, 302
Corradini, Corrado, 190, 192–3
Corto Maltese – Mū, 334
Cotentin, 125
Courtney, Geoffrey, 173
Courtney, Roger, 62, 64, 140, 173–4
Crankshaw, Tony, 329
Cree, 208
Cresta Run, 21
Crete, 63–4, 141, 152–72, 177–8, 186, 196, 217, 228, 242–4, 259, 261, 267, 287–302, 308, 332–4, notes 267, 292, 445, 476
  Free Crete, 289, 297–8, 300
Creux, 131, 133
Croatia, 261, 268, 306
Crotty, Bombardier, 328, notes 577, 583
Crouch, Freddie, 319–20, 323–4, 334, 336, note 577
Cuillin Sound, 67
Cumberland, 114
Curaçao, 16–7
Cyclades, 230, 232, 241, 244
Cyprus, 178, 184, 188, 191, 194, 202–203, 221, 247

D'Arcy, Mick, 188, 241, 223, 247
Daiyir, 26–8

Dakar, 82, 88, 90
Dalmatia, 288, 306, 327–8
Dalton, Hugh, 52
Dane, Estrid, 3, 112, 115
Dane, Peter, 112, 115
Danzig, 17
Dardanelles, 193
Dartmouth, 87
De Gaulle, Charles, 102
de la Billière, Peter, 132
Delentas, Antonis, 246
Denmark, x, xii, 25, 27–8, 38, 48–9, 52, 58, 74, 80–1, 113, 179–80, 225, 241–2, 286, 327, 331–6
Deremen, 221–2, 224
Derrible Bay, 129
Desgrange, André, 78, 87, 98, 111, 125, 127, note 210
Devon, 75, 77, 114, 139
Diamantopoulos, George, 284
Dida *see* Kristine Carlsen
Dieppe, 109, 121–2, 134–5
Dimitri, 274
Dinesen, Thomas, 3
Dismore, Leonard H., 105–106
Distinguished Conduct Medal, 259
Dixcart Bay, 129
Dixcart Hotel, 131–3, 135
Djibouti, 23
Dobrski, Julia *see* Dolbey
Dodecanese, 44, 64, 177, 205, 232
Dodson, D.S.L., 278–9, 281–2, 284
Dog Tom, 309
Dolbey, Major (Julian Dobrski), 182–4
Dorchester, 138
Doundoulakis, Helias, note 496
Dracunda, 190
Dramia, 294
Drozitis, 159
Dubno, note 22
Duboki, 257
Dubrovnik, 256
Duckett, Miss, 135
Dudgeon, Patrick Laurence, 128, 173
Dunbabin, Thomas J., 243–4, 288, 290, 295
Dunkirk, 7, 39, 76, 207, 212
Durban, 24, 38
Durnford-Slater, John, 41
Dutch West Indies, 16
Duurlo, Ebba, 286
Duurlo, Sven Peter, 286
Dyonisios, 295

EAC *see* East Asiatic Company
East Asiatic Company, 6–7, 9, 11, 15, 37
Eastern Front, 22, 109, 113, 122, 153, note 22
Eddie's Bar, 286
Eden, Anthony, 103
Egypt, 61, 63, 142, 145–6, 156, 194, 226, 239, 260, 359
Eisenhower, Dwight D., 145, 177, 181
El Alamein, 140, 142
En dansk soldat, Major Anders Lassen, V.C., M.C., 333
Eleusis, 268
Eliotis, Dimitri, 158–9
Elsinore, 74
Emborio, 238
Enigma, 14
Epanomi, 278
Epirus, note 518
Episkopi, 291
Equatorial Guinea, 91
Esslinger, Heinrich, 133
Estonia, 287
Étaples, 39
Eton, 329
European Hospital, Lagos, 104
Evangelismos, 159
Evison, Ernest, 79, 87, 98
Exmoor, 114

Fairbairn, William, 33–4, 69–70
Fakse Ladeplads, 334
Faliron, 274, 276
Falmouth, 16
Famagusta, 221
Fanizza, Lieutenant Colonel, 184
Faroe Islands, 67
Farrant, Ralph, 32
Felmy, Helmuth, 165
Fermor, Patrick Leigh, 157, 167, 242–3, 288, notes 267, 293, 444
Fernando Po, 85, 91–2, 95–9, 101–104, note 173
Ferrara, 303–304, 306, 310
Ferris, Leslie, 197, 201
Field, Philippa, 105, 338
Fielding, Sean, 243
Filedem, Note 267
Filibusters, 333
Finland and Finnish Winter War, xii, 20–2, 24, 31, 74, 242, 287
Fiorana, 325
Fira, 233–4, 236–7
Firth of Forth, 32
Fitzroy Tavern, 115
Fleves, 269, 273
Flint, Jimmy, 129–30
Flore, 54
Florina, 275
Folegatti, Giuseppe, 313, 315, note 573

Foot, M.R.D., 133
Forcados, 102
Forster, Eric, 129
Fort William, 33
Fosecchie, 320
Fourni, 207
Fox, SBS officer, 328
Franck, Børge, 79–80, 85, 98, 308
Franck, Louis, 90–1, 97
Frandsen, A.G., 49
Fraser, Simon, Lord Lovat, 32–3
Frede, 9
Frederik, HRH Crown Prince, 334, 336
Free Crete, 289, 297–8, 300
Free French, 102, 141, 148
Freetown, 82, 87–9, 97–8, 106, 111
French Guinea, 92
Fresemann, First Lieutenant, 198–201
Fricke, Kurt, 241
Frogman Corps, 334, 336
Funen, 5

Gambia, 93
Gambut, 245
Garda, Lake, 182
Gargano Peninsula, 255, 328
Gavin, James 'Jim', 32
Gazala, 140
Geneva Convention, 134
Georg, Prince, 8
George II, King of Greece, 63, 290
Georgia, 310
Georgios, Nereanos, note 279
Georgioupolis, 287, 294, 297
Giannotti, Captain, 183
Gibraltar, 7, 18, 141–2
Glanville, Blake, 77–8, 80
Glaser, Lieutenant, 229
Glenfinnan Monument, 334
Glyfa, 245
Godden, B. (W 51), 103, note 173
Gorgopotamos, note 374
Gorizia, 304
Gossensass, 327
Gothic Line, 303
Gran Sasso, 175
Grayson, Major, 72
Great Bitter Lake, 140
Greaves, Sidney, 155, 160–3, 165, 168, 172, note 281
Grech, Tony, 209
Green, Freddie, 307, 320, 324, notes 577, 580
Green, Maurice, 219
Greenland, 8, 79
Greenlands, 112

Groman, Second Lieutenant, 294–5
Groppi's Restaurant, 171–2
Gryllakis, Manolis, 246–7
Gubbins, Colin McVean, 13–14, 31–2, 52, 73, 78, 82, 85, 90, 109–10, 134
Guernsey, 41, 42, 127, 133, 144
Guernsey Evening Star, 130
Guise, C.A.L. (W 10), 96, 98, 102
Gulluk, 221
Gumley Hall *see* Special School (Gumley Hall)
Gümüslük, 209
Gurna, 209
Gwynne, John, 138–9
Gyparis, Pavlos, 198

Haakon VII, King of Norway, 31
Haifa, 141, 148, 178, 182, 188, 214, 293, note 539
Halck, Jørgen, 225–6, 333, note 408
Halki, 179, 191–2, 194–5, 223–4, 228–30, note 421
Hall, H.R., 209
Hall, Tony, 111, 114, 125–7, note 210
Hambleden, Patricia Smith, Viscountess, 112, 115, 121, 145
Hambleden, William Smith, Viscount, 112, 115
Hamburg, 15–17, 36
Hamilton-Hill, David, 270–2
Hammer, Kjeld Mogens Aage, 48–9, 53–5
Hamson, Dennis, 211–12, note 374
Hampshire, 55
Hanau, Juliua (Caesar), note 174
Hancock, Hank, 188, 207, 244, 246, 281, note 460
Handfast Point, 87
Hansen, Colonel, note 217
Hansen, Curt Carlis, 80
Harare, 191
Harris, Jack, 235, 249
Harrow, 79
Haslev, 336
Haslev High School, 5
Hastings, Stephen, 152, note 531
Hayes, Graham, 78–9, 85, 88, 92, 94, 98, 111, 123–7, 338, note 210
Hellings, 111, 125, 127, note 210
Helwan, ix, 224–5
Helsingborg, 25
Henderson, Patsy, 188, 223, 234, 236, 244, 247
Henley-on-Thames, 112
Henshaw, J.C., 256–7, 259, 274, 280–1, 284, 291, 294, note 513
Heraklion, 141, 154–5, 157, 164, 166, 171–2, 244, 287–94, 297–301, note 293

Hereford, 334
Herlufsholm, 4–6, 334
Herm, 144
Hertfordshire, 59
Hesse, German Lieutenant, 234, 237
Heyman, Brigadier, 182
Hitler, Adolf, 109, 121, 134–5, 185, 229, 287, 303, note 22
Hoch, Ján Ludvik (Ian Robert Maxwell), 111
Hoegh-Guldberg, Fritz Emmerich, 113
Hoffmann, Else, ix, 224–5
Hoffmann, Vagn, ix, 224–5
Hog's Back, 129–30
Holland, J.F.C., 13, 32
Holland America Line, 87
Hollingworth, Ralph C., 50, 52–3, 59, 111
Holmegård, 334
Holmes, Richard 'Dick', 72, 169, 172, 209, 214, 251–2, 257, 259, 264, 266
Hooper, Keith, 298
Hortet, note 210
Hortiatis, 282
Hotel Excelsior, 307
Hotel Grande Bretagne, 268, 286
Hotel Saint Georges, 182
How to Use High Explosives, 14
Høvdingsgaard, 1, 4
Howard, Francis, 111, 123, 125–7
Hube, Hans-Valentin, 174
Hughes, Stanley Raymond, 321, 323–4, 334, 336, note 577
Hummer, Able Seaman, 36
Hungary, 261, note 235
Hunter, note 476
Hunter, Private, note 577
Hunter, Tom, 313, 329, 334
Hydra, 274

I streng fortrolighed, note 408
Iatrides, John O., 283
Icaria, 207, 230, 247
Imerovigli, 234, 237
Imperial War Museum, 334
India, 23, 177–8
Indian Ocean, 38
Ingeborg, Princess, 74
Inverailort House, 33
Invergowrie, 334
Inverlair, 56
Inverness-shire, 55–6, 67
Ios, 230, 241, note 450
IRA, 13
Iraklion, *see* Heraklion
Iran, 26
Iraq, 151

Isbrandtsen, Hans, 25, 27–8
Ismolco, 25–7
Israel, 334
Istanbul, 212
Italian East Africa, 174
Italy,
    Kingdom of Italy declares war on Germany, 182
    Social Republic of Italy (RSI), 182, note 527
    War with Turkey in 1912, 44
Iversen, Werner Michael, 49–50, 53–4, 57–60, 72–3, 138
Ivory Coast, 104
Izmir, 175, 193, 212

Jaeger Corps, 334, 336
Jarrell, Porter, 195, 209, 244, 247, 253
Jeffers, H.H., 100, 104
Jellicoe, George, x, 21, 62, 64, 140–2, 147–50, 153, 181–4, 186–7, 205, 208–10, 221, 226, 255, 260, 263, 267–9, 273, 275, 278, 284, 293, 296, 331, 336, notes 300, 313–14, 371, 478, 481, 539
Jellicoe, John, 21
Jellicoe, Nicholas, 339
Jensen, P.B., 260
Jersey, 41, 127
John, interpreter, 234
John Holt & Co., 96
Jones, Ray W., 155, 160–7, 172, 230, notes 279, 281
Jordan, 65
Jørgen, sailor on *Eleonora Mærsk*, 43
Jørgensen, Alfred, 79, 81, 85, 87, 98
Just, Corporal, 133

Kabrit, 140, 146–8
Kalamaki, 273
Kalithea, 193
Kalymnos, 188, 207–208, 227
Karasovici, 256
Kardamyli, note 267
Karfopoulos, Charis, 158
Karpathos, 177–9, 217, 228
Karsten, Ellen (Ellen Branth), 115, 145–6, 305
Karsten, Elli, 115
Karsten, Henning, 115
Karsten, Henrik O., 305–306
Karyotakis, Spyridon, 165
Kasos, 179, 217
Kasoulis, Stefan M., 209, 223, 230, 233–5, 238, 249
Kastelli, Kastelli Pediada, 14, 154–5, 157–9, 163–6, 168, 172, 230, 291, 334

Kastellorizo, 179, 184–5, 187–8, 191, 198, 202, 213, 221, 229, notes 314, 421
Katsikas, Lieutenant, 223
Katsounas, 156
Kavala, 279–80
Kefalos (Leros), 196–7
Kefalos (Paros), 245, 247
Keir, xi, 32
Kemp, Peter, 32–3, 51, 111, 114, 123–4, 133, 137–9, 144–5, note 235
Kenyon, Colonel, 196
Kesselring, Albert, 174
Kesterton, Sergeant, 182–4
Keyes, Roger, 42, 108
Kiervasili, 221
Kingston, Sergeant, 235–7, 239, 249
Kioste, 194
Kirk, Geoffrey, 238–9, 241, notes 434, 437
Klagenfurt, 329
Kleemann, Ulrich, 184–5, 198, note 313
Klepp, Ernst, note 527
Klotz, Corporal, 133
Knudsen, Danish consul, 25, 35
Knudsen, Svend Ove Bent, 308
Koinsky racconta...due o tre cose che so di loro, 334
Kokkinos *see* Tzouanakis, Giorgis
Kongsøre, 334
Korçë, 276
Kos, 177–9, 185–8, 191–2, 194, 196–7, 205, 207–208, 217, 221, 261, 287
Koumasa 156
Kozani, 275
Kreipe, Heinrich, 242–4, notes 442, 444, 476
Kriezotou Street, 283
Kritsotakis, Manolis, 160
Kurds, 216
Kusadasi, 211, 213–14, note 379
Kythera, 263–4, 269

L'Agnese va a morire, note 567
La Jaspellerie, 130
La Maddalena, 175
La Spezia, 303–306
Lagos, 82, 89–90, 92, 95, 97–102, 104, 106
La Jaspellerie, 130
Lake, Peter Ivan (W 53), 103, note 173
Lake Comacchio *see* Comacchio
Lamonby, Kenneth, 154–7, 164–71
Lang, C.A., 27–9, 37, 43
Lange, Werner, 241–2
Langley, Mike, 132, 240, 381, note 437
Langton, Tom, 148, 151
Laos, note 235
Lapraik, J. (Ian) Neilson, 151, 182, 188–92, 194–5, 198–9, 201, 203, 207, 222, 255, notes 319, 320

Lassen, Anders,
  Alcohol, 16, 23, 36, 43, 46, 60, 150, 157
  Amphetamine, 234, 254, 272
  Benzedrine *see* amphetamine
  Bow and arrow, 83–4, 114, 131
  Character, temper, viii, 5–6, 11, 15, 18, 36, 43, 45, 59–60, 73, 79, 92, 138, 150, 169, 180, 189, 199, 208, 212, 214, 220–1, 225–6, 241, 245–6, 249, 252–4, 259–60, 264, 271, 278, 281, 286, 289–90, 293–6, notes 531, 577
  Cover name, 145
  Danes, Denmark, 179–80, 225, 293, 307
  Death, 321–2
  Decorations, viii, 143, 145, 171–2, 180, 200, 207–208
  Discipline, 79, 150, 214, 252, 264, 271, 286, 311
  Dog, 214, 220, 224, 293, 308–309
  Dress, 226, 301
  Driving, 152, 274, 278, 289, note 531
  Family, childhood, background, 1–6, 11, 16, 57, 73, 111–12, 128, 327, 331–2
  Fighting, 18, 23, 36, 80, 199, note 437
  Friends, 11, 15, 80–1, 112, 128, 145, 208, 127–8, 188, 224–6, 230, 252–3, 290, 293, 296
  Germans, 106, 120–1, 200, 220–1, 225, 241, 260, 294, note 437
  Greeks, 157, 209, 241, 296
  Health, 58–9, 80, 194–5, 199, 220, 343
  Hospitalized, 59, 180, 188, 220, 254, 224
  Hunting, 2, 9, 71, 106, 112, 114
  Killing, 81, 120–1, 131, 133–4, 162, 180, 199–200, 209, 220–1, 226, 230, 241, 260, notes 437, 513
  Knife, 92, 241, note 437
  Languages, accent, 16, 57, 73, 83, 161, 271
  Leadership, x, 212–13, 240, 249, 252, 258–60, 264, 271, 282, 296, 307–308, 311, 318, 320
  Looks, 221
  Money, xii, 17, 223, 231, 270, 285, 307
  Patriotism, viii, 25–8, 48–9, 54, 80–1, 225, 241
  Plans, aspirations, viii, xii, 9, 11, 22, 38, 48, 54, 286, 290, 307
  Rank, 104, 111, 188, 270, notes 232, 482
  Reputation, 71, 189, 246, 252, 260, 263, 272, 281
  Reward for capture, 226, note 408
  Sailor, xii, 7–19, 22–31, 35–8, 43–5, 85–8, 98–102, 124–5, 129, 314
  School, 4–6
  Shooting, 2, 79, 138

Index 389

State of mind, 83–4, 92, 127, 169, 181, 225, 253
Strength, stamina, speed, viii, 71, 152, 157, 199, 212, 245, 252, 320
Stress, 112, 169, 252–3, 272, 302
Superiors, 214, 249, 259, 270, 293, note 577
Tactics, 159, 199, 234, 240, 245, 258–9, 282–3, 285
Teeth, 36, 115, 227
Training, 111–12, 120, 37, 54–60, 67–111, 138, 151–2, 157, 240, 289, 308
Weapons, 231
Women, 36, 46, 125, 171, 214, 226–7, 274, 276, 290
Wounded, 194–5, 199, 224, 343
Lassen, Bente (Bente Bernstorff-Gyldensteen), 1, 11, 332, 339
Lassen, Emil Victor Schau, 1–6, 22, 74, 112, 332, 334
Lassen, Estrid *see* Estrid Dane
Lassen, Frants, 1, 2, 4–6, 9, 11, 22, 113, 121, 139, 143–4, note 236
Lassen, Jenny, 3, 112
Lassen, Suzanne Marie (née Raben-Levetzau), 1–3, 5–6, 16, 22, 30, 36, 74, 113, 132–3, 146, 331–4, 336, 341, notes 279, 524
Lassen Hoiuse, 334
Lassengården, 334
Lawrence, T.E., 13
Lawson, Andrew, 145
Laycock, Robert, 62–3, 331
Le Bar Alexis, 115
Le Havre, 108
Le Touquet, 41
Leavesden Hospital, 59
Lebanon, 151–2, 215, 220, 226
Leeds, 76
Lefka Ori, 287
Lefkes, 246
Lehniger, Richard (Leonard), 111, 127
Leicestershire, 72
Leonidas, 332
Leonard *see* Lehniger, Richard
Leros, 79, 179, 185–8, 190–1, 194, 203, 205–11, 214, 217–21, 260–1, 287, note 356
Les Casquets, 123–4
Les Moulins, 125
Levitha, 208–16
Liberia, 82, 90, 92–3
Libya, 63–4, 140–2, 147, 245
Lili Marlene, 307
Limassol, 184
Lindsay, Martin, 20

Lindsay, T.G., 54, 57–9
Lippett, Richard (W 25), 96–7
Lipsi, 179, 228, 363, note 450
Lipsos, 207–10
Lisbon, 113, 175
Lisso, 179
Little Sark, 129
Liverpool, 17, 106
Ljubjana Pass, 217
Lochailort, 33, 42, 67, 69, 70
Lodwick, John, 328, 333, note 595
Lofoten, 61, 134
Löhr, Alexander, 197
Lolland, 3
London, 31, 49, 50, 53–5, 59, 63, 74, 79, 112–15, 128, 145, 305
Longastrino, 325
Longovardas, 248
Loopy, 92
Loutra, 165
Lovat, Lord, 32, 33
Luhr, 97
Lukas, Michael, 193, 196
Lumley Beach, 89, 92, 95, 97
Lundby, 5, 6
Lunn, C.D.O., 6
Lussu, Emilio. 173, notes 301, 356
Luxembourg, 35
Lynmouth, 114

Macaskie, Frank, 268
Macbeth, 203–204
Macedonia, 285, note 489
Maclean, Fitzroy, x, 148, 150–1
Macpherson, note 476
La Maddalena, 175
Madeira, 88
Madrid, 66, 99, 102
Mærsk-Møller, C., 26–7, 29
Major Anders Lassen Medal for Valour, 336
Malaya, 49, 58, 97
Maleme, 141, 165, 287, 291
Mallaig, 33
Malta, 141–2, 178, 205, 330
Manchester, 55
Maniotopoulos (interpreter), 278
Mantzarides, 279
March-Phillipps, Gustavus Henry, 75–9, 81–2, 85, 88, 91, 92, 97–9, 102, 104–106, 109–12, 114, 116–19, 121, 123–8, 253
Marco, 78
Marcos, 207
Mariani, Francesco, 324, note 589
Maris, Miron, 156
Marmara, 245–6
Marmissa, 246

Maroulakis, Chrysanthos, 191, 227
Marpissa, 245, 247–8
Mascherpa, Luigi, 187, 206, 209
Mashonaland East, 191
Massa Carrara, 303
Massa Lombarda, 303
Mather, David Carol MacDonnell, 140
Maule, Henry, 283
Mavrikis, Jason, 278–80
Maxwell, Ian Robert *see* Hoch, Ján Ludvik
Mayfair, 115
Mayfield, Bryan, 32, 33
Mayne, Robert Blair 'Paddy', 148
MC *see* Military Cross
McLeod, Alec, 278–80
McLeod, RN 203
McCreery, Richard, 303–306, 329
Medcalfe, Private, note 577
Megalo Mikra, 277, 285
Megara, 271
Megathon, 271
Melbourne, 19, 20, 23, 26, 336
Memorial Cemetery at Ryvangen, 334, 336
Menate, 325
Menday, R.P., 316–17
Mention in Despatches, 152
Merenberg, Georg von, 248, note 448
Mern School, 4
Mersa Matruh, 154–5, 165, 171
Mersinjek, 239
Messina Strait, 181
Mexico, 16
Michael, King of Romania, 256
Michalis, note 267
Michie, Charles W., 95, note 173
Milan, 327
Military Cross, x, 13, 34, 78, 143, 145, 171–2, 200, 207–208, 226, 266, note 374
Military Medal, 172, 259, 266–7
Miller, J.D. 'Dusty', 44–6, 128, 253
Milner-Barry, Walter, 154, 197, 203, 223–4, 268, 275, 286, 289, 293, 327, notes 427, 531
Milos, 237, 287
Miri, 23
Mitford, Terence Bruce, 216
Modugno, 306–307
Moldavia, note 267
Møller, A.P., 12, 15, 38
Møller, Arnold Peter, 25–6
Møller, Børge, 46, 53, 60
Molloy, Esther, 145, note 240
Monopoli, 255, 327–30
Monte Sant'Angelo, 255, 288, 307, 309
Montgomery, Bernard Law, 288
Moosburg, 230

Most Secret (novel), 75, 82
Moukhtari, 159–60, 162
Moulton, Suzanne (Nina), 3
Mountbatten, Louis, 108–10, 136–7, 145
Muglia, 199–200
Mull, 151
Müller, Friedrich-Wilhelm, 209, 242–4, notes 292, 445
Munich, 217
Murajo, 202
Muravera, 173
Murray, H., 329
Museum of Danish Resistance, 334
Mussolini, Benito, 44, 175, 177, 182, 197, 327
Muus, Flemming, note 236
Mykonos, 230, 241

Nab Tower, 117, 127
Næstved, 15
Naples, 181, 329–30
Napoleon, 324
Narvik, 20
Nasmyth, Jan, 79, 85
Nathenas, Andreas, 299
Naxos, 230, 244, 248
Nazareth, 180
Nea Kameni, 233
Nea Potidaea, 278
Netherlands, 35, 40, 327
Nereanos, Georgios, note 279
New York, 25–6
New Zealand, 63, 332
Newcastle, 46, 48, 50, 53–4, 60, 87
Newmarket, 21
Nicholson, Jack, 155, 158, 160–3, 165, 168, 172, 209, 213, 223, 235–6, 238–40, 244, 247, 249, 259, notes 281, 437
Nicoto, 263
Nigeria, 82, 90, 92, 95, 98, 100, 104–105, 191, 289
Niko, 238
Nile, 62, 142
Nipiditos, 157–8, note 269
Nisyros, 179, 191, 198, 227, note 450
Nita, 226
Niven, David, 21
Normandy, 41, 78, 108, 125, 217, 244, 255, note 210
North Africa, 63–5, 77, 115, 122–3, 144–5, 153, 159, 177, 191, 242, note 260
North Sea, 17, 109
Northampton, 54
Northwest Highlands, 32, 42, 54
Norway, 20, 31–2, 35, 39, 45–6, 75, 80, 115, 122, 217, 225, 242, 332–3

Norway, Nevil Shute *see* Shute, Nevil
Nyhavn, 74, 113, 327

O'Brien-Twohig, Joseph Patrick, 268
O'Connor, Richard Nugent, 63
O'Kane, Patricia, 226
O'Reilly, Sean, 188, 223–4, 234–6, 240, 252–3, 321–3, note 577
Oban, 46
Occhipinti, Andrea, 190, 192
Ogden-Smith, Bruce, 128
Ogden-Smith, Colin, 124–5, 128, 139
Oh, Mabel, Darling Mabel, 327
Old Harry Rocks, 87
Olga, 226
Ollerup, Academy of Physical Education, 6, 8
Olokemeji, 90, 97–8, 105–107
Omaha Beach, 125
Opoczynski, Abraham *see* Orr, Adam
Organisation Todt, 120
Orr, Adam, 111, 123, 125, 127, note 210
Ortona a Mare, 181
Osborne, Lithgow, 38
Osborne, Lillie (Lila) (née Raben-Levetzau), 38
Oslo, 31, 332
Ostellato, 310, 315
Oswald, Peter, 133–4
Ottana, 174
Ottoman Empire, 44
Owen, David Lloyd, note 356
Oxford, 79
Oxland, Major, 292

Page, Miss, 135
Paignton, 139
Palestine, 40, 148, 226, 248, 260, note 385
Palia Kameni, 233
Panagia, 156
Pandeli Bay, 209
Pano, Poulies, 158
Panorama, 279, 281–2
Panormitis, 190–1, 198, 204, 227
Papadakis, General, 291
Papandreou, Georgios, 261, 263, 273
Paphos, 188
Paradisi *see* Villanova
Paris 21, note 210
Parker, Sergeant, 278–9
Paros, 230, 242, 244–8, 259, 281, note 448
Partisan Leader's Handbook, The, 13–14, 109
Partridge, Private, 240
Paterson, 328
Patmos, 179, 207, 227–8
Patras, 267, 269, note 542
Patterson, Ian, 267–8, 278

Pearl Harbor, 97
Pedersen, P. Juel, 18, 25, 26, 27–9, 35, 43
Pedi Bay, 198–200
Peloponnese, 64, 263, 267, 269–70, note 354
Perantinos, Dimitris, 246
Percival, Captain, 289
Perdika, 272
Perissa Monastery, 233, 238, 241
Perkins, Frank 'Buzz' Colbourn, 78–9, 85, 88–9, 92, 98, note 235
Perkins, Harold B., note 235
Persia, 151
Persian Gulf, xii, 19, 23, 25, 29, 177
Petersgaard, 113
Petit Dixcart, 130
Petougakis, Michaelis, 160
Petrakis, Georgios, 291
Petrakogiorgis *see* Petrakis, Georgios
Petsamo, 242
Peza, 164
Pinckney, Philip, 128–30, 132, 145–6, 149
Pipo, 214, 220, 224, 293, 308–309
Piraeus, 64, 267–9, 272–4, 276, 289
Piso Livadi, 247
Pittard, Frances, 130–1, 135
Plocice, 256
Po, River and Delta, 303–4, 306, 309, 317, 326
Po Plain, 306
Podias, Giannis, 291, 294, 296
Point Château, 129
Pointe de Barfleur, 117
Pointe de Fouli, 118
Poland, 13, 40, notes 210, 236
Polygyros, 279
Pomford, Doug, 189, 251
Pongo River, 92
Ponza, 175
Poole, 74, 77, 79–80, 88, 105, 110, 114, 334
Poros, 269–70, 272–3
Port Elizabeth, 38
Port en Bessin, 125
Port Said, 7, 18–19, 141
Port Sudan, 7
Port Tewfiq, 19
Portland, Portland Bill, 17, 110, 123–4, 128, 132
Porto Garibaldi, 310–11, 313, 315, 319–20, 326
Portolago Bay, 210
Portomaggiore, 325–6
Portsmouth, 19, 110, 116–17, 119, 127
Portugal and Portuguese colonies, 82, 88, 90, 92–3
Portuguese Guinea, 92
Poulies, 157–8, note 269

Powys, Fennimore, note 408
Pratt, Hugo, 334
Princess, Pub in Newcastle, 46
Pritchard, C.H.V., 277
Prodromos, 245–6
Prout, Leslie, 78–9, 87, 98, 146
Præstø Fjord, 334
Punta Furana, 173
Pyle, Ernie, 216, 287
Pyrenees, 6
Pyrialas, Theodor, 245

Quebec, 178
Queen Olga Avenue, 282–3

Raben-Levetzau, Frederik, 2
Raben-Levetzau, Lillie *see* Osborne, Lillie
Raben-Levetzau, Siegfried Victor, 6, 10, 15, 113
Raben-Levetzau, Suzanne Marie *see* Lassen, Suzanne
Raibosola, 320
Ramsey, Winston, 132
Ravenna, 303–306, 309, 312–13, 323, 325, note 577
Red Sea, 7
Redborn, Gunner, 132
Redfern, Alan. G., 190–1, 196, 202, 209, notes 330, 356
Reed, Howard, 260
Rees, Noel, 193–4, 211
Reeves, Signaller, 240
Rehe, Captain, 195, 223
Reichenheim, Peter *see* Dane, Peter
Reno River, 303, 310, 312, 318, 326
Rethymnon, 289, 298–9, 297
Reventlow, Eduard, 43, 74, 112, 145, 179–80
Rhodes, 63–4, 153, 160, 177–9, 182–6, 190–1, 193, 195, 197–200, 203–205, 217, 224, 228–30, 233, 242, 244, 261, 287, 295, 328, notes 313–14, 426
Rhodes (city), 183–5, 190, 198, 200
Rhodesia, 191
Rice, Digger, 208
Rigopoulos, Rigas, note 421
Rickards, C.J.M., 290, 297
Ride of the Valkyries, 312
Ringway, 55, 59, 114, 138
Ritchie, Neil, 65
Road to the Isles, 33
Roberts, Edward, 321, 323–4, 334, 336, note 577
Robinson, Muriel Lilian, 49
Robinson, Joseph Henry 'Tim', 129
Røder, H.C., 27
Romania, 177, 217, 256, 261, note 267
Rome, 181–2, 307–308, 328, 336, note 313

Rommel, Erwin, 63–4, 142
Rooney, Mickey, 137
Roosevelt, Franklin D., 144, 178, 205
Rosyth, 32
Rowe, Lieutenant, 164, 168, 172
Royal Hotel, 53, 59
Royal Victoria Patriotic School, 54, 139
Rufus, 2
Russel Quay, 78
Russell Square, 53
Russian Civil War, 13
Rye and Dry Club, 115

Sælen, Frithjof, 333
Saint-Jouin-Bruneval, 108
Saint-Nazaire, 109
Sainte-Honorine-des-Pertes, 125
Salamis, 268
Salerno, 181
Samaria, 302
Salonika, 284, *see also* Thessaloniki
Samos, 186–8, 190, 205, 209–14, 217, 220, 227, 261, 274, note 371, 379, 385, 421
San Menaio, 328
Sănătescu, Constantin, 256
Sandhurst, 21
Sange paa Rejsen, 333
Sant'Alberto, 318, 320, 323
Sant'Angelo *see* Monte Sant'Angelo
Sant'Antonio, 326
Santa Isabel, 91, 95–7, 99, 101–102
Santerno, 306
Santorini (Thira), 213, 230–41, 249, 258–9, 308, notes 430, 434, 460
Sarakino, 161
Sardinia, 153–4, 172–5, 217, 226
Saria, 217, 230
Sark, 42, 127–32, 134–5, 155, 338
Saronikos, 264
Scagliocca, 313
Scapa Flow, 32
Scarborough, 174
Schalburg, C.F. von, 22
Schau, Emil Victor, 2
Scobie, Ronald, 260, 263
Scotland, 32, 44–5, 59, 61, 114, 129, 138–9, 334
Sedgwick, A.C. 'Shan', 268
Segura, José, 104
Seine, 125
Selbys, Charles August, 3
Seligman, Adrian, 178, 219
Selwyn College, 100
Senegal, 82
Senio, 306, 324
Sesklio, note 4

Sfakia, 63
Shanghai, 34, 70
Shatt al Arab, 26
Shaw, Private, note 577
Shepheard's Hotel, 140, 148, 172
Shohet, Viv, 213
Shute, Nevil, 75, 82
Sibbet, Busty, 240, 244, 246
Siciliy, 145, 153, 155, 167, 173–4, 177, 181, 355
Sierra Leone, 82, 89, 92
Singapore, 23, 37–8, 97
Sjolte, 334
Skala, 233
Skaramagas, 268
Skiathos, 277
Skipworth, Lieutenant, 256
Skopelos, 277
Skov, R., 27
Skye, 33
Skygholt, 6, 11
Smith, I.C.D., 34
Smith, Kenneth (Ken) Herbert, 324, note 577
Sofia, 241
Sofoulis, Kyriakos, 245–7
Sognefjord, 31
Soldarelli, Mario, 187, 190, 211, note 379
Solomon, Martin, 280–1, 285
Sorrento, 328
Souris, Nikos, 156
South Africa, 23, 38, 43, 45, 62, 93, 95, 104–105
Southampton, 21
Soviet Union, xii, 20, 177, 217, 242, 256, 280, notes 22, 210, 235, 504
Spain, Spanish colonies, 6, 66, 90–1, 96–7, 99, 102–104, 127, 153, notes 173, 210, 235
Spanish Civil War, 6, 13, 32, note 235
Spanoyannis, 163
Sparky *see* Bennike, Arne
Specht, Captain, 103
Spetsai, note 476
Spiliotopoulos, Panagiotis, 268, 273, notes, 476, 481
Spit, 310–12, 315, 317, 324–5, 579
Sporades, 276, 278
St. Catherine's Point, 119
St. Honorine des Pertes, 125
St. James, 115
St. Laurent gap, 125
St. Michael Monastery, 191
St. Moritz, 21
Stacey, David, 32
Stalin, Josef, 261, 280
Stallen, 203
    see also Stellin, Dion John 'Stud'

Stardust, 92
Starup, C.J., 60, 73, 80
Stauffenberg, Claus von, note 22
Steinertz, Captain von, 225, note 408
Stella, barmaid, 46–7, 49
Stellas, Christos, 245
Stellas, Manolis, 245
Stellas, Nikolas, 245–7, note 363
Stellin, Dion John 'Stud', 192–3, 195–6, 203, 319, 328–9, 332
Stephenson, Les, 259, 296, 307, 313, 319–22, notes 577, 583, 584
Stevens, J.M., note 537
Stintino Peninsula, 173
Stirling, David, x, 21, 32–3, 62, 64–5, 140–1, 145, 147–8, note 539
Stirling, William 'Bill', x, 32, 33, 136, 138, 145, note 221
Stockbridge, Ralph H., 244
Stockholm, 139
Stokes, Horace, 129
Stowell, Hugh, 220
Street, Vivian, 147–8
Stroumboula, 245
Student, Kurt, 165
Suda, 297
Suez, 19, 62, 140, 148
Sumatra, 38
Sunda Strait, 23
Sutherland, David, x, 141, 148, 152, 154–6, 159–60, 164–6, 168–72, 184, 186–8, 196–7, 207–209, 222–3, 228, 230, 240–4, 248–9, 275, 278, 289, 293, 324, 328–31, note 427
Sweden, 20, 25, 74, 121, 179, note 210
Swizzle Stick, 115
Switzerland, 76, 327
Sykes, Eric, 33–4, 69–70
Symi, 184, 188–204, 207, 217, 220, 227, notes 314, 320
Syria, 61, 148, 211, 214–15
Syrna, 232, 239
Syros, 230

Tabel, Lieutenant Colonel, 245–6
Tangier, 175
Taranto, 263
Tate, Winifred Susanne, 81
Taylor, 98
Tel Aviv, 150, 289
Thanos, Captain, 230, note 427
Tharissa, 234
Thebes, 267
Thessaloniki, 197, 276–85, 287, 291, 336, 338, notes 496, 518, 535
Thira *see* Santorini

Thirasia, 233
Thompson, Private, note 577
Thott, Axel, 113
Tigani, 210–12
Tilney, Robert A., 209–10
Tilos, 179, 191–2, 194, 217, 227
Timm, Corporal, 229
Tinos, 245
Tito, Josip Broz, 151, 275
Tobruk, 140, 207
Tocqueville, 119
Tod, Ronnie J.F., 41, 263, 270, 273, 311, 329
Tomasi, Ettore, 317, 320, 322–3, 332, note 580
Tottenham, Denis, 79, 81, 85, 89, 98, 111, 128–9
Tourlos, 272
Trafford, Sam, 234–5, 249, 279, 282
Trasimeno, Lake, 305
Treasure Island, 223
Trieste, 217, 304, 327
Tripiti, 156, 165, 167, 171–2
Truscott, Lucian K., 305–306
Tsigantes, Kristoudolos, 147, 208, 253, 332
Tsigonias, Panagiotis Emmanuel, 246
Tsiknakis, Lefteris, 156
Tsoutsouras, 171
Tuckey, Allan, 229–30, note 421
Tunisia, 145
Turin, 327
Türkbükü, 221
Turkestan, 310
Turkey, 145, 175, 177–8, 185, 191, 193–4, 197, 202–203, 207, 209–11, 214–17, 220–2, 226, 229, 242, notes 379, 385
Turnbull, D.J.T., 148, 182, 184, 186, 188, 218
Turnbull, First Lieutenant, 319, 322, notes 577, 583–4
Tuxpan, 16
Tvermose, Jørgen, 80
Tymbaki, 141, 154, 156, 164–5
Tzouanakis, Giorgis 'Kokkinos', 157, 160

Udine, 327
Umbria, 305
Umuahia, 104
Upper Wharfsdale, 76
Unvle John *see* Barbaiannis
Unge Anders Lassen, 333
USA, xii, 21, 38, 97, 302
USSR *see* Soviet Union

Valavani, 156
Valle Bertuzzi, 310
Valle Fattibello, 320
Valle Isola, 310
Valle Ponti, 310
Valle Trebba, 310
Valli di Comacchio, 309–10, note 568
Vathy, 210, 212–13
Vaughan, Charles T., 138
VC *see* Victoria Cross
Venice, 93, 327, 330
Verney, John, 20, 147–51, 172–3, note 300
Verona, 304, 327
Via Romea, 310
Via Veneto, 307
Vichy France, Vichy French colonies, 44, 82, 88, 90, 92, note 210
Victor, The, 334–5
Victora Cross, viii, x, 3, 328–9, 331, 334, 336, note 4
Vienna, 217, 277
Vietinghoff, Heinrich von, 303, 325–6
Viganò, Renata, note 567
Villanova, 193, 196
Vittorio Emanuele III, 175
Vourvoulos, 234, 236–8
Vrellianakis, Manolis, 156

W5, 89
W10 *see* Guise, C.A.L.
W25 *see* Lippett, Richard
W51 *see* Godden, B.
W53 *see* Lake, Peter Ivan
Waite, Sergeant, 320, 321, note 577
Waldheim, Kurt, note 427
Walter, Arthur R., 180
Wandsworth, 54, 139
Warre, Captain, 129
Warren, Ian, 92, 111, 138–9
Warsaw, 13
Watkins, Corporal, note 577
Watson, Lieutenant, 266
Watson, E.H, 288
Waugh, Evelyn, 21, 39, 62, 255
Weinreich, Senior Corporal, 133
Wellington Club, 115, 145
Westerman, Percy, 15, 80
Weymouth, 17
White Mountains *see* Lefka Ori
White's Club, 21
Wichfeld, Varinka (Muus), 11, note 236
Wight, 117, 119, 125, 127
Willemstad, 16
Williams, Alan, 125, 127
Williams (SBS private), 244, note 577
Wilson, Maitland, 183–4, 187
Wingate, R.S.L., 90
Winter, Tom, 79, 87, 98, 111, 123, 125, 127, note 210

Winter War *see* Finland
Wolfson, Commander, 211
Wöllner, Kurt, note 408
Workman, Sergeant Major, 328, notes 577, 583
Wraxall Manor, 138
Wright, Leslie 'Red', note 214
Wright, Roger, 209, 264, 266–7

Xeropotamos, 166

Yedi Atala, 228
Yedi Atdullah, 221
Yorkshire, 174
Yoruba, 105
Young, Lieutenant, 168, 171
Young, Second Lieutenant, 129
Yugoslavia, 63, 153, 242, 255–6, 261, 267, 275–6, 302, note 235

Zadar, 306
Zahedi, Fazlollah, 151
Zante, 64
Zealand, 1, 3, 12
Zervakos, Philotheos, 248
Zervas, Colonel, notes 476, 518
Zografakis, Kimon, 155–7, 159–61, notes 281, 295
Zorilla, Augustin, 97

Civilian ships
Athenia, 17
Bibundi, 101, 307
British Consul, 43–6, 60, 128, 253
Danmark, 8
Duchessa d'Aosta, 85, 91–104, 307, 332
Eleonora Mærsk, xii, 15–20, 23–7, 29–30, 35–8, 43–4, 83, 128, 253, 332
Esperia, 198–200
Fionia, 7–9, 11, 15–16, 44, 83, 332
Geneviève, 82
I'm Alone, 77
Jessie Mærsk, 27
Likomba, 91–2, 95, 97, 99, 101–103, 307
Mary Kingsley, 97
Nuneaton, 98–9, 101–102
Pommern, 78
Strathmore, 87
Tasmania, 27
Vendia, 17
Vikingland, 332
Vulcan, 98–102

Government Departments, non-military organizations, companies, etc.
Admiralty, 37, 53, 82, 223, 332
Arriba, 102
BBC, 25, 27, 166, 327
Colonial Office, 104
Commando Veterans Association, 336
Daily Express, 331
Danish Club, 58, 145
Danish Council, 49, 53, 72, 115
Directorate of Military Training, 33
Foreign Ministry (German), note 504
Foreign Office, 52, 103, 151
Grand Council of the Fascist Party (Italy), 175
International Non-Intervention Commission, 6
International Transport Workers' Federation, 25
King's College, Lagos, 100
Ministry of Economic Warfare, 52
Ministry of Supply, note 221
Ministry of Trade (Danish), 25
National Liberation Committee for Northern Italy (CLNAI), 327
National Union of Seamen, 46, 53, 60
New York Times, 268
NUS *see* National Union of Seamen
Pan Am, 106
Red Cross, 74, 195, 282, 300, note 210, 236
SAS Regimental Association, 334
Special Forces Club, 334
War Office, 13, 21, 33, 41, 51, 52, 83–4, 104, 114, 331, notes 444, 524
Wilkinson Sword, 34

Codenames of operations, etc.
Accolade, 177
Albumen, 154–72, note 279
Ambassador, 41
Aquatint, 125, 127
Barclay, 153
Barricade, 116–20, 122–3, 133, 134, 143
Basalt, 128, 132, 134, 142, note 214
Batman, 137
Biting, 108
Bodyguard, 217
Branford, 124–5, 143
Buckland, 306, 324
Bullfrog, 219
Chariot, 109
Collar, 41
Craftsman, 306, 327
Dryad, 123–5, 128
Eisbär, 196
Erratic, 193
Fahrenheit, 136
Fireeater, 219
Freikorps Rescue, 270

Fry, 313, 316, 318–19, 325, note 563
Hardihood, 175
Harpoon, 141–2
Hawthorn, 172–4, note 300
Health Able, 256
Husky, 155, 173
Impact, 318
Impact Plain, 325
Impact Royal, 325
Impact Slam, 325
Jeanne, 284–5
Jubilee, 121–2, 136
Knife, 31–3, 111
Leopard, 205
Lever, 317–18
Manna, 263, 267
Marigold, 173
Mincemeat, 153
Noah's Ark, 261, 275, note 471
Overlord, 217, 223, 227, 242
Postmaster, 84, 97–105, 109, 143, 338, note 173
Pussyfoot, 144
Roast, 311–13, 316
Rodell, 182
Rutter, 109, 121–2
Second-Undercut, 280
Torch, 122, 144
Trianda, 198
Vigorous, 141–2
Yak, note 221
Zeppelin, 217, 230

Military units, corps, commands, HQs, intelligence organisations, etc.
Allied Commands
Allied Forces HQ, 263, 275, 299, 328–9
Army Groups
XV Army Group, 301
XXI Army Group, 288
Commonwealth Commands, etc.
Chiefs of Staff Committee, 39, 109, 144, 175, 177, 187 note 221
Combined Operations Directorate *see* Combined Operations H.Q.
Combined Operations H.Q., 40, 42, 51, 108–10, 120, 127, 136–8, 144–5, 331
Directorate of Combined Operations *see* Combined Operations H.Q.
Home Forces, 120
Home Guard, 33, 80
Imperial General Staff, 39
Land Forces Adriatic, 255, 272–3
Middle East Command, 65, 163, 177–8, 182, 186–7, 205, 210–11, 218, 273, 299, note 221

Territorial Army, 31, note 542
Armies
British Expeditionary Force, 17
Eighth Army, 142, 148, 181, 195, 300, 303–306, 311–12, 315, 317, 324–9, note 577
Ninth Army, 219, 242
Tenth Army, 242
Army Corps
II Corps, Polish, 327
III Corps, 188, 260, 280, 288–9, note 470
V Corps, 324
XIII Corps, 63
ANZAC, 63, 296
Divisions
4th Indian Infantry Division, note 470
5th Airborne Division, 280
8th Indian Division, 177–8
34th Infantry Division, 280
46th Infantry Division
56th (London) Infantry Division, 318, 326
57th Infantry Division, 280
78th Infantry Division, 326
Brigades
2nd Independent Parachute Brigade Group, 277, note 470
7th Indian Infantry Brigade, 284–5
9th Armoured Brigade, 305
23rd Armoured Brigade, note 470
24th Guards Brigade, 313
38th (Irish) Brigade, 326
102 Royal Marines Brigade, 136
139th Infantry Brigade, note 470
167th (London) Infantry Brigade, 318
183rd Infantry Brigade (Adriatic Brigade), 268
234th Infantry Brigade, 178, 205
Adriatic Brigade *see* 183rd Infantry Brigade
Highland Brigade, 271
Regiments, battalions, and smaller units
1st Parachute Battalion, 78–9
3rd King's Own Hussars, 115
4th Independent Parachute Battalion, 273, 275
27th Lancers, 305
42nd Field Company Royal Engineers, 316, 319
Buffs (Royal East Kent Regiment), 72–3, 105, 308
Cameron Highlanders, 151
Coldstream Guards, 20, 64, 140
Durham Light Infantry (DLI), 196–7
Highland Light Infantry, 267
Irish Guards, 54, 188, note 267
London Irish Rifles, 111
Lovat Scouts, 33

Index 397

Parachute Regiment, 108
RAF Regiment, 267, 275
   2908 Squadron, 267
Rhodesian African Rifles, 191
Royal West Kent regiment, 187
Scots Guards, 20–1, 31–3, 136, 140, 152
Snowballers *see* Scots Guards
Royal Marines
Royal Marines, 40, 153, 255, note 214
   40 (RM) Commando, 267, 311–13, 326
   43 (RM) Commando, 311–12, 326
   102 Royal Marines Brigade, 136
Corps, Services, etc.
64 British General Hospital, 220
Airborne Engineers, 275
Army Ski School, 151–2, 220
CSDIC, 171–2, 243
Combined Services Detailed Interrogation Centre *see* CSDIC
FANY, 76
First Aid Nursing Yeomanry *see* FANY
Field Security Section, 148
Land Warfare Centre, 336
Middle East Staff College, 293, note 539
Military College of Science, 76
No. 1 Parachute Training School, Ringway, 55, 59, 114, 138
Parachute Training School, No. 1, 55, 114
Returned Stores Depot (RSD), 329
Royal Army Medical Corps, RAMC, 216
Royal Army Service Corps, RASC, 305
Royal Artillery, 89
Royal Corps of Signals, 216
Royal Electrical and Mechanical Engineers, REME, 76, 216, 259, 329
Royal Engineers, 277, 316, 319
WAAF (Women's Auxiliary Air Force), 307
Commando forces and raiding units
1 Demolition Squadron *see* Popski's Private Army
1 Special Force, 173
2nd Commando Brigade (2nd Special Service Brigade), 311, 313, 315–17, 319, 329
2 Commando, 311, 312, 326
3 Commando, 41–2, 61
4 Commando, 41, 61
5 Commando, 41
6 Commando, 41
7 Commando, 41, 61, 76, 77
   B Troop, 76
8 (Guards) Commando, 41, 61–3
9 (Scottish) Commando, 41, 263, 271, 311, 317
   Troop 4, 317

11 (Scottish) Commando/Independent Company, 41, 42, 61, note 70
12 Commando, 127–8, 137
40 (RM) Commando, 267, 311–13, 326
43 (RM) Commando, 311–12, 326
51 Commando, 148
62 Commando *see* SSRF
Achnacarry School (Commando Depot/ Commando Basic Training Centre), 138
Advanced HQ A-Force, 66
Commandos, 34, 39–42, 61–5, 67, 76 109–10, 120, 134–6, 255, 264, 300, note 214, 217
COPP (Combined Operations Pilotage Parties), 312
Folboat Section, 62, 64, 140, 147, 173 *see also* Special Boat Section
Greek Sacred Squadron, 147–8, 208, 211–12, 216, 218–19, 230, 242, 244–6, 253, 255, 263, 338, notes 450, 458
Hieròs Lókhos *see* Greek Sacred Squadron
Holding Unit Special Forces, 149, 216
Independent Companies, 31, 41–2
Kalpaks, 216
Knife force, 33, 111
Layforce, 62–5, 77, 140, 148
L Detachment *see* SAS
Long Range Desert Group *see* LRDG
LRDG, 145, 159, 188, 190–1, 203, 207–209, 216, 255–7, 259–60, 263–4, 267, 277, 279, 288, notes 238, 330, 470
   S1 Patrol, 191
Maid Honor Force, 77, 79–81, 98, 102, 105, note 173
Middle East Commando, 64
Popski's Private Army (PPA), 145, 159 note 238
Raiding Forces HQ, (RFHQ), 148, 182, 187–8, 208, 215–18, 221, 223, 227–8, 244, 255, 277, note 450
Raiding Support Regiment, 216, 263
Royal Marine Boom Patrol Detachment, 216
SAS, xi, 64–6, 140–2, 145–8, 151–2, 159–60, 173, 178, 196, 251, 329, 334
   1 SAS Regiment, 145, 147–8
      B Squadron, 147
      C Squadron, 148
      Free/Fighting French Squadron, 147–8
      Special Boat Squadron, 147–8
   2 SAS Regiment, 145, 173
   22 SAS Regiment, 334
   23 SAS Regiment, 334
      D Squadron, 334
   L Detachment, 65, 140, 145

SBS, 33, 105, 147–8, 220, 223 292 note 379
  Amphetamine, 234, 254, 272
  Benzedrine *see* amphetamine
  Detachments, Squadrons, Groups, ad hoc units, 148, note 396
    HQ (present), 334
    HQ Squadron, 286, 293
    L Detachment/Squadron, 148, 151, 154, 172, 220, 222, 226, 228, 267, 278, 306, 327, 329
    M Detachment/Squadron, 148, 151, 182, 188, 248, 255, 263–4, 269, 276–7, 280, 285, 288, 306–309, 311, 313, 316, 319, 324–5, 327–9, 331, note 320
    S Detachment/Squadron, 148, 152, 154, 197, 207, 220, 222, 228, 249, 256, 276, 278, 293, 306, 328–9, note 450
    Senforce, 287–301, 308, note 524
    Z Group, 173
  Discipline, 149, 214, 224, 251, 270, 272, 307, 327–8
  Esprit de corps, morale, fatigue 149–50, 250, 272, 302, 307, 324. 327–8
  Patrols,
    B Patrol, 155, 157, 164, 167, 169–70, 172
    C Patrol, 155, 157, 169–70, 172
    D Patrol, 156, 164, 168
    Guard's Patrol, 188
    Irish Patrol, 188, 207, 214, 230, 288, note 361
    J Patrol, 230, 241, 244, 248
    K Patrol, 230, 241, 244, 256
    O Patrol, 256
    P Patrol, 230, 244, 248, 252
    Q Patrol, 244, 248
    Y Patrol, 319–20, note 577
    Z Patrol, 230, 234, 248
    Bluebell, 172, 174
    Daffodil, 172
    Hyacinth, 172
    Jasmine, 172
    Mistletoe, 172, 174
    Periwinkle, 172, 174
  Reputation, 226, 251–2, 263, 329
  RTU, 250
  Spirit and style, 149–50, 172, 214, 231, 250, 272, 307, 324
  Training, 141, 151–2, 250, 307–8
  Uniform, 247, 251, 301
  Weapons, 170, 231–2
Small Scale Raiding Force *see* SSRF
Special Air Service *see* SAS
Special Air Service Brigade *see* SAS

Special Boat Section, 64, 140, 173
Special Boat Service *see* SBS
Special Boat Squadron, 148, notes 379, 396 *see* SBS
Special Raiding Squadron *see* SRS
SRS, 148, *see* SAS
SSRF, 109–12, 115–17, 123, 125, 127–8, 135–9, 142–5, 154, 217, note 214
Z Force, 62

Ad hoc units, staffs, departments, etc.
Bucketforce, 267, note 481
Creteforce, 300, note 553
Force 1, 316
Force 2, 316
Force 133, 288, 292, 299, 301
Force 292, 177
Force J., 136
Foxforce, 263, 267, 269, 273
Fryforce, 316–17
Glisforce, 284–5
Kelforce, 277–8, 282, 284–5
Lagos Defence Force, 98, 100
Layforce, 62–5, 77, 140, 148
Nigerian Local Defence Volunteers, 98, 100
Pompforce, 275–6
RASC Regiment, 306
Scrumforce, 276–80, 282, 284
Senforce *see* SBS
Senior Military Officer Crete, 300, note 533

Naval units, commands, etc.
Department of Miscellaneous Weapons Development (DMWD), 81–2
No. 1 Submarine Flotilla, 64
42nd Motor Launch Flotilla, 187–8
Coastal Command, 136
Commander-in-Chief Mediterranean, 330
Force 120, 261
Levant Schooner Flotilla (LSF), 178, 188, 190, 218–21, 278, note 450
Portsmouth Command, 116
Z Force, 62
Catterick, 290, 297
Fridtjof Nansen, 80
Geneviève, 82
HDML 1083, 223
HDML 1377 239
Hornet, 117
Illustrious, 108
LS1, 230, 232, 238–9
LS3, 220–1
LS5, 220–1
LS7, 208, note 367
LS9, 220–1
LS10, 220

Index 399

LS11, 230, 232, 238–9, note 434
LS24, 229–30, notes 421, 428
LS Hedgehog, 190
Maid Honor, 75, 77–98, 106, 110, 128, 331, notes 165, 173
Medway, 64
ML458, 276, 278
ML361, 155, 168, 171
MTB 344, 115–19, 123–9, 131–2, 136
N63 (Tigris) 78
Porcupine, 141
Prince of Wales, 97
Repulse, 97
Strathmore, 87
Stuyvesant, 87
Tewfik, 220–4, 228, 230, 236, 239, 247, 248, 252–3
Tigris (N63), 78
Truant, 32
Violet, 101, 102

Air Forces
Balkan Air Force, 275
Desert Airforce, 243
No. 1 Parachute Training School, 55, 114
Royal Air Force, RAF, 42, 44, 49, 73, 75, 178, 196–7, 201, 203, 205, 209, 218, 232, 245, 254, 256, 267, 288, 301, note 64
South African Air Force (SAAF), 196–7, 313

Intelligence, sabotage, paramilitary, etc. organisations and schools
6 District, 288–9
'A' Force, 65–6, 153, 279–80
Directorate of Military Intelligence, 13
Electra House, 52
Inter Services Liaison Department *see* SIS
Inter-Services Research Bureau *see* ISRB
ISLD *see* SIS
ISRB *see* SOE
Maid Honor Force, 79, 81, 110, note 173
MI(R), 13–14, 31–3, 39, 42, 51–2
MI5, 74, 214
MI6 *see* SIS
MI9, 193, 208, 211, 213
Military Intelligence (Research) *see* MI(R)
Secret Intelligence Service *see* SIS
SIS, 51–2, 143–4, 193, note 210
SOE, 51–2, 54
    Belgium Department, 111
    Danish Department, 59
    Cooler, 56
    Country Section Schools, 56
    Department M (SOE), 110
    Force 133, 288, 292, 299, 301
    Frawest (French West Africa), 90
    Group A Schools, 55
    Group B Schools, 55
    Holding Schools, 56, 72
    Neucols, 90, 95–6
    No. 1 Special School, No. 1 Special Training School *see* STS 1
    Olokemeji (SOE school), 90, 98, 105–107
    Paramilitary School Arisaig House (STS 21) *see* STS 21
    Paramilitary Schools, 55, 59, 67, 71
    PERO, 90
    Political and Economic Research Organization *see* PERO
    Polish Section, note 235
    Preliminary Schools, 55
    Special Training Centre Lochailort *see* STC Lochailort
    Special Training School *see* STS
    Specialist Schools, 56
    STC Lochailort, 33, 42, 67, 69, 70
    STS 1, 54, 56, 308
    STS 21, 55, 59–60, 67, 69–72, 83, 131, 162, 308
    STS 21–25, 55, 59–60, 67
    STS 41 (Gumley Hall), 72–4 79
    STS 62 *see* SSRF (Commando forces and raiding units)
    STS 62c (Wraxall Manor, an outstation of Anderson Manor), 138
    Technical Research and Development Station, 81
    W Mission, W Section (SOE), 82, 103
    West African department, 82
Special Operations Executive *see* SOE
Station 62 *see* SSRF (Commando forces and raiding units)

France
Various units
Chasseurs Alpins, 21
Free/Fighting French Squadron *see* SBS

Poland
Various units, etc.
II Corps, 327
Expeditionary Force for Norway, 31

Greece
Various organisations and units
Andartes *see* Partisans
EAM/ELAS, 261, 263–4, 268, 270, 273, 279, 280–5, 288–91, 296–300, 302, 332, notes 472, 475–6, 481, 504, 513, 518, 537
EDES, notes 476, 518
EOK, 288–91, 297–9
EPON, 283
Free Greek forces, 194, 202, 211–12

Genarmerie, 300
Greek Sacred Squadron, 147–8, 208, 211–12, 216, 218–19, 230, 242, 244–6, 253, 255 263, 338, notes 421, 448, 450
Hieròs Lókhos *see* Greek Sacred Squadron
Kanaris, 297
KKE, notes 504, 518
Partisans, 294, 300, 302
Royal Hellenic Navy, 263
Security Battalions, 267

Italy
Divisions
Infantry Division Cuneo, 211–12
Brigades
24th Legione MVSN, 187, 211
28th Garibaldi Brigade ('M. Gordini'), 312–13, 316, 318, 325–6
35th Garibaldi Brigade ('Mario Babini'), 312
Regiments
8th Infantry Regiment, note 379
27th Artillery Regiment, note 379
Police
Carabinieri, 190, 192, 194–5, 201, 205, 228, note 338
Guardia di Finanza, 190, 194, 205, 228
Harbour police, 185
Police, 223

Other Units, etc.
Arditi (WWI), 40
National Liberation Committee for Northern Italy (CLNAI), 327

Navy and Air Force
Italian Navy, 190
Italian Airforce, 196

Intelligence
Servizio Informazioni Militare (SIM), 184

Poland
II Polish Corps, 327

Germany
Army Groups and higher commands
Army Group Africa, 153
Army Group E, 197, 229–30, 242, 277, 287, notes 426, 427
Commander-in-Chief Italy, 174
Commander-in-Chief Southern Greece, 165
Wehrmacht High Command (OKW), 165, notes 217, 426, 428
Army and Air Corps
XI Flying Corps, 165
Afrika Korps, 63, 171, note 354

Divisions and Brigades
7th SS Volunteer Mountain Division Prinz Eugen, 153
10th Panzer Division, 121
22nd Infantry Division, Airborne Infantry Division, Airborne Division, 163, 196, 242, note 292
29th Panzergrenadier Division, 317, 325–6
42nd Jäger Division, 326
90th Light Division, note 260
90th Panzergrenadier Division, 153, note 260
114th Jäger Division, 310
133rd Fortress Division, note 527
162nd (Turkestan) Infantry Division, 310, notes 569, 581
319th Infantry Division, 131
Division Brandenburg, 196, 212, 222, 229, 242
Fortress Division Crete, 287
Sturmbrigade Reichsführer SS, 153
Sturm-Division Rhodos, 184, 197 notes 426, 428
Regiments, battalions and other minor units
9th Infantry Regiment 'Potsdam', note 22
15th Panzergrenadier Regiment, 325
71st Panzergrenadier Regiment, 325
129th Armoured Reconnaissance Battalion, 317, 325
303rd Infantry Regiment, 313, notes 569, 581
314th Infantry Regiment, note 569
329th Infantry Regiment, note 569
538th Infantry Regiment, 131
587th Infantry Regiment, 119
Brandenburg Regiment, 212, 222
Grenadier Regiment Rhodos, 198
Jäger Regiment 1 'Brandenburg', 212
Pila Company 780, 229
Pioneer Landing Company 780 *see* Pila Company 780
Post 4, 119–20, 134
Various units, organizations, etc.
Arab Free Corps, 270
Battlegroup Müller, 209
Fortress Crete, 153, 244
Fortress Kos, 261
Fortress Leros, 261
Fortress Rhodes, 261
GFP (Geheime Feldpolizei), 294
Küstenjäger, 222, 229, 242
  see also Division Brandenburg
Makedo-Romanians, 242
Pirate detachments, 242
Platzkommando Paros, 248

SD (Sicherheitsdienst), 229, notes 22, 217
Stalag 7, 229
Stalag VIIIB, note 210
Stalag XIB, note 210
Naval units and commands
9th Torpedo Boat Flotilla, 218
21st Anti-Submarine Flotilla, 218
Admiral Ägäis, 241, 277
Kriegsmarine, 242, 287
Marinegruppenkommando Süd, 153, 201, 204, 241
Esperia, 198–200
Gradisca, 277
Malona, 229
Parma, 198, 200
Schleswig-Holstein, 17
Tirpitz, 109
Air Force
Luftwaffe, 16, 158, 161, 196, 205, 207, 210, 239, 245, 287

USA
Armies
Fifth Army, 181, 303–304, 306, 327
Seventh Army, 327
Various army units
755th Armored Battalion
Air Force
USAAF, 205
Intelligence
Office of Strategic Services (OSS), 173, 277, 288, note 301
Yugoslavia/Croatia
Partisans, 257–8
Ustashi, 258